Collaborative Dynamic Capabilities for Service Innovation

Mitsuru Kodama
Editor

Collaborative Dynamic Capabilities for Service Innovation

Creating a New Healthcare Ecosystem

Editor
Mitsuru Kodama
Nihon University, College of Commerce
Tokyo, Japan

ISBN 978-3-319-77239-4   ISBN 978-3-319-77240-0 (eBook)
https://doi.org/10.1007/978-3-319-77240-0

Library of Congress Control Number: 2018936619

© The Editor(s) (if applicable) and The Author(s) 2018
This work is subject to copyright. All rights are solely and exclusively licensed by the Publisher, whether the whole or part of the material is concerned, specifically the rights of translation, reprinting, reuse of illustrations, recitation, broadcasting, reproduction on microfilms or in any other physical way, and transmission or information storage and retrieval, electronic adaptation, computer software, or by similar or dissimilar methodology now known or hereafter developed.
The use of general descriptive names, registered names, trademarks, service marks, etc. in this publication does not imply, even in the absence of a specific statement, that such names are exempt from the relevant protective laws and regulations and therefore free for general use.
The publisher, the authors, and the editors are safe to assume that the advice and information in this book are believed to be true and accurate at the date of publication. Neither the publisher nor the authors or the editors give a warranty, express or implied, with respect to the material contained herein or for any errors or omissions that may have been made. The publisher remains neutral with regard to jurisdictional claims in published maps and institutional affiliations.

Printed on acid-free paper

This Palgrave Macmillan imprint is published by the registered company Springer International Publishing AG part of Springer Nature.
The registered company address is: Gewerbestrasse 11, 6330 Cham, Switzerland

Preface and Acknowledgments

The world's hi-tech companies have a growing need to develop new products and services based on new technology achieved through the "convergence" of different existing technologies—an approach to developing new products and services that will differentiate their own from those of other companies.[1] This is because of the many cases where the integration of technology in one field with that of another has resulted in the successful development of new products and services based on novel ideas. Therefore, there is a growing need for business strategies that provide for convergence, that is, the integration and consolidation of different technologies, the development of products and services that span different industries, and the construction of new business models.

Furthermore, the evolution of ICT has brought about temporal and spatial contractions in business processes and supply chains in all industries. In addition to enhancing management efficiency and accelerating decision-making, ICT has spawned new business models that crisscross and integrate different industries. For example, the realization of diverse e-businesses and the creation of new content (particularly for smartphones and tablet PCs, an area in which Google and Apple have had the most impact in the world of ICT) have brought about business innovation not only in technical areas, such as the development of ICT, but also in the creation of new markets through the integration of knowledge sourced from diverse players.

In addition, NTT DOCOMO's i-mode (the world's first mobile phone business model, developed in Japan), Sony's and Nintendo's game devices (PlayStation/DS/Wii and Pokemon Go using smart devices), and rapidly growing social networking services (SNS) such as Facebook and Twitter, as well as various kinds of social games, have brought about innovation in both product development technology and services resulting from the creation of new markets (contents, applications, game software). These product and service innovations have also facilitated co-creation and co-evolution in the ICT industry as a whole through the formation of dynamic "business ecosystems" as new value chains. Internet businesses, SNS, social games, and so on, using mobile telephones and smartphones have grown from the dynamic construction of these business ecosystems developed through co-creation and co-evolution (e.g., Kodama 2000, 2007, 2008, 2009).

The convergence of different technologies and industries is progressing rapidly in a wide range of hi-tech areas, including smartphones, radio-frequency identifications (RFIDs), smart grids, solar cells, computerization of cars, environmental cars, semiconductors, biotechnology, and life sciences. Moreover, the sophistication and diversity of such technologies and dramatic developments in ICT are forcing companies to consider more complex business models.

Amid today's dramatically changing business environments—with their rapid technological innovations and short product life cycles, mature markets in developed countries and expanding markets in emerging countries, progress in ICT, and the search for new business models—it is essential for companies to explore the development of new technologies and the construction of new business models. Companies must also pursue business innovation to offer new value to customers through drivers such as the integration of different technologies and the creation of ICT businesses across various industries, which requires more than just integration and consolidation of the different kinds of internal specialist knowledge. For companies to achieve this, the integration of different kinds of knowledge from external companies will also be vital.

The questions then are: What kind of organizational strategies and actions should a company adopt to generate new products, services, and business models through convergence? In other words, how can ICT businesses that integrate different technologies and intersect industries be created? What kind of leadership and management is required to achieve this? These are some of the many issues facing hi-tech and global corporations in this regard.

While detailed strategies of individual industries and companies vary, the key concept in corporate activities for adapting to convergence lies in new "asset orchestration" (or knowledge creation/integration) through the demonstration of dynamic capabilities (Teece 2007, 2014). Furthermore, the corporate and organizational platform that supports this asset orchestration process is the formation of business communities that originate in the Japanese concept of *ba*, or place (Nonaka and Takeuchi 1995; Nonaka and Konno 1998; Kodama 2005; Nonaka et al. 2014), and those unique, inherent capabilities of their practitioners (leaders and managers) and organizations that are difficult to replicate.

Promoting the asset orchestration process does not just mean integrating (orchestrating) diverse kinds of knowledge (assets) across different organizations and areas of specialization within a company. The most critical issue in this process is demonstrating dynamic capabilities for integrating (orchestrating) assets within a company and superior assets dispersed throughout the world by engaging in strategic collaboration with outstanding partners (ecosystem partners) via global networks. These unique corporate capabilities, which accelerate asset orchestration through strategic collaboration within and outside companies, and which are hard to replicate, are referred to as "collaborative dynamic capabilities," and are a key theoretical concept of this book. Collaborative dynamic capabilities developed through strategic collaboration among companies across boundaries within and outside companies to promote the processes of co-creation and co-evolution, and led to the creation of value chains as new business models. One of the objectives of this book is to shed light on the macro and micro elements of collaborative dynamic capabilities that create new services in this era of convergence.

In the field of business and management research, a theme of increasing interest in theoretical and practical research focusing on strategic theory in particular is that of the aforementioned "dynamic capabilities." Thus, in environments where convergence of technologies and services is advancing across industries, companies and groups of companies must demonstrate collaborative dynamic capabilities to bring about sustainable growth in business ecosystems through service innovation. Hence, through an analysis of these processes from the perspective of strategic management and innovation, this book offers new knowledge on both the theoretical and practical aspects. The case studies in this book look at e-healthcare businesses that are gaining global attention, with original research examples of some of the most advanced service innovations in the world, not seen in other research to date.

The book's contributors are researchers from different fields (healthcare and hospital management, environmental management, risk management, information technology and systems, supply chain management, and innovation and technology management). Thus, this volume offers a unique analysis using the knowledge of different specializations through a common theoretical framework (collaborative dynamic capabilities) for the e-healthcare business model.

This book would not have been completed without deep and detailed interactions with numerous practitioners, to whom the authors would like to extend their gratitude. We would also like to express our thanks for the Nihon University College of Commerce Multidisciplinary Research Grant (2016–2017).

Concerning the publication of this book, the Editor wishes to extend his appreciation to Liz Barlow, Head of Business, Publisher Scholarly Business and Management, Maddie Holder, Commissioning Editor, and Lucy Kidwell, Senior Editorial Assistant from Palgrave Macmillan, who provided tremendous support.

Tokyo, Japan   Mitsuru Kodama

Note

1. In this context, convergence, meaning merging or concentration, means the concentration or integration of technologies and media. Examples include the integration of telecommunications and broadcasting, of telecommunications and electric power, and of mobile phones and diverse media (such as music and games).

References

Kodama, M. (2000). New Multimedia Services in the Education, Medical and Welfare Sectors. *Technovation, 20*(6), 321–331.

Kodama, M. (2005). New Knowledge Creation Through Leadership-Based Strategic Community—A Case of New Product Development in IT and Multimedia Business Fields. *Technovation, 25*(8), 895–908.

Kodama, M. (2007). *Project-Based Organization in the Knowledge-Based Society* (Vol. 12). London: Imperial College Press.

Kodama, M. (2008). *New Knowledge Creation Through ICT Dynamic Capability Creating Knowledge Communities Using Broadband*. Charlotte: Information Age Publishing.

Kodama, M. (2009). Boundaries Innovation and Knowledge Integration in the Japanese Firm. *Long Range Planning, 42*(4), 463–494.

Nonaka, I., & Konno, N. (1998). The Concept of "*Ba*": Building a Foundation for Knowledge Creation. *California Management Review, 40*(1), 40–54.

Nonaka, I., & Takeuchi, H. (1995). *The Knowledge-Creating Company*. New York: Oxford University Press.

Nonaka, I., Kodama, M., Hirose, A., & Kohlbacher, F. (2014). Dynamic Fractal Organizations for Promoting Knowledge-Based Transformation—A New Paradigm for Organizational Theory. *European Management Journal, 32*(1), 137–146.

Teece, D. J. (2007). Explicating Dynamic Capabilities: The Nature and Microfoundations of (Sustainable) Enterprise Performance. *Strategic Management Journal, 28*(13), 1319–1350.

Teece, D. J. (2014). The Foundations of Enterprise Performance: Dynamic and Ordinary Capabilities in an (Economic) Theory of Firms. *The Academy of Management Perspectives, 28*(4), 328–352.

Contents

1 **Collaborative Dynamic Capabilities: The Dynamic Capabilities View**   1
Mitsuru Kodama

2 **Service Innovation Through Collaborative Dynamic Capabilities: A Systems Approach**   47
Mitsuru Kodama

3 **E-healthcare Service Innovations: In Depth Case Studies in Japan**   91
Mitsuru Kodama

4 **Quality Improvements and Cost Reductions in Healthcare: Accountable Care Organizations from the Perspective of Collaborative Dynamic Capabilities and Leadership**   113
Toshiro Takahashi

5 **Realization of a Health Support Ecosystem Through a Smart City Concept: A Collaborative Dynamic Capabilities Perspective**   135
Nobuyuki Tokoro

6	**Business Model Changes Through Collaborative Dynamic Capabilities Through Insurance Company Use of IT (InsurTech) in the Medical and Health Sectors** *Futoshi Okada*	153
7	**Telemedicine System Developments Through Strategic Collaboration Between Industry, Government and Academia** *Rumiko Azuma and Mitsuru Kodama*	163
8	**Pharmacy Service Innovation from the Standpoint of Collaborative Dynamic Capabilities** *Takuya Akikawa*	203
9	**Building Healthcare Ecosystems Through Strategic Collaboration Across Different Industries** *Mitsuru Kodama*	225
10	**Boundaries Synchronization and Capabilities Congruence: Discussion and Implications** *Mitsuru Kodama*	271
11	**Conclusions and Issues for Future Research** *Mitsuru Kodama*	335

Index 353

Notes on Contributors

Takuya Akikawa is an associate professor at Nihon University. He received his PhD from Sensyu University and has his Japanese public qualification as a Small and Medium Enterprise Management Consultant. His research interests focus on the realization factor of supply chain management and logistics management. His research has been published in many journals, including the *International Journal of Production Economics* and the *International Journal of Logistics Research and Applications*.

Rumiko Azuma is an associate professor at the College of Commerce, Nihon University, Japan. She received her PhD in engineering from University of the Ryukyus. Her current research interests include educational data analysis for learning support systems, theory of decision-making in engineering approaches, and text mining.

Mitsuru Kodama is Professor of Innovation and Technology Management at the College of Commerce and Graduate School of Business Administration, Nihon University. His research has been published in international journals such as *Long Range Planning*, *Organization Studies*, *Journal of Management Studies*, *Technovation*, *R&D Management*, and *Information Systems Management*, among others. He has published 12 books in English, including *Collaborative Innovation* (2015), *Winning through Boundaries Innovation* (2014), *Competing through ICT Capability* (Palgrave Macmillan, 2012), *Knowledge Integration Dynamics* (2011), *Boundary Management* (2009), and *Knowledge Innovation* (2007).

Futoshi Okada is a professor at the College of Commerce, Nihon University. He specializes in risk management and insurance, with a focus on mutual and co-operative insurance. His most recent work, a joint paper titled "Mutual insurance and co-operative Kyosai in Japan" is due to be published in 2018.

Toshiro Takahashi is a professor at Nihon University's Graduate School of Business Administration and College of Commerce. He specializes in hospital management, in particular hospital management evaluation, methods and improvements (*kaizen*), and the use of a balanced scorecard. He is chairman of the Japan Association for Healthcare Balanced Scorecard studies, an executive of the Nippon Academy of Management and the Japan Academy of Management, and a board member of the Japan Society for Healthcare Administration. He has edited, authored or co-authored 27 books and 134 articles and has been an editorial board member and/or a reviewer for a number of journals. He has extensive international experience, serving as a consultant to and/or presenting academic and governmental courses, in Taiwan, Vietnam, and Canada.

Nobuyuki Tokoro is Professor of Business Administration at the College of Commerce and Graduate School of Business Administration, Nihon University. His research has been published in international journals, including *Asian Business and Management* among others. He also has published several books in Japanese.

List of Figures

Fig. 1.1	Business innovation through collaborative DC	5
Fig. 1.2	Realization of synergies through "capabilities synthesis"	11
Fig. 1.3	The Capabilities Map: the DC and OC view	22
Fig. 1.4	The strategic innovation system	30
Fig. 2.1	Capabilities congruence through the assets orchestration process	53
Fig. 2.2	Capabilities congruence inside and outside of a company—the systems view	57
Fig. 2.3	Internal and external consistency of capabilities congruence—a dynamic strategic management framework from the systems view	60
Fig. 2.4	Corporate boundaries, assets orchestration, capabilities congruence—systems view	65
Fig. 2.5	Collaborative DC through strategic innovation loop synchronization	71
Fig. 2.6	Strategic innovation loop synchronization through boundaries synchronization	79
Fig. 2.7	The co-creation and co-evolution model for service innovations and business ecosystems	83
Fig. 3.1	NTT DOCOMO healthcare business development—supporting action phase (2008–2017). (Source: Created by the authors from DOCOMO publications)	98

Fig. 3.2	Capabilities map in a strategic innovation system in NTT DOCOMO—supporting action phase (2008–2017)	102
Fig. 3.3	Collaborative DC through strategic innovation loop synchronization centered on DOCOMO and Omron Healthcare	107
Fig. 5.1	Concept of the local comprehensive care system at Fujisawa SST	141
Fig. 5.2	The process of value co-creation	148
Fig. 7.1	The transforming business models of telecommunications carriers around the world (fixed and mobile networks)	166
Fig. 7.2	Building business ecosystems through collaborative DC	169
Fig. 7.3	Creating strategic communities among innovative customers and collaborating partners. (*IC* innovative customer, *CP* collaborating partners, *SC* strategic communities)	177
Fig. 7.4	Community asset orchestrating cycle among innovative customers and collaborating partners through the strategic communities creation	182
Fig. 7.5	Formation of strategic community and networked SCs	189
Fig. 7.6	Networked strategic communities at the big project	190
Fig. 7.7	Video-Net in Katsurao village, Fukushima Prefecture [conceptual diagram]	192
Fig. 7.8	Capabilities synthesis through collaborative DC of community leaders	195
Fig. 8.1	Conceptual model	211
Fig. 9.1	General trading company business model. (Source: Mitsubishi and Mitsui publicly released materials)	227
Fig. 9.2	Mitsubishi corporation's business model: comparison with other business structures. (Source: Mitsubishi Corp.'s publicly released materials)	228
Fig. 9.3	The transforming business model of Mitsubishi—the healthcare business case	231
Fig. 9.4	Mitsui healthcare ecosystem—global healthcare network. (Source: Created by the authors from Mitsui publications)	235
Fig. 9.5	Mitsubishi corporation's business model by category. (Source: Created from Mitsubishi Corp.'s publicly released materials)	237
Fig. 9.6	General trading company capabilities map	239

Fig. 9.7	Mitsubishi corporation's multi-layered functions (basic and new). (Source: Created from Mitsubishi Corp.'s publicly released materials)	240
Fig. 9.8	General trading company asset orchestration map. (Note: Asset orchestration architecture: → "vertical integrated architecture," "horizontal integrated architecture" and "linkage relationship architecture"; *SD* strategy drivers, *MD* management drivers)	243
Fig. 9.9	Asset orchestration process map. ([Legend] Asset orchestration architecture: → "Vertical integrated architecture," "Horizontal integrated architecture" and "Linkage relationship architecture"; *SD* strategy drivers, *MD* management drivers)	246
Fig. 9.10	Linkage relationship architecture	258
Fig. 9.11	General trading company strategic innovation system	260
Fig. 9.12	Collaborative DC through boundaries synchronization	261
Fig. 10.1	Theory and characteristics of boundaries between main player(s) and partner(s). (Note: This figure was generated based on Kodama (2007a))	272
Fig. 10.2	Asset orchestration by forming SC between the main player and partner(s)	281
Fig. 10.3	Boundaries synchronization between main player(s) and partner(s) on the capabilities map—strategic innovation loop synchronization	284
Fig. 10.4	Congruence of the five capabilities among players	296
Fig. 10.5	Internal and external congruence through orchestration of co-specialized assets (The TSMC business model)	299
Fig. 10.6	TSMC's DC through asset orchestration	301
Fig. 10.7	Leader teams, project and line networks in NTT DOCOMO	304
Fig. 10.8	Strategic innovation based on *ba* and SC triad model. (Source: Excerpted from Figure 4, Nonaka et al. (2014))	309
Fig. 10.9	Co-specialization through convergence	314
Fig. 10.10	Operational capabilities of Dell's virtual integration through the orchestration of co-specialized assets	317
Fig. 10.11	Leadership capabilities—leadership interaction across different companies—leadership structures formed from multiple companies (middle-management layer)	320

Fig. 11.1	Assets orchestration processes and microstrategy processes	341
Fig. 11.2	Asset orchestration through dynamics of paradoxical SC formation. (Explanatory note: Loosely coupled network and tightly coupled network SC (SC-1 to SC-*N*) co-exist at each step of strategy execution. These network relationships change dynamically along the time axis according to environmental changes or deliberate corporate strategies)	346

List of Tables

Table 5.1	Fujisawa SST council	144
Table 7.1	Asahikawa Medical University Hospital telemedicine initiatives	174
Table 8.1	Profile of respondents	212
Table 8.2	Measurement model and descriptive statistics	214
Table 8.3	AVE and correlation matrix	217
Table 8.4	Results of hypothesis tests	217
Table 8.5	Total effects on ICC	218
Table 8.6	Paths of controlled variables	218
Table 9.1	Vertical integrated architecture	249
Table 9.2	Horizontal integrated architecture	254

List of Boxes

Box 1.1	"Capabilities Synthesis"—A New Theoretical Concept—The Synergy of Three Elements Based on Business Model Matching, Optimized Profit Structure Generation and Co-specialization	7
Box 1.2	Concept of Strategic Communities (SC)	11
Box 9.1	Mitsubishi's Business Transformation and Its Healthcare Business	229
Box 9.2	Mitsui Healthcare and Medical Businesses	231
Box 9.3	The Asset Orchestration Process Map	245
Box 9.4	Asset Orchestration Thinking	248
Box 11.1	The Asset Orchestration Process for the Four Specific Factors	341

1

Collaborative Dynamic Capabilities: The Dynamic Capabilities View

Mitsuru Kodama

1.1 The Need for Collaborative Dynamic Capabilities

Superior core technologies at the cutting edge of industries such as ICT, energy, cars, electronics, semiconductors, biotechnology, pharmaceuticals, and material science are dispersed among companies, organizations, and even individuals throughout the world. Innovation using these superior core technologies is a wellspring of new products and services. A strategic goal for hi-tech companies has been the development of products through ongoing innovation in individual technologies. However, a host of demands have been placed on manufacturing industry, including: demands for high-function, high-performance products; offers on low-priced products; extensive product lines; and short product development cycles (e.g., Kodama 2007c). At the same time, diversified customer

---

M. Kodama (✉)
Nihon University, College of Commerce, Tokyo, Japan
e-mail: kodama.mitsuru@nihon-u.ac.jp

requirements and values have created user needs arising from new product values such as "disruptive technology" (Christensen 1997).

In world markets, where demand from emerging countries is growing, new marketing and creative product strategies have become an urgent issue for global companies. Moreover, when developing new products and services, global hi-tech companies need to differentiate them based on the "convergence" of different technologies. This stems from the evidence of the cases where the integration of technology in one field with that of another has resulted in successful new products and services based on novel ideas. Therefore, there is a growing need for business strategies that provide for convergence, that is, the integration and consolidation of different technologies, the development of products and services that intersect different industries, and the construction of new business models.

Furthermore, the evolution of ICT has brought about temporal and spatial contractions in business processes and supply chains in all industries. In addition to enhancing management efficiency and accelerating decision-making, ICT has spawned new business models that crisscross and integrate wide range of industries, such as e-businesses, and new content (particularly for smartphones and tablet PCs, an area Google and Apple have dominated the world of ICT), and that have brought about business innovation in technical areas, such as the development of ICT and the creation of new markets through the integration of knowledge sourced from diverse players.

In addition, NTT DOCOMO's i-mode (the world's first mobile phone-internet business model, developed in Japan) (Kodama 2002), Sony's and Nintendo's game devices (PlayStation/DS/Wii and Pokemon Go using smart devices)(Kodama 2007c) and rapidly growing social networking services (SNS), such as Facebook and Twitter, and various kinds of social games, have brought about innovations in product development technology and service innovations through new marketing in newly created markets (for content, applications, game software). Moreover, these product and service innovations have facilitated co-creation and co-evolution across the ICT industry through the formation of dynamic "business ecosystems" as new value chains. Internet businesses, SNS, social games, and so on using mobile telephones and smartphones start out through the dynamic construction of business ecosystems developed through co-creation and co-evolution (e.g., Kodama 2001, 2007a, 2009b, 2012, 2014, 2015, 2017b).

The convergence of such different technologies and industries is progressing at a rapid pace in a wide range of hi-tech areas, including smartphones, radio-frequency identification (RFID), smart grids, solar cells, automotive computerization, environmental vehicles, semiconductors, biotechnology, and life sciences. Furthermore, the sophistication and diversity of these technologies, and the dramatic developments in ICT are forcing companies to come up with more complex business models.

In today's rapidly changing business environment—with its high-speed technological innovations and short product life cycles, mature markets in developed countries and expanding markets in emerging countries, progress in ICT and the search for new business models—it is essential for companies to explore the development of new technologies to construct new business models. Companies must also pursue business innovation to offer new value to customers through the integration of different technologies and the creation of ICT businesses across various industries. This requires more than just the integration and consolidation of different kinds of specialist knowledge within each company—a vital element is the integration of different kinds of knowledge from other companies.

For example, in Japan, where the mobile phone market has already reached saturation, mobile phone carriers such as NTT DOCOMO and SoftBank have been forced to search for new business. Therefore, these companies need strategies that enable them to transition from saturated markets like the mobile phone market to new business models.

Market saturation is due to a number of issues common to developed countries: (1) the number of mobile phone subscribers is close to that of the population; (2) cut-throat competition among carriers over user charges; (3) increases in handset prices (due to increased development costs); (4) penetration of number portability (lowering of the barrier to switching carriers); (5) entry of new operators (mobile virtual network operators); and (6) increase in communications traffic (increase in content accompanying the increased use of smartphones).

Therefore, mobile phone carriers have to develop new value for customers. For example, in response to changes in the business environment, NTT DOCOMO is aggressively developing new mobile phone businesses in the ICT industry as well as social support services that cross different industries. To achieve this, it is constructing a technology platform to enhance the efficiency of information circulation via mobile devices, including smartphones and tablets, in areas such as ecology, safety and security, and healthcare; while Softbank is pursuing the acquisition of US companies to gain domination in world markets as it strives to make the transition into new service businesses.

The question then is: What kind of organizational strategies and actions should a company adopt to generate new products, services and business models through "convergence," that is, the creation of ICT businesses that integrate different technologies and span industries? In addition, what kind of leadership and management is required to achieve this? There are many issues for hi-tech and global corporations to consider in this regard.

While the detailed strategies of individual industries and companies vary, the key concept behind corporate activities for adapting to convergence lies in "asset orchestration" (or knowledge creation) through the demonstration of dynamic capabilities (DC) (Teece 2007, 2014). Furthermore, the corporate and organizational platforms that support this asset orchestration process are the formation of business communities which originate in the Japanese concept of *ba*, or place (Nonaka and Takeuchi 1995; Nonaka and Konno 1998; Kodama 2005) and those unique, inherent capabilities of their practitioners (leaders and managers) and organizations, which are difficult to replicate (see Fig. 1.1).

The asset orchestration process is not simply a process of integrating (orchestrating) diverse kinds of knowledge (assets) across different organizations and areas of specialization within a company. The most critical issue in this process is demonstrating DC for integrating (orchestrating) assets within a company and superior assets dispersed throughout the world by engaging in strategic collaboration with outstanding partners (ecosystem partners) via global networks. These unique corporate capabilities, which accelerate the asset orchestration process through strategic collaboration within and outside companies, and which are hard to replicate, are referred to as "collaborative dynamic capabilities" and are a key theoretical concept of the book. Collaborative DC developed through strategic collaboration among companies across the boundaries within and outside companies to promote the processes

Collaborative Dynamic Capabilities: The Dynamic Capabilities...

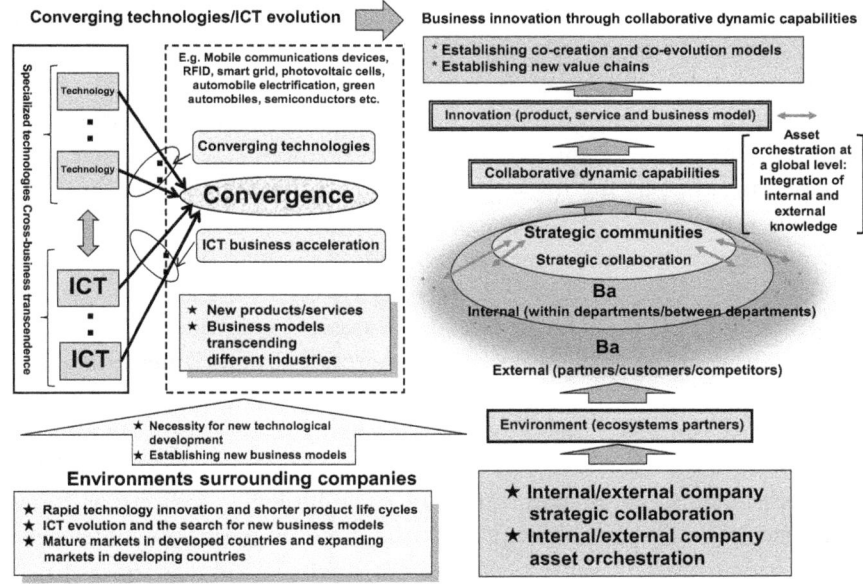

Fig. 1.1 Business innovation through collaborative DC

of co-creation and co-evolution and led to the creation of new business models and value chains (see Fig. 1.1).

1.2 The Central Concept of Collaborative Dynamic Capabilities

This book describes the theoretical concept of collaborative DC which consists of the following three main core theories:

> (1) building enduring relationships of trust through strategic collaboration with ecosystem partners,
> (2) realizing co-specialization with ecosystem partners, and
> (3) realizing capabilities synthesis with ecosystem partners.

The first aspect of the core theory is the corporate action taken to build enduring relationships of trust for strategic collaboration through the discovery and cultivation of ecosystem partners. The second aspect is the achievement of co-specialization through the asset orchestration of the knowledge (intangible and tangible assets) of those ecosystem partners. Co-specialization exists in various forms, such as: between assets (e.g., technologies and techniques); of strategies and organizations; of strategies and processes (e.g., operations); between technologies; and co-specialization of technologies and other parts of value chains. In groups of companies that promote ecosystem strategies in particular, achieving co-specialization with the assets of the individual companies is of vital importance.

The third aspect of the core theory is the achievement of capabilities synthesis through the asset orchestration process (see Box 1.1). Capabilities synthesis refers to the maximization of capabilities, including the company's own and those of its stakeholders (ecosystem partners), which creates a broad-based business ecosystem to achieve service innovation. Capabilities synthesis can be achieved through optimizing the asset orchestration process, the core function of DC.

The capabilities of companies and industries that realize these three main elements are collectively referred to as collaborative DC in this book. Furthermore, shedding light on the elements of macro and micro collaborative DC to create new services in the convergence era is one of the objectives of this study.

Existing research on DC focuses on the characteristics of sustainable competitiveness, mainly within the same industry, and maintaining this competitiveness, as well as the differences in competitiveness between companies. However, very little research has been done on DC within and among companies, and between industries, for creating business ecosystems through new service innovations and growing sustainably in convergence environments where the integration of technologies and services across different industries is moving ahead. On the other hand, collaborative DC form the foundation of the main core theoretical framework for achieving success in ecosystem strategies, and one of this book's core theories is the concept of "capabilities synthesis" between different companies and industries.

For example, IBM and P&G are typical examples of global corporations with innovation strategies based on collaborative DC. The formation of business communities that originate in *ba*, and community leaders who promote the sustainable growth of these business communities, are vital business elements for accelerating the asset orchestration process to realize new innovation in a convergence era through high-quality collaborative DC that intersect within and outside companies. *Ba* and business communities serve as important platforms for companies to evolve knowledge (intangible and tangible assets) at the same time as actively searching for excellent knowledge worldwide and promoting the integration (asset orchestration) of that knowledge with their own core knowledge (see Fig. 1.1).

One of the forms of business community described in this book is the "strategic community (SC)" (see Box 1.2). The authors, based on their research over a prolonged period, clarify that the formation of SCs begins in *ba* (see Fig. 1.1)

Box 1.1 "Capabilities Synthesis"—A New Theoretical Concept—The Synergy of Three Elements Based on Business Model Matching, Optimized Profit Structure Generation and Co-specialization

In considering capabilities synthesis, this book takes a close look at e-business ecosystems and presents case studies of service innovations they have achieved. First, the "multi-sided platform (two-sided platform) model" (Eisenmann et al. 2006) has at least two different types that can be clearly distinguished as business development models in which customers who play important and interdependent roles in those relationships simultaneously participate. Businesses that use this platform also provide high-value products and services to those customers. As well as saving transaction costs between different customers, these platforms also offer product and service diversity, and are typified by the online shopping systems used by eBay, Yahoo, Amazon, and so on (which match seeds and needs), advertising supported services like the Google search engine, and credit card services, such as Visa. More examples of this business model include newspapers that link advertisers with subscribers, and health maintenance organizations (a type of American health insurance system that links up patients with treatment organizations).

(continued)

Box 1.1 (continued)

In addition, convenience stores such as 7-Eleven use the business synergies of the multi-sided platform model formed from partnerships with different businesses to offer services such as financial services via ATM machines, distribution services like home delivery, and fee collection services for utility bills. Another example of the multi-sided platform model is Japan's JR, a rail and transport business that introduced Sony's non-contact FeliCa integrated circuit (IC) card into their train passes (Suica card), and installed Suica card readers in train stations and in surrounding convenience stores, restaurants, cafés, bookstores, and clothing stores. Thus encompassing a wide range of commercial entities and successfully creating new markets. Unlike online shopping, the convenience store and Suica card cases are examples of real-world shopping with a multi-sided platform model that created network effects among multiple clients (e.g., Shapiro and Varian 1998).

Ecosystem partners in this kind of multi-sided platform model position their businesses in various ways. For example, in the world of broadband and mobile telephone services, platform innovators such as telecommunications carriers and Internet service providers not only create information communications networks consisting of communications lines and nodes to transmit data, voice, and video, but also build systems that enable timely digital content delivery to end users in combination with the relevant financial transactions, authentication, and content searching capabilities necessary for information distribution. This type of information distribution platform makes use of application and content innovators to provide end users with a wide range of products and services—content innovators in broadband delivery services (for music, broadcast, video, books, games, corporate information, etc.) or value-added services (education, medical social welfare, etc.) offer a wide range of diverse applications.

Among the more prominent examples of success with this model are NTT DOCOMO's i-mode, Sony's and Nintendo's game businesses, the social networking website Facebook, and the online auction site eBay, but there are also web portals throughout the world that use this multi-sided platform model to provide a wealth of other e-commerce services. Most platforms in this model, such as Google and Amazon, offer open access to participants and external partners (the open, multi-sided platform model), although innovators offering platforms such as i-mode, or for games (such as Sony and Nintendo), or Apple's AppStore for its iPhone, engage in strict and thorough quality control of the services, applications, and content they provide on their platforms, and administer and regulate external partners. This book defines this semi-open multi-sided platform model by contrasting it with open platforms. Apple's AppStore is now an example of a semi-open multi-sided platform model, although it was initially a strongly vertically integrated organization that controlled its application and content innovators.

(*continued*)

Box 1.1 (continued)

Application and content innovators use the platforms (technology, products, services, etc.) provided by platform innovators to provide end users with products and services, such as B2B, B2C, and even B2B2C. However, fixed business rules exist in the semi-open multi-sided platform model between application, content, and platform innovators. In NTT DOCOMO's i-mode platform strategy of bundling various application services and content, co-ordination and collaboration based on fixed rules are very important.

In the multi-sided platform model, strategic collaboration between ecosystem partners is crucial because they require adequate communication, collaboration, and co-ordination to respond to platform innovators' technological improvements, product and service innovations, and changes to product and service specifications (or platform specifications). The process of platform users' strategic collaboration with platform innovators is also important, regardless of whether the platform is open or closed. Likewise, to invigorate a platform and maximize its network effects, platform innovators must engage in the important process of co-ordination and collaboration with external application and content innovators, who are important complementary players in this type of business process.

The multi-sided platform is also a core business model of the business ecosystem. The word "ecosystem" usually refers to biological systems but business ecosystems are similar in that they emerge from the mutual synergies between multiple corporate and organizational groups, while transactions between participants in the ecosystem influence other participants through network effects. In recent years, open platform ecosystem business models have become more widespread, such as open operating systems or Google's open social model. These enable profits from external partner innovation activities to be shared and promise profits from network effects while expanding the customer base. In contrast to the vertically integrated platform model, open platforms have the benefit of lower negotiation and adjustment costs with external partners.

In some cases, incorporating partially closed elements as a semi-open platform can serve to regulate access to the ecosystem (screening external partners, licensing, etc.) and can control the degree of ownership rights to the platform (for example, the level of external partner investment), which enables optimal advancement of innovation (quality and quantity), and quality control for the ecosystem.

Various business models require some elements of co-ordination and collaboration between individual ecosystem partners to bring about win-win business structures. The nature of strategic collaboration implies the creation of business models matched to create optimized profit structures for all involved. Platform innovators, who play an essential role in these business models in optimizing the profit structure, have to be mindful of corporate activities purely for their own profit (for example, overexpansion of

(continued)

Box 1.1 (continued)

the company's business domain through vertical integration of its platform, or giving favor to or ignoring certain application and content innovators). As mentioned, the most important element in maintaining and developing a business ecosystem is the deep strategic collaboration brought about by a resonance of values and trust building, which promotes the co-creation and co-evolution of these new business models.

Furthermore, there are three synergies that arise between ecosystem partners during the co-creation and co-evolution processes. The first is "business synergy." This refers to ecosystem partners working together for individual business model optimization through mutual creative assessment and alignment through matching processes. Importantly, ecosystem partners collaborate mutually and strategically to bring new and higher value to customers (target users and end users). Ecosystem partners must also be able to assess whether costs can be more efficiently reduced by using another company's knowledge (assets) instead of their own knowledge (asset). For example, the cases of convergence mentioned earlier are cases of business synergies arising from the mutual integration and optimization of business models with partner companies to create new markets through alliances with different businesses.

The second is "technology synergy," which decides whether ecosystem partners can mutually integrate technical knowledge to realize new products and services. An example of this is Google, a company that encouraged the merging of hardware and software technologies of its global device and mobile phone manufacturing partners with its Android OS. The collaboration of Google and Sony is a case of technology synergy using Android OS to develop next-generation Internet television with Sony's TV development capabilities and rich content (movies, music, etc.), combined with Google's software development capabilities.

The third is "partnership synergy." This synergistic element refers to ecosystem partners mutually and strategically collaborating to reinforce each other's strengths while supplementing each other's weaknesses to bring about higher levels of synergy and creativity. Long-term partnerships built on collaborative activities establish shared values and trust among all parties involved and contribute to the asset orchestration process; while partnership synergies can serve to improve the ecosystem partners' reputations. These three synergies are also the result of the co-specialization mentioned earlier.

Achieved through business model matching, the creation of optimal profit structures, and co-specialization, these synergistic elements result from capabilities synthesis within companies, between companies, and between industries. Underlying the realization of capabilities synthesis is the formation of business communities (SCs, discussed in Box 1.2), these are organizational platforms for maximizing the asset orchestration process, which makes their formation crucial (see Fig. 1.2).

(continued)

Box 1.1 (continued)

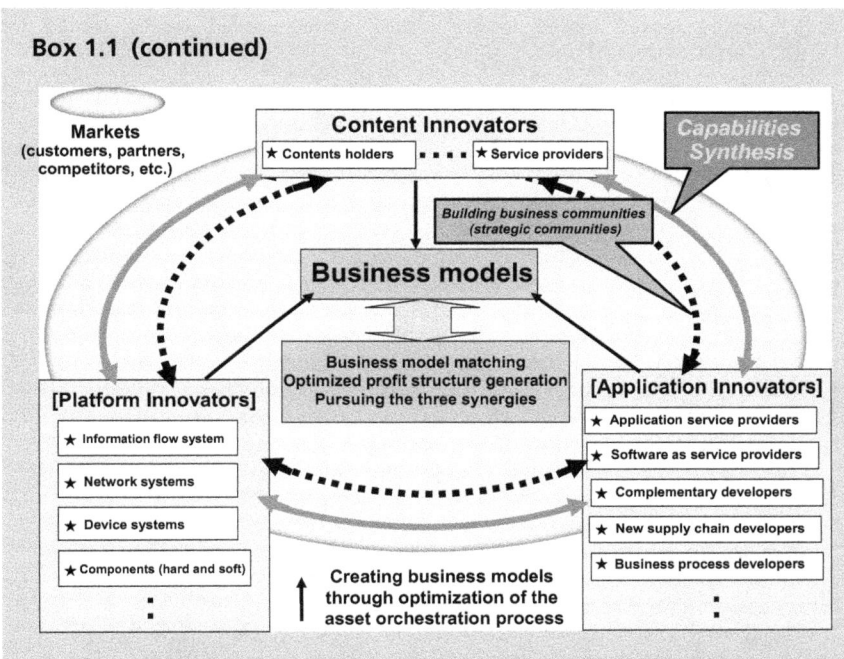

Fig. 1.2 Realization of synergies through "capabilities synthesis"

Box 1.2 Concept of Strategic Communities (SC)

SCs have characteristics of *ba* (Nonaka and Takeuchi 1995; Nonaka and Konno 1998) and are defined as follows (Kodama 2005, p. 28).

Strategic communities are based on the concept of *ba* as shared spaces for emerging relationships that serve as a foundation for knowledge creation. Participating in a *ba* means transcending one's own limited perspectives or boundaries and contributing to the dynamic process of knowledge creation. In strategic communities, members (including customers) with different values and knowledge consciously and strategically create *ba* in shared contexts that are always changing. New knowledge and competencies are formed by the organic merging and integration of communities to form *ba* to address multiple new eventualities. From a practical aspect, strategic communities are viewed as informal organizations with elements consistent with both the resource-based view of emergent shared-context learning and the planned strategic-based view of planning for a target market position.

(continued)

Box 1.2 (continued)

Furthermore, noting that SCs have characteristics of small-world structures in network theory, Kodama (2009a, p. 469) makes the following observation:

> SCs are groups forming small-world structures where practitioners in diverse specializations realize innovations aimed at solving the issues facing them and implement problem-solving and creative strategies. Short connections between nodes (people are the first unit nodes) and local clustering are features of small-world structures. For example, short paths among nodes of practitioners in different organizations enable easier access to other practitioners within a firm or based in other firms, including customers. Each node in a small-world structure is embedded in a local cluster. This clustering then enhances the possibility of fostering reliable accessibility. A small-world structure can be formed by either randomly rewiring a portion of an existing regular network or attaching each new node to a "neighborhood" that already exists.

In this way, SCs have characteristics of *ba* or small-world structures as networks, but in practice they also have characteristics of pragmatic boundaries (Carlile 2004). For example, Kodama (2005, p. 40) states that in actual business activities SCs actuate boundaries.

The third principle is that the SC provides pragmatic boundaries, allowing actors in different contexts to transform existing knowledge. A variety of problems or issues are posed within pragmatic boundaries, and actors are challenged with solving these problems and issues, and then creating new knowledge. The actors of an organization thus require practical yet creative confrontations or conflicts and also political negotiation skills. Hence, innovation or creativity emerges on the boundaries between the disciplines and specializations of different organizations.

On the other hand, Taifi and Passiante (2012, p. 2125), who discuss new products and service development through strategic community creation, note the following in regard to the importance of the formation of SCs in the automotive sector:

> The case study provides and analyzes the structural characteristics and success factors of an SC of after-sales services firms in the automotive sector. The study shows that it is important to have entities—more precisely SCs—dedicated to the after-sales services firms for the integration of their technical knowledge in the innovation process. The SC plays a key role, which is to contribute to the development of both the products and the services of the automaker. The paper contributes to the literature on the SC, and is an example of significant inter-organizational collaboration and innovation.

(continued)

> **Box 1.2 (continued)**
>
> In other words, knowledge integration (asset orchestration) through strategic collaboration between companies is important in service innovations.
>
> The concept of SCs has been practiced in the healthcare sector with the following results: The SC has taken the form of a temporary inter-organizational collaboration structure composed of health professionals, first-level managers, general practitioners, specialized doctors, and non-profit representatives. The SC approach has appeared to be an efficient strategy for taking action. It has been appropriate for cases where inter-organizational collaboration has clearly declined, and where several other attempts had failed, and where the care trajectory involved vulnerable clients who had to travel between different service points for their required care.
>
> From the perspective of previous research, it seems SCs are organizational platforms for developing core assets within and outside a company and actively searching for superior assets in the world to achieve asset orchestration of core assets within the company.

This book presents the theoretical concept of collaborative DC that achieve new service innovations in the convergence era and provides detailed case studies. The underlying questions are: What must a company do to generate new service innovations across different industries? What elements of collaborative DC generate new services and lead to sustainable corporate growth (as well as sustainability in relationships between companies and industries) in the convergence era? This book addresses these holistic research questions from the viewpoint of academic research in strategic and innovation management.

1.3 Theory Background: Dynamic Capabilities

The fundamentals of the theoretical model of collaborative DC in this book begin with a capabilities theory centered on the DC of existing research. The resource-based theories focused on independent capabilities for companies and organizations (e.g., Penrose 1959; Richardson 1972; Wernerfelt 1984; Rumelt 1984; Barney 1991) have developed as strategy theory frameworks from the viewpoints of microeconomics and organizational economics. These resource-based theories and Porter's (1980) competition strategy theory enable a detailed analysis of strategic positioning and the relationship between competitive excellence and the internal resources already owned by companies in slowly changing environments and industries. However, it is difficult to analyze how companies in rapidly changing hi-tech industries within competitive environments, such as the ICT and digital sectors, create new competitive excellence.

The theory of DC has been developed and refined, and has become a fundamental theory that clarifies the mechanisms for sustainable growth through corporate strategic innovation (e.g., Teece et al. 1997; Teece 2007, 2014). Teece et al. (1997, p. 516) assert that DC are defined as the firm's ability to integrate, build, and reconfigure internal and external competences to address rapidly changing environments. DC thus reflect an organization's ability to achieve new and innovative forms of competitiveness given path dependencies and market positions (Leonard-Barton 1992). In addition, Teece (2014, p. 332) states that strong DC enable an enterprise to profitably build and renew its resources and assets, both within and beyond its boundaries, reconfiguring them as needed to innovate and respond to (or bring about) changes in markets and in business environments more generally.

As micro core functions these DC can usefully be broken down into three primary clusters: (1) identification, development, co-development, and assessment of technological opportunities in relationship to customer needs (sensing); (2) mobilization of resources to address needs and opportunities, and to capture value from doing so (seizing); and (3) continued renewal (transforming). Engagement in continuous or semi-continuous sensing, seizing, and transforming is essential if a company is to sustain itself as customers, competitors, and technologies change (Teece 2007, 2014).

Regarding the domain in which DC are applied, Teece et al. (1997) claimed that DC are important for sustainable company-level competitive advantage, especially in high-velocity markets. Strong DC enable an enterprise and its top management to develop conjectures about the evolution of consumer preferences, business problems, and technologies, to validate and fine tune them, and then to act on them by realigning assets and activities to enable continuous innovation and change (Teece 2014).

From this perspective, and as a subtheme of this book, by achieving the creation of new services in the convergence era, DC can be considered as dynamic business processes that should be demonstrated in the convergence era with its rapidly changing business environments and/or high levels of uncertainty.

In the dynamic environments of "hypercompetition" (D'Aveni 1994) or "next-generation competition" (Teece 2012a, b) in the convergence era that has been gaining attention, the theoretical concept of DC is crucial for companies to drive "ecosystems strategies" (Teece 2014). Moreover, asset orchestration (see Teece 2007), a core function of DC, is reinforced by the organizational processes of: (1) co-ordination/integration; (2) learning; and (3) reconfiguration (Teece et al. 1997). This asset orchestration has a major influence on processes and outcomes for service innovations.

However, there is scant existing theoretical and practical research (qualitative and/or quantitative) on the relationship between DC and ecosystems strategies, or on the details of optimizing the asset orchestration process, which functions at the core of DC in the convergence era. Therefore, this book presents new practical and theoretical knowledge of collaborative DC, and makes novel contributions to the research on innovation and technology management for new services in the convergence era, an area that looks set for rapid growth.

1.4 Literature Review and Theory Background: Capabilities Map Concept

Resource-based theories focused on independent capabilities for companies and organizations have developed as strategy theory frameworks from the viewpoints of microeconomics and organizational economics (e.g., Penrose 1959; Richardson 1972; Wernerfelt 1984; Rumelt 1984; Barney 1991). These resource-based theories and Porter's (1980) competition strategy theory enable a detailed analysis of strategic positioning and the relationship between competitive excellence and a company's internal resources in slowly changing environments and industries.

However, this analysis is difficult in rapidly changing hi-tech industries within competitive environments, such as the ICT and digital sectors.

The theory of DC has been developed and refined, and has become a fundamental theory that clarifies the mechanisms for sustainable growth through corporate strategic innovation (e.g., Teece et al. 1997; Teece 2007, 2014). Teece et al. (1997, p. 516) assert that DC are defined as a firm's ability to integrate, build, and reconfigure internal and external competences to address rapidly changing environments. Hence, DC reflect an organization's ability to achieve new and innovative forms of competitive advantage given path dependencies and market positions (Leonard-Barton 1992). In addition, Teece (2014, p. 332) states that strong DC enable an enterprise to profitably build and renew the resources and assets that lie both within and beyond its boundaries, reconfiguring them as needed to innovate and respond to (or bring about) changes in the market and in the business environment more generally.

DC can usefully be broken down into three primary clusters of micro core functions: (1) identification, development, co-development, and assessment of technological opportunities in relationship to customer needs (sensing); (2) mobilization of resources to address needs and opportunities, and to capture value from doing so (seizing); and (3) continued renewal (transforming). Engagement in continuous or semi-continuous sensing, seizing, and transforming is essential if the firm is to sustain itself as customers, competitors, and technologies change (Teece 2007, 2014).

On the other hand, regarding the domain in which DC are applied, Teece et al. (1997) claimed that DC are important for sustainable company-level competitive advantage, especially in high-velocity markets. In addition, strong DC allow an enterprise and its top management to develop conjectures about the evolution of consumer preferences, business problems, and technology, to validate and fine tune them, and then to act on them by realigning assets and activities to enable continuous innovation and change (Teece 2014). From this perspective DC can be considered as important dynamic business processes that should be demonstrated in business environments that are rapidly changing and/or have a high degree of uncertainty, as seen in Domains I, II, and III in the Capabilities Map in Fig. 1.3 described in Sect. 1.5.

In the dynamic environments of "hypercompetition" (D'Aveni 1994) or "next-generation competition" (Teece 2012a, b), the theoretical concept of DC is crucial for companies to drive "ecosystems strategies" (Teece 2014). Moreover, asset orchestration (Teece 2007), a core function of DC, is reinforced by the organizational processes of: (1) co-ordination/integration; (2) learning; and (3) reconfiguration (Teece et al. 1997). Asset orchestration has effects on performance in the individual domains of the Capabilities Map (see Fig. 1.3).

Teece (2007, 2014) clearly distinguishes these DC from "ordinary capabilities" (OC hereinafter). Teece (2014, p. 330) states that "Ordinary capabilities have also been called static (Collis 1994), zero-level (Winter 2003), first order (Danneels 2002), and substantive (Zahra et al. (2006). The zero-, first-, and second- typology is used by Easterby-Smith and Prieto (2008) and Schilke (2014). The more common usage seems to be equating first-order with ordinary." Hence, these OC generally fall into three categories: administration, operations, and governance. As specific details of corporate activity, OC enable a company to perform an activity on an ongoing basis, using more or less the same techniques on the same scale to support existing products and services for the same customer population. Such a capability is ordinary in the sense of maintaining the *status quo* (that is, not out of the ordinary; Winter [2003]) (Helfat and Winter 2011).

Nevertheless, OC which pursue efficiency in terms of a company's best practices and "doing things right," are not to be underestimated—they are often fundamental and can support competitive advantage for decade-long periods (Teece 2014). In other words, OC are valid functions in relatively stable and gently changing environments with low levels of uncertainty, but they cannot ensure corporate sustainability over the long term. However, in large traditional companies running many businesses, there will always be some business domains in which these OC must be demonstrated. It is crucial to demonstrate OC in businesses in relatively stable environments where environmental change is gradual and there are low levels of uncertainty. OC are particularly important in Domain IV (see Fig. 1.3, low uncertainty, slow environmental change).

Accordingly, companies must apply OC and systematically and analytically formulate and implement strategies under relatively stable or slow-moving conditions with little business uncertainty. "Learning before doing" (Pisano 1994), that is, formulating and implementing detailed strategy planning and policies, is a key element of OC in market structures with clear corporate boundaries to capture/place into the players in value chains.

In contrast, DC have been reinterpreted by many researchers, including Eisenhardt and Martine (2000), who present them as

> The firm's processes that use resources—specifically the processes to integrate, reconfigure, gain and release resources—to match and even create market change. DC thus are the organizational and strategic routines by which firms achieve new resource configurations as markets emerge, collide, split, evolve, and die (p. 1107)

These scholars recursively derived the concept of corporate DC required for both slow and high-speed environments. They went on to suggest the importance of "learning by doing" with simple rules to emphasize results rather than prior training and implementation processes, especially in fast-moving environments, where uncertainty arises and an industry's corporate borders become vague (Eisenhardt and Sull 2001). However, Eisenhardt and Martin (2000) claimed that DC are inherently unsuited to creating sustainable advantage and that they are likely to break down in high-velocity markets.

Nevertheless, regarding the Eisenhardt and Martin (2000) statement that "dynamic capabilities would break down in high-velocity environments because of the instability of the simple rules (basically, semi-improvised managerial actions)," Teece (2014, p. 339) argued from a rational perspective on the real business environment, that:

> In high-velocity environments, the business enterprise may well be particularly reliant on the sensing and seizing instincts and actions of the CEO and the top management team. To the extent that this is so, the capabilities will, of course suffer from a degree of instability because their longevity depends logically on the tenure of entrepreneurs/managers/leaders.

In rapidly changing environments that require the dynamic spiral of thought and action, not only should top management but also project leaders and their team members be agile enough to show/use DC in front line processes to create new business, as they engage regularly in trial and error towards their strategic objectives (both prudent and bold—these are deliberate but sometimes emergent) (e.g., Kodama 2005). The concept of "simple rules" is one standard of judgment that should be considered by business practitioners in some complex dynamic business processes, depending on the situation.

In contrast to Eisenhardt and Martins' theory (2000), Teece (2014, p. 432) asserts that

> Eisenhardt and Martin's (2000) article misinterpreted (or reframed) the DC framework by claiming that all capabilities, including DC, can ultimately be characterized by best practice and hence imitated. In essence, Eisenhardt and Martin conflated two concepts that benefit from being analytically separated, namely OC and DC. OC and DC are quite distinct, both analytically and in practice.

This interpretation of DC has attracted differing opinions among researchers.

According to some researchers, this interest in strategy theory has evolved toward a dynamic structure that reflects current corporate activity. For example, O'Connor (2008) respects the DC theory of Eisenhardt and Martine (2000), and mentions that a large number of major innovations, including radical ones, developed gradually from slow (or very slow) market environments, and were implemented over a period of years to decades. Thus. the concept of DC is described as a theory that can be evaluated and applied to both market speed and business uncertainty (including risk) characterized by radical innovation.

Helfat and Winter (2011) assert that slow changes, projects currently in progress, and relatively peaceful external environments should be incorporated into research on DC. This is because DC should not be limited to brand new businesses, environments moving rapidly, or radical changes. There are plenty of cases of new product development, such as Intel's MPU, that are essentially cases of DC derived from ongoing businesses in relatively peaceful environments. Many of these businesses seem to be demonstrating routine OC, expanding the size and scope of their corporate resources at the same time as forming business ecosystems to achieve major economic effects through radical innovation. Technological innovations, as for the MPU, involve many scientists, engineers, and business partners in a wide range of different fields (electronic design automation (EDA) vendors, semiconductor manufacturing equipment manufacturers, etc.), and are driven by R&D processes in conditions of high business uncertainty (including risk) and novelty. In other words, in these environments, demonstrating DC is of particular importance in the Domain I → II shift (business environment with high uncertainty), as described in the Capabilities Map in Fig. 1.3.

O'Connor (2008) used the term "MI (major innovation) dynamic capability" for capabilities that promote the "exploration" process (March 1991) to achieve major innovation (radical and really new innovation) under conditions of uncertainty and high risk. MI DC differs from other capability theories that emphasize the evolution of the original exploitation activity process (e.g., King and Tucci 2002; Nelson and Winter 1982; Winter 2000) (March 1991). MI DC responds to highly uncertain situations, regardless of the speed of market movement, and embraces the concept of DC in high-speed (and high uncertainty) markets as mentioned by Eisenhardt and Martine (2000).

Realistically speaking (and drawing on the author's practical experience as a project leader), many radical innovations are established during the stages of discovery or invention in slow- and very slow-moving basic scientific research and technological development environments. The developed core technologies and provisional business models based on discovered or invented ideas are later adopted and exploited in products and services through improvisation and trial and error processes (including weeding-out processes) involving trial manufacture, experiment, and incubation. Product and service markets are gradually established. Then new products and services anticipated or forecast for the growth markets become the competitive markets for other companies (the timing of other companies entering the market depends on individual businesses). The market environment becomes fast-moving, and companies accelerate their investment in the necessary resources.

O'Connor and DeMartino (2006) undertook long-term observation and analysis of radical innovation in major US corporations, and indicated the importance of three-phase management (discovery, incubation, and acceleration) as a radical innovation development framework. They then named the ability to implement these processes the "breakthrough innovation capability," and suggested that building this capability into a company is a key management system that leads to successful radical innovation (O'Connor et al. 2008).

This three-phase management (discovery, incubation, and acceleration) is used in projects in large corporations (and venture enterprises) to develop new products, services, and businesses. Different capabilities are required from practitioners (and organizations such as project teams) in the business processes in each of the three phases, depending on the degree of business uncertainty and environmental change being faced. DC function robustly in response to the externalities of uncertainty and environmental change, and are also a framework for demonstrating difficult-to-imitate competitiveness. Hence, managing these three phases with "MI dynamic capability" (O'Connor 2008) and "Breakthrough Innovation Capability (the three phases of discovery, incubation, and acceleration)" (O'Connor et al. 2008) can be described with the three DC functions (sensing, seizing, transforming), which can be applied in highly uncertain and rapidly changing environments.

Previous research, such as Teece's DC framework and O'Connor's MI innovation capability, and so on, positioned around the two axes of uncertainty and change led to the situation illustrated by the Capabilities Map in Fig. 1.3, which shows the relationship between previous research and the three development phases of O'Connor and DeMartino (2006).

This chapter names these three management phases of discovery, incubation, and acceleration as Domains I, II, and III, to describe the stages leading from invention or proposal to the commercialization of new technologies and businesses. These three domains are business fields in which DC are demonstrated (and OC also need to be demonstrated in Domain III, see Sec. 1.5.3). In contrast, OC function in pursuit of best practices in stable environments with low uncertainty and slow change (Domain IV) (Teece 2007, 2014). Here there is stra-

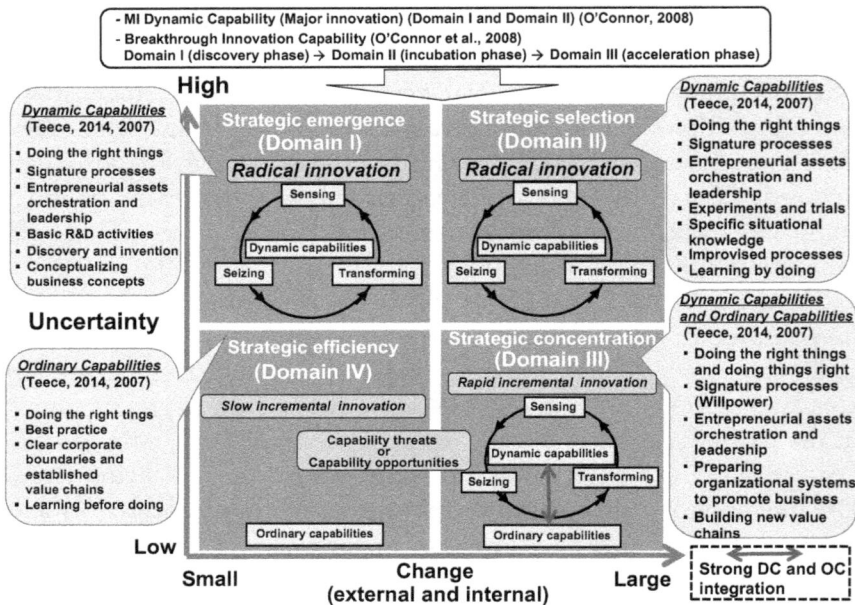

Fig. 1.3 The Capabilities Map: the DC and OC view

tegic uncertainty beyond the four elements of markets, technology, organization, and resources mentioned by Leifer et al. (2000); and change is not only limited to the external elements of market speed and industrial technology speeds, but it also corresponds to the internal elements of a company's own strategy, organization (organizational revamping), technology, operation, and leadership. Section 1.5 describes the characteristics of capabilities in each of the domains, and a capabilities system that integrates these domains.

1.5 Strategic Innovation Systems: DC and OC

In light of the theoretical concepts in the existing research, and from the perspective of DC and OC, this section analyzes the various capabilities required of diverse divisions in corporations (R&D, new business development, project teams, existing line organizations, etc.) as they face a range of business contexts daily. It also presents a "strategic innovation system" as a new theoretical framework, which includes a framework for building DC to achieve service innovations through strategic collaborations with stakeholders, such as partnering corporate players.

1.5.1 DC in Domain I

Slow or very slow environmental change with high uncertainty (Domain I) observed at the initial stage of radical innovation is the technology creation stage that arises from new ideas, business concepts, discoveries, and inventions, and corresponds to the "discovery phase" of O'Connor and DeMartino (2006). In this domain, the exploration process is advanced through the MI dynamic (or breakthrough innovation) capability mentioned above. The role of sensing in this domain is significant. To achieve radical innovation, R&D in large corporations (research laboratories, development centers, new business development organizations, etc.) must seek out and detect latent market potential with sensing, and continuously or semi-continuously set down and execute medium- to long-term R&D plans through the seizing and transforming processes.

The basic research and creation of ideas at the source of new strategic innovation will take longer as the ratio of scientific elements and degree of technological difficulty rises (depending on the field). Achievements in Domain I are largely due to the creative thinking and actions of middle managers and staff in company R&D and business development divisions (Nonaka 1988; Kodama 2005), but substantial commitment and strategic engagement needs to be made by top- and upper-level managers based on a policy of "doing the right things" (Teece 2014). Moreover, there are important "signature processes" (Bruch and Ghoshal 2004) in large traditional (leading) corporations that are difficult for other companies to copy and that raise the quality of R&D, which this author calls "strategic emergence."

In the asset orchestration process in Domain I, practitioners need to pursue reconfiguration/transformation through learning via hypotheses verification in line with R&D objectives and the co-ordination/integration of a wide range of intangible assets. Hence, there are diverse patterns for asset orchestration. There are still many cases of traditional companies with conventional hierarchical systems for closed innovation centered on internal laboratories and development divisions (Japanese manufacturing is a typical example) (e.g., Kodama 2009b). To develop incremental innovation or to sustain innovation through accumulated path-dependent knowledge closed innovation is still an important process (Christensen 1997). Closed innovation also plays a critical role in traditional hi-tech fields such as heavy electrical, nuclear power generation, aviation, vehicle equipment, machine tool, medical equipment, and semiconductor manufacturing equipment.

In contrast, in industries in which technologies are rapidly advancing, such as ICT, the best technical achievements and know-how are spreading across the globe. In these fast-moving environments open innovation is adopted (Chesbrough 2003), partial core intangible assets are incorporated from externalities, and hence processes to merge and integrate these assets with intangible assets, both within and outside of companies, are critical (e.g., Kodama 2009b). In these processes it is particularly important that the co-ordination and integration of various resources (as in asset orchestration) is performed by top and leading middle managers in an entrepreneurial fashion (Teece 2007).

In Domain I companies must consider what business model they should choose. Should they adopt a vertical integration model with the aim of finally bringing about core technologies, such as components, or completed items, such as products and services? Or should they focus on an area of specialization through a horizontal disintegration-type industrial structure? Or should they reinforce technologies while searching out strategic alliances (strong or weak ties) with other companies? Or should they build a new value chain through the co-ordination and integration of intangible assets, which are the strengths of this and other companies, via a strategic collaboration across different types of business? Thus, practitioners have to allow for an expanded diversification of asset orchestration and concentrate on learning through trial and error activities.

In Domain I companies have to hypothetically test their corporate boundaries in response to strategic objectives or business environments and attempt to reconfigure/transform entrepreneurial asset orchestration through trial and error processes. If it is advantageous to develop or manufacture in-house, then it is better to configure a vertical value chain model with a focus on creativity (Kodama 2009b). In contrast, there are many cases in which a company should abandon its in-house development efforts and focus on efficiency, not only through strategic outsourcing but also through strategic alliances, joint developments, and M&A to acquire and access external intangible assets. The important thing in this kind of asset orchestration process is "co-specialization" (Teece 2007), which raises levels of synergies of business elements, such as core technologies. The process of co-specialized asset orchestration is an important factor in raising a company's dynamic internal and external congruence in capabilities (Kodama 2018).

1.5.2 DC in Domain II

As core technologies and business concepts migrate from the slow-moving environment of Domain I to rapidly changing in-house (or occasionally external) acquisition of human resources, and the maintenance and upgrading of organizations for business incubation, there is a shift to a dramatically transforming Domain II environment that sustains speed of change and uncertainty. This domain promotes DC for exploration processes (MI dynamic or breakthrough innovation) (O'Connor 2008). It corresponds to the incubation phase of hypothetical setups, experiments, and assessments mentioned by O'Connor and DeMartino (2006). Learning through trials and experiments also leads to less risk and uncertainty in markets and technologies, and to a greater probability of success for incubation for radical innovation (O'Connor et al. 2008). Then top and middle management make decisions to select and bring to market rigorously tested and evaluated products, services, and business models.

In Domain II (the incubation phase), the role of seizing is important in commercial development divisions on the business side for achieving radical innovation. Commercialization divisions must use the sensing function to match technical innovations with markets (latent customer needs, etc.), while engaging in seizing and transforming radical innovations for the commercial development of new businesses, new technologies, and new processes. Thus, practitioners must pursue entrepreneurial strategies

(Minzberg 1978), demonstrate commitment, and make strategic contributions based on the basic policy of "doing the right things." Moreover, the quality of signature processes unique to a company that were required in Domain I are more strongly reflected in this domain. This is because of the, so-called, "valley of death" (Branscomb et al. 2001; Markham 2002; Merrifield 1995), which can be a serious impediment to commercializing the outcomes of R&D. The capability to surmount these hurdles is largely down to these rarefied signature processes unique to companies.

O'Connor et al. (2008) confine this incubation domain to trial experiment and assessment models, but in many cases business activities go beyond trial experiments in uncertain and dramatically changing, fast-moving environments and commercial businesses are launched, where companies may boldly take up risky challenges. In this domain, there are often cases where the excessive trust and commitment of leaders and managers lead to strategies to create business through trial and error while it is still unclear whether newly developed ideas or prototypes have the potential for building new business models and value chains. These are typified by cases in the new online business world where products are both trialed and launched in dramatically changing domains of general high risk and uncertainty. Hence, the key is to select and implement promising, valuable businesses. The author calls this domain "strategic selection."

In Domain II the asset orchestration process entails selecting and narrowing down the diverse intangible and tangible assets trialed and experimented on in the strategic emergence domain. The level of completeness of asset orchestration of products, services, and business models is raised through: (1) co-ordination/integration; (2) learning; and (3) reconfiguration. Depending on circumstances, there are cases where it is necessary for a corporation to rethink its corporate boundaries (both vertical and horizontal) or its relationships with other companies, such as partnerships, and to realign or reconfigure its assets.

1.5.3 DC and OC in Domain III

If the new businesses (products and services) chosen through strategic selection in Domain II have prospects for the future and somewhat reduced uncertainty, they shift to Domain III, a domain of lower uncertainty, although external (environmental) and internal change is ongoing. Domain III is the stage in which the radical innovations incubated (or partially commercialized) in Domain II enter a growth trajectory; it corresponds to the "acceleration phase" mentioned by O'Connor and DeMartino (2006). According to O'Connor et al. (2008), this is where the exploitation process is promoted by breakthrough innovation capability, and the building and optimizing of processes and value chains for the selected new businesses are achieved.

New business functions are then wholly or partially transferred to the appropriate business divisions to accelerate commercialization (or else new business divisions are established, or made independent as external ventures), and further resources are invested in through the strategic commitment of top and middle management to "doing the right things." The author calls this domain "strategic concentration." A large number of product and service development projects for major corporations have invested management resources through asset orchestration in commercialization through this kind of shift from strategic selection to strategic concentration (e.g., Kodama 2005, 2007d).

In Domain III, where environmental change is very fast and competition with other companies is fierce, the role of transforming the business side is important for surviving the so-called "Darwinian Sea" (e.g., Dismukes 2004). The "Darwinian Sea" metaphor illustrates a burgeoning of new organisms in competition with each other in rough seas and being culled and implies evolution in business. As time passes, newly developed products and businesses burst into competitive environments with other companies with this shift into Domain III. Nevertheless, while the degree of shift into a competitive environment depends on the industry or the features of a product, the actual birth of a competitive market means that uncertainty in the environment, in other words the market, becomes low. Divisions that are positioned upstream of the value chain at the business side (such as product planning and technical development) also function to sense and detect changes in newly created markets and to establish robust value chains through seizing and transforming for upgrades and improvements through quick and incremental innovation (sustainably advancing technologies) of new products and businesses that have been successfully commercialized. For this purpose, practitioners pursue entrepreneurial strategies (including deliberate and emergent strategies), to demonstrate commitment and strategic engagement based on the basic policy of "doing the right things."

In Domain III there is significant dependence on the "willpower" (Bruch and Ghoshal 2004) of the unique signature processes of a company to win out over the competition. Willpower is the energy and concentration in the thinking and actions that come with a sense of purpose. Energy means vigor, and concentration directs energy toward a particular outcome. For practitioners the most important factor is to paint a clear scenario of their intended strategy in their minds and to then dedicate themselves to planning so as to bring their strategy into being in the midst of stiff competition.

In this domain, much of the burden is carried by the unique and highly rarefied signature processes of a company through willpower. A strategy can be defined as "a coherent set of analyses, concepts, policies, arguments and actions that respond to a high-stakes challenge" (Rumelt 2011, p. 6), just as Teece (2014, p. 314) argued. The best strategic activities require: (1) a diagnosis; (2) a guiding policy; and (3) coherent action brought about by the unique signature processes of a company based on willpower (Rumelt 2011). At the time of writing the smartphone market is in the Domain III stage, as the completion level of products and services is raised for commercialization, and upgrades, improvements, and new versions as rapid incremental innovation, through the processes of asset orchestration are promoted and concentrated to complete value chains.

However, in Domain III, to get new products, services, and businesses off the ground, win out over the competition, and survive the Darwinian Sea, robust value chains must be configured. Organization supervisors and staff in product planning and technical development divisions upstream of the business side in the value chain must demonstrate strong DC. In contrast, leaders and staff in routine divisions downstream in the value chain (sales, technical management, procurement, manufacturing, after support, etc.) need to thoroughly reinforce operations management through strong OC. These downstream divisions require strong OC to get their current products (and their successor upgraded and improved versions) on the market, win out amid stiff competition, and turn a profit. Thus, the capabilities required in Domain III are essentially different to those required in Domains I and II since the strong integration of DC and OC is of particular importance (see Fig. 1.3).

1.5.4 OC in Domain IV

A great deal of existing business is positioned in Domain IV, in slow-moving market environments with low uncertainty and low rates of change. Incremental innovation is promoted to systematically enhance business efficiency through the exploitation process, which comprises activities to improve existing business by using mainstream organizations that demonstrate inherent OC (Teece 2007, 2014).

In Domain IV, the weight on DC diminishes, and the focus shifts to the demonstration of best practice through OC. In existing traditional line organizations (business units, etc.) slow changes in existing markets are observed, existing operations in formal organizations are executed through path-dependent, planned, carefully considered, and deliberate strategies in business divisions, and they demonstrate strict, top-down, centralized leadership (Kodama 2004). In Domain IV, to drive slow incremental innovation through strengthened OC, high performance must be brought about by evolving routines through higher-order learning to generate short-term profits in response to internal and external changes (King and Tucci 2002; Benner and Tushman 2003; Winter 2000; Amburgey et al. 1993; Nelson and Winter 1982). Promoting Domain IV process management accelerates an organization's speed of response to achieve incremental innovation (Benner and Tushman 2003). However, there is always a danger that product lineups in Domain IV could be threatened by emergent technical innovations. The author calls this domain "strategic efficiency."

Many businesses in Domain IV (products and services) are those that have survived the competitive environment of Domain III and that have come into Domain IV later, which entails the conversion of old and new businesses over long periods of time (Markides 2001). In other words, this means replacing the strategic concentration from Domain III, arrived at through the path of radical innovation (Domain I → Domain II → Domain III), with the strategic efficiency of Domain IV (in other words, conversion of new and old business). The simultaneous management of existing and new strategic positions discussed by Markides (2001) is combined in Domains III and IV, and in shifting from an old position to a new one, existing businesses initially positioned in Domain III are replaced by new businesses that have grown and accelerated in Domain III (through the Domain I → Domain II → Domain III shift), which means existing businesses in Domain III shift to Domain IV.

In describing the dynamics of the shifts between domains in the Capabilities Map, of particular importance are the strategic actions in Domains III and IV that aim for sustainable corporate growth through ongoing strategic innovation. According to the "capabilities lifecycles" framework of Helfat and Peteraf (2003), to uncover capabilities opportunities to achieve further radical innovation, and to handle capability threats as they arise, companies drive new DC in Domains III and IV, and

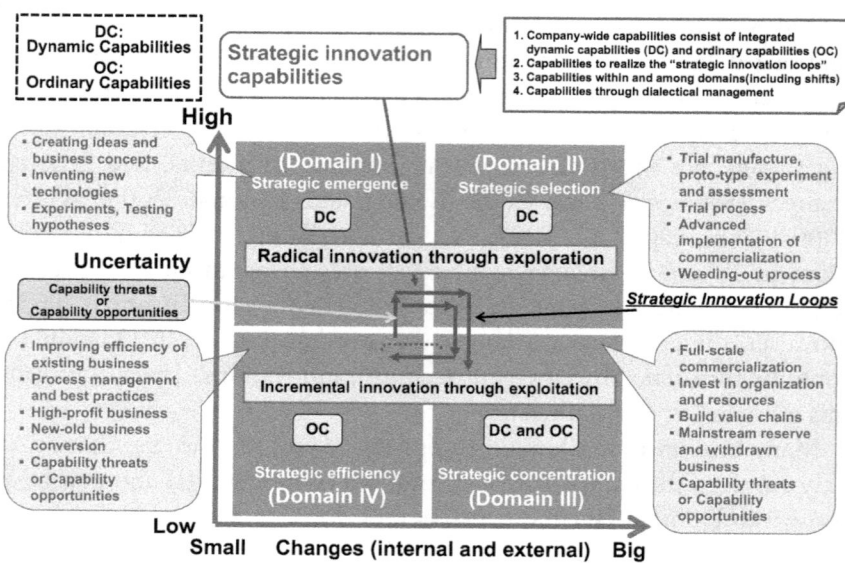

Fig. 1.4 The strategic innovation system

then shift into Domain I (see Figs. 1.3 and 1.4). In other words, as discussed in Sec. 1.6, leading corporations engage in a spiraling of strategic activities between these four domains (Domain I → Domain II → Domain III → Domain IV → Domain I and/or Domain III → Domain I ...) to achieve strategic innovation through interaction with dynamic changes in the environment. The author calls this corporate system of achieving strategic innovation a "strategic innovation system." The following section describes the strategic innovation loop and strategic innovation capability that make up this strategic innovation system.

1.6 "Strategic Innovation Loop" and "Strategic Innovation Capability"

When considered from the viewpoints of corporate exploration and exploitation processes based on radical and incremental innovations, and the time axis in a business context, the four domains form a continuous loop (see Fig. 1.2). The strategic emergence (Domain I) and selection (Domain II) domains, which are exploratory processes through DC (asset orchestration), are the core processes for radical innovation processes. "Strategic concentration (Domain III)" is the acceleration phase indicated by O'Connor and DeMartino (2006). This phase rapidly sets up new product, service, and business models or market strategies through the exploratory processes of strategic emergence and selection, and shifts the domain from one of exploration to one of exploitation. Strategic concentration initiates paths to newly generated radical innovations that differ from the existing business of the strategic efficiency domain (Domain IV).

In the strategic concentration domain, newly generated business always undergoes major internal or external change in its initial phase. At this stage, businesses transform their internal elements aimed at building optimal value and supply chains in response to external change. This is the strategic concentration domain in which strong integration of DC and OC are required, as described above.

Businesses that succeed in establishing themselves in markets from among these strategically concentrated businesses, which are subject to major change, achieve stability as mainstream operations shift to the slow-moving (or small) "strategic efficiency" domain, while promoting still greater operational and business process efficiency measures, either become part of the existing mainstream lineup or undergo business integration (which promotes still greater business process efficiency through strong OC).

However, businesses subject to major external changes in markets and technologies following mainstream growth, and major internal changes in areas such as strategy, organization, technology, operations, and leadership (for example, ICT industries in broadband and smartphones, online businesses, or digital consumer electronics) always become positioned in this strategic concentration domain. Put another way, businesses growing in a mainstream direction become deployed in one or both of the strategic concentration and efficiency domains. Although new business in the strategic concentration domain is the "mainstream reserve," this does not mean that all business can grow in a changing mainstream environment, and some businesses have to withdraw. This is especially true of the ICT industry.

In this way, the flow of radical innovation for major corporations shifts from Domain I to Domain II, then to Domain III (where some businesses undergoing major changes maintain their position), and finally to Domain IV (see Fig. 1.4). Many businesses in Domain IV (products and services) are those that have survived the competitive environment of Domain III, which entails the conversion of old and new businesses over long periods of time (Markides 2001). In other words, this means the replacement of strategic concentration businesses in Domain III, arrived at through the path of radical innovation (Domain I → Domain II → Domain III), with existing strategic efficiency businesses in Domain IV (the conversion of new and old business). As described above, the simultaneous management of existing and new strategic positions discussed by Markides (2001) is combined in Domains III and IV, and in shifting from an old position to a new one, existing businesses initially positioned in Domain III are replaced by new businesses that have grown and accelerated in Domain III (though the Domain I → Domain II → Domain III shift), which means existing businesses in Domain III shift to Domain IV.

Realistically however, although major corporations promote strategically innovative projects, only some survive to become success stories through the natural selection process involved in the shift from Domains I to III. Amabile and Khaire (2008) note a number of cases where outstanding ideas and business models born in Domain I have been diluted and ended in failure after a major corporation employed a different management organization to commercialize them. This is one issue associated with radical innovation that major corporations face. As the domain shifts can be observed within organizations at the micro level, and because there is feedback through the interactions between each domain and spiral feedback loops at the macro level, this model also includes the chain-linked model of Kline (1985).

The most important inter-domain shift is that from III and/or IV to I. This is the path that creates radical new innovations (see Fig. 1.4). In the Capabilities Lifecycles of Helfat and Peteraf (2003), large corporations involved in businesses in Domains III and IV that are seeking out new capability opportunities and directly facing capability threats also need to take strategic action through the demonstration of DC. This is characterized by accelerated environmental and internal interactions and the creation of new ideas, technological inventions, and discoveries based on high-quality tacit knowledge (Nonaka and Takeuchi 1995). This knowledge is cultivated through the practice of researchers, engineers, marketers, and strategy specialists in shifting from Domains I through IV (accumulating and integrating new practice through existing business practice and incremental and radical innovation) via the "transformational experience" of shifting from previously existing business routines with strategic innovation (King and Tucci 2002; Amburgey et al. 1993). King and Tucci (2002) suggested that the transformational experience of practitioners involved in continual (Katz and Allen 1982) and large-scale (Tushman and Romanelli 1985; Amburgey et al. 1993) organizational innovation in product development teams leads to continuous new product innovation and can overcome rigid organizational inertia. Put another way, it enhances the potential for embedding new DC in organization members to create new strategic non-routines that transform organizations and achieve radical innovation.

While excessive adherence to existing knowledge (e.g., Kodama 2009b) can become a hindrance, the absorption of knowledge from different sectors and industries, and from scientific, technological, and marketing viewpoints, and the knowledge integration process can trigger new radical innovations. Various innovation theories, including the importance of shedding the "mental model" (e.g., Spender 1990), the focus on "peripheral vision" and "boundary vision" (Kodama 2011; Kodama and Shibata 2016), the challenge of achieving "cross innovation" (Johansson 2004), and "destructive innovation" (Christensen 1997) confer precious insights into innovation processes, but more detailed theory building is yet to be undertaken. The author proposes that the evolution and diversification of high-level, strategic non-routines, through the formation of strategic communities (see Box 1.2) in Domains III and IV, fundamentally promote DC (asset orchestration) while inducing the shift to Domain I arising from the incremental innovation and integration of new knowledge (assets) inside and outside the company (Kodama 2009b), and increase the probability of achieving new knowledge integration as radical innovation.

The author would like to explain the *three new insights* obtained from this framework and use them as a basis for explaining strategic innovation capabilities. The first insight is that outstanding companies deliberately hold a dynamic view of capabilities (including some emergent elements) and drive the loops in continuous shifts (strategic innovation loops, see Fig. 1.2) from Domain I → Domain II → Domain III → Domain IV → Domain I and/or Domain III → Domain I. This dynamic view of capabilities co-establishes the different modes of the exploratory and exploitative processes and can secure long-term corporate growth (e.g., March 1996; Benner and Tushman 2003; Tushman and O'Reilley 1997). These two processes (March 1991; Holland 1975) do not employ opposing strategic activities; rather, companies must implement a strategy while skillfully balancing their strategic activities in a mutually complementary way (He and Wong 2004).

Zollo and Winter (2002) propose a knowledge evolution process based on adjusted evolutionary theory. The continuous routine activity seen within this process can trigger a shift from the exploitation to the exploration process, while experiential knowledge accumulated from learning activities can also be an element in creating new DC (corresponding to a shift from Domain III and/or Domain IV to Domain I). The author explains how the recursive processes and co-evolution of these different modes simultaneously challenge corporations and drive process routines.

Furthermore, regarding short- and long-term strategies and organizational reform, Dixon et al. present a theoretical framework of the "dynamic capabilities cycle" derived from an in-depth longitudinal case study on a Russian oil company. They cite two capabilities to be demonstrated by the company in its short- and long-term development processes: the first is "adaption dynamic capabilities" as exploitation activities to regularly polish its extant knowledge (i.e., OC) to respond to environmental changes, and gain a temporal, short term competitive edge; the second capability is "innovation dynamic capabilities" as exploration activities to acquire sustainable, long-term competitiveness through unique new creative ideas and action (i.e., DC). These researchers named these patterns for strategy execution the "dynamic capabilities cycle" in which leading companies cyclically demonstrate these two different capabilities through time (both asynchronously and synchronously).

In contrast to the DC theory of dynamic resources reconfiguration, divestment, and integration to handle environmental changes (Teece et al. 1997), the DC cycle offers a model that takes into account capability factors to further achieve radical new innovation, such as exploration (March 1991) or path creation (Graud and Karne 2001).

The second insight is that observing large corporations at selected times reveals the constant presence of each of the four domains with their different business contexts. In large corporations, multiple projects oriented to strategic innovation function as layered strategic innovation loops on different time axes. Top and middle management must therefore manage appropriately within each domain and it is key that they smoothly implement the domain shift through a strategic innovation loop. Different strategies, organizational structures, technology, operations, and leadership are required within each domain.

In this discussion one especially important question is how the asset orchestration process can create the skills and expertise for strategic emergence (Domain I, the new discovery and invention domain), using accumulated experiential knowledge (which arises from diverse high-level strategic non-routines through DC via continuous strategic innovation loops) and then absorb and integrate new knowledge outside the company. Regardless, learning through higher-order routines (Amburgey et al. 1993; Nelson and Winter 1982; Winter 2000) alone does not make it easy to shift from Domain III and/or Domain IV to Domain I.

Teece (2014, p. 338) said "First, I reject the notion that dynamic capabilities reside *only* in high-level routines," and continued that "creative managerial and entrepreneurial acts (e.g., creating new markets) are, by their nature, often non-routine." In the same vein Teece (2014, p. 332) quotes Steve Jobs, the late CEO of Apple, who said "Innovation has nothing to do with how many R&D dollars you have. When Apple came up with the Mac, IBM was spending at least one hundred times more on R&D. 'It's … about … how much you get it'."

In another interview about product development at Apple (Burrows 2004), Jobs described it as a blend of routine and creative acts: "Apple is a very disciplined company, and we have great processes. But that's not what it's about. Process makes you more efficient. But innovation comes from people meeting up in the hallways or calling each other at 10:30 at night with a new idea, or because they realized something that shoots holes in how we've been thinking about a problem."

That means Apple's processes are based in OC. However, even if a new product development entails a number of routine components, Jobs said that at least one thing has to be different. Those different things are the non-routine establishment of strategies and activities by entrepreneurs. Hence, new product development projects at Apple, through the prioritization of the future, based on a deep market understanding gained through Jobs' own sensing and his insatiable obsession to achieve easy-to-use products with attractive designs and advanced technologies (co-specialization through asset orchestration integrating hardware, software, applications, and contents) was a driving force in the company's success. The creative acts of seizing and transforming brought about through diverse strategic non-routine activities at Apple also hint at the secret of what Jobs described as "getting it" (Teece 2012a, b). Thus, as a chain of creative actions, asset orchestration itself can be described through the demonstration of DC.

From the research conducted into the divisions in corporations that achieve innovations as new products or businesses (including the authors' direct and indirect involvement) (e.g., Kodama 2002, 2005, 2006,

2007a, b, c, d, e), the authors would like to present the hypothesis that DC are generally demonstrated by practitioners through strategic non-routine activities via the configuration of informal organizations (or informal networks, which are also strategic communities), whereas OC are mainly demonstrated by practitioners through routine business in formal organizations.

Our accumulated research to date clarifies that, depending on the characteristics of a business and the environmental circumstances, the characteristics of informal organizations change in accordance with changes of characteristics in boundaries (knowledge and organizational boundaries) in and between organizations (between practitioners at the micro level) (Carlile 2002, 2004; Kodama and Shibata 2014a, b). As detailed in case studies in this book, absorbing and integrating new knowledge (assets) or capabilities, in other words promoting asset orchestration through DC, entails the formation of strategic communities with pragmatic boundaries to promote strategic non-routing activities (see Box 1.2).

The third insight is that the analysis of in-depth longitudinal case studies in this book suggests that the exploration and exploitation processes are especially interactive. It has been argued that organizations within major corporations undertaking radical innovation should either be isolated physically and organizationally from the mainstream organization, or they should operate as independent venture companies (e.g., Hill and Rothaermel 2003; Benner and Tushman 2003; Burgelman and Sayles 1988; Kanter 1985). But an appropriate interface with existing organizations is also potentially significant for accelerating radical innovation from the viewpoint of strategy and resource integration (e.g., Heller 1999; Kodama 2003). Questions of organizational design are arguably more important in achieving strategic innovation, such as: How much should a new business integrate with, or separate from, existing businesses? Is it better to have complete separation, complete integration, or something in between? (e.g., Christensen 1997; Burgelman and Sayles 1988; Good and Campbell 2002; Tushman and O'Reilley 1997).

Much previous research discussed management processes and organizational divisions, such as: the two distinct archetypes of exploratory and exploitative, or incremental or radical (e.g., Greenwood and Hinings 1993; Tushman and O'Reilley 1997); and the ambidextrous organization (e.g., O'Reilley and Tushman 2004). However, little detailed analysis has been done on the interfaces and interactions between management elements, such as strategy, organizational structure, technology, operation, and leadership, which differ in each archetype (e.g., Kodama 2003, 2004). Nevertheless, the co-establishment and co-existence of these two archetypes within the same large corporation, and the skillful management of strategic contradiction (Smith and Tushman 2005), creative abrasion (Leonard-Barton 1995), and productive friction (Hagel III and Brown 2005) to create synergies are also important elements of successful strategic innovation. The co-existence of contradictions highlights the important roles not just of the top management (Smith and Tushman 2005; Tushman and O'Reilley 1997), but also of middle management and staff (Govindarajan and Trimble 2005). The author calls this "dialectical management" (Kodama 2003, 2004, 2017a).

Based on these three insights above, strategic innovation capabilities is a concept that embraces the following *four capabilities*: The (1) all the capabilities of a company integrating DC and OC; (2) the capabilities to implement spiral strategic innovation loops; (3) capabilities within and among domains, including shifts; (4) and capabilities to achieve the co-existence of two the different archetypes through dialectic management (see Fig. 1.4). Moreover, strategic innovation capabilities embrace the existing dynamic and MI DC (or breakthrough innovation capability) concepts mapped in Fig. 1.3, while aiming to expand the concept of DC and OC for individual product development projects in large corporations in the direction of innovation capabilities for the corporate or management system. This book calls the kind of management system that uses strategic innovation capabilities to activate spiraling strategic innovation loops and to maintain the existing business while establishing strategic innovation business the "strategic innovation system" (see Fig. 1.4).

From the concepts of the Capabilities Map, DC and OC, strategic innovation capabilities, and the strategic innovation loop, Chap. 2 discusses a framework for collaborative DC, the core theory of this book, from the perspective of a systems approach.

1.7 Chapter Summary

This chapter has presented an overview of the theoretical concept of collaborative DC, an important corporate capability within and between companies and industries aimed at building business ecosystems. The chapter also introduced the concept of a Capabilities Map of corporate capabilities to handle uncertainty and speed of change in environments; it observed and analyzed the characteristics of capabilities in the map from the perspective of DC and OC; and presented a "strategic innovation system" as a dynamic theoretical framework for maintaining sustainable corporate competitiveness.

References

Amabile, T. M., & Khaire, M. (2008). Creativity and the Role of the Leader. *Harvard Business Review, 86*, 100–109.

Amburgey, T., Kelly, D., & Barnett, W. (1993). Resetting the Clock: The Dynamics of Organizational Change and Failure. *Administrative Science Quarterly, 38*(1), 51–73.

Barney, J. (1991). Firm Resources and Sustained Competitive Advantage. *Journal of Management, 17*(1), 99–120.

Benner, M., & Tushman, M. (2003). Exploitation, Exploration, and Process Management: The Productivity Dilemma Revisited. *Academy of Management Review, 28*(2), 238–256.

Branscomb, L. M., Auerswald, P. E., & Chesbrough, H. W. (2001). *Taking Technical Risks*. Cambridge, MA: MIT Press.

Bruch, H., & Ghoshal, S. (2004). *A Bias for Action: How Effective Managers Harness Their Willpower, Achieve Results, and Stop Wasting Time*. Boston: Harvard Business Press.

Burgelman, R. A., & Sayles, L. R. (1988). *Inside Corporate Innovation*. New York: Simon and Schuster.

Burrows, P. (2004). The Seed of Apple's Innovation. *Business Week*, 12.

Carlile, P. (2002). A Pragmatic View of Knowledge and Boundaries: Boundary Objects in New Product Development. *Organization Science, 13*(4), 442–455.

Carlile, P. (2004). Transferring, Translating, and Transforming: An Integrative Framework for Managing Knowledge Across Boundaries. *Organization Science, 15*(5), 555–568.

Chesbrough, H. (2003). *Open Innovation*. Boston: Harvard Business School Press.

Christensen, C. M. (1997). *The Innovator's Dilemma: When New Technologies Cause Great Firms to Fail*. Boston: Harvard Business School Press.

Collis, D. J. (1994). Research Note: How Valuable Are Organizational Capabilities? *Strategic Management Journal, 15*(S1), 143–152.

D'Aveni, R. A. (1994). *Hypercompetition: Managing the Dynamics of Strategic Maneuvering*. New York: Free Press.

Danneels, E. (2002). The Dynamics of Product Innovation and Firm Competences. *Strategic Management Journal, 23*(12), 1095–1121.

Dismukes, J. P. (2004). Accelerate Radical Innovation-Now! *Research Technology Management, 47*(5), 2.

Easterby-Smith, M., & Prieto, I. M. (2008). Dynamic Capabilities and Knowledge Management: An Integrative Role for Learning? *British Journal of Management, 19*(3), 235–249.

Eisenhardt, K., & Martine, J. (2000). Dynamic Capabilities: What Are They? *Strategic Management Journal, 21*(10–11), 1105–1121.

Eisenhardt, K., & Sull, D. (2001). Strategy as Simple Rules. *Harvard Business Review, 79*, 106–116.

Eisenmann, T., Parker, G., & Van Alstyne, M. (2006, October). Strategies for Two-Sided Markets, *Harvard Business Review, 84*, 92.

Garud, R., & Karnoe, P. (2001). Path Creation as a Process of Mindful Deviation. In R. Garud & P. Karnoe (Eds.), *Path Dependence and Creation* (pp. 1–38). London: Lawrence Erlbaum.

Goold, M., & Campbell, A. (2002). *Designing Effective Organizations: How to Create Structured Networks*. San Francisco: Jossey-Bass.

Govindarajan, V., & Trimble, C. (2005). *Ten Rules for Strategic Innovations*. Boston: Harvard Business School Press.

Greenwood, R., & Hinings, C. (1993). Understanding Strategic Change: The Contribution of Archetypes. *Academy of Management Review, 36*(5), 1052–1081.

Hagel, J., III, & Brown, J. S. (2005). Productive Friction. *Harvard Business Review, 83*(2), 139–145.

He, Z., & Wong, P. (2004). Exploration Vs. Exploitation: An Empirical Test of the Ambidexterity Hypothesis. *Organization Science, 15*(4), 481–494.

Helfat, C. E., & Peteraf, M. A. (2003). The Dynamic Resource-Based View: Capability Lifecycles. *Strategic Management Journal, 24*(10), 997–1010.

Helfat, C. E., & Winter, S. G. (2011). Untangling Dynamic and Operational Capabilities: Strategy for the (N)everchanging World. *Strategic Management Journal, 32*(11), 1243–1250.

Heller, T. (1999). Loosely Coupled Systems for Corporate Entrepreneurship: Imaging and Managing the Innovation Project/Host Organization Interface. *Entrepreneurship, Theory and Practice, 24*(2), 25–31.

Hill, C., & Rothaermel, F. (2003). The Performance of Incumbent Firms in the Face of Radical Technological Innovation. *Academy of Management Review, 28*(2), 257–247.

Holland, J. (1975). *Adaption in Natural and Artificial Systems*. Ann Arbor: University of Michigan Press.

Johansson, F. (2004). *The Medici Effect*. Boston: Harvard Business School Press.

Kanter, R. (1985). Supporting Innovation and Venture Development in Established Companies. *Journal of Business Venturing, 1*(1), 47–60.

Katz, R., & Allen, T. (1982). Investigating the Not Invented Here (NIH) Syndrome: A Look at the Performance, Tenure, and Communication Patterns of 50 R & D Project Groups. *R&D Management, 12*(1), 7–12.

King, A., & Tucci, L. (2002). Incumbent Entry into New Market Niches: The Role of Experience and Managerial Choice in the Creation of Dynamic Capabilities. *Management Science, 48*(2), 171–187.

Kline, S. J. (1985). Innovation Is Not a Linear Process. *Research Management, 28*(4), 36.

Kodama, M. (2001). Creating New Business Through Strategic Community Management. *International Journal of Human Resource Management, 11*(6), 1062–1084.

Kodama, M. (2002). Transforming an Old Economy Company Through Strategic Communities. *Long Range Planning, 35*(4), 349–365.

Kodama, M. (2003). Strategic Innovation in Traditional Big Business. *Organization Studies, 24*(2), 235–268.

Kodama, M. (2004). Strategic Community-Based Theory of Firms: Case Study of Dialectical Management at NTT DoCoMo. *Systems Research and Behavioral Science, 21*(6), 603–634.

Kodama, M. (2005). Knowledge Creation Through Networked Strategic Communities: Case Studies in New Product Development. *Long Range Planning, 38*(1), 27–49.

Kodama, M. (2006). Knowledge-Based View of Corporate Strategy. *Technovation, 26*(12), 1390–1406.

Kodama, M. (2007a). *The Strategic Community-Based Firm*. London: Palgrave Macmillan.

Kodama, M. (2007b). *Knowledge Innovation – Strategic Management as Practice*. Cheltenham: Edward Elgar Publishing.

Kodama, M. (2007c). *Project-Based Organization in the Knowledge-Based Society*. London: Imperial College Press.

Kodama, M. (2007d). Innovation and Knowledge Creation Through Leadership-Based Strategic Community: Case Study on High-Tech Company in Japan. *Technovation, 27*(3), 115–132.

Kodama, M. (2007e). Innovation Through Boundary Management—A Case Study in Reforms at Matsushita Electric. *Technovation*, 27(1–2), 15–29.

Kodama, M. (2009a). Boundaries Innovation and Knowledge Integration in the Japanese Firm. *Long Range Planning, 42*(4), 463–494.

Kodama, M. (2009b). *Innovation Networks in Knowledge-Based Firm –Developing ICT-Based Integrative Competences*. Cheltenham: Edward Elgar Publishing.

Kodama, M. (2011). *Interactive Business Communities*. Farnham: Gower Publishing.

Kodama, M. (2012). *Competing Through ICT Capabilities*. London: Palgrave Macmillan.

Kodama, M. (2014). *Winning Through Boundaries Innovation –Communities of Boundaries Generate Convergence*. London: Peter Lang.

Kodama, M. (Ed.). (2015). *Collaborative Innovation: Developing Health Support Ecosystems* (Vol. 39). London: Routledge.

Kodama, M. (2017a). *Developing Holistic Leadership: A Source of Business Innovation*. London: Emerald.

Kodama, M. (2017b). Developing Strategic Innovation in Large Corporations—The Dynamic Capability View of the Firm. *Knowledge and Process Management, 24*(4), 221–246.

Kodama, M. (2018). *Sustainable Growth Through Strategic Innovation: Driving Congruence in Capabilities*. Cheltenham: Edward Elgar Publishing.

Kodama, M., & Shibata, T. (2014a). Strategy Transformation Through Strategic Innovation Capability—A Case Study of Fanuc. *R&D Management, 44*(1), 75–103.

Kodama, M., & Shibata, T. (2014b). Research into Ambidextrous R&D in Product Development–New Product Development at a Precision Device Maker: A Case Study. *Technology Analysis & Strategic Management, 26*(3), 279–306.

Kodama, M., & Shibata, T. (2016). Developing Knowledge Convergence Through a Boundaries Vision—A Case Study of Fujifilm in Japan. *Knowledge and Process Management, 23*(4), 274–292.

Leifer, R., McDermott, M., O'Connor, C., Peters, S., Rice, M., & Veryzer, W. (2000). *Radical Innovation: How Mature Companies Can Outsmart Upstarts*. Cambridge, MA: Harvard Business School Press.

Leonard-Barton, D. (1992). Core Capabilities and Core Rigidities: A Paradox in Managing New Product Development. *Strategic Management Journal, 13*(2), 111–125.

Leonard-Barton, D. (1995). *Wellsprings of Knowledge: Building and Sustaining the Source of Innovation*. Cambridge, MA: Harvard Business School Press.

March, J. (1991). Exploration and Exploitation in Organizational Learning. *Organization Science, 2*(1), 71–87.

March, J. (1996). Continuity and Change in Theories of Organizational Action. *Administrative Science Quarterly, 41*(2), 278–287.

Markham, S. K. (2002). Moving Technologies from Lab to Market. *Research Technology Management, 45*(6), 31–36.

Markides, C. (2001). Strategy as Balance: From "Either-Or" to "And". *Business Strategy Review, 12*(3), 1–10.

Merrifield, B. D. (1995). Obsolescence of Core Competencies Versus Corporate Renewal. *Technology Management, 2*(2), 73–83.

Mintzberg, H. (1978). Patterns in Strategy Formation. *Management Science, 24*, 934–948.

Nelson, R., & Winter, S. (1982). *An Evolutionary Theory of Economic Change*. Cambridge, MA: Belknap Press.

Nonaka, I. (1988). Toward Middle-Up-Down Management: Accelerating Information Creation. *Sloan Management Review, 29*(3), 9–18.

Nonaka, I., & Konno, N. (1998). The Concept of "*ba*": Building a Foundation for Knowledge Creation. *California Management Review, 40*(1), 40–54.

Nonaka, I., & Takeuchi, H. (1995). *The Knowledge-Creating Company*. New York: Oxford University Press.

O'Connor, G. (2008). Major Innovation as a Dynamic Capability: A Systems Approach. *Journal of Product Innovation Management, 25*(2), 313–330.

O'Connor, G., & DeMartino, R. (2006). Organizing for Radical Innovation: An Exploratory Study of the Structural Aspects of RI Management Systems in Large Established Firms. *Journal of Product Innovation Management, 23*(2), 475–497.

O'Connor, G., Leifer, R., Paulson, P., & Peters, P. (2008). *Grabbing Lightning: Building a Capability for Breakthrough Innovation*. San Francisco: Jossey-Bass.

O'Reilly, C., & Tushman, M. (2004). The Ambidextrous Organization. *Harvard Business Review, 82*(4), 74–82.

Penrose, E. T. (1959). *The Theory of the Growth of the Firm*. New York: Wiley.

Pisano, G. (1994). The Governance of Innovation: Vertical Integration and Collaborative Arrangements in the Biotechnology Industry. *Research Policy, 20*(3), 237–249.

Porter, M. (1980). *Competitive Strategy: Techniques for Analyzing Industries and Competitors*. New York: Free Press.

Richardson, G. B. (1972). The Organisation of Industry. *The Economic Journal, 82*(327), 883–896.

Rumelt, R. (1984). Toward a Strategic Theory of the Firm. In R. Lamb (Ed.), *Competitive Strategic Management* (pp. 556–570). Englewood Cliffs: Prentice Hall.

Rumelt, R. (2011). *Good Strategy/Bad Strategy: The Difference and Why It Matters*. New York: Crown Business.

Schilke, O. (2014). Second-Order Dynamic Capabilities: How Do They Matter? *Academy of Management Perspectives, 28*(4), 368–380.

Shapiro, C., & Varian, H. R. (1998). *Information Rules*. Boston: Harvard Business School Press.

Smith, S., & Tushman, M. (2005). Managing Strategic Contradictions: A Top Management Model for Managing Innovation Streams. *Organization Science, 16*(5), 522–536.

Spender, J. C. (1990). *Industry Recipes: An Enquiry into the Nature and Sources of Managerial Judgement*. Oxford: Basil Blackwell.

Taifi, N., & Passiante, G. (2012). Speeding Up NPSD Through Strategic Community Creation: Case of Automaker After-Sales Services Partners. *The Service Industries Journal, 32*(13), 2115–2127.

Teece, D. J. (2007). Explicating Dynamic Capabilities: The Nature and Microfoundations of (Sustainable) Enterprise Performance. *Strategic Management Journal, 28*(13), 1319–1350.

Teece, D. J. (2012a). Next-Generation Competition: New Concepts for Understanding How Innovation Shapes Competition and Policy in the Digital Economy. *Journal of Law Economics and Policy, 9*(1), 97–118.

Teece, D. J. (2012b). Dynamic Capabilities: Routines Versus Entrepreneurial Action. *Journal of Management Studies, 49*(8), 1395–1401.

Teece, D. J. (2014). The Foundations of Enterprise Performance: Dynamic and Ordinary Capabilities in an (Economic) Theory of Firms. *The Academy of Management Perspectives, 28*(4), 328–352.

Teece, D. J., Pisano, G., & Shuen, A. (1997). Dynamic Capabilities and Strategic Management. *Strategic Management Journal, 18*, 509–533.

Tushman, M. L., & O'Reilly, C. A. (1997). *Winning Through Innovation.* Cambridge, MA: Harvard Business School Press.

Tushman, M., & Romanelli, R. (1985). Organizatinal Evolution: A Metamorphosis Model of Convergence and Reorientation. *Research in Organizational Behavior, 7*(2), 171–222.

Wernerfelt, B. (1984). A Resource-Based View of the Firm. *Strategic Management Journal, 5*(2), 171–180.

Winter, S. (2000). The Satisficing Principle in Capability Learning. *Strategic Management Journal, 21*(10–11), 981–996.

Winter, S. (2003). Understanding Dynamic Capabilities. *Strategic Management Journal, 24*(10), 991–995.

Zahra, S. A., Sapienza, H. J., & Davidsson, P. (2006). Entrepreneurship and Dynamic Capabilities: A Review, Model and Research Agenda. *Journal of Management Studies, 43*(4), 917–955.

Zollo, M., & Winter, G. (2002). Deliberate Learning and the Evolution of Dynamic Capabilities. *Organization Science, 13*(3), 339–351.

2

Service Innovation Through Collaborative Dynamic Capabilities: A Systems Approach

Mitsuru Kodama

2.1 Capabilities Congruence Through Asset Orchestration Processes

In the knowledge economy, diverse human knowledge is the source of valuable products, services, and business models that can give a company new competitiveness. Through convergence across different technologies and industries, co-specialized asset orchestration has the potential to produce new products, services, business models, and value chains as new strategic models that span many boundaries. To configure new businesses, companies need to rediscover the process business perspective of creating new intangible assets by transcending organizational boundaries, both in and between companies, to dynamically share and integrate the intangible assets of people, groups, and organizations.

Thus, the formulation and implementation of overall strategic processes must be optimized by dynamic asset orchestration across multiple

---

M. Kodama (✉)
Nihon University, College of Commerce, Tokyo, Japan
e-mail: kodama.mitsuru@nihon-u.ac.jp

organizational boundaries (which also means knowledge integration), through internal congruence [Insight-1] of the capability elements that make up the corporate system—"(1) strategy capabilities, (2) organization capabilities, (3) technology capabilities, (4) operation capabilities, (5) leadership capabilities"—and external congruence in capabilities with the environment [Insight-2] (Kodama 2018).

In the process of R&D and new technologies selection for innovation, the cognitive capabilities of management are of great importance in responding to dynamic external environments, such as business opportunities. Practitioners must use their sensing functions to seek out, filter, and analyze opportunities, and is dependent on the cognitive capabilities of individual practitioners, particularly the leader organizations in management.

Helfat and Peteraf (2015) have discussed how heterogeneity in the cognitive capabilities of top management teams brings about disparities in organizational performance in changing conditions. According to their reviews of theories in cognitive psychology, cognitive science, social psychology, cognitive neuroscience, and behavioral decision theory, important aspects of cognitive capabilities are fixed to certain contexts. It has also been argued that these aspects can affect the heterogeneity of cognitive capabilities (e.g., Ericsson and Lehmann 1996).

Following many years of management research, Helfat and Peteraf (2015) assert the importance of cognitive capabilities that form the foundation of mental processes (or mental models) in managers at the top of organizations, and present evidence from research by Rosenbloom (2000) at NCR Corporation and by Tripsas and Gavetti (2000) at Polaroid. It is also suggested that top managers should strengthen "paradoxical cognition" (Smith and Tushman 2005) to be able to simultaneously pursue exploration and exploitation (March 1991), while heeding warnings from the many cases where an unwitting or inappropriate reliance on specialist past knowledge becomes a hindrance in the search for new technologies and strategies (Miller and Ireland 2005). Leading management research confirms that heterogeneity in the cognition of top management teams affects the heterogeneity of approaches to strategic change and its outcomes.

The role of intuition, as a cognitive capability in leading practitioners, is significant and much awareness and inspiration comes from deep interactions between stakeholders (customers, business partners, etc.). To demonstrate the cognitive capability of intuition, practitioners must have boundaries vision capabilities (Kodama 2011; Kodama and Shibata 2016) to be able to acquire new insights from complex and diverse boundaries. The concept of boundaries vision capabilities is a new proposition that entails capability to integrate dissimilar knowledge—the ability to orchestrate intangible assets (knowledge integration) and boundaries architecture—the ability to achieve corporate design for new business models by defining new corporate boundaries by integrating dissimilar boundaries, and boundaries innovation—the process of innovation across the boundaries between companies and industries (Kodama 2009a), and so forth (Kodama 2011).

In recent years, it has become necessary to design open innovation (Chesbrough 2003) to expand the breadth of the search for business opportunities through joint research systems between industry, government, and academia that transcend the boundaries between corporate organizations, and to grasp customer needs by bringing in the best technologies from the outside through leading middle management and by management layers co-operating with suppliers, or hybrid innovation—an intermediate between open and closed innovation (Kodama 2011). In the era of convergence, as discussed in Chap. 1, important managerial considerations include new knowledge about the dynamic strategic processes of drawing up grand designs for new boundaries architecture and configuring new business models with "boundaries architects" using their boundaries vision capabilities.

Practitioners have to face these issues in their strategic thinking and actions, focusing on wide-ranging boundaries to orchestrate different intangible assets (and co-specialized assets) to bring about service innovations. Since entering the 21st century, the best core technologies of the world's cutting-edge businesses have become dispersed around the globe and so innovations are now occurring all over the world. Accordingly, going forward in this era of convergence, in which valuable co-specialized assets bring about wealth, management that integrates intangible assets (i.e., assets orchestration through dynamic capabilities [DC]) dispersed within and outside of organizations, and with customers in multi-perspective open systems, will become increasingly important. Thus, in order to create new products, services, and business models, the concepts of open and hybrid innovation are of major importance in knowledge economy to develop and accumulate competitive intangible assets in a company, and at the same time to orchestrate the company's intangible assets (and co-specialized assets) with those of other companies.

As discussed, in the sensing process, demonstrating boundaries vision capabilities, which are also a form of cognitive capabilities of intuition, is extremely important for practitioners to uncover the best intangible assets (and co-specialized assets). For example, Apple's foray into the music distribution and smartphone business and Fujifilm's foray into the cosmetics business (Kodama and Shibata 2016) are also results of the demonstration of (1) boundaries vision capabilities. Moreover, to create new markets or new value in dynamically changing markets, practitioners have to demonstrate (2) context architect capabilities, (3) boundaries consolidation capabilities, and (4) strategy architect capabilities.

"Context architect capabilities" refer to the ability of innovators to generate new meaning between different contexts. Differences arise on the boundaries between different contexts (Carlile 2002, 2004), and these differences give rise to further diversity and contradictions of contexts. Overcoming contradictions originating in contextual diversity dynamically gives rise to new contexts, which enables sharing of specific contexts (Kodama 2006). To overcome these contradictions, the execution of dialectical and creative dialogue (Kodama 2007b; Kodama and Shibata 2014b), creative confrontations or abrasion (Leonard-Barton 1995), productive friction (Hagel III and Brown 2005) and political negotiating practice (Brown and Duguid 2001), and so forth among practitioners are important factors.

To achieve their business visions or missions, the context architect capabilities of practitioners enables the creation and practice of new concepts though constructive and creative dialogue on questions such as why things are the way they are, how things should be, and how to achieve certain objectives. As a result, the quality of these specific contexts in turn determines the quality of the knowledge produced. In the Apple case mentioned, creating new markets is a vision for the future; to achieve this, collaborating partners, with their range of backgrounds and skills, questioned themselves and each other to bring about and share specific contexts.

Boundaries consolidation capability entails the building and rebuilding of strategic communities (Kodama 2005) rooted in the aforementioned specific contexts. "Practitioners" does not mean simply anybody, but rather a certain number of people who evince strongly the innate human capability of constantly pursuing self-improvement (Kodama 2006). This also means specific practitioners who have 'common knowledge' (shared language and knowledge) (e.g., Star 1989), as expressed in the contexts of engineers. These people use their own ideas and beliefs to proactively bring about specific contexts to build and rebuild strategic communities. "Specific practitioners" denotes executives and managers in managerial levels of an organization, executives and managers in partner companies, and leading customers.

These practitioners build strategic communities to create valuable new knowledge through the formation of human networks. The authors term this behavior and capability of certain practitioners to link specific organizational and knowledge boundaries together and network them "boundaries consolidation capabilities." Furthermore, these strategic communities are reconfigured over time by practitioners in response to strategic objectives. Accordingly, these can more precisely be considered "specific strategic communities that change."

Hence, "strategy architect capabilities" are practitioners' capabilities to formulate and implement strategy through the dynamic formation of strategic communities to bring about new business models through "context architect capabilities" and "boundaries consolidation capabilities." Strategy architect capabilities include the know-how and skills to draw a grand design of strategy and then actualize it. A factor of strategy architect capabilities is the ability to skillfully use and integrate different strategy-making processes.

For example, for innovation in uncertain environments, in the Domain I → Domain II shift on the Capabilities Map, practitioners continuously create concepts of new business models (frameworks for new products, services, and businesses, etc.) with imagination and creativity. In these activities, emergent strategies (Mintzberg and Walters 1985) are executed through the formation of multiple emergent external strategic communities (ESCs) with external strategic business partners, including customers. Emergent strategies are those created by practitioners through the process of trial and error at the workplace level (various cases including divisions near customers and middle management layers) as they recognize changes in the environment that they did not predict. However, in reality, strategy-making processes in corporations are generally intended or deliberate, whereas the details of strategy are emergent. In the authors' long practical corporate experience, strategy-making processes have characteristics that are simultaneously planned and emergent (e.g., entrepreneurial strategies (Mintzberg 1978)) (Kodama 2007a).

The two types of organizational forms (emergent and traditional organizations) in "strategic community-based firms" (discussed in Kodama 2007a) have paradoxical elements. Emergent organizations pursue creativity and autonomy, on the other hand, traditional organizations pursue efficiency and control. Thus, there is always conflict and friction between these organizations. These factors are hindrances to the integration of the knowledge of formal organizations, internal strategic communities (ISCs), and ESCs. Nevertheless, "leadership teams" (Kodama 2005a, 2017a) drive this synthesis. These leadership teams are formed from leaders (the CEO, executives, division managers, senior management, project leaders, and managers, etc.) at all management levels within the company (top and middle management layers and teams, cross functional teams, and task forces). Leadership teams bring about DC and ordinary capabilities (OC) across entire corporations through the synthesis and integration of knowledge in the two types of formal organizations and/or ISCs. To achieve a strategic community-based firm, it is important that leadership teams simultaneously combine and synthesize these apparently contradictory creative and planned strategic methods. Leadership teams at Apple are characterized by their combination of both creativity and efficiency (Kodama 2017a).

Managers in leadership teams engage in deep dialogue to select strategies and tactics that will genuinely enable innovation to flourish, which are then executed through the leadership of those managers. Synergy of leadership enabled by collaboration among managers at all management levels—including the CEO and executives—focuses on dialectical dialogue, promotes carefully selected and planned deliberate strategies, and achieves synthesis of the knowledge and strategies of different organizations. Underlying the achievement of DC in these leadership teams is the dynamics of knowledge strategy enabled through abduction, described later. Strategy architect capabilities also refer to executing the abduction process of strategy formulation and implementation through the building and rebuilding of ISCs and ESCs. This is strategy view in the context of the strategic community-based firm.

These four above capabilities drive the three processes of sensing, seizing, and transforming, and achieve capabilities congruence between capabilities elements (co-specialized assets) of strategies, organizations, technologies, operations, and leadership through co-specialized asset orchestration in the corporate system. In addition, these four capabilities achieve the optimization of capabilities (capabilities congruence) through the dynamic knowledge integration processes of assets (both intangible and tangible) inside and outside of the corporation (Kodama 2000, 2003, 2004, 2007c, d, 2009a) and knowledge convergence processes (Kodama 2014) (Fig. 2.1).

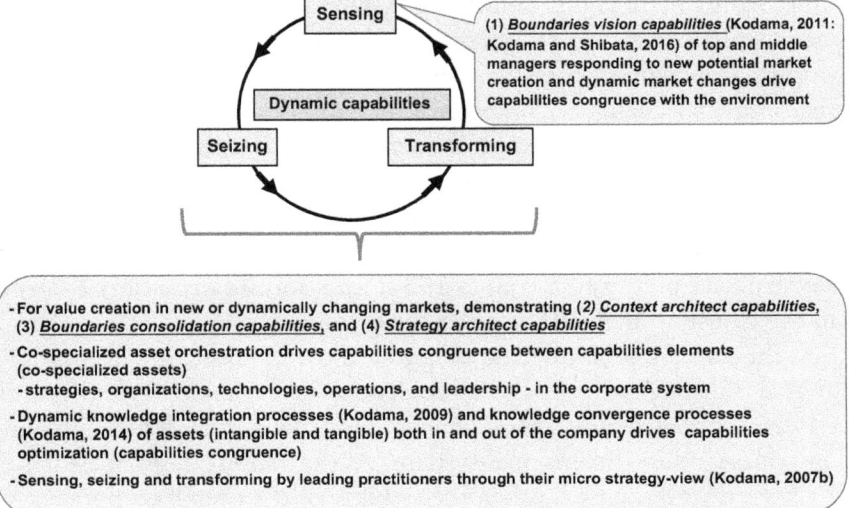

Fig. 2.1 Capabilities congruence through the assets orchestration process

2.2 Capabilities Congruence In and Out of Corporations: The Systems View

Kodama (2018) presents the concept of capabilities congruence in a framework for a dynamic strategic management theory to achieve sustainable growth through strategic innovation. From the perspective of systems theory, the concept of capabilities congruence is also the state of adaptation or fit of capabilities demonstrated by a corporation as a system. Put differently, adaptation or fit means the "most stable state" of a corporation system demonstrating its capabilities (e.g., Kramer and de Smit 1977).

In general, a system can be said to be stable when it returns (or reaches) to a condition that is given or selected following a disruptive state. A dynamically stable system such as a corporate system entails "purposive (purposeful) property" (Kramer and de Smit 1977; Checkland 1980), which makes efforts to shift the system from a particular state to a desirable one. A system for which stability can be maintained even in changing environments is called an "ultra-stable system" (e.g., Kramer and de Smit 1977).

Corporate systems have internal selection mechanisms that can be used to orient the system toward stability when environments change. Additionally, there is the "multi-stable system" that includes conditions under which exist groups of corporate systems consisting of multiple partners in business ecosystems. For ecosystem stability in the face of environmental change, maintenance of stable states with ecosystems is required in individual corporate systems and, at the same time, stability must be achieved through co-ordination via interaction between subsystems in individual corporate systems. This is because systems are integral entities in which interactions occur at the interfaces between their parts as a character of a system (Capra 1996; Kast and Rosenzweig 1972)—a change in a subsystem affects other subsystems.

At the same time, individual corporate systems consisting of multiple internal subsystems (e.g., the aforementioned capabilities elements of strategies, organizations, technologies, operations, and leadership) are compound, multi-dimensional systems. As the various internal elements of a system work on each other, the stability of the overall corporate system is maintained through interactions with the environment (the business ecosystem) while corporate system assets (tangible and intangible) are dynamically reconfigured to change internal systems structures and functions. Cannon (1932) called this quality of organisms "homeostasis." Homeostasis refers to the process of constantly maintaining physical and energetic conditions in an organism, and describes a system condition in which this is achieved through dynamic interaction (von Bertalanffy 1960). Homeostasis enables organisms to maintain a dynamic balance by themselves, and is thus also a self-regulatory mechanism that can change their variables within an acceptable range.

A corporate system, on the other hand, is also a "self-organizing system" (Mesarovic 1962) that can purposefully reform its structure and conversion functions so that it can maintain its current state of stability through adaption or move to a new stable state in response to environmental change through transformation of its internal parts, and at the same time influence the environment. Systems thinking requires attention be paid to the fundamental structural units of a system as well the basic principles on which it is founded—systems can be both open and closed.

However, in the literature on strategic theory, as a state of adaptation, congruence only appears as states (or processes) at certain times in corporate systems, and finding one-time congruence (fit) is not the ultimate goal of corporate activity (Miles and Snow 2001). In other words, after achieving congruence, corporations, as self-organizing systems, must adapt to changes in the external environment or in internal corporate elements. To achieve dynamic stability of corporate systems (and stability of capabilities) in each domain and in the Domain I → Domain II → Domain III shifts in the Capabilities Map, a corporate system must be self-organizing.

In addition, viewed in the perspective of capabilities, corporations that achieve sustainable growth do not only need congruence for dynamically changing environments, but also must enable congruence between multiple different capabilities through co-ordination, alignment, and realignment between different capabilities elements in companies. Thus, large companies simultaneously engage in incremental and radical innovation by demonstrating DC through forming strategic communities as dynamic informal organizations to bring about DC, as discussed in Chap. 1, and strategic innovation capabilities (Kodama 2017b; Kodama and Shibata

2014a). The concept of capabilities congruence is the most important managerial factor in achieving sustainable growth over the long term.

Here, capabilities congruence is a requisite for DC (and strategic innovation capabilities) with which a corporation systematically and continuously brings about both incremental and radical innovation. Put differently, in a large corporation, capabilities congruence entails optimizing capabilities both within a company and broadly across business ecosystems configured to include all stakeholders to achieve strategic innovation for sustainable growth.

This capabilities congruence can be achieved through asset orchestration, a core function of DC. As the functions of asset orchestration, Teece (2014, p. 333) presents the organizational processes of (1) co-ordination/integration (2) learning, and (3) reconfiguration. Further, Kodama (2018) proposes the processes of capabilities congruence as a fourth function. This chapter discusses capabilities congruence between different business partners comprising business models for service innovations.

2.3 Capabilities Congruence Through Dynamic Capabilities In and Out of Corporation: A Framework for Dynamic Strategic Management in the Systems View Perspective

In the view of strategic management as a dynamic process, corporate systems (capability elements in a company such as strategies, organizations, technologies, operations, and leadership) must change dynamically to adapt to dynamically changing environments surrounding corporations (for example markets, technologies, competition and co-operation, and structures) (Kodama 2011, 2018). The borders or corporate boundaries between environments and corporate systems define the relationships with environments and company business models (Kodama 2009b). In the systems view, changes in environments bring about changes in corporate boundaries and simultaneously affect individual elements of capabilities in corporate systems. Conversely, changes to the individual capability elements in corporate systems (either active or passive) bring about changes to the corporate boundaries of a company, and in turn also affect the environment.

Teece (2007b) argues that, in the same manner that markets (or environments, ecosystems) form corporations, the activities of co-ordination and resource allocation by business persons form markets (or environments, ecosystems). In other words, companies and markets are in co-eval relationships (see Fig. 2.2). Thus, good asset orchestration by business persons with technical aptitude (i.e., DC) enables a company to create favorable external environments, which as a result ties in with raising "evolutionary fitness" (Helfat 2007; Helfat et al. 2007).

Furthermore, Teece (2007a) states that in a multi-national enterprise, one of the core functions of management is to develop and implement

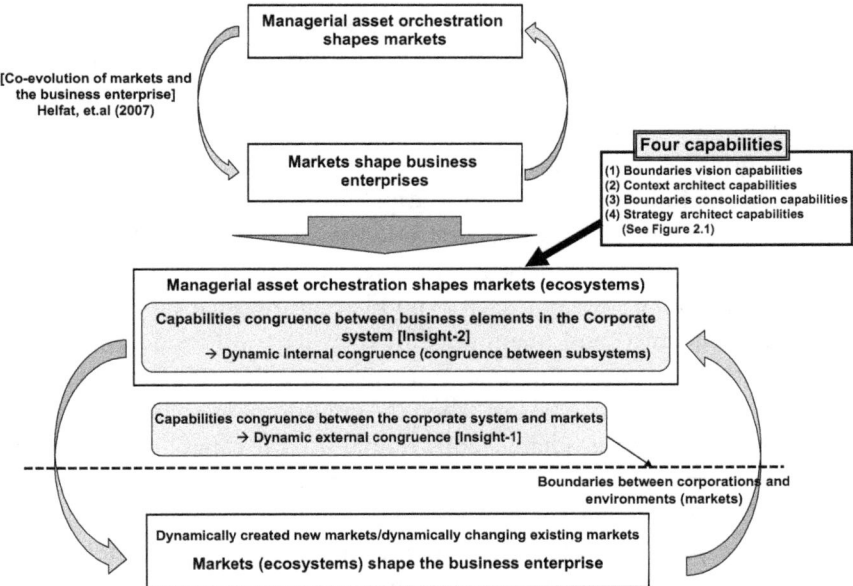

Fig. 2.2 Capabilities congruence inside and outside of a company—the systems view

the company's unique strategies, which means they must "fit" assets, structures, and processes globally (and their individual internal elements), while the company management team must also decide one the technological opportunities and customer needs that the company is addressing while securing the resources and assets needed to execute strategy. Hence, the capabilities to proactively adapt, redeploy, and reconfigure in an entrepreneurial fashion gives meaning to "orchestration," and thus to "dynamic capabilities."

In the systems view, in a different interpretation, there is a necessity for practitioners to intentionally change business elements related to capabilities such as strategy, organizations, technologies, operations, and leadership in corporate systems, to bring congruence to the boundaries between capability elements so that corporations can adapt to changing environments (or ecosystems) (the creation and implementation of environment adaption strategy is discussed in Chap. 9), or actively work on the environments (or ecosystems) and create new environments (creation and implementation of environment creation strategy is also discussed in Chap. 9). Hence, Kodama (2018) identifies that not only the capabilities congruence between corporate systems and markets (ecosystems) (dynamic external congruence) [Insight-1] but also capabilities congruence between capabilities elements in corporate systems (dynamic internal congruence (congruence between subsystems)) [Insight-2] are required. The function that achieves capabilities congruence both in and outside of companies is asset orchestration through DC (see Fig. 2.2).

Nevertheless, even if diverse management capabilities (capabilities elements in corporate systems), such as good organizational capabilities and so forth, are formed and maintained, if they are routines dominated by stable patterns or OC, companies must take into account the possibility that their advantage may be lost when the environment changes. In other words, companies must change and reconfigure the capabilities elements of the corporate system ((1) strategy capabilities, (2) organization capabilities, (3) technology capabilities, (4) operation capabilities, and (5) leadership capabilities) through the demonstration of the aforementioned DC (sensing → seizing → transforming), in step with changes in the broader environment. To achieve this, companies should unceasingly renew their resource bases by integration, alignment, and realignment of their diverse resources (capabilities) (Kodama 2018).

Actually, on the forefront of business where DC must be demonstrated (the front line of business where strategic non-routine activities are executed through DC rather than the routine work involving OC), practitioners face the questions "what product strategies match the latent needs of users?" "what form should organizations and operations take to achieve strategic objectives?" "What is required for technical elements to achieve target products or business models?" "what kind of leadership do company leaders and managers need to enact to achieve new strategies?" "in what way does the awareness of staff need to be reformed?" and "how do in-house processes need to be reformed?"

However, Kodama (2017a) identifies that business elements such as strategy, organizations, technologies, operations, and leadership exist in different contexts, while practitioners have dissimilar thought worlds (e.g., Dougherty 1992) and individual mental models (e.g., Markides 1999) based on their own different contexts and empirical knowledge, and that the perspectives on environments and the individual elements of capabilities that make up a corporate system vary from practitioner to practitioner. Accordingly, "knowledge boundaries" (Kodama 2007a), which are constraints between practitioners, naturally occur as barriers to congruence between these capabilities elements. However, Kodama (2017b) also asserts that practitioners driving innovations and business transformation have to see knowledge boundaries not as limitations, but as triggers that can bring about new capabilities.

In the systems view, regarding the processes of change in environments and corporate systems, the important proposition for dynamic strategic management is congruence on boundaries between environments and corporate systems [Insight-1], congruence on the boundaries between individual capabilities elements in corporate systems [Insight-2], and how practitioners use the aforementioned boundaries vision capabilities to recognize boundary changes through their sensing functions, and to bring about boundaries congruence through their context architect, boundaries consolidation, and strategy architect capabilities.

In rapidly changing environments, as stated in Kodama (2017b), practitioners need to engage in effective corporate management to achieve environment adaptation and creation strategies. Hence, by demonstrating DC (sensing → seizing → transforming), business people should engage in the dynamic practice of bringing congruence to the boundaries between environments and corporate systems [Insight-1] and bringing congruence to the boundaries between the individual capabilities elements within the corporate system [Insight-2].

For a company to develop and grow sustainably, practitioners must create new products, services, and business models with a competitive edge by engaging in the processes of changing strategic management over time (i.e., DC congruence processes, which are either gradual or rapid), executed through DC that are difficult for other companies to copy. Here, the concept of capabilities congruence by asset orchestration mentioned earlier and the execution of the concept is crucial (See Fig. 2.3).

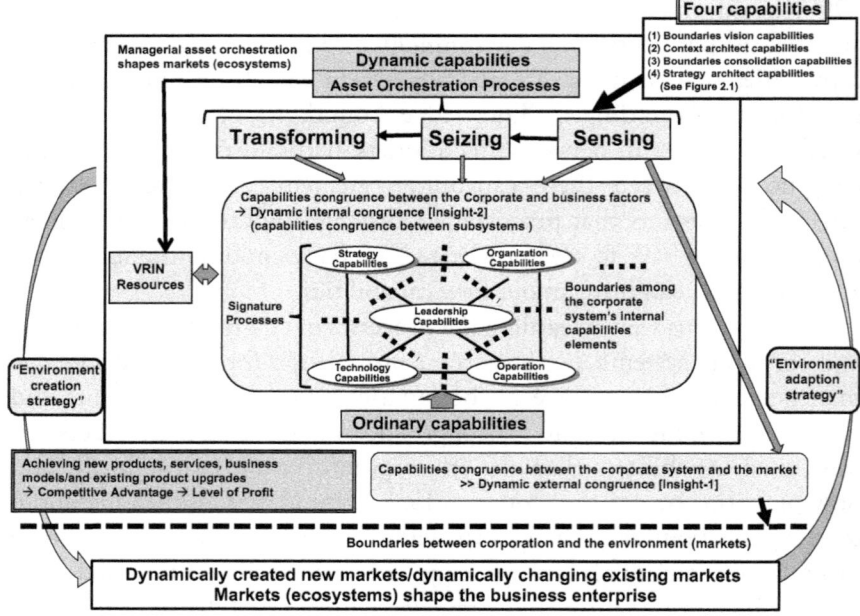

Fig. 2.3 Internal and external consistency of capabilities congruence—a dynamic strategic management framework from the systems view

Despite that, Teece (2014, p. 334) states that "Dynamic capabilities do not operate alone. They must be coupled with effective strategizing to bring about competitive advantage." Teece emphasizes evolution in which DC are interlocked with business environments and strategies, and presents Rumelt's (2011) three strategy kernels as this "effective strategy." However, as identified by Kodama (2017b), regarding effective strategizing functions while being deeply interconnected with the four capabilities beyond strategy of organization, technology, operation, and leadership. Hence, in addition to those capability factors, Kodama (2017b) identifies the corporate system in which not only the elements of "strategizing," in other words strategy capabilities (strategy processes) but also other four capabilities elements are added, as shown in Fig. 2.3, and states that DC function properly in corporate systems in which congruence between the individual capabilities elements has been achieved.

These five capabilities can also be interpreted as "signature processes" (Gratton and Ghoshal 2005). Signature processes are intangible assets that are difficult for other companies to copy, and are rooted in company history and the individual thinking and actions of staff members, which also satisfy the VRIN standards of Barney (1991) (Teece 2014, p. 333) (See Fig. 2.3).

Furthermore, Teece (2014, p. 334) also asserts that "In short, the joint presence of strong dynamic capabilities, VRIN resources, and good strategy is necessary and sufficient for long-run enterprise financial success." Teece (2014, pp. 340–341) also says that

> "In short, VRIN resources, in and of themselves, are inherently valuable by definition, but they do not generate long-term enterprise value (or military prowess) on their own. For long-term growth and survival of the enterprise, they must be cleverly managed, or orchestrated, by a dynamically capable management team pursuing a good strategy. This also means that the resource-based view of the firm needs dynamic capabilities to explain how assets get deployed and how rent streams get extended and renewed,"

which can be interpreted as DC and VRIN resources being in a complementary relationship. Kodama (2018) also clearly positions the role of VRIN resources in the capabilities congruence framework.

In Fig. 2.3, OC are described as foundation of five capabilities elements. On this point, Teece (2014, p. 334) says

> Strong OC (operations, administration, governance) must be accessed by the enterprise, but they need not necessarily be owned. Managing a plethora of OC can undermine dynamic capabilities. In other words, OC are not sufficient for long term financial success—they may not even be necessary.

OC are required for the fast and slow incremental innovation in Domains III and IV respectively in the Capabilities Map. Moreover, strong integration of DC and OC in Domain III is an indispensable factor in winning out over competitor companies in fast-moving environments. OC are the basic skills of business persons in large corporations, and advance routines to achieve company-unique best practices (they may be copied by other companies) through higher-order learning (Winter 2003) (even business people and upper managers in venture companies must focus on demonstrating appropriate OC as company growth, because the volume of formulaic routine work increases as companies get bigger). Therefore, OC are fundamental to all five capabilities as tangible and intangible assets that cannot be ignored.

As well as all the above, companies have to constantly strengthen their strategic positions by actively and dynamically changing their corporate governance structures and corporate boundaries in evolving environments (or in environments that they themselves have created). Research on corporate boundaries describes corporate governance structures and corporate boundaries decision-making as dependent on various factors such as transaction costs perspective, capabilities and competences perspective, and identities. Thus, in building value chains as strategic objectives, decision-making about what type of business activity should be carried out within a company, or what type of resources should be accessed externally through what type of agreements with the market are elements of corporate strategy that are important not only for large corporations but for ventures too (e.g., Pisano 1991; Kodama 2009a).

Santos and Eisenhardt (2005) describe four specific factors that determine corporate boundaries (efficiency, power, competence, and identity). In corporate activities, these four factors, those of cost (efficiency), autonomy (power), growth (competence), and consistency (identity) are basic business issues that managers must question, and are serious issues that determine corporate boundaries. In reducing costs in recent years particularly, determining corporate boundaries by strategic outsourcing has become even more prevalent as a way of making corporate activity more efficient. Moreover, the *keiretsu* networks typical of the auto industry and rooted in long-term trust with contractor companies promote influence through power in corporate activities as well as autonomy for subcontractor companies. Here, "competence" is replaced with "resource," and "power and identity" is replaced with "value."

In addition, the following can be said from research implications regarding competence identified by Santos and Eisenhardt (2005). In deciding these corporate boundaries, boundaries conception of the creativity views centered on corporate leaders (Kodama 2009a) drives the creation of new business and expansion of business territory, and self-creation for competitiveness (creative abilities) through orchestration of co-specialized assets, which leads to the achievements of strategies for corporate creativity over the long term. Deciding these corporate (organizational) boundaries is an important factor in business to define the boundaries between the company and the environment so as to create, develop, and grow new business ecosystems.

Furthermore, in recent years the smartphone, mobile phone applications and contents, game, and semiconductor design/manufacturing business models (fabless/foundry models) have been characterized by the creation of new environments as business ecosystems through co-evolution processes with stakeholders, which has massive impacts on the boundaries between many businesses and industries. For all of these industries and stakeholders, the boundary conception of the "dialectic view" for market expansion centered on leader companies and main follower companies (Kodama 2009a) combines competition and corporation (strategic synergies, or the aforementioned strategy capabilities demonstration), and brings about innovations through orchestration of co-specialized assets. The five elements of boundary conceptions, efficiency, resources, value, creativity and the dialectic, are management drivers that determine corporate boundaries (vertical and horizontal) (Kodama 2009a, b).

The systems view perspective, with which corporations consider congruence between the corporations and the environments, how to dynamically change corporate boundaries and apply them to the environments of ecosystems that have already been created (or create new environments as ecosystems, see Fig. 2.3), is an important aspect of executing corporate strategy. In other words, this is the importance of dynamic congruence between environments (ecosystems) and corporate systems. Accordingly, companies must optimally design their vertical (value chains to achieve strategic objectives, as defined by the companies) and horizontal (expansion and diversification of business domains) boundaries to set down and achieve the strategic objectives of their sustainably competitive products, services, and business models. To manage corporate boundaries with congruence with the environments of ecosystems (external congruence in capabilities) [Insight-1], management should be optimized through "capabilities congruence" (internal congruence in capabilities) [Insight-2] within a corporate system consisting of the aforementioned capabilities elements of (1) strategy capabilities, (2) organization capabilities, (3) technology capabilities, (4) operation capabilities, (5) leadership capabilities (See Fig. 2.4).

To achieve this, as mentioned, the most important factors are capabilities congruence (dynamic external congruence) between the corporate system and markets (ecosystems) achieved by orchestrating co-specialized assets through internal and external capabilities networks both in and outside of the company and capabilities congruence (dynamic internal congruence, capabilities congruence with subsystems) between each capabilities element in a corporate system. Hence, this refers to the importance of congruence both inside and outside of a company by orchestrating different co-specialized assets, which is described by the new [Insight-3] stated at the beginning of this chapter.

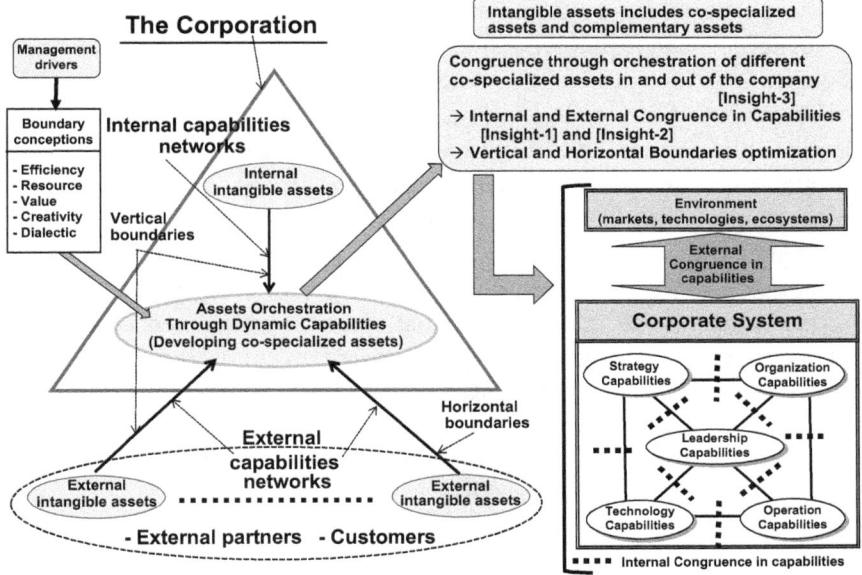

Fig. 2.4 Corporate boundaries, assets orchestration, capabilities congruence—systems view

2.4 Conditions for Capabilities Congruence Between Different Stakeholders in Business Ecosystems: A Systems Approach

Internal and external congruence in capabilities ([Insight-1] and [Insight-2]), and congruence through orchestration of different co-specialized assets both in and out of a company [Insight-3] were presented as a theoretical framework for maximizing capabilities through capabilities congruence in a company, as discussed above. However, in the systems view, Insights-1, -2, and -3 alone are insufficient for maximizing capabilities through capabilities congruence between different business partners involved in business models formed for service innovations, which are the theme of this book.

This chapter takes a systems approach to derive conditions of capabilities congruence in business ecosystems consisting of a main company and groups of partner companies in relationships with that company, all aiming to achieve a service innovation. As there is almost no practical academic application in innovation research and business ecosystem research through the knowledge of systems theory, this area holds promise for the future. For example, if systems theory is applied effectively, it can be used to clarify various system relationships such as the relationships between certain elements in service innovations and business ecosystems, groups of corporate systems as subsystems that constitute a business ecosystem, interactions between elements within subsystems and groups of corporate systems. Hence, it is necessary to indicate conditions for achieving capabilities congruence in business ecosystems from the four standards required with systems theory (e.g., von Bertalanffy 1960), as described below (details are discussed in Chap. 10).

(1) The system is identifiable, and its elements are interdependent;
(2) The effect of the whole is greater than the sum of the parts;
(3) Homeostasis is achieved through interaction and networking with the larger organization; and
(4) There is a clear purpose in the larger business ecosystem in which individual corporate systems are embedded.

Consideration is required from the following perspectives on groups of corporate systems comprising business ecosystems, from these four standards. For example, with strategic innovation in large corporations, the success of those innovations is heavily influenced by the complex interactions between each subsystem that makes up the corporate system (e.g., the subsystem elements of (1) strategy capabilities, (2) organization capabilities, (3) technology capabilities, (4) operation capabilities, (5) leadership capabilities). At the same time, it is necessary to define the corporate systems that make up business ecosystems, and the subsystems that affect strategic innovation in the overall business ecosystem. As well as that, the characteristics of subsystems and the interactions between them, and the dynamically changing conditions of individual subsystems (corporate systems) and whole systems (business ecosystems) responding to environments must be thoroughly analyzed. Systems theory (Capra 1996; Felix 2003; von Bertalanffy 1968) and complex adaptive theory (Stacey 1995) enable the above perspectives to be treated comprehensively. O'Connor's (2008) clarification of radical innovation systems in large corporations describes the validity of systems theory and presents a number of propositions on subsystem interactions.

First, this section reviews the main existing research on business ecosystems, positions players that comprise business ecosystems and considers their roles, and discusses important managerial factors that shape sustainable growth of service innovations and business ecosystems.

2.4.1 Existing Research and the Concept of Sustainable Business Ecosystems

There is some existing research on the various players that make up business ecosystems. Moore (1996) defines business ecosystems as organic organizational entities in business worlds, economic communities supported by organizations that are mutually interlocked, and organizations of individuals. These economic communities generate value for customers through products and services. Members of these communities include suppliers, main producers, competitors, and other stakeholders (expressed using the ecosystem metaphor of co-operative networks consisting of investors, partners, suppliers, and customers).

Iansiti and Levien (2004) in their advancement of Moore's (1993, 1996) research (Moore first applied the idea of biological ecosystems to business contexts), define business ecosystems as consisting of customers, suppliers, leading producers, competitors, and other stakeholders, and classify four roles of companies in business ecosystems in terms such as existence, value generation, and value acquisition. First, there is a keystone role central to a business ecosystem. As an enabler, the keystone's influence is powerful. Second are dominators, and third are the lords of the hubs. Although companies that play these roles influence the ecosystem, those that retain most of their value in-house do not contribute much to the ecosystem. Fourth are the niche players. Niche players constitute the majority of the ecosystem, and thus play a role in bringing about innovation in it.

So, from these classes of players, looking at the roles of players in terms of generating value, the company that plays the key role has to attend to balancing value generation and value acquisition, because this brings profit to the whole business ecosystem. These researchers emphasize the importance of a keystone corporation at the center of the companies in a business ecosystem. The "keystone" means the company that clarifies issues, helps other companies to understand, plays a co-ordinating role among all the companies, and hence is a highly influential component of the ecosystem.

Furthermore, Kodama (2009b, 2015) states that the key to achieving sustainable innovation is enacting the spiral of the four stages of Moore (1993) with the leader and follower companies at the core. Kodama (2009b) describes collaborative innovation through co-ordination by the leader company and thinking and action through dialectic view among members of innovation communities is a key ingredient in achieving co-evolution (Kodama 2009a). The business models centered on leader corporations such as Apple, Google, Microsoft, Sony Computer Entertainment, and NTT DOCOMO are classic examples of these sorts of business ecosystems.

On the other hand, from the viewpoint of corporate evolution and the theory of corporate strategy, leader corporation and related stakeholder companies acquire new knowledge and capabilities through exploration activities (March 1991), and create ecosystems as new markets in the stages of "birth" and "self-renewal," which is also the process of the birth of innovation achieved by new knowledge creation (or knowledge integration). As well as this, the "expansion" and "leadership" stages are equivalent to the "knowledge utilization" process, in which stakeholder companies centered on leader corporations polish their existing knowledge and capabilities, and drive exploitation activities (March 1991) to expand and grow the newly created ecosystem. In this vein, in the process of creating, developing, and growing an ecosystem, Kodama (2015) describes the importance of developing the activities spiral of exploration and exploitation through co-ordination and collaborative innovation by the groups of companies (or groups of organizations) that comprise the ecosystem.

In addition, Gawar and Cusumano (2002) discuss the importance of infrastructure and rules called a "platform" to bring together multiple and different user groups to trigger innovation. Hence, they define business ecosystems as systems consisting of platforms and complementary products. Similar to Iansiti and Levien (2004), this kind of business ecosystem has a focus on a structure consisting of a central corporation and peripheral companies.

Based on game theory, Brandenburger and Nalebuff (1997) made four classifications of peripheral players of a corporation as its customers, complementary producers, competitors, and suppliers, and clarified their interdependent relationships, the competition and co-operation between companies, as a value correlation diagram of mutual dependencies (ValueNet). In addition, definition of a business ecosystem entails a dynamic structure consisting of multiple organizations mutually linked with each other, and further defines these organizations as small companies, large companies, universities, laboratories, and public institutions as well as other groups that influence the system.

Meanwhile, Teece (2007) assert limitations on the details of players participating in business ecosystems, and that they include customers, suppliers, and complementary goods providers as well as regulatory agencies, standards development organizations, judicial authorities, and education and research institutions, if they are crucial for value generation. In this context, Adner and Kappor (2010) focus on the importance of suppliers, complementary products, complementary producers, and complementary resources (e.g., Teece 1986; Milgrom and Roberts 1990) among the players involved in value generation, and present their relationships.

Thus, as described above, while there is a diversity of interpretations of the concept of the business ecosystem from researchers, it is possible to interpret value generation in business ecosystems as the result of strategic collaboration among all the players, centered on the activities of the pioneering leadership of the main player(s). Moreover, in the process of creating, developing, and growing an ecosystem, while developing the activities spiral of exploration and exploitation through collaborative innovation among the groups of companies (or groups of organizations) that comprise the ecosystem is important, the details of the mechanisms and processes of this sort of collaborative innovation are unclear. In particular, in clarifying collaborative innovation, presumably there is deep involvement of collaborative DC among stakeholders, although there remain many unsolved areas such as how the existing DC theories are related.

Hence, this chapter simplifies classifications as main players and multiple other collaborative players, and discusses how collaborative DC are brought about through the interactions of the capabilities of those respective main players and collaborating players. Moreover, the authors would like to attempt to analyze and consider the main business factors of co-creation and co-evolution for creating, growing, and developing service innovations and business ecosystems from the systems approach.

2.4.2 Capabilities Congruence Between Various Players: A Systems Approach

A business ecosystem can be thought of as a composite system consisting of various corporate systems (main players and groups of collaborating partners) as subsystems with ultra-stable characteristics (e.g., Kramer and de Smit 1977). These subsystems have to achieve capabilities congruence between their respective partial environments ([Insight-1], [Insight-2], and [Insight-3]). However, when dynamic changes occur in these partial environments, if it is possible to absorb and adapt to these changes through interactions between corporate systems, which are subsystems, and the environment, and within corporate systems, then the assertions of [Insight-1], [Insight-2], and [Insight-3] will be satisfied (e.g., Kramer and de Smit 1977). Nevertheless, when significant changes occur that bring about new business ecosystems such as new service innovations, it is necessary to seek out stable conditions of new capabilities congruence for the entire system (a business ecosystem formed from the integrated systems of all the group companies).

On the other hand, at this time, while the business ecosystem, a composite system, is subjected, if a corporate system which is a subsystem (e.g., a main player) causes significant changes between environments, it will have significant influence on other corporate systems as subsystems (collaborating players). Hence, when this happens, inevitably there is a necessity to make efforts to bring congruence to capabilities in subsystems ([Insight-1], [Insight-2] and [Insight-3]) through the interactions of capabilities between the subsystems (the corporate systems). The interactions of capabilities between the various subsystems (between corporate systems) is equivalent to capabilities congruence between the various stakeholders [Insight-4], while dynamic congruence with the Capabilities Map in corporate systems is important (see Fig. 2.5).

Hence, as with three factors of the collaborative DC discussed in Chap. 1, capabilities congruence among stakeholders [Insight-4] consists of:

(1) building enduring relationships of trust through strategic collaboration with ecosystem partners;
(2) realization of co-specialization with ecosystem partners;
(3) the realization of capabilities synthesis with ecosystem partners.

However, for this reason, among stakeholders shifting between domains must be synchronized when stakeholders are in the individual stages of domains I to IV. For example, when main player demonstrates DC to execute incubation process such as R&D for new services or pro-

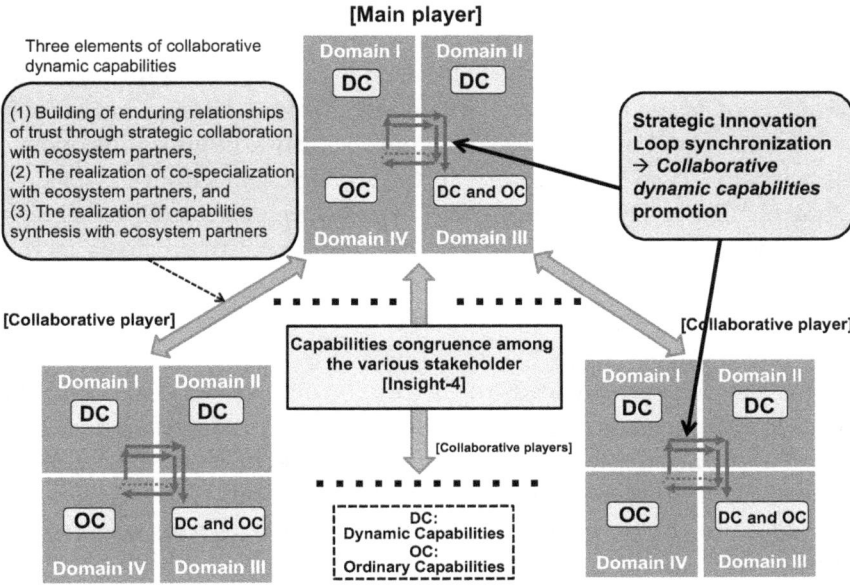

Fig. 2.5 Collaborative DC through strategic innovation loop synchronization

totype services in Domains I and II, collaborating players must also simultaneously share the context and demonstrate DC with the main player, and execute incubation process. If there is only commitment based on routines with OC for new service R&D and trial services in the Domain I and II stages, it is highly unlikely that capability synergies between partners (synthesis) will occur. As background, there are in fact cases of routine execution through normal OC by half-hearted management or as a sideline by existing stakeholder organizations.

Accordingly, to achieve new services that have elements of radical innovation, service innovations have to be effected by specialist organizations or project teams separate from existing organizations (e.g., Kodama 1999, 2002; Leifer et al. 2000). In the above four perspectives on systems theory, the first perspective, "(1) The system is identifiable, and its elements are interdependent" means specialized organizations that are to take charge of radical innovation must be defined in corporate systems of main players and collaborating players.

In addition, in the strategic selection stage of Domain II, the situation that arises among stakeholders regarding important decision-making about commercializing experimental and trial service processes and results is of particular importance. Hence, context mismatches among stakeholders can hinder achievement of capability synthesis in the strategic selection stage. Furthermore, in the strategic concentration stage of Domain III, the key is implementation of resources across all stakeholders. However, it can be difficult to achieve capability synthesis in the strategic concentration stage if there is insufficient resource input from a certain stakeholder in the collaboration among stakeholders and if strong DC and OC are lacking.

Thinking in this way leads to the proposition that it is necessary to synchronize the strategic innovation loops of the Capabilities Map with capabilities congruence among stakeholders [Insight-4]. Synchronization of strategic innovation loops drives collaborative DC. According to the aforementioned systems theory, systems are integral entities characterized by the interfaces (interactions) between their parts (Capra 1996; Kast and Rosenzweig 1972). If one part changes, it affects others. Thus, in systems thinking, attention must be paid to both the fundamental structural units of the system as well as the basic principles of its organization. One of the four system standards mentioned above, that of "(3) Homeostasis is the self-regulatory mechanism that allows organisms to remain in dynamic balance, with their variables fluctuating between certain tolerance limits," must also be satisfied. Open systems like corporate systems tend toward homeostasis. In other words, constantly changing equilibrium is useful for a system to keep in step with its environment.

However, caution is required because conditions where capabilities congruence has been achieved between corporate systems through the functioning of homeostasis are cases where the differences of the characteristics of capabilities between initial systems are few. As mentioned, the problem is that if there is a situation in which there is only commitment by collaborating players based on routines with OC for new service R&D and trial services in the Domain I and II stages, it is highly unlikely that capability synergies between partners (synthesis) will occur. In such cases, managers and project leaders in these interacting corporate systems requires six factors—high involvement, high embeddedness, resonance of values, trust building, common interests, and awareness through improvised learning, and so forth (discussed later). These factors drive the formation of strategic communities based on *ba* (more correctly, ESCs) (Kodama 2005a, b).

Nonaka and Takeuchi (1995) describe the characteristics of superior *ba* as (1) commonsense, (2) self-transcendence, (3) and self-organization. Among the six factors, resonance of value and trust building are factors that foster common perceptions among partners. Furthermore, the factors of common interests and awareness through improvised learning encourage self-transcendence in partners. Moreover, the factors of high involvement and high embeddedness accelerate self-organization among partners. This self-organizing characteristic of a corporate system drives capabilities congruence between corporate systems.

Homeostasis and self-organization of corporate systems as open systems serve to bring about a state of equilibrium in which the synchronization of strategic innovation loops among stakeholders on the Capabilities Map (in other words, congruence of capabilities among stakeholders in each domain) is constantly changing. Homeostasis and self-organization, which synchronize strategic innovation loops, achieve

[Insight-4] at the same time as bringing capabilities congruence to subsystems (corporate systems) ([Insight-1], [Insight-2] and [Insight-3]). These mechanisms bring adaptability (or congruence) as maximum stability to the complex systems (multi-stable systems) of business ecosystems.

Synchronization of strategic innovation loops between corporate systems brings about collaborative DC in business ecosystems, and brings about the aforementioned three factors:

(1) building of enduring relationships of trust through strategic collaboration with ecosystem partners;
(2) realization of co-specialization with ecosystem partners;
(3) realization of capabilities synthesis with ecosystem partners.

In particular, the achievement of co-specialization and capability synthesis has the potential of establishing a proposition—to satisfy one of the four aforementioned system standards, that of "(2) the effect of the whole is greater than the sum of the parts." (Details of this discussion are given in Part III: Results and Discussion of this book).

In open systems theory, systems with semi-permeable boundaries avoid descending into disorder by continuously taking in flows of energy and matter to survive (von Bertalanffy 1968, 1972). Similarly, individual corporate systems (main players and collaborating players) are open systems that require interaction with larger systems that incorporate these corporate systems (in other words, business ecosystems). Thus, conditions are satisfied for one of the four aforementioned standards, that of "(4) There is a clear purpose in the larger business ecosystem in which individual corporate systems are embedded."

Furthermore, individual corporate systems require self-governance, networking through interaction between corporate systems (as strategic communities), and learning and innovation through DC or strategic innovation capabilities through feedback loops. Open systems are not the same as closed systems, in that they adapt to changes in the environment in which they are positioned, and they are self-regulating, self-adjusting, and self-renewing, which enables them to avoid falling into disorder, and instead move toward order (Capra 1996; Felix 2003; von Bertalanffy

1968). In contrast, closed systems have clear boundaries, can easily fall into disorder, be broken apart, and finally collapse (Capra 1996).

On the other hand, open systems are self-regulating and self-organizing, and work to renew themselves and survive by constantly transforming their elements through "autopoiesis" (Maturana and Varela 1980). As Felix (2003) indicates, some types of systems learn through single-loop feedback. However, there are cases where the system is strengthened for long-term survival or this is not possible if there are changes. Questions arise on the aim of systems with double-loop learning (e.g., Argyris and Schon 1978). If a system strays from a proper state, change begins and the system attempts, as quickly as is possible, to adapt to a new desirable state (passively or actively—environment adaptive strategies and environment creation strategies). This also includes jumps in system states (or discontinuity), depending on the level of environmental change.

In addition to that, Von Bertalanffy (1968) outlines the concept of aiming for disequilibrium as flow equilibrium instead of aiming for equilibrium in many complex systems. For example, the shift from Domains III and/or IV to Domain I on the Capabilities Map describes the case of a corporate system transforming itself toward disequilibrium to generate innovation, and these orientations can actually be seen in observations of large corporate systems. Flow equilibrium management systems can be characterized by equilibrium with constant movement. With both unrelenting positive and negative feedback, strategic direction can be given to corporate systems in rapidly changing and unpredictable environments (equivalent to the shifts between domains in the Capabilities Map).

In addition, Stacey (1995) presented the necessity of systems to operate as complex adaptive systems in conditions far removed from equilibrium, to bring about actions that are creative and transformative and can continually change. It is possible to establish the proposition that the system characteristics of autopoiesis and complex adaptive systems may be factors to satisfy one of the four aforementioned system standards, that of "(2) The effect of the whole is greater than the sum of the parts." (Details of this discussion are given in Part III: Results and Discussion of the book.)

Furthermore, important factors in achieving capabilities congruence among stakeholders [Insight-4] through synchronization of the strategic innovation loops are the mechanisms of "boundary synchronization," which are the strategic micropractices of practitioners within organizations (or within companies) and between organizations (or between companies).

2.5 Co-creation and Co-evolution by Linking Radical Innovation Through Exploration and Incremental Innovation Through Exploration

To achieve new service innovations, the shift from Domain IV and/or Domain III → Domain I → Domain II → Domain III is required. In particular, the role of sensing in Domain I is important. Sensing enables main and certain collaborating players in R&D organizations and so forth to seek out and detect potential new markets, while the setting down of plans for R&D over the mid- to long term in R&D organizations is enabled by the sensing and transforming processes.

Furthermore, the role of seizing of main and certain collaborative players involved with the commercialization side in Domain II is particularly important. In departments involved in commercial development, sensing is performed to match markets and technical innovations, while seizing and transforming are performed to develop and commercialize new businesses, technologies, and processes.

Here, in Domain I → Domain II, DC centered on main players and certain collaborating partners serve to execute radical innovation and commercialize new services. In addition, initiatives to expand markets through partnership and collaboration with many collaborative players is crucial for launching and growing new services, and bringing about business ecosystems.

Moreover, the role of transforming the business division side of main and collaborative players is critical in Domain III, where environmental changes are rapid and competition is severe. Particularly, departments involved in service planning and technical development at the business division side have to use sensing to detect changes in new markets, and have to establish robust value chains by sustainably advancing services (including their technical elements) through seizing and transforming to upgrade and improve new businesses shifted from Domain II to Domain III. While market expansion reduces uncertainty, rapid incremental innovation through strong DC and OC in Domain III with the participation of collaborative partners serves to grow business ecosystems.

As discussed in Chap. 1, differing from other three domains, the weight of DC in Domain IV is lower, and mainly best practices are demonstrated through OC. The existing organizations of main players and collaboration partners (business division, etc.) detect gentle changes in existing markets and execute deliberate service strategies through planning and careful consideration with path dependency in business divisions to achieve slow incremental innovation.

The shifts between domains (Domain I → Domain II → Domain III) entails the important aspect of integrating (or linking) radical and incremental innovation strategies. The integration of strategies in business ecosystems is achieved through capabilities congruence among stakeholders [Insight-4], through the synchronization of strategic innovation loops between stakeholders on the Capabilities Map. Synchronization of strategic innovation loops among stakeholders plays a role in driving collaborative DC.

In Domains I and II, main players and certain collaborating partners form ESCs, and continuously promote emergent and entrepreneurial strategies, and establish new markets by attracting the interest of many end-users and other partners for a new service innovation. Then, to further grow a service, main players and certain collaborating partners encourage the participation of other collaborating partners to expand the business ecosystem, and at the same time form ISCs with their internal exiting business organizations, and take actions to genuinely expand new services born in Domain I → Domain II as the main business of the company (or there are cases of these businesses becoming subsidiaries as venture enterprises within corporations). For this, the demonstration of strong DC and OC in Domain III drives genuine rapid incremental innovation through deliberate strategies making use of an organization's capabilities at an organizational scale across entire companies (or groups of companies), to grow the new markets triggered by the emergent and entrepreneurial strategies in Domain I ➔ Domain II.

By "context synchronizing" on service innovations between different ISCs and ESCs, practitioners in main and collaborating player companies must dynamically and concurrently share knowledge about strategic objectives and problems and issues for the achievement of strategy. Context synchronization entails concurrently and interactively sharing strategic contexts related to co-creation through strategic collaboration among partners for service innovations. Hence, practitioners bring about practical synchronization in practitioners themselves and between practitioners to materialize shared strategic contexts. The microstrategic mechanism of boundary synchronization, which is context synchronization and practical synchronization, achieves capabilities congruence among stakeholders [Insight-4] through the synchronization of strategic innovation loops and win-win positive feedback.

The important thing to grasp here is that, in collaborating player organizations there are ISCs similar to the may player ISCs and ESCs that bridge main players and collaborating players. Interlocked with context and practical synchronization in main players, and also in collaborating players, context and practical synchronization is simultaneously carried out through keeping pace with the boundaries synchronization in main players.

For example, software and application vendors, content providers, telecommunications carriers, communications equipment vendors, and components manufacturers involved in close collaboration with Apple and Google made comments such as the following:

> We are always watching the strategies of Apple and Google. For example, what kind of platforms will Apple and Google build in the future, and what kind of new services are they conceiving? What kind of functions are they going to include in their next and subsequent smartphones? We exchange opinions with main players as appropriate, to try to uncover current states and future trends. Thus, when main players take new strategic actions, we also have to follow and execute new strategies (a senior manager of an application and content provider).

Service Innovation Through Collaborative Dynamic Capabilities... 79

As equipment and components vendors not only do we make terminals exactly to specifications for the Google OS (Android), but we also have to co-ordinate other players who are involved regarding new technical specifications or quality etc. to match improvements to smart phone hardware and software. Then, we share road maps for future terminal developments (including semiconductors and software used within them) with each other to develop terminals in step with Google's service strategies (a senior manager of an equipment manufacturer).

Practitioners in collaborative partner companies not only continually share contexts, but also bring congruence to practical aspects of executing strategies with main players in ESCs established with main players and in their own ISCs. Thus, all collaborating players including main players match timing and pace of strategy formulation and implementation with each other through context and practical synchronization (see Fig. 2.6).

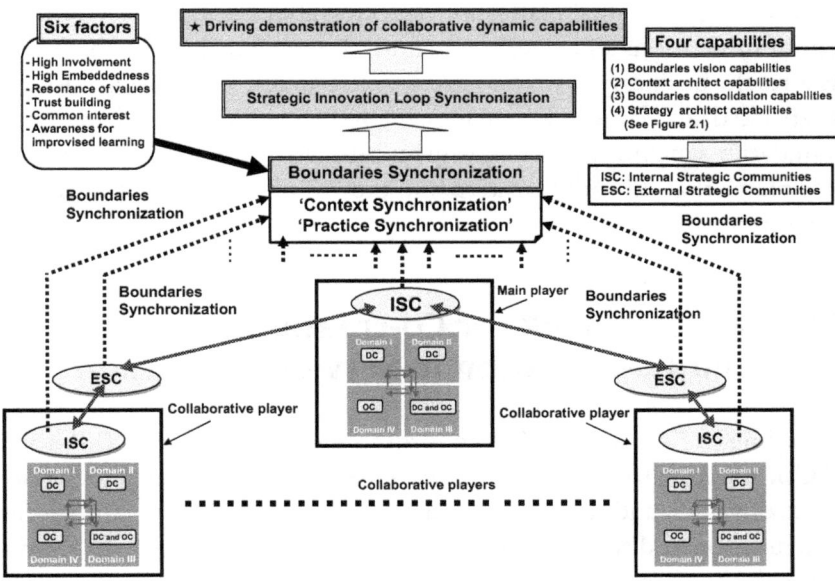

Fig. 2.6 Strategic innovation loop synchronization through boundaries synchronization

In the practical aspect, practitioners who commit to strategic objectives through participation in ISCs and ESCs need to align themselves chronologically with the pitch and rhythm of achievement of business objectives of the individual strategies as actions in strategic communities (ISCs and ESCs) to achieve business models. In executing business in ISCs and ESCs, practitioners of main and collaborating companies align their thoughts and actions, carry out strategies as actions in each of their strategic communities with a certain pitch and rhythm, and concurrently achieve objectives. This mechanism is a factor of practical synchronization. From a different perspective, context and practical synchronization drives the building and rebuilding of ISCs and ESCs among player companies and the configuration of optimized vertical and horizontal boundaries. Thus, this brings about optimized boundaries congruence (capabilities congruence) for all players and the three synergies (business, technology, and partnership synergies) (see Fig. 1.2 and Box 1.1 in Chap. 1).

As discussed above, as a new perspective, ISCs and ESCs bring about dynamic context and practical synchronization for practitioners, and are informal organizational platforms that bring about integrations (or linking) of innovations strategies (Domain I → Domain II → Domain III). As a result, business ecosystems grow, the scale of collaborating partners is expanded, and large hubs emerge centered on main players. Large-scale boundaries synchronization thus gives birth to and co-evolves business ecosystems that drive the creation and growth of new markets of service innovations (see Fig. 2.6).

2.6 A Framework for Co-creation and Co-evolution in Service Innovation

According to Kodama (2005a), to form strategic communities (ISCs and ESCs), the four factors of high involvement, high embeddedness, resonance of values, and trust building are crucial. Furthermore, through the aforementioned discussion, the authors would like to present two more factors for the generation of new service innovations through integration of dissimilar knowledge by forming ESCs across different industries and different types of businesses. First, there is the discovery of common interest among practitioners. Common interest is an enabler that generates new meaning from dissimilar contexts on dissimilar knowledge boundaries, and is thus a factor in the production of new contexts. While common interest has commonalities with common knowledge (e.g., Carlile 2002, 2004), it is not merely a factor in driving the enactment of tasks such as projects among different technically specialized areas and so forth through the medium of IT tools. Common interest is an enabler that can bridge dissimilar fields with absolutely no relationship between them, and exists in the shared values of a variety of human and social values. New innovations have a tendency to come about on organizational and knowledge boundaries between practitioners with differing organizational regulations or differing areas of specialization (Leonard-Barton 1995); hence, common interest promotes practitioner awareness and inspiration and brings about new creative ideas and breakthrough innovations with dissimilar knowledge (e.g., Johansson 2004).

Second is awareness from improvised learning. Many researchers have reported on the importance of improvisation as a concept particularly in the product development process (e.g., Brown and Eisenhardt 1995; Eisenhardt and Tabrizi 1995; Kamoche and Cunha 2001; Kodama 2007a). Improvisation in the field of new product development or pioneering new business is characterized by disciplined imagination and creativity. To build and rebuild the aforementioned strategic communities, practitioners need to demonstrate imagination and creativity in in-house procedures and routines, in fixed business customs between companies and in industries and in the discipline of the partnership model established (these are distinct, depending on the industry structure or corporate culture). Thus, practitioners must improvise hypothetical verification with trial and error, learn from each other, and acquire new awareness to solve problems, uncover issues, and create new ideas and concepts themselves. This is the process of gaining awareness through improvised learning.

For example, in the process of making strategy through abductive reasoning, practitioners engage in serial hypothetical verification by executing emergent strategies (or entrepreneurial strategies). The concept of "abduction," to enable the exploration of the unknown, is a transcendent method of thinking and practice that is neither deduction nor induction, and was proposed by Charles Sanders Peirce (1839–1914), an American who founded the field of thought known as pragmatism. In short, this is a knowledge methodology that entails: (1) organizationally grasping latent factors or mechanisms that bring about new value opportunities in the process of sharing tacit knowledge with the market (or environment): (2) creating specific models that lead to prospects and execution in shareable markets: and (3) correcting hypotheses in those processes, and leading to justification and theorizing of knowledge to solve problems when they are faced.

Improvised learning processes through trial and error gives practitioners new awareness, and promotes actions for refining favorable strategies and their full-fledged execution. As described in Sect. 2.1, arousing "autonomous action with discipline" or "disciplined imagination and creativity" in subordinates by leadership teams of middle managers (e.g., Kodama 2005a, b) drives building and rebuilding of strategic communities and restructuring of business processes through the strategy-making process using abduction, and triggers new idea generation and execution of problem solving. The practitioner thoughts and actions of execution of dialectical and creative dialogue (Kodama 2007b), creative confrontations or abrasion (Leonard-Barton 1995), productive friction (Hagel III and Brown 2005), political negotiating practice (Brown and Duguid 2001), and so forth are important factors in the improvised learning process. Here, there is little compromise consensus. Practitioners engage in repeated and thorough discussions and dialogue among themselves, and uncover the essence of strategy from the dynamic interaction of concepts and ideas based on their own subjective beliefs with objective data.

The six factors of high involvement, high embeddedness, resonance of values, trust building, common interest, and awareness through improvised learning discussed in this section raise the level of the aforementioned boundaries synchronization as context and practice synchronization, and at the same time drive the formation of strategic communities by practitioners. These six factors and boundaries synchronization enable the abductive reasoning process through the improvised learning of practitioners, and link radical innovation strategies (exploration) with incremental innovation strategies (exploitation) (Domain I → Domain II → Domain III). As a result, synchronization

Service Innovation Through Collaborative Dynamic Capabilities... 83

of strategic innovation loops is achieved, and the three factors of collaborative DC are brought about. Thus, the collaborative DC of stakeholders optimize vertical and horizontal boundaries as a strategy driver, optimize boundaries congruence (capabilities congruence), and bring about the three synergies (business, technology, and partnerships synergies) (see Fig. 1.2 and Box 1.1 in Chap. 1).

Business ecosystems are built through new service innovations brought into being by the above processes, and win-win relationships among all stakeholders are achieved. This is the model of co-creation and co-evolution in service innovation. In addition, to drive these processes, five management drivers are to be executed by certain practitioners with certain contexts and certain strategy views, who must have the four qualities of boundaries vision capabilities, context architect capabilities, boundaries consolidation capabilities, and strategy architect capabilities (See Fig. 2.7).

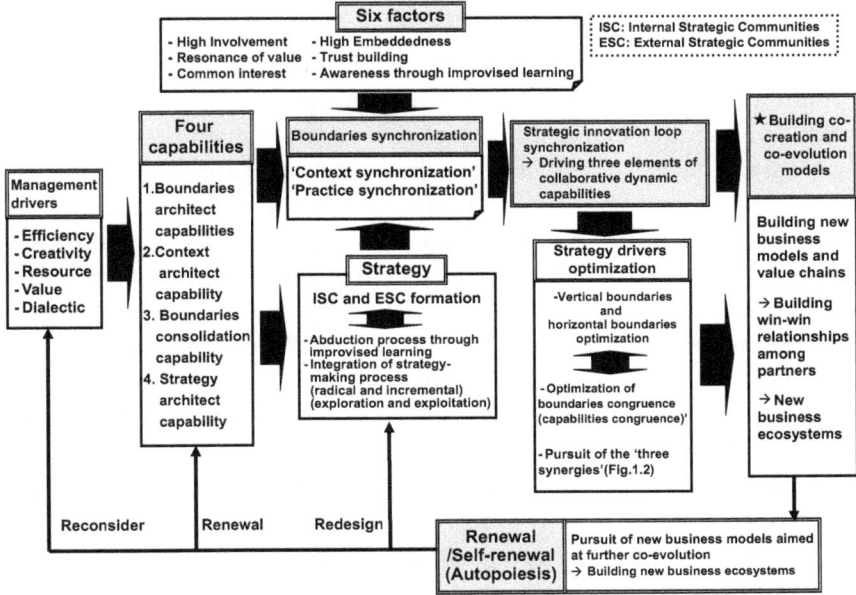

Fig. 2.7 The co-creation and co-evolution model for service innovations and business ecosystems

Service innovations centered on smartphones are examples of the constant advancement of this co-creation and co-evolution model. According to Moore (1993), a business ecosystem is an economic community supported by a foundation of interacting organizations and individuals—the organisms of the business world. Moore suggests that a company should not be viewed as a member of a single industry but "as part of a business ecosystem that crosses a variety of industries," and highlighted the importance of co-evolving the capabilities amongst the business ecosystem members. Apple, Google, and mobile telecommunications carriers around the world pursue new business models to co-create and co-evolve through co-ordination and collaboration with their diverse collaborating partners. As a result, new business ecosystems are formed. In the systems theory discussed previously, open systems are self-regulating and self-organizing. Open systems work to renew themselves and survive by constantly transforming their elements through "autopoiesis" (Maturana and Varela 1980). In these recursive processes, feedback loops are formed for renewal and self-renewal of the business ecosystem, and stakeholders reconsider the aforementioned management drivers in one's company, renew the four capabilities, and redesign strategies making processes to rebuild strategic communities (ISCs and ESCs) and execute new radical innovation as Domain III and/or Domain IV → Domain I → Domain II.

From the perspective of network theory, business ecosystem formulation is rooted in not only the formulation of "small-world structures" as strategic communities (ISCs) and the networking of these in companies such as Apple or Google, but also the formulation of multiple small-world structures as strategic communities (ESCs) with external partner companies, different businesses and customers, and the networking of these. Centered on Apple or Google, which create hubs, these massive clusters of small-world structures trigger the aforementioned boundaries synchronization, and players resonate their contexts and practice (See Fig. 2.6). Thus, for Apple and Google the way they create links with certain customers and external partners and form clusters of small-world structures has been key. Huge amounts of small-world structures have been created in companies, with external partners and across different industries for the birth of these smartphone business models. Hence, Apple and Google demonstrate collaborative DC with their external partners and with different industries to co-create and co-evolve new business ecosystems.

2.7 Chapter Summary

This chapter has derived four propositions for conditions of capabilities congruence in business ecosystems consisting a main company and groups of partner companies in relationships with that company to achieve a service innovation, as described below.

(1) Dynamic external congruence [Insight-1]
(2) Capabilities congruence between managerial elements of the corporate system [Insight-2]
(3) Congruence through orchestration of different co-specialized assets in and out of the company [Insight-3]
(4) Capabilities congruence among the various stakeholders [Insight-4]

These four propositions have qualitatively been shown to satisfy the four standards required in systems theory.

In addition, to co-create and co-evolve new business models by demonstrating collaborative DC, the chapter has presented the necessity for synchronization of strategic innovation loops on the Capabilities Map in player companies that are building business ecosystems. Thus, the chapter has clarified important factors in achieving capabilities congruence among stakeholders [Insight-4] through synchronization of the strategic innovation loops as mechanisms of "boundary synchronization," which are the strategic micropractice of practitioners within organizations (or within companies) and between organizations (or between companies).

References

Adner, R., & Kapoor, R. (2010). Value Creation in Innovation Ecosystems: How the Structure of Technological Interdependence Affects Firm Performance in New Technology Generations. *Strategic Management Journal, 31*(3), 306–333.

Argyris, C., & Schon, D. (1978). *Organizational Learning: A Theory of Action Approach*. Reading: Addison-Wesley.

Barney, J. (1991). Firm Resources and Sustained Competitive Advantage. *Journal of Management, 17*(3), 99–120.

Brandenburger, A. M., & Nalebuff, B. J. (1997). *Co-opetition: A Revolution Mindset that Combines Competition and Cooperation: The Game Theory Strategy that's Changing the Game of Business*. New York: Doubleday.

Brown, J. S., & Duguid, P. (2001). Knowledge and Organization: A Social-Practice Perspective. *Organization Science, 12*(2), 198–213.

Brown, S. L., & Eisenhardt, K. M. (1995). Product Development: Past Research, Present Findings, and Future Directions. *Academy of Management Review, 20*(2), 343–378.

Cannon, W. B. (1932). Homeostasis. *The Wisdom of the Body*. New York: Norton.

Capra, F. (1996). *The Web of Life: A New Synthesis of Mind and Matter*. London: Harper Collins.

Carlile, P. (2002). A Pragmatic View of Knowledge and Boundaries: Boundary Objects in New Product Development. *Organization Science, 13*(4), 442–455.

Carlile, P. (2004). Transferring, Translating, and Transforming: An Integrative Framework for Managing Knowledge Across Boundaries. *Organization Science, 15*(5), 555–568.

Checkland, P. B. (1980). The Systems Movement and the "Failure" of Management Science. *Cybernetics and Systems, 11*(4), 317–324.

Chesbrough, H. (2003). *Open Innovation*. Boston: Harvard Business School Press.

Dougherty, D. (1992). Interpretive Barriers to Successful Product Innovation in Large Firms. *Organization Science, 3*(2), 179–202.

Eisenhardt, K. M., & Tabrizi, B. N. (1995). Accelerating Adaptive Processes: Product Innovation in the Global Computer Industry. *Administrative Science Quarterly, 40*, 84–110.

Ericsson, K. A., & Lehmann, A. C. (1996). Expert and Exceptional Performance: Evidence of Maximal Adaptation to Task Constraints. *Annual Review of Psychology, 47*(1), 273–305.

Felix, R. (2003). A Proposed Taxonomy of Management Systems. *System Research and Behavioral Science, 20*(1), 21–29.

Gawer, A., & Cusumano, M. A. (2002). *Platform Leadership: How Intel, Microsoft, and Cisco Drive Industry Innovation* (pp. 29–30). Boston: Harvard Business School Press.

Gratton, L., & Ghoshal, S. (2005). Beyond Best Practice. *MIT Sloan Management Review, 46*(3), 49–57.

Hagel, J., III, & Brown, J. S. (2005). Productive Friction. *Harvard Business Review, 83*(2), 139–145.

Helfat, C. E. (2007). Stylized Facts, Empirical Research and Theory Development in Management. *Strategic Organization, 5*, 185–192.

Helfat, C. E., & Peteraf, M. A. (2015). Managerial Cognitive Capabilities and the Microfoundations of Dynamic Capabilities. *Strategic Management Journal, 36*(6), 831–850.

Helfat, C. E., Finkelstein, S., Mitchell, W., Peteraf, M. A., Singh, H., Teece, D. J., & Winter, S. G. (2007). *Dynamic Capabilities: Understanding Strategic Change in Organizations*. Oxford: Blackwell.

Iansiti, M., & Levien, R. (2004). *The Keystone Advantage: What the New Dynamics of Business Ecosystems Mean for Strategy, Innovation, and Sustainability*. Boston: Harvard Business School Press.

Johansson, F. (2004). *The Medici Effect*. Boston: Harvard Business School Press.

Kamoche, K., & Cunha, M. P. E. (2001). Minimal Structures: From Jazz Improvisation to Product Innovation. *Organization Studies, 22*(5), 733–764.

Kast, F. E., & Rosenzweig, J. E. (1972). General Systems Theory: Applications for Organization and Management. *Academy of Management Journal, 15*(4), 447–465.

Kodama, M. (1999). Customer Value Creation Through Community-Based Information Networks. *International Journal of Information Management, 19*(6), 495–508.

Kodama, M. (2000). New Multimedia Services in the Education, Medical and Welfare Sectors. *Technovation, 20*(6), 321–331.

Kodama, M. (2002). Transforming an Old Economy Company Through Strategic Communities. *Long Range Planning, 35*(4), 349–365.

Kodama, M. (2003). Strategic Innovation in Traditional Big Business. *Organization Studies, 24*(2), 235–268.

Kodama, M. (2004). Strategic Community-Based Theory of Firms: Case Study of Dialectical Management at NTT DoCoMo. *Systems Research and Behavioral Science, 21*(6), 603–634.

Kodama, M. (2005a). Knowledge Creation Through Networked Strategic Communities: Case Studies on New Product Development in Japanese Companies. *Long Range Planning, 38*(1), 27–49.

Kodama, M. (2005b). How Two Japanese High-Tech Companies Achieved Rapid Innovation Via Strategic Community Networks. *Strategy & Leadership, 33*(6), 39–47.

Kodama, M. (2006). Knowledge-Based View of Corporate Strategy. *Technovation, 26*(12), 1390–1406.

Kodama, M. (2007a). *The Strategic Community-Based Firm.* London: Palgrave Macmillan.

Kodama, M. (2007b). *Knowledge Innovation – Strategic Management as Practice.* Cheltenham: Edward Elgar Publishing.

Kodama, M. (2007c). *Project-Based Organization in the Knowledge-Based Society.* London: Imperial College Press.

Kodama, M. (2007d). Innovation and Knowledge Creation Through Leadership-Based Strategic Community: Case Study on High-Tech Company in Japan. *Technovation, 27*(3), 115–132.

Kodama, M. (2009a). Boundaries Innovation and Knowledge Integration in the Japanese Firm. *Long Range Planning, 42*(4), 463–494.

Kodama, M. (2009b). *Innovation Networks in Knowledge-Based Firm –Developing ICT-Based Integrative Competences.* Cheltenham: Edward Elgar Publishing.

Kodama, M. (2011). *Interactive Business Communities.* Fanham: Gower Publishing.

Kodama, M. (2014). *Winning Through Boundaries Innovation—Communities of Boundaries Generate Convergence.* London: Peter Lang.

Kodama, M. (Ed.). (2015). *Collaborative Innovation: Developing Health Support Ecosystems* (Vol. 39). London: Routledge.

Kodama, M. (2017a). *Developing Holistic Leadership: A Source of Business Innovation.* Bingley: Emerald.

Kodama, M. (2017b). Developing Strategic Innovation in Large Corporations—The Dynamic Capability View of the Firm. *Knowledge and Process Management, 24*(4), 221–246.

Kodama, M. (2018). *Sustainable Growth Through Strategic Innovation: Driving Congruence in Capabilities.* Cheltenham: Edward Elgar Publishing.

Kodama, M., & Ohira, H. (2005). Customer Value Creation Through Customer-as-Innovator Approach—Case Study of Development of Video Processing LSI. *International Journal of Innovation and Learning, 2*(1), 175–185.

Kodama, M., & Shibata, T. (2014a). Strategy Transformation Through Strategic Innovation Capability–A Case Study of Fanuc. *R&D Management, 44*(1), 75–103.

Kodama, M., & Shibata, T. (2014b). Research into Ambidextrous R&D in Product Development–New Product Development at a Precision Device Maker: A Case Study. *Technology Analysis & Strategic Management, 26*(3), 279–306.

Kodama, M., & Shibata, T. (2016). Developing Knowledge Convergence through a Boundaries Vision—A Case Study of Fujifilm in Japan. *Knowledge and Process Management, 23*(4), 274–292.

Kramer, N., & De Smit, J. (1977). *Systems Thinking—Concepts and Notions.* Leiden: M Nijhoff Social Sciences Division.

Leifer, R., McDermott, M., O'Connor, C., Peters, S., Rice, M., & Veryzer, W. (2000). *Radical Innovation: How Mature Companies Can Outsmart Upstarts.* Cambridge, MA: Harvard Business School Press.

Leonard-Barton, D. (1995). *Wellsprings of Knowledge: Building and Sustaining the Source of Innovation.* Cambridge, MA: Harvard Business School Press.

March, J. (1991). Exploration and Exploitation in Organizational Learning. *Organization Science, 2*(1), 71–87.

Markides, C. (1999). *All the Right Moves: A Guide to Crafting Breakthrough Strategy.* Boston: Harvard Business School Publishing.

Maturana, H. R., & Varela, F. J. (1980). Problems in the Neurophysiology of Cognition. In *Autopoiesis and Cognition* (pp. 41–47). Dordrecht: Springer.

Mesarovic, M. D. (1962). On Self Organizational Systems. In M. Yovits, G. T. Jacobi, & G. D. Goldstein (Eds.), *Self-Organizing Systems* (pp. 9–36). Washington, DC: Spartan Books.

Miles, R. E., & Snow, C. C. (2001). *Fit, Failure & the Hall of Fame.* New York: Free Press.

Milgrom, P., & Roberts, J. (1990). The Economics of Modern Manufacturing: Technology, Strategy, and Organization. *The American Economic Review, 80*, 511–528.

Miller, C. C., & Ireland, R. D. (2005). Intuition in Strategic Decision Making: Friend or Foe in the Fast-Paced 21st Century? *The Academy of Management Executive, 19*(1), 19–30.

Mintzberg, H. (1978). Patterns in Strategy Formation. *Management Science, 24*(4), 934–948.

Mintzberg, H., & Waters, J. A. (1985). Of Strategies, Deliberate and Emergent. *Strategic Management Journal, 6*(3), 257–272.

Moore, J. (1993). Predators and Prey: A New Ecology of Competition. *Harvard Business Review, 71*(3), 75–86.

Moore, J. (1996). *The Death of Competition: Leadership and Strategy in the Age of Business Ecosystems.* New York: Harper Business.

Nonaka, I., & Takeuchi, H. (1995). *The Knowledge-Creating Company.* New York: Oxford University Press.

O'Connor, G. (2008). Major Innovation as a Dynamic Capability: A Systems Approach. *Journal of Product Innovation Management, 25*(2), 313–330.

Pisano, G. (1991). The Governance of Innovation: Vertical Integration and Collaborative Arrangements in the Biotechnology Industry. *Research Policy, 20*(3), 237–249.

Rosenbloom, R. S. (2000). Leadership, Capabilities, and Technological Change: The Transformation of NCR in the Electronic Era. *Strategic Management Journal, 21*, 1083–1103.

Rumelt, R. (2011). *Good Strategy/Bad Strategy: The Difference and Why It Matters*. New York: Crown Business.

Santos, F. M., & Eisenhardt, K. M. (2005). *Constructing Markets and Organizing Boundaries: Entrepreneurial Action in Nascent Fields* (Working paper). INSEAD.

Smith, S., & Tushman, M. (2005). Managing Strategic Contradictions: A Top Management Model for Managing Innovation Streams. *Organization Science, 16*(5), 522–536.

Stacey, R. (1995). The Science of Complexity: An Alternative Perspective for Strategic Change Process. *Strategic Management Journal, 16*(6), 477–495.

Star, S. L. (1989). The Structure of Ill-Structured Solutions: Boundary Objects and Heterogeneous Distributed Problem Solving. In L. Gasser & M. N. Huhns (Eds.), *Distributed Artificial Intelligence* (pp. 37–54). London: Pitman.

Teece, D. J. (1986). Profiting from Technological Innovation: Implications for Integration, Collaboration, Licensing and Public Policy. *Research Policy, 15*(6), 285–305.

Teece, D. J. (2007). Explicating Dynamic Capabilities: The Nature and Microfoundations of (Sustainable) Enterprise Performance. *Strategic Management Journal, 28*(13), 1319–1350.

Teece, D. J. (2014). The Foundations of Enterprise Performance: Dynamic and Ordinary Capabilities in an (Economic) Theory of Firms. *The Academy of Management Perspectives, 28*(4), 328–352.

Tripsas, M., & Gavetti, G. (2000). Capabilities, Cognition, and Inertia: Evidence from Digital Imaging. *Strategic Management Journal, 21*, 1147–1161.

von Bertalanffy, L. (1960). Principles and Theory of Growth. *Fundamental Aspects of Normal and Malignant Growth, 493*, 137–259.

Von Bertalanffy, L. (1968). General System Theory. *New York, 41973*(1968), 40.

Von Bertalanffy, L. (1972). The History and Status of General Systems Theory. *Academy of Management Journal, 15*(4), 407–426.

Winter, S. (2003). Understanding Dynamic Capabilities. *Strategic Management Journal, 24*(10), 991–995.

3

E-healthcare Service Innovations: In Depth Case Studies in Japan

Mitsuru Kodama

3.1 Service Innovations for Co-creation and Co-evolution: The Case of NTT DOCOMO

In the modern world, networks are being increasingly configured to share medical, welfare, and healthcare-related information using mobile terminals such as smartphones and tablet computers. In developed Western countries, an increasing amount of information is exchanged about care advice, citizens are offered counseling and medical and healthcare consultations, information is exchange among communities (including doctors, carers, helpers, volunteers, and the able-bodied), and in social networking. Meanwhile, the smart cities concept, which entails the integration of these various information networks, is moving ahead in developed countries.

M. Kodama (✉)
Nihon University, College of Commerce, Tokyo, Japan
e-mail: kodama.mitsuru@nihon-u.ac.jp

Modern healthcare services are often passive or intermittent and focus on disease. However, the Organisation for Economic Co-operation and Development (OECD) (2013) has noted that new healthcare services must engage more proactively in prevention and focus on quality of life and well-being. Modern medicine is centered on hospitals and doctors. This model must be transformed to a patient-centered approach, so that patients can receive a variety of care while at home (Kodama 2000, 2001, 2002, 2008). This model must also incorporate wider social networks, as households and local society can act as important contributors to the health and well-being of individuals. Care must be tailored to meet the different requirements, needs, and circumstances of individuals, therefore, when dealing with factors that contribute to health, illness, and recovery, patients must be engaged as partners (OECD 2013, p. 34).

The OECD (2013) cites the development of meaningful service innovations as one of the main challenges for the future in the latest literature reporting on the state of development of e-healthcare in its member states. Regarding the benefits that e-healthcare services will bring to their recipients and the bearers of their costs, the OECD (2013) suggests that these services should be considered in broader interdisciplinary contexts rather than in terms of simple healthcare benefits.

In light of these pioneering e-healthcare services, which are gaining attention around the world, NTT DOCOMO INC. (DOCOMO hereinafter) has made an effort to transform itself from its historical role as a mobile communications company to become an "added value co-creation company," following a philosophy of shifting from competition to co-creation. The company has named this initiative "+d" (pronounced "plus dee") and is putting +d efforts into fields such as medical and healthcare, education and learning, agriculture, and the Internet of Things. This entails initiatives to make people's lives more convenient and that will invigorate regions to solve social issues through strategic collaboration with partners such as governments, businesses, and research institutions. DOCOMO's knowledge assets (tangible and intangible) underpin its mobile networks, customer base, safe transaction systems, and i-mode. The company believes it can co-create new social value and new businesses by working with its partners as they use these knowledge assets in conjunction with their wisdom and expertise.

3.1.1 The E-healthcare Service Innovation Challenge

DOCOMO's first initiative in the healthcare and medical field was to launch a "wellness support" service in June 2009 to provide ongoing support for health instruction and management. Vital data—such as bodyweight, body composition, and blood pressure—are collected via health devices and mobile telephones with built-in pedometers, then stored in a wellness support server (a vital data collection platform). By linking the collected vital data to healthcare services, institutions, or healthcare-related companies, effective services can be efficiently achieved.

DOCOMO went through the following processes from conceptualization to launching a commercial service. This new project began in October 2007. What could be done with a mobile phone for healthcare, taking into account the specific medical examinations and health guidance businesses due to start in Japan in April 2008? What kind of support was possible? Project members began by holding hearings with existing healthcare equipment manufacturers and healthcare service providers. Comments were made about how healthcare services developed for use with personal computers had problems with ease of use and continual use. Hence, project members uncovered the potential for mobile phones to contribute to ease of use.

Service providers involved in health information, in recording functions and communities through websites, and so on, had issues with collecting day-to-day health information from customers to enrich healthcare services. DOCOMO felt confident that it could contribute to building a better service since not only do mobile telephones have simple communication functions, but they also provide support for daily life, and health is an important part of that support. Thus, the company began with building services for "wellness support." After announcing this service in the press, there were many inquiries from outside the company and project members realized that there were many companies wanting to engage in health promotion.

Through dialog with a wide range of users, project members found many stakeholders who wanted to make consumers healthy (people involved in medicine, government, and the healthcare business), and many individuals who wanted to be healthier. Project members became convinced that they could combine services to meet both of these needs and build a new healthcare market. By making it easier for more consumers to manage their health, the team was confident that perceptions of healthcare management would change. Thus, through dialog with healthcare equipment manufacturers and healthcare service providers, project members had used their "sensing," a function of their dynamic capabilities (DC).

Project members believed that DOCOMO was in a neutral position and could convert the measurement data produced by the different technologies of healthcare equipment manufacturers to a standard format, which would enable standardized operations and be of great value to the generation of a new market. Project members also embraced the idea that, as a telecommunications carrier and intermediary, DOCOMO could also provide services to bring users together.

To build this new service concept it would be necessary to develop and maintain an infrastructure that enabled users to easily manage their medical examinations and daily healthcare data while regularly checking it. At the time, providers were managing individuals' healthcare data, but the project team believed that if users themselves were able to manage various services and their healthcare data then e-healthcare services would broaden. Thus, as they tried to match the needs of those who wanted to be healthy with the needs of those who wanted to make people healthy, they began the process of "seizing" by setting down specifications for the development, testing, verifying, and commercializing of a new service.

For the DOCOMO project team to achieve a wellness support service, it had to drive strategic collaborations with a diverse range of partner companies (IT vendors, healthcare equipment manufacturers, healthcare promotion service providers, governments, and private companies such as Asahi Kasei Life Support, NTT Resonant, NTT-IT, Omron Healthcare Co. Ltd. [Omron Healthcare hereinafter], Konami Sports & Life, Konami Sports Club, Tanita, WM, Best Life Promotion, Wing Style/Casio Information Systems, and NEC Mobiling). It was crucial not only to complement the IT technology with mobile telephones, but also to incorporate the concept of interconnecting the new service with real-time communications.

Through experimentation and trials of the service, project members became aware that users were not looking for "technology," so they aimed to design an interface that was convenient from the user's perspective. Since various problems always appear as a service becomes operational and the number of its users increases, the project team oriented themselves toward seizing and transforming while adapting to changes in e-healthcare service market conditions because of the time required to embed new values.

An initiative in April 2008, focusing on health guidance for metabolic syndrome (two or more states of visceral fat obesity combined with hypertension, hyperglycemia, or hyperlipidemia), started DOCOMO out on the verification and testing of its wellness platform in June 2008, closely linked to the core collaborating partners, Omron Healthcare and NTT data. In November 2008, DOCOMO conducted monitoring surveys of a limited number of people through strong linkages with Shiseido Health Insurance Union and the local government of Kamakura city, Kanagawa prefecture. Questionnaire results reported that about 70% of citizens surveyed had increased awareness of their own health management through the visualization of their measurement results, clarifying the usefulness of mobile telephones as a tool for forming the habit of taking measurements daily. Project members confirmed that roughly the same 70% of participants intended to personalize the service with their vital data.

In the trial in Kamakura city, DOCOMO built linkages with systems from NTT-IT, and through trials of FeliCa-compatible, publicly operated, body composition analyzers (a prototype), gained two high appraisals from public health workers and nurses: (1) reduced workload in manually inputting measurement results; and (2) shortened response times enabled by utilizing vital data acquired in advance, and the ability to provide guidance and advice for improvements in a timely manner.

Through the project team's demonstration of DC (sensing → seizing → transforming), and experiments and verification through trial and error, the team was able to verify the extremely high benefits of using the mobile phone, a personal tool, to collect vital data regularly. FeliCaPlug, a technology for instantaneously transferring measurement information from healthcare devices to a mobile phone, was announced by DOCOMO at CEATEC JAPAN 2009. This technology enables inclusion in previously problematic healthcare devices thanks to its compact, low cost, and low power consumption. By building this technology into healthcare devices it greatly improved the ability of many consumers to easily record and store data from healthcare devices on their mobile telephones. The demonstration of DC to achieve the development, verification, testing, and commercialization of this new service was instrumental in the formation of a new company.

(a) Establishing DOCOMO Healthcare and New Service Developments

DOCOMO Healthcare, Inc., was established in July 2012. DOCOMO and Omron Healthcare are the main shareholders, with 66% and 34% respectively. DOCOMO aimed to achieve a "smart life" using mobile technology and the cloud, while Omron Healthcare aimed to develop new devices to visualize a variety of physiological data from devices such as body composition analyzers, the company's world-leading blood pressure monitors, and sleep pattern analysis meters.

DOCOMO Healthcare's smart life-centered corporate vision is "Connecting individual's health with society." DOCOMO has the mobile technologies and applications required to build such a mechanism and has enabled a complementary relationship with Omron Healthcare to build "new world views," rather than proceeding with new businesses by themselves. With the target of producing a service to provide continuous customer value from a user's perspective, both companies spent about a year preparing for the establishment of the new company. DOCOMO Healthcare is aiming to build a completely new healthcare culture through alliances with many other partner companies.

In this way, DOCOMO Healthcare achieves co-specialization and capabilities synthesis by developing businesses that make use of the service and device developments strengths of both DOCOMO and Omron Healthcare. The company's "moveband" automatically measures and sends data on the number of steps, distance traveled, calories consumed, amount of sleep time, and sleep conditions to enable regular checking of daily activities and health via an application. The measurements taken by this device make use of Omron Healthcare's precision technologies.

Meanwhile, using the service development capabilities of DOCOMO, the company has taken the initiative to contribute to general health by providing peripheral complementary services centered around the moveband, such as: the *karada no kimochi* (body feeling) app to support beauty, diet, and pregnancy using information obtained from the menstrual cycle and matched to daily rhythms; the *karada no tokei* (body clock) app to provide healthcare information on sleep, meals, diet, and prevention of lifestyle-related illnesses.

Based on Omron Healthcare's technological strengths, the company offers reassuring and highly reliable healthcare devices (sensors and components), including blood pressure monitors and a women's thermometer. In the future, Omron Healthcare will require services to bring these devices together and create new value.

Omron Healthcare's culture of manufacturing highly reliable devices and DOCOMO's corporate culture of creating services have completely different investment concepts, sense of speed, and relationships with customers. Omron Healthcare's difficulties lie in building mechanisms as services, which requires a strategic collaboration with DOCOMO. Thus, the three factors of strategic collaboration, co-specialization, and capability synthesis bring about collaborative DC.

(b) Strategy Through DOCOMO's Midterm Vision 2015

DOCOMO's midterm vision 2015 was not limited to healthcare, it included policies on eight new service areas: M2M (machine to machine); aggregation platforms; finance and transactions; media and content; commerce; medical and healthcare; safety and security; and the environment and ecology. Underlying DOCOMO's thinking is that as a telecommunications carrier merely providing telecommunications lines as a "dumb pipe" business, it is difficult to produce differentiation from communications revenues, and that competition in the mobile markets of the future will be severe. Therefore, for telecommunications carriers, these eight new areas will be one of the new business fields in the future. Hence, DOCOMO's 2015 midterm vision included the concept of the company being a "smart life partner," representing a new axis for DOCOMO to focus on users and partner them in creating smart lives.

One of the new fields is medical and healthcare, on which DOCOMO is focusing. Because health is key to a smart life it is important to develop services in the four core categories of diet, exercise, sleep, and healthcare (see Fig. 3.1). As a way of mutually linking services in these four categories DOCOMO has set up "Radishbo-ya," handling health and organic foods, and "ABC Cooking Studio" to provide recipes and dietary education. The company's exercise services include the smash hit "Billy's Bootcamp" and TRF's dance exercise DVD "Ez Do Dancercize" produced with collaborating partners through Oak Lawn's "Shop Japan."

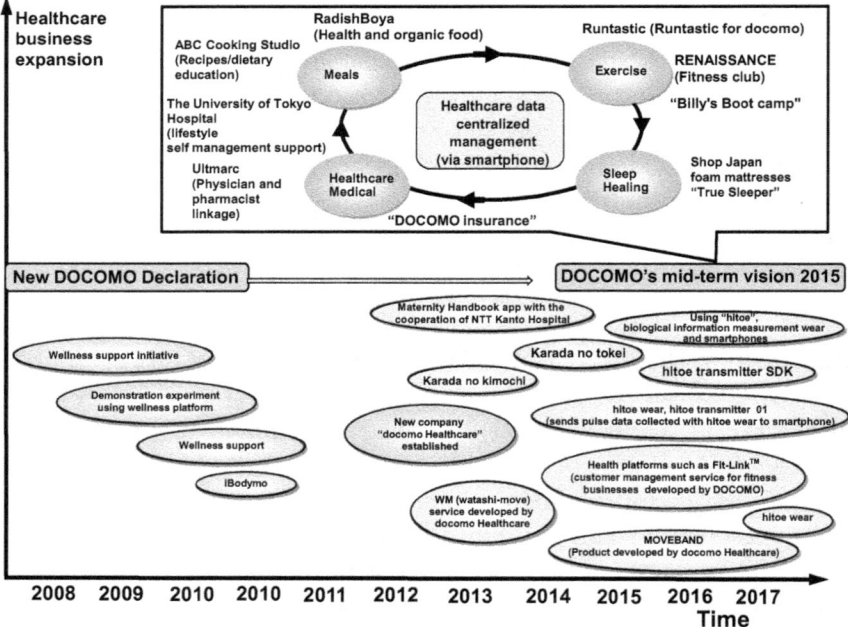

Fig. 3.1 NTT DOCOMO healthcare business development—supporting action phase (2008–2017). (Source: Created by the authors from DOCOMO publications)

Other new DOCOMO services include: the Shop Japan "True Sleeper" foam mattress; healthcare insurance; courses in partnership with University of Tokyo Hospital on supporting self-management of lifestyle-related disease; and "Ultmarc" to connect doctors with pharmacists. And it is healthcare data that connects all of these (see Fig. 3.1).

As a telecommunications carrier DOCOMO offers smartphones, while Toray and NTT (a company with shares in DOCOMO) developed and commercialized "hitoe," a conductive fiber fabric that enables the acquisition of biometric data (such as pulse rate and electrocardiogram waveform) just by the user wearing it. DOCOMO began providing new services using smartphones and biometric data measuring wear made from hitoe in 2014. In December 2015, DOCOMO produced a software development kit (SDK) called "hitoe transmitter SDK" to enable providers to develop services by freely utilizing biometric data measured by the hitoe fabric.

The hitoe transmitter SDK enables free use of pulse, acceleration, and electrocardiogram biometric data acquired through hitoe wear and hitoe transmitter 01 (a device developed by DOCOMO to transmit pulse data acquired with hitoe wear) using smartphones. The data can then be analyzed for stress, posture, walking conditions, and variations in walking time balance. Providers can develop services using this biometric information for effective training, regularly check user conditions using the stress estimation, and provide them to users.

As a result of joint development and experimentation, DOCOMO has engaged in strategic collaborations with NTT Data MSE, Kyoto University, and Kumamoto University to develop a system to detect driver sleepiness, using hitoe wear to acquire the biometric information (pulse data). Demonstration and verification testing of the effectiveness of this system began in May 2016 in co-operation with a transport company. NTT Data MSE developed a special application for smartphones that uses a new sleep detection algorithm developed by Kyoto and Kumamoto universities. By sending pulse data acquired with hitoe wear and the hitoe transmitter 01 to a smartphone with the special app installed, driver sleepiness on long-haul night drives can be detected, drivers can be alerted, and managers can be alerted by email. This system thus helps prevent drivers from falling asleep at the wheel.

The physiological data measured with moveband and hitoe can easily be collected through a smartphone. The centralized collection and management of personal health record data means that DOCOMO and DOCOMO Healthcare can use the data to suggest new health-centered lifestyles. As well as using moveband and hitoe, data can be collected from scales, thermometers, sleep meters, and so on provided by the partner company Omron Healthcare. Individual users become aware that they can use the data into the future. Hence, DOCOMO is aiming to develop diverse interactive services for a world in which items are connected through smartphone hubs and wearables are connected directly.

DOCOMO has teamed up with Austrian mobile fitness company Runtastic to produce the "Runtastic for docomo" running record service. The Runtastic app has had more than 100 million downloads, and as DOCOMO has cemented a firm partnership with this global player, it can offer appropriate services to users. This means DOCOMO can deploy more co-ordinated services as a complete set consisting of the three elements of exercising in a real place, net services, and sales. DOCOMO has begun the "iBodymo" net service, which covers walking and aspects of diet, rather than just exercise; it also offers *karada no tokei* (body clock), a healthcare service that uses the body's internal clock in relation to lifestyle. Hence, if one exercises, surely one is also concerned about diet and nutrition, which creates a cycle of the four aspects of diet, exercise, sleep, and healthcare/medical (see Fig. 3.1).

DOCOMO also has a stake in health spatial informatics at the University of Tokyo and is engaged in cross-functional research—based on the belief that ICT can be used for self-managed diabetes support and a quick exchange of information between emergency transportation and hospitals to speed up treatment, even if only by a second. The company also provides a "maternity handbook" app in partnership with Hakuhodo and with the co-operation of NTT Kanto Hospital.

In May 2015 DOCOMO and Renaissance formed a business alliance to provide new healthcare services to improve user health by linking DOCOMO's platform for managing and using physiological and health data to fitness clubs all over the country, instructors, exercise know-how, and health programs owned by Renaissance. This is part of DOCOMO's +d initiative to co-create new value with collaboration partners. The healthcare platforms include: "WM (watashi move)," a service developed by DOCOMO Healthcare; "Fit-Link," customer management service for fitness businesses developed by DOCOMO; and healthcare management and prevention support services using wearable devices such as moveband (a product developed by DOCOMO Healthcare). Hence, DOCOMO and Renaissance will provide total healthcare services for individuals, businesses, and governments nationwide, both in and out of fitness facilities, using ICT to contribute to improved health.

As the main player, DOCOMO's strategic action is characterized by its expansion of a new business ecosystem of e-healthcare through strategic collaboration with a diverse range of collaborating partners, including Omron Healthcare and DOCOMO Healthcare.

The following sections analyze the collaborative DC of DOCOMO and its collaborating partners as a result of the challenge of the new e-healthcare businesses that began with the new DOCOMO declaration of April 2008 and the "supporting action phase (2008–2017)" through mobile telephones (see Fig. 3.1).

3.2 DOCOMO Strategic Innovation System: Supporting Action Phase (2008–2017)

Figure 3.2 illustrates DOCOMO's businesses in the supporting action phase (2008–2017) on the Capabilities Map. New services based on 3.9G mobile communications systems (LTE: 4G compliant with IMT-Advanced) and smartphones had been commercialized through Domain I → Domain II processes in the previous phase (before 2008) and moved to Domain III in this phase. Hence, the conventional 3G i-mode services that had been the main business in Domain III in the previous phase were shifted to Domain IV in this phase. A strong integration of DC and ordinary capabilities (OC) was required in Domain III in this phase for upgrading versions of high-speed packet communication services in the rapidly changing competitive environments of mobile telecommunications carriers (other companies also pursued 3.9G mobile telecommunications services and commercialized them). On the other hand, in the

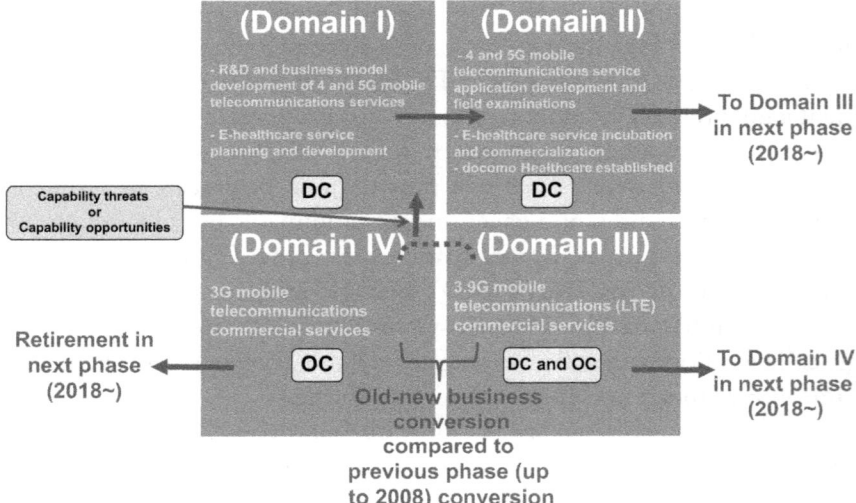

Fig. 3.2 Capabilities map in a strategic innovation system in NTT DOCOMO—supporting action phase (2008–2017)

slow-moving business environments of Domain IV, OC were demonstrated to maintain the existing sunset 3G mobile telecommunications i-mode service businesses (and gradually retrench, leading to retirement in the next phase following 2018). Thus, with the new businesses based on LTE and smartphones in Domain III, and the 3G i-mode services in Domain IV, DOCOMO's 3.9G (LTE) and 3G businesses were both positioned as its existing businesses in this phase (see Fig. 3.2).

In this phase, with technical accumulation over many years from the existing 3G and 3.9G mobile telecommunications services in Domains III and IV, DOCOMO was induced to shift from Domain III (and/or IV) to Domain I for R&D on the coming 4G and 5G mobile telecommunications systems. With the objective of achieving further radical innovation, DOCOMO is uncovering capabilities opportunities for the 4G and 5G mobile telecommunications systems, and driving new DC in Domains III and IV to achieve the shift to Domain I. Thus, for its subsequent technical challenges, DOCOMO simultaneously engaged in R&D for: 4G (with roughly ten times the communications speed of LTE) and 5G mobile telecommunications services to be commercialized by 2020; new service and business planning and development; and trial experiments and business verification of these by shifting from Domain I to Domain II.

Notably, DOCOMO is engaging in experiments and technical developments with major global vendors to achieve 5G joint developments, such as: experimental trials of chip sets required for 5G terminals with Intel; developing devices to measure the results of 5G experiments with Keysight Technology, Rohde, and Schwarz; efficient communication systems technologies with Panasonic; and 5G communications technologies with Qualcomm. DC are notably demonstrated in Domains I and II, particularly in the R&D departments (see Fig. 3.2).

DOCOMO had to engage in DC demonstrations on how to use this new infrastructure to generate new markets. Underlying this is that mobile telecommunications carriers face the potential of their businesses becoming a "dumb pipe." In future, it will be difficult to produce revenue differentiated from the provision of lines of communication, and competition in mobile markets will be severe. Thus, as DOCOMO faces "capability threats," or opportunities to uncover "capability opportunities," one of its new business territories has become the e-healthcare business.

Accordingly, DOCOMO's strategic objectives are to develop new businesses (social support services) in the areas of environment, ecology, safety and security, and health management to produce value in new areas for the sustainable growth of society. With its base of roughly 54 million customers, DOCOMO continues to work on solutions to social problems. By advancing its strengths in networking, mobile terminals, and services, and by widening the use of mobile phones and smartphones—with their characteristics of mobility, real time, and personal devices—DOCOMO aims to enhance its contribution to enabling efficiency in individual actions and consumption, and to raising the productivity of society.

These new R&D activities through DC, and co-creation activities through a wide range of strategic collaborations, are crucial for DOCOMO's e-healthcare businesses. Project members aiming to create new healthcare businesses enacted sensing, seizing, and transforming in the highly uncertain environments of the Domain I → Domain II stages.

The role of DC in Domain I is particularly important. Sensing enables DOCOMO's project team in charge of R&D to seek out and detect potential new markets in e-healthcare, meanwhile setting down and executing plans for R&D over the mid- to long term through the seizing and transforming processes. These processes are equivalent to marketing and R&D activities to achieve the various DOCOMO-centered healthcare information services enabled by the wellness support service, moveband, and hitoe as described in Sect. 3.1.1.

As in Domain I, the project team's DC play a significant role in Domain II. The team demonstrated sensing to match technical innovations with healthcare markets, and executed seizing and transforming processes to orchestrate tangible and intangible assets in DOCOMO and Omron Healthcare through DC to develop, trial, and test new businesses and technologies, to provide full-fledged commercial services, and to establish the new DOCOMO Healthcare. From 2016 onward, other companies have become involved in these e-healthcare businesses, and the market is gradually growing. For the next phase, from 2018 onward, DOCOMO, Omron Healthcare, and DOCOMO Healthcare are promoting full-scale businesses in the environments of Domain III (see Fig. 3.2).

As discussed in Sect. 2.1 in Chap. 2, in the shift from Domain I → Domain II in the Capabilities Map, project members have to demonstrate imagination and creativity to achieve new innovations in environments of uncertainty, such as the e-healthcare business. Project members are continuously creating to achieve concepts of new business models (frameworks for new products, services, and businesses). Emergent strategies are executed through the formation of multiple emergent external strategic communities (ESC) with partners, including customers (Mintzberg and Waters 1985). Emergent strategies are created by practitioners through trial and error at workplace level (including divisions near customers and middle management layers) as they recognize changes in the environment that they did not predict. DOCOMO's e-healthcare business is a case of pioneering a business through the formation of multiple emergent ESCs with external strategic business partners, including customers.

The structure of DOCOMO's strategic organizations are an example of Kodama's "strategic community-based firm," discussed in Sect. 2.1 (2003, 2004, 2005, 2006, 2007a, b, d, 2009a, b). DOCOMO generally has two types of organizational form (emergent and traditional): emergent organizations are those that aim to plan, develop, and commercialize the company's e-healthcare businesses; while traditional organizations are those that target the maintenance and development of current businesses. There are paradoxical elements in terms of the pursuit of creativity and autonomy in emergent organizations as opposed to the efficiency and control in traditional organizations. Thus, there is always conflict and friction between these organizations, which hinders the integration of the knowledge of formal organizations or internal strategic communities (ISCs) and ESCs. Nevertheless, the leadership teams in DOCOMO drive this synthesis (Kodama 2004, 2007c, 2010, 2014, 2017).

The leadership teams are formed from leaders (the CEO, executives, division managers, senior management, project leaders, and managers) at all management levels within the company (individuals and teams from top and middle management layers, cross-functional teams, and task forces). Leadership teams bring about DC and OC across entire corporations through the synthesis and integration of knowledge in both types of formal organization (emergent and traditional) and in internal strategic communities. To achieve a strategic community-based firm, it is important that leadership teams combine and synthesize these apparently contradictory creative and planned strategic methods.

3.3 Collaborative DC Through Strategic Innovation Loop Synchronization

On analyzing the process of commercialization of the DOCOMO-centered e-healthcare businesses, it can be said that the shifts between domains were synchronized between stakeholders (DOCOMO, Omron Healthcare, and many other collaborating players, such as NTT data), in the individual stages of Domain I → Domain II. For example, when the main players, DOCOMO and Omron Healthcare, demonstrated DC to execute incubation processes, such as R&D, for new or prototype services in Domain I → Domain II, collaborating players simultaneously shared the context with the main players (context synchronization) and demonstrated DC with the main players, and executed an incubation process (practice synchronization). In other words, "boundaries synchronization" occurred among the group of mutually related companies as in the "context synchronization" and "practice synchronization" discussed in Chap. 2. The mechanism of "boundary synchronization," the strategic micropractice of practitioners within organizations (or companies) and between organizations (or companies) drives the synchronization of strategic innovation loops and achieves "capabilities congruence among stakeholders" [Insight-4].

In Domains I and II, the main players, DOCOMO and Omron Healthcare, form ESCs with certain collaborating partners to continuously promote emergent and entrepreneurial strategies that attract the interest of many end-users and other partners for the e-healthcare service innovations, and to create new markets. The important perspective here is that, in collaborating player organizations, there are ISCs similar to the main player ISC and ESCs that bridge main players and collaborating players. Interlocked with the boundaries synchronization of context and practice synchronization in main players, context and practice synchronization between collaborating players is simultaneously carried out to keep pace with that of the main players.

To further grow a service, main players and certain collaborating partners encourage the participation of other collaborating partners to expand the business ecosystem, at the same time forming ISCs, and fully expanding new businesses born in Domain I → Domain II to be the company's main business. In this way, the main players established a new company, DOCOMO Healthcare, as an in-house venture.

As discussed in Chap. 2, homeostasis and self-organization of corporate systems as open systems serve to bring about a state of equilibrium in which the synchronization of strategic innovation loops among stakeholders (main players and collaborating players) on the Capabilities Map (the congruence of capabilities among stakeholders in each domain) is constantly changing. Homeostasis and self-organization, which synchronize strategic innovation loops, achieve [Insight-4] at the same time as bringing capabilities congruence to subsystems (corporate systems—main and collaborating players) ([Insight-1], [Insight-2], and [Insight-3]). These mechanisms bring adaptability (or congruence) for maximum stability of the complex systems (multi-stable systems) in e-healthcare business ecosystems.

E-healthcare Service Innovations: In Depth Case Studies in Japan

At DOCOMO and Omron Healthcare, new services with radical innovation elements are achieved by specialist organizations, or project teams, separate from existing organizations. In the strategic selection stage of Domain II, important decision-making comes from stakeholders regarding commercializing experimental and trial service processes and results. Notably, this led to the DOCOMO and Omron Healthcare decision to establish the new DOCOMO Healthcare company.

Synchronization of the strategic innovation loops on the Capabilities Map was promoted among DOCOMO, Omron Healthcare, DOCOMO Healthcare, and many other collaborating players (such as NTT Data), and hence "capabilities congruence among stakeholders [Insight-4]" was achieved. This synchronization of strategic innovation loops drives collaborative DC (see Fig. 3.3).

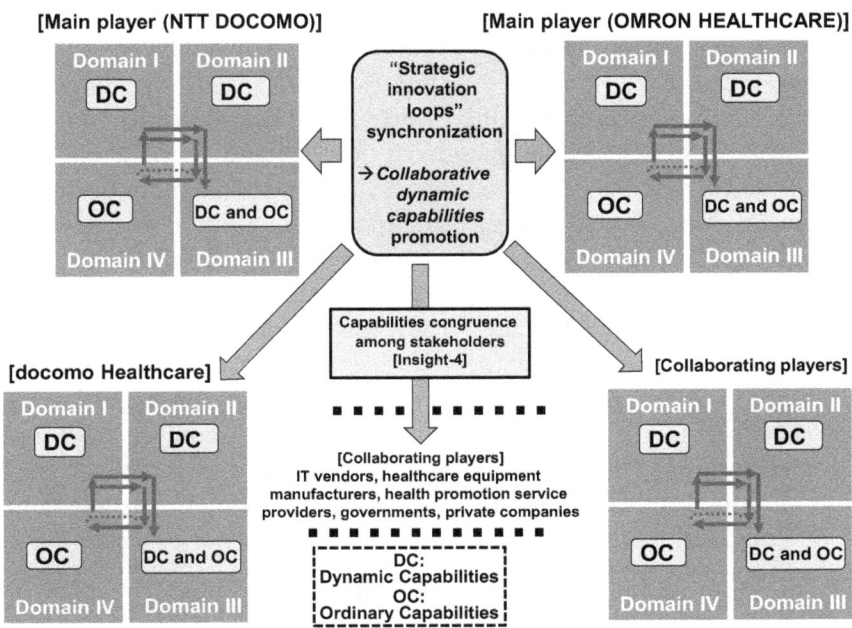

Fig. 3.3 Collaborative DC through strategic innovation loop synchronization centered on DOCOMO and Omron Healthcare

3.4 The Six Factors Driving Strategic Innovation Loop Synchronization

As discussed in Sect. 2.6 in Chap. 2, managers and project leaders in both corporations required six factors to synchronize strategic innovation loops (high involvement, high embeddedness, resonance of values, trust building, common interests, and awareness through improvised learning).

Project leaders engaged in launching the new business, DOCOMO Healthcare, cited that the most important point of launching a new business was "a worldview of new business." These project leaders indicated that it was important to explain this "new worldview" in a single phrase to both in-house and external practitioners and bring about empathy both inside and outside of the company, in other words, the importance of "resonance of values." Project leaders also cited that "the integration of five values" was important for the concept of "business with built-in social value," and spoke of the importance of providing new value to society and users.

Project members need to think through the most important customer and business values, including convergence values, to bring about new ideas. Project members also cited that the concept of "aiming for the big picture but starting with small things" was important for business. Aiming for the big picture was the "worldview," whereas starting with small things justified the hypothesis of the generation of the assumed (five) values. Project leaders cited that it was important to bring together the wisdom of all project members for these concepts.

In addition, project members need to quickly and, on a small scale, repeatedly engage in trial and error through "common interest" and "awareness through improvised learning." Project leaders from DOCOMO and Omron Healthcare also said moving ahead by doing things the same way is no good, the key was to get project members not to see failure as failure, but to learn that the pattern would not lead to success.

In the new DOCOMO Healthcare company, DOCOMO and Omron Healthcare brought their mutual strengths, based on trust building between their companies, and developed a business of products and services that complemented weaknesses by converging manufacturing with services. This triggered the generation of co-specialization—an element of collaborative DC. DOCOMO Healthcare is including new collaborative partners centered on itself and is bringing about a business ecosystem to further develop markets. Important to which is the promotion of sustainable collaborative innovation between the main and collaborating partners (Kodama 2015, 2017). The key to promoting this is, according to project leaders, "a worldview of business" as the big picture, "execution" of the little things, and thinking about social and technical aspects in parallel with business and customer profit.

In DOCOMO Healthcare, the high involvement and high embeddedness of project members in both companies are key to thoroughly executing new collaborative processes to bring about the three factors of collaborative DC and synergies in both companies. To succeed with the new business, project members have to take a broad view of matters when conceptualizing business, at the same time scrutinizing details when taking initiatives to formulate business. These factors generate collaborative DC that bring together the wisdom and collaboration of both companies.

Furthermore, DOCOMO, Omron Healthcare, and DOCOMO Healthcare have formed (external) strategic communities originating in the formation of *ba* among them. Among the six factors discussed above, resonance of values and trust building are factors that foster common perceptions among collaborating partners and project members. Furthermore, the factors of common interests and awareness through improvised learning encourage self-transcendence in collaborating partners and project members. Moreover, the factors of high involvement and high embeddedness accelerate self-organization among collaborating partners and project members.

Common perceptions, self-transcendence, and self-organization drive the formation of *ba* and strategic communities (both internal and external), and bring about boundaries synchronization between the main players—DOCOMO, Omron Healthcare, and DOCOMO Healthcare—and many other participating companies—the collaborating players—as context synchronization and practice synchronization.

In this way, close strategic collaboration among players achieves the synchronization of strategic innovation loops and capabilities congruence through boundary synchronization, and achieves the three factors of collaborative DC. Hence, this dynamic strategic process drives co-creation and co-evolution to build new business models and value chains, as discussed in Fig. 2.7 in Chap. 2.

3.5 Conclusion

This chapter has observed and analyzed details of a service innovation to plan, develop, and provide healthcare support services with involvement from many collaborating partners, enabled by the strategic collaboration between DOCOMO, a Japanese mobile telecommunications carrier, and Omron Healthcare, a major healthcare business, and the use of the resources of both companies. This chapter has also observed and analyzed collaborative innovation with the involvement of groups of companies across different industries (main and collaborating players) and the building of business ecosystems from the perspective of collaborative DC.

This chapter has clarified a microstrategic mechanism of boundaries synchronization as context and practice synchronization among groups of companies across different industries (main and collaborating players) to promote collaborative DC through the synchronization of strategic innovation loops to achieve capabilities congruence among stakeholders [Insight-4], leading to co-creation and co-evolution.

References

Kodama, M. (2000). New Multimedia Services in the Education, Medical and Welfare Sectors. *Technovation, 20*(6), 321–331.
Kodama, M. (2001). New Regional Community Creation, Medical and Educational Applications Through Video-Based Information Networks. *Systems Research and Behavioral Science, 18*(3), 225–240.
Kodama, M. (2002). Strategic Partnership with Innovative Customers: A Japanese Case Study. *Information Systems Management, 19*(2), 31–52.
Kodama, M. (2003). Strategic Innovation in Traditional Big Business. *Organization Studies, 24*(2), 235–268.

Kodama, M. (2004). Strategic Community-Based Theory of Firms: Case Study of Dialectical Management at NTT DoCoMo. *Systems Research and Behavioral Science, 21*(6), 603–634.

Kodama, M. (2005). Knowledge Creation Through Networked Strategic Communities: Case Studies in New Product Development. *Long Range Planning, 38*(1), 27–49.

Kodama, M. (2006). Knowledge-Based View of Corporate Strategy. *Technovation, 26*(12), 1390–1406.

Kodama, M. (2007a). *The Strategic Community-Based Firm*. London: Palgrave Macmillan.

Kodama, M. (2007b). *Knowledge Innovation—Strategic Management as Practice*. Cheltenham/Northampton: Edward Elgar Publishing.

Kodama, M. (2007c). *Project-Based Organization in the Knowledge-Based Society*. London: Imperial College Press.

Kodama, M. (2007d). Innovation and Knowledge Creation Through Leadership-Based Strategic Community: Case Study on High-Tech Company in Japan. *Technovation, 27*(3), 115–132.

Kodama, M. (2008). *New Knowledge Creation Through ICT Dynamic Capability Creating Knowledge Communities Using Broadband*. Charlotte: Information Age Publishing.

Kodama, M. (2009a). Boundaries Innovation and Knowledge Integration in the Japanese Firm. *Long Range Planning, 42*(4), 463–494.

Kodama, M. (2009b). *Innovation Networks in Knowledge-Based Firms: Developing ICT-Based Integrative Competences*. Cheltenham/Northampton: Edward Elgar Publishing.

Kodama, M. (2010). *Boundary Management: Developing Business Architecture for Innovation*. Berlin: Springer.

Kodama, M. (2014). *Winning Through Boundaries Innovation: Communities of Boundaries Generate Convergence*. London: Peter Lang.

Kodama, M. (Ed.). (2015). *Collaborative Innovation: Developing Health Support Ecosystems* (Vol. 39). London: Routledge.

Kodama, M. (2017). *Developing Holistic Leadership: A Source of Business Innovation*. London: Emerald.

Mintzberg, H., & Waters, J. A. (1985). Of Strategies, Deliberate and Emergent. *Strategic Management Journal, 6*(3), 257–272.

OECD. (2013). *ICTs and the Health Sector: Towards Smarter Health and Wellness Model*. Paris: OECD.

4

Quality Improvements and Cost Reductions in Healthcare: Accountable Care Organizations from the Perspective of Collaborative Dynamic Capabilities and Leadership

Toshiro Takahashi

4.1 Introduction

In 2012, the American Board of Internal Medicine (the ABIM Foundation), in conjunction with nine American medical associations and consumer groups, produced a series of lists called "Five Things Physicians and Patients Should Question" totaling 45 items that aimed to reduce unnecessary examinations and treatments.[1] This Choosing Wisely campaign was designed for doctors and patients to query the necessity of examinations and treatments and to effectively reduce healthcare costs. With the advances, diversification, complexity, and increasing costs of healthcare in developed countries, it has become necessary to determine the appropriacy of duplicate examinations and the selection of medicines and treatments during hospitalization.

T. Takahashi (✉)
Nihon University, College of Commerce, Tokyo, Japan
e-mail: t.toshiro@nifty.com

Under US President Donald Trump, the national health insurance scheme devised by the Democrats under the previous Obama Administration was questioned, and up to 20 million or more people could end up without any health insurance. It has thus become increasingly important to study the mechanisms of the broad aims of the so-called Obamacare.

Even though the United States has a focus on private health insurance, the reforms of healthcare systems under Obamacare had placed healthcare providers under pressure to control healthcare costs while raising quality. But that in itself was not enough—there were patients who had fallen between different disciplines in hospital treatments specialized for different organs. In addition, places need to be established where physicians can provide scientific treatments based on clinical data, and where patients can be made aware that they are responsible for their own health and can meet and discuss so that high-quality physicians can train as family doctors.

First, this chapter describes healthcare system reforms in the United States and evaluates the effectiveness of Accountable Care Organizations (ACOs)—organizations that have adopted an integrated healthcare provision model to handle these reforms. Then, from the perspective of collaborative dynamic capabilities (DC) and leadership, this chapter observes and analyzes the management systems that ACOs must operate to succeed in this new healthcare provision model.

4.2 Organizations Intent on Quality Improvement and Cost Reductions: US System Reforms

In the United States, the Patient Protection and Affordable Care Act (PPCAC) has been law since 2010, with the aims of lowering costs and improving healthcare quality through:

(1) Bundled payments (Medicare bundled payments)
(2) ACOs[2]
(3) Patient-centered medical homes (PCMH) (Filson et al. 2011).

ACOs appeared with Obamacare as a mechanism in which healthcare providers partner with each other and insurers to provide services while reducing costs by effective use of healthcare resources, but do they really reduce costs? The ACO model has been introduced into Medicare and gives the impression of a network organization created with the discretionary participation of healthcare providers for the chronically ill, such as primary care doctors, hospitals, and pharmacists. In light of that, this chapter evaluates the existing research.

The shared saving programs operating in the United States aim to improve the quality of healthcare for Medicare fee-for-service basis beneficiaries and to reduce unnecessary costs through smooth co-ordination and co-operation among healthcare providers. Providers, hospitals, and suppliers, who satisfy certain qualifications can either establish an ACO or participate in one by joining a shared savings program.

As an integrated healthcare provision model, ACOs are hospital networks of provider groups consisting of primary care physicians, nurses, specialists, and hospitals with joint responsibilities for the quality and cost of citizens' healthcare (Korda and Eldridge 2011). Eligible ACOs include practitioner networks, medical group companies, acute care hospitals staffed by physicians suitable for ACOs and joint ventures between hospitals and specialists (Burtley et al. 2012).

As a new healthcare model, not much research has been done on ACOs. However, they are predicted to reduce costs mainly by shortening hospitalization times and reducing rates of rehospitalization (Korda and Eldridge 2011). Thus, similar to PCMHs, it is expected that ACOs will catalyze the adoption of stronger incentive models (Conrad and Perry 2009).

4.3 ACO Evaluation

An ACO is a type of integrated healthcare service provision model consisting of family doctors, nurses, healthcare specialists, and hospitals, characterized by a joint responsibility for the quality and costs of local healthcare. However, there is not much research that evaluates the effectiveness of ACOs on healthcare cost reductions or quality improvements.

One integrated report, based on case studies on the evolution of four diverse healthcare organizations into ACOs, has identified the following (Van Citters et al. 2012):

(1) When forming an ACO, existing functions of provider organizations are used, although there are many cases requiring new resources in fields such as governance, leadership, and physician contributions. Reasonable efforts are taken to establish relationships with doctors (e.g., physician contributions in decision making) and deepen their involvement in the ACO model (e.g., focusing on economic incentives).
(2) Because these case studies deal with the initial stages of ACO development, it is still unclear whether they have achieved healthcare improvements or overall cost reductions.

Physician Group Practice Demonstrations (PGPD, a model of treatment by physician groups) managed by the Centers for Medicare & Medicaid Services are regarded as precursors that became the cornerstone of ACO design (Berwick and Hackbarth 2012). According to one analysis of PGPD projects, generally effectiveness is low and there is no consistency in terms of cost, although wide-ranging healthcare quality improvements were recognized (Wilensky 2011). Moreover, according to Berwick and Hackbarth (2012), from an analysis by Colla et al. (2012) using a highly sophisticated analysis model, there was an overall slowdown in the rate of cost increases at all PGPD bases compared to a control group (Berwick and Hackbarth 2012), which was recognized as significant savings for patients with dual qualifications—"patients with dual qualifications" is a definition of vulnerable patient groups covered by both Medicare and Medicaid due to age, physical disabilities, or poverty. Cost reduction effects for these patients have been indicated (Colla et al. 2012; Berwick and Hackbarth 2012). For patient groups without dual qualifications, the annual cost reduction per person was not shown to be very significant. In addition, research on the Medicare Shared Saving Program shows that while ACOs do improve quality, their effectiveness on cost savings is relatively small (McWilliams et al. 2016).

4.4 Organizations of Hospitals and Doctors

Burns and Muller (2008) analyzed hospital–physician relationships (HPR) focusing on hospital–physician economic integration and analyzed HPR targets. In the complex regulatory environments in which they are based, Burns and Muller (2008) proposed three types of hospital–physician relationships: non-economic integration—hospital efforts to register doctors; economic integration—remuneration payments for management by physicians and improvements to clinical services; and clinical integration—co-ordination of patient treatment through hospital organizational structures and systems. They focused on the influence of economic integration on clinical integration. With economic integration, there are several possible categorizations that combine risk and advantage:

(1) the physician-participating P4P (pay for performance) model (e.g., Medicare PGPD) for improvements to clinical care requiring collaboration;[3]
(2) the hospital-awarded P4P model (e.g., Medicare Hospital Quality Demonstration Initiative) for improvements where physician collaboration might be necessary;
(3) physicians as fixed-rate hospital employees with fixed-rate guarantees for certain treatments and 90-day follow-up periods to share risk (e.g., Geisinger Health System).

According to Burns and Muller (2008), the main purpose of the hospital–physician relationship is not to reduce costs and improve healthcare, but to focus on solving quantities and revenues. The evidence-based economic integration model is either weak or non-existent. The reviewed literature does not demonstrate a strong connection between economic integration and clinical integration.

According to research that verifies the relationship of hospital–physician alliances there is a recognized connection between slightly higher treatment rates and high patient expenditures in integrated payroll models with hospital–physician alliances. This research indicates almost no evidence that hospital–physician alliances enable the measurement of patient treatments or alliance achievements (Madison 2004).

As an alternative method of distributing results hospital–physician collaborations and joint ventures are described as follows:

(1) An ambulatory surgery center (ASC) is a hospital–physician joint venture investment business (Burns and Muller 2008), where ASC healthcare revenues are distributed according to the ASC ownership ratio (Thompson and Reedstrom Bishop 2007).
(2) In physician management service contracts, physician groups contracted to specific hospitals manage some of that hospital's business (Thompson and Reedstrom Bishop 2007).

Accordingly, physician governance in organizations and investment ratios will be important keywords in the future.

4.5 ACO Effectiveness

The new American ACO model is also aligned with evidence-based healthcare and evidence-based management: these organizations bundle evidence and use it; physicians and hospitals unite to engage in gain sharing and measure the quality of healthcare. Moreover, an ACO is a mechanism for ongoing value improvement of care, as well as for risk sharing with hospitals and Medicare.

Basically, the structure of ACOs provides solutions to traditional healthcare issues such as rapid cost increases, higher patient demands, and increases in chronic illnesses associated with societal aging. This structure is therefore favored by administrations creating healthcare policies because they are expected to achieve accountability and maximum integration to meet bureaucratic demands. In other words, from the perspective of integration, they are systems that theoretically unify physicians and hospitals and split the burden of accountability. However, confirmation is required as to whether these actually function well. In the United States, the evidence is mounting that ACOs can achieve cost reductions and healthcare quality improvements. There have also been discussions about their broader potential effects.

There are more than 100 healthcare provider organizations under ACO contracts and the Affordable Care Act, with laws in 12 states supporting ACOs (Dixon and Poteliakhoff 2012). According to evaluations, major cost reductions were achieved in primary organizations (among ten healthcare groups, four achieved reductions of US$36.2 million) (Mechanic 2011). Evaluations of initial programs from 1991 indicated healthcare quality improvements and cost reductions through a payback system based on fee-for-service (Mechanic 2011).

There are other evidence-based opinions of ACOs. For example, the late Uwe Reinhardt, professor of healthcare economics at Princeton University who carried out a long-term study of Kaiser Permanente, said that an ACO is an organization close to Kaiser Permanente, although nobody had actually had that experience (Reinhardt 2011). Professor Smith of the University of California says that an ACO is like a unicorn, a fictional organism with mystical powers that nobody has actually seen.[4] According to another evaluation, one of the pitfalls of ACO development is an overestimation of its powers (Singer and Shortell 2011).

Thus, there have been many successes and many failures. Reasons for these failures include an overestimation of ACO capabilities, bad governance, taking on too much risk with gain sharing, and doing things prematurely.

However, in terms of healthcare institutions burdened with accountability, the ACO concept has significance in the United States. As described above, ACOs give responsibility for healthcare quality and costs to physicians and hospitals and encourage comprehensive patient care. This shared intent and hospital accountability could promote the integration of medical records through electronic media, which would bring in more players and means these initiatives should yield results quickly and progress steadily. Thus, there are demands for the unification of various standards of electronic medical records. Insurers, healthcare providers, pharmaceutical companies, and healthcare equipment manufacturers are extremely interested in using evidence-based results and knowledge for new business. Many have already begun investment and implementation in light of the business insights gained from the evidence. Hence, the conditions exist to produce results through open innovation among hospitals, physicians and companies (Chesbrough 2003). There is increased willingness among many stakeholders to shift to models that scientifically integrate results and knowledge, which promotes investment for integration.

However, shifting to these industrial business models has the danger of defining the status and direction of the healthcare industry.

General discussion about the potential effects of ACOs as combinations of healthcare providers and institutions for the management of healthcare-related events, could be of interest to other countries. They appeal to policymakers because they are able to transfer risk and achieve maximum integration and accountability, while improving healthcare quality and cost and patient safety.

4.6　ACO Organizational Forms and Issues

An ACO uses the existing functions of provider organizations, although in many cases new resources—in fields such as governance, leadership, and physician contributions—are required. Efforts need to be made to establish relationships with doctors (e.g., physician contributions to decision-making) and to deepen their involvement with the ACO model (e.g., through rewards).

ACOs are mechanisms that contract with family doctors, hospitals, and specialized medical professionals, and that co-operate with external in-home care, psychiatric care, rehabilitation services, and so on in the locality. This ensures patient safety, reduces costs, and improves healthcare quality through hospital–physician integration.

ACOs based on the integrated healthcare provision model are hospital networks of provider groups consisting of primary care physicians, nurses, and other specialists, and hospitals with joint responsibilities for the quality and cost of healthcare for citizens (Korda and Eldridge 2011).

Eligible ACOs include practitioner networks, medical group companies, acute care hospitals with ACO-qualified physicians on duty, and joint ventures between hospitals and specialists (Burtley et al. 2012). As a new healthcare model, ACOs are expected to lower costs, mainly by shortening hospitalization times and reducing rates of rehospitalization, although there is not much research on these (Korda and Eldridge 2011).

Family doctors contract with one ACO, while specialists can contract with multiple ACOs. Patients contract with one family doctor, making them the one that patients consult on visits.

ACO activity needs to be considered through three basic infrastructure elements. First, the ACO must be accountable to the locality and be able to control costs and improve quality through the capabilities of healthcare institutions and service providers. Second, using shared savings to reduce costs and improve quality—there are incentives available through performance standards related to the quality of care, giving top priority to patients, and providing remunerations that suppress medical expense increases. Third, measuring healthcare and economic achievements to the satisfaction of citizens, medical institutions, medical specialists, and administration in the ACO locality; and in ways their funders can understand.

Generally, alliances and collaborations among hospitals, specialists, and local doctors need to: prevent rehospitalization; prescribe appropriately and in a timely manner for chronic illnesses; use local home-nursing when beds are not available in hospitals; and raise overall patient satisfaction through realistic co-ordination by care managers.

In theory, modern ACOs start among hospitals and doctors only. Some have reached a second stage that requires proactive contributions from both hospital and family doctors. In those few that have reached a third stage, pharmacists and so on also make proactive contributions. In reality, this model of progress remains unclear because ACOs are still developing and are including a wider range of providers. Furthermore, local social healthcare and nursing is still not completely integrated, which will be solved by co-ordinating with local care managers and creating better delivery mechanisms.

4.7 Discussion

4.7.1 The Perspective of Collaborative Dynamic Capabilities and Leadership for Successful ACO Healthcare Services

US healthcare reforms are creating stiff competition for modern hospital management. After many years of soft competition and reasonably predictable business conditions the US healthcare industry underwent a shift after health insurance reform legislation in March 2010. The reforms emphasized value based care (VBC) to provide the best quality at the lowest possible costs. The challenge for hospitals is how to achieve VBC. Hence, healthcare quality and cost reforms have become a central theme of healthcare insurance systems.

Porter and Lee (2013, pp. 50–51) stated:

> In healthcare, the days of business as usual are over. Around the world, every health care system is struggling with rising costs and uneven quality despite the hard work of well-intentioned, well-trained clinicians. Health care leaders and policy makers have tried countless incremental fixes—attacking fraud, reducing errors, enforcing practice guidelines, making patients better "consumers," implementing electronic medical records—but none have had much impact.

Thus, indecision about the issues of cost and quality remain in the medical workplace.

> It's time for a fundamentally new strategy. At its core is maximizing value for patients: that is, achieving the best outcomes at the lowest cost. We must move away from a supply-driven health care system organized around what physicians do and toward a patient-centered system organized around what patients need. We must shift the focus from the volume and profitability of services provided—physician visits, hospitalizations, procedures, and tests—to the patient outcomes achieved. And we must replace today's fragmented system, in which every local provider offers a full range of services, with a system in which services for particular medical conditions are concentrated in health-delivery organizations and in the right locations to deliver high value care.

The new challenge for healthcare institutions is to raise the quality of healthcare, surgeries, and treatments while reducing costs to achieve VBC, which requires unique management structures and skills. Without considering quality, cost reductions are easy, while quality improvements are easy if there are no restrictions on cost. This illustrates the importance and difficulty of acquiring the capabilities to improve both of these diametrically opposed factors simultaneously, as discussed above by Porter and Lee (2013).

Healthcare insurance reforms also include Medicare rehospitalization payment policies and bundled billing experiments (in hospitals where patients are hospitalized, given outpatient care, physician care, and care after release from hospital under certain conditions). Hence, healthcare institutions have to provide patients with high-quality care at low cost through efficient and effective co-ordination and collaboration with healthcare providers. Such ACOs are one form of strategic organization with the potential to simultaneously improve healthcare and lower costs.

Following changes in the US healthcare business environment, Agwunobi and Osborne (2016) identified the importance of a DC framework for healthcare institutions similar to that in private companies (particularly cutting-edge global and hi-tech companies). They cited the case of the Yale New Haven Health System and identified difficult to imitate processes, and structures and skills enabled by DC, that improved the quality of healthcare systems, surgeries and treatment while lowering costs in one of this institution's businesses (2016, p. 144).

The organizational capabilities required in an ACO are the DC of individual organizations and the collaborative DC among stakeholders. Collaborative DC are those that skillfully lead intellectual resource exchange among dissimilar actors so that new value is created. The concept of collaborative DC requires the three elements of: (1) building relationships of trust through strategic collaboration; (2) asset cospecialization; and (3) capabilities synthesis among the ecosystem partners in the ACO.

In these trust relationships among stakeholders, including patients, it is crucial to embed deep relationships between family physicians (primary care), medical institutions (hospitals), specialists, and patients in the provision of medical services. For example, strategic co-ordination and collaboration activities are required among providers to provide high-quality healthcare services appropriate for patients with chronic illnesses. Co-ordination and collaboration among a number of healthcare providers brings about collaborative DC, and capabilities synthesis of stakeholder capabilities accelerates cospecialization to enable high-quality healthcare services with cost benefits to patients.

This section discusses existing research on the leadership providers need to demonstrate in these collaborative DC. Shortell et al. (2014) and Colla et al. (2014), who classified many ACO models, identified the importance of "institutional leadership" (e.g., Selznick 1957) for ACO leaders. Here, "institution" refers to shared values based on an organization's philosophy or mission. Hence, for business managers, it is important to: demonstrate leadership that transcends traditional leadership with its focus on subordinates and hierarchies; inject values across all organizations; and align the vectors of organizational members' activities.

Teece (2014) asserts that if there is wise leadership, DC will be reinforced, particularly "Phronetic" leadership (Nonaka and Toyama 2007). *Phronesis* is an ancient Greek word that means practical knowledge and wisdom.

Through case studies on new hi-tech product development and the first large-scale healthcare experiment in a doctorless village in Japan, Kodama identified the necessity for leaders to have "dialectical leadership" to combine various opposing challenges (e.g., healthcare costs and quality) (Kodama (2005a, b). Kodama identified a theoretical framework to achieve business innovation, which entails combinations of "integrated, centralized leadership," "autonomous, decentralized leadership," "directive control (strategic leadership and forceful leadership)," and "participative control (creative leadership and servant leadership)" as important factors of that dialectical leadership for middle managers and project leaders.

Kodama (2017) refers to the importance of a "holistic leadership" that includes the three structural elements of leadership in both public and private organizations (centralized, distributed, and dialectical) to achieve innovation in business. To drive this holistic leadership and create a foundation for value and community it is necessary to have both practical wisdom (*phronesis*) and institutional leadership.

The original concept of *phronesis* advocated by Aristotle includes the ideas of prudence, practical reason, and practical wisdom. Practical wisdom, as the cornerstone of holistic leadership, can be seen as the "ability of leaders to resonate values and build mutual trust, make the right decisions and seek out the best course of action to execute specific strategies to create new knowledge" (Kodama 2017).

To deliver VBC, ACOs need to form *ba* (Nonaka and Takeuchi 1995) in which creative and constructive dialog among ACO leaders creates values for visions and targets that resonate both within and between organizations. This establishes strategic partnerships through institutional leadership among ACO leaders. Practical wisdom is the engine that creates a new platform of value creation so that ACO leaders can engage in strategic thinking and action.

However, sharing visions and objectives with others to provide value-based care and building a platform of resonance of value is not so simple. Complex business models, challenges, and processes need to be conceptualized and clearly identified to attract the interest and motivation of others. ACO leaders need to build win-win relationships with others, which is crucial for the future of healthcare services. In other words, it is necessary to bring about synergies among core competences (capabilities synthesis) and compensate for each other's weaknesses through the demonstration of DC. For this reason, it is important to seek out business models that consider other parties as functions influence each other in value chains and value networks, and that influence each other's business—but not by enabling some stakeholders to control others.

To summarize, demonstrating holistic leadership through practical wisdom is the engine to sustainably bring about DC and collaborative DC. ACO leaders have to form platforms to resonate values at organizational levels for a variety of members, both within and outside the organization, to enable VBC.

4.7.2 New Perspectives from Practical Aspects

There are a number of key issues that can be observed in discussions of healthcare quality and cost systems (Takahashi 2017). This section considers how we should face reforms. Healthcare providers need objective information about what they are doing, how to make improvements, and then how move rapidly toward those improvements. Even if we know that it is important to change our actions, our past experiences can make it difficult to make such changes. In general, incentives are important, while measurements and reportage often lead to improvements. These are the complexities of changing actions.

In Ontario, Canada, measuring and reporting on healthcare quality and costs is understood to be crucial to healthcare (Takahashi 2014a). Individual provinces create health insurance systems in line with the Canada Health Act to provide a universal health coverage that applies even when moving between provinces; they also motivate healthcare personnel to improve their performance. However, there are many cases where workers do not know how they are performing or how they are being assessed. Even if overall performance data is released, nothing changes unless workers understand how they are contributing, and their position within the whole. This is a common situation around the world.

As a result of a range of research in Ontario in Canada, we found that when performance levels are understood at physician and hospital levels they are improved. At the same time, healthcare workers—physicians, nurses, and office managers—are motivated to improve and they think about what they are doing, what they should be doing, and how to make even greater improvements.

Key to simultaneously improving both healthcare quality and costs in healthcare systems are these three points, which are not new, but are often forgotten:

(1) In public organizations, it is necessary to make public announcements on goals for improvement.
(2) Plans to achieve those goals must be established, publicized, and linked to remuneration; the achievement of targets must be reported; and it is important to clarify the processes.
(3) Physicians with power must maintain consistency in clinical improvement leadership and improvement goals—in the healthcare industry, the key to robust improvement is leadership that avoids the dogmatism of power (Brown et al. 2012; Brown 2015).[5]

As regards (1), the influence of centralized leadership is strong. Sharing the culture and values widely in an organization enables an effective sharing of tacit knowledge among employees and promotes the creation of organizational knowledge. In fact, based on the philosophy of their founders, those private companies that outperform others have put a lot of energy into thoroughly infusing their unique company (or organization) culture and values.

The sharing of organizational culture and values brings about systems and rules unique to the company or organization and embeds unique corporate (or organizational) thinking and perceptions, and hence behavior patterns in employees. The role of creating, promoting, and sharing this unique culture and values among employees is given to the organization's top leaders (CEOs and senior management) and centralized leadership. This centralized leadership brings about institutional leadership as a foundation for creating and building communities.

Regarding (2), the influence of distributed leadership is strong. Management systems that clarify the processes for achieving strategic targets and the incentives will motivate employees and promote their autonomous and decentralized actions. Employees are inspired by perspectives and processes that are flexible in applying rules, and that allow exceptions and improvised solutions. Leading business practitioners have a good understanding of when to (productively) bend rules, and they understand the time and place for improvisation. The creative, solution-finding activities of these business practitioners are largely carried by distributed leadership.

Regarding (3), the influence of dialectical leadership is strong. The space between creating strategic goals and their execution is brimming with gaps and contradictions. It is extremely difficult to be consistent in achieving upgrades, improvements, and innovation. Sometimes, leaders demonstrate centralized leadership based on rules and regulations, sometimes the solutions are not possible based on rules alone. On the other hand, to do the right thing, ethical improvisation induces distributed leadership by promoting autonomous decentralized activities depending on dynamic contexts before and after changes in circumstances. This is an issue of striking a balance between centralized and distributed leadership in an organization. The thoughts and acts of these sorts of leaders are important factors in dialectical leadership.

In summary, leaders and employees need to skillfully use and combine holistic leadership, which includes centralized, distributed, and dialectical leadership.

However, many hospitals overlook these three factors when attempting to set out a new strategy. If these three fundamentals are not executed well, new endeavors will not be successful and will not have the appeal of specific incentives. Hence, hospitals must set down management strategies that include the above three factors and properly execute them.

Going forward, the healthcare industry will continue to grow with a patient-centric view and evidence-based knowledge—foundation building is already underway within the United States Federal Government in many fields in which the use of evidence-based results and knowledge is a prerequisite. From a scientific perspective, the above three fundamentals lead to the incorporation and acceptance of ICT and innovation as strategy.

In line with the larger framework of government healthcare policy, feedback to individual hospitals must clarify objectives, methods, evidence, and target values, while hospitals must foster individual strategic awareness in their staff members. The Balanced Score Card uses this logic (Takahashi 2011a, b, 2014b; Takahashi et al. 2011) and is an effective hospital management strategy applicable to new organizational forms, such as ACOs. It entails using ICT, open innovation, and convergence in alliances and collaborations in healthcare, welfare, hospitals, corporations, and so on (Kodama 2015).

If attempting innovation with ICT, convergence, alliances, and so on, in healthcare management, substantive evidence must be collected and bundled, organizations and human capabilities must be built and measured, and consideration must be given to incentives in organizations. Moreover, hospitals need a good clinical culture managed by physicians through holistic leadership, and it is important that patients (citizens) can trust those physicians. In other words, the trust of physicians has to be engendered first.

4.8 Conclusion

This chapter has described ACOs—which are modern American strategic organizations aiming for healthcare quality improvements and cost reductions—their current state, has evaluated them and their effectiveness, and the challenges they face. ACOs have the potential to provide high-quality care at low cost through efficient and effective co-ordination and collaboration among healthcare providers. An ACO is one form of strategic organization with the potential to simultaneously improve healthcare and lower costs. This chapter has presented three factors for improving healthcare quality and costs in healthcare systems. To drive these three factors, it is crucial that organizational leaders demonstrate collaborative DC through holistic leadership based on practical wisdom.

Acknowledgment The author expresses gratitude to Justin Peffer of the Ontario Ministry of Health and Long-Term Care (MOHLTC) and Professor Adalsteinn Brown of the University of Toronto for their co-operation.

Notes

1. While reductions in healthcare expenses could amount to billions of dollars, there are questions as to whether these should be limited to the healthcare actions of physicians.
2. Under the PPCAC, introduced by the Obama administration in March 2010, ACOs were established as new healthcare service supply systems in Medicare. They are characterized by incentives to increase revenues by reducing costs and are accountable for both the quality and cost of the healthcare they provide. Medicare ACOs also focus on integration and continuity of care, based on primary care. ACOs could also influence business models for insurers. Shared saving programs operating in the United States aim to reduce unnecessary costs and improve healthcare quality for Medicare fee-for-service beneficiaries through smooth co-ordination and co-operation among providers. Those providers, hospitals, and suppliers who satisfy certain qualifications, can either establish an ACO or participate in one by joining a shared savings program. Hence, ACOs aiming for an integrated healthcare provision model are hospital networks of provider groups consisting of primary care physicians, nurses, specialists, and hospitals with joint responsibilities for the quality and cost of healthcare. As a new healthcare provision model the ACO promises to reduce costs by shortening hospitalization times and reducing rates of rehospitalization (Takahashi 2017).

3. P4P is defined as measurements using evidence-based standards and methods to formulate healthcare work incentives to provide high-quality care. In other words, this is an incentive system involving healthcare institutions paying high remunerations to both improve the quality of healthcare and more effectively use healthcare expenditures. P4P has been led by private health insurers in the USA looking for greater efficiency in medical expenditure. In the American health insurance system, public health insurance is only paid to the elderly or low income earners—other patients sign up for private health insurance for medical expenses. For this reason, insurance companies are compelled to drive down high medical expenses. P4P measurements include clinical indicators, patient satisfaction levels, levels of IT implementation, outcome indexes for guideline compliance rates, and mortality and complication rates are used with clinical indicators.
4. This finding is due to personal communication from Professor Smith.
5. This is knowledge gained from the ideas of Professor Adalsteinn Brown in discussions with the author. For details please see Brown et al. (2012) and Brown (2015).

References

Agwunobi, A., & Osborne, P. (2016). Dynamic Capabilities and Healthcare. *California Management Review, 58*(4), 141–161.

Berwick, D. M., & Hackbarth, A. D. (2012). Eliminating Waste in US Health Care. *JAMA, 307*(14), 1513–1516.

Brown, A. D. (2015). The Challenge of Quality Improvement at the System Level. Whither COO? *Healthcare Quarterly, 17*(Special Issue), 48–51.

Brown, A. D., Baker, G. R., Closson, T., & Sullivan, T. (2012). The Journey Toward High Performance and Excellent Quality. *Healthcare Quarterly, 15*(Special Issue), 6–9.

Burns, L. R., & Muller, R. W. (2008). Hospital-Physician Collaboration: Landscape of Economic Integration and Impact on Clinical Integration. *Milbank Quarterly, 86*(3), 375–434.

Burtley, C., Jacobs, L., & The Camden Group. (2012). *Physician-Hospital Integration 2012: How Health Care Reform in Reshaping California's Delivery System*. Oakland: California HealthCare Foundation.

Chesbrough, H. (2003). *Open Innovation*. Boston: Harvard Business School Press.

Colla, C. H., Wennberg, D. E., Meara, E., Skinner, J. S., Gottlieb, D., Lewis, V. A., et al. (2012). Spending Differences Associated with the Medicine Physician Group Practice Demonstration. *JAMA, 308*(10), 1015–1023.

Colla, C. H., Lewis, V. A., Shortell, S. M., & Fisher, E. S. (2014). First National Survey of ACOs Finds that Physicians Are Playing Strong Leadership and Ownership Roles. *Health Affairs, 33*(6), 964–971.

Conrad, D. A., & Perry, L. (2009). Quality-Based Financial Incentives in Health Care: Can We Improve Quality by Paying for It? *Annual Review of Public Health, 30*, 357–371.

Dixon, A., & Poteliakhoff, E. (2012). Back to the Future: 10 Years of European Health Reforms, *Health Economics, Policy and Law, 7*(Special Issue 01), 1–10.

Filson, C. P., Hollingsworth, J. M., Skolarus, T. A., Clemens, J. Q., & Hollenbeck, B. K. (2011). Health Care Reform in 2010: Transforming the Delivery System to Improve Quality of Care. *World Journal of Urology, 29*, 85–90.

Kodama, M. (2005a). Knowledge Creation Through Networked Strategic Communities: Case Studies on New Product Development in Japanese Companies. *Long Range Planning, 38*(1), 27–49.

Kodama, M. (2005b). New Knowledge Creation Through Dialectical Leadership: A Case of IT and Multimedia Business in Japan. *European Journal of Innovation Management, 8*(1), 31–55.

Kodama, M. (Ed.). (2015). *Collaborative Innovation: Developing Health Support Ecosystems* (Vol. 39). London: Routledge.

Kodama, M. (2017). *Developing Holistic Leadership: A Source of Business Innovation*. London: Emerald Publishing.

Korda, H., & Eldridge, G. N. (2011). Payment Incentives and Integrated Care Delivery: Levers for Health System Reform and Cost Containment. *Inquiry, 48*(4), 277–287.

Madison, K. (2004). Hospital-Physician Affiliations and Patient Treatments, Expenditures, and Outcomes. *Health Service Research, 39*(2), 257–278.

McWilliams, J. M., Hatfield, L. A., Chernew, M. E., Landon, B. E., & Schwartz, A. L. (2016). Early Performance of Accountable Care Organizations in Medicare. *New England Journal of Medicine, 374*(24), 2357–2366.

Mechanic, R. (2011). Opportunities and Challenges for Episode-Based Payment. *New England Journal of Medicine, 365*(9), 777–779.

Nonaka, I., & Takeuchi, H. (1995). *The Knowledge Creation Company: How Japanese Companies Create the Dynamics of Innovation*. New York: Oxford University Press.

Nonaka, I., & Toyama, R. (2007). Strategic Management as Distributed Practical Wisdom (Phronesis). *Industrial and Corporate Change, 16*(3), 371–394.

Porter, M. E., & Lee, T. H. (2013). The Strategy that Will Fix Health Care. *Harvard Business Review, 91*(12), p. 24.

Reinhardt, U. (2011). The Many Different Prices Paid to Providers and the Flawed Theory of Cost Shifting: Is It Time for a More Rational All-Payer System? *Health Affairs, 30*(11), 2125–2133.

Selznick, P. (1957). *Leadership in Administration: A Sociological Interpretation*. Berkeley: University of California Press.

Shortell, S. M., Wu, F. M., Lewis, V. A., Colla, C. H., & Fisher, E. S. (2014). A Taxonomy of Accountable Care Organizations for Policy and Practice. *Health Services Research, 49*(6), 1883–1899.

Singer, S., & Shortell, S. M. (2011). Implementing Accountable Care Organizations—Ten Potential Mistakes and How to Learn from Them. *JAMA*. Published online August 9, 2011. https://doi.org/10.1001/jama.2011.1180.

Takahashi, T. (Ed.). (2011a). *Healthcare Balance Scorecard Research Business Practice Edition* (in Japanese). Tokyo: Seisansei-shuppan (Japan productivity center).

Takahashi, T. (2011b). The Potential of Healthcare BSC Activities in Local Society—Towards Sustainability Healthcare Balanced Scorecard Development (in Japanese). *Healthcare Balanced Scorecard Research, 8*(1), 20–41.

Takahashi, T. (2014a). Research on CSR and BSC for Sustainable Hospital Management (in Japanese). *Journal of Business, Nihon University, 83*(4), 107–141.

Takahashi, T. (2014b). Observations of the Reform Process of the Hospital Funding System in Ontario, Canada (in Japanese), *Journal of Business, Nihon University 83*(3), 49–80.

Takahashi, T. (2017). Research on Healthcare Quality Improvements and Cost Reductions: Accountable Care Organization (ACO) and Pay for Performance (P4P). Is It Possible to Aim for Simultaneous Health Care Cost Control and Quality Improvements? (in Japanese). *Journal of business, Nihon University, 86*(4), 33–71.

Takahashi, T., Brown, A. D., & Nakano, T. (2011). Healthcare BSC Usage Potential in Healthcare Policy (in Japanese). *Healthcare Balanced Scorecard Research, 8*(2), 26–55.

Teece, D. J. (2014). The Foundations of Enterprise Performance: Dynamic and Ordinary Capabilities in an (Economic) Theory of Firms. *The Academy of Management Perspectives, 28*(4), 328–352.

Thompson, R. C., & Reedstrom, J. (2007). Opportunities for Physitcian-Hospital Collaborations and Ventures. *Spine, 32*(11S), S27–S32.

Van Citters, A. D., Larson, B. K., Carluzzo, K. L. Gbemudu, J. N., Kreindler, S. A., Wu, F. M., et al. (2012). *Four Health Care Organizations' Efforts to Improve Patient Care and Reduce Costs* (Toward Accountable Care, Case Study Series). The Commonwealth Fund.

Wilensky, G. R. (2011). Lessons from the Physician Group Protection Demonstration—A Sobering Reflection. *New England Journal of Medicine, 365*(18), 1659–1661.

5

Realization of a Health Support Ecosystem Through a Smart City Concept: A Collaborative Dynamic Capabilities Perspective

Nobuyuki Tokoro

5.1 Introduction

With higher awareness of climate change, efforts to solve the problem through the development of new technologies and innovations have been gaining momentum around the world. The smart city construction analyzed in this chapter is one of those efforts. A smart city is a next-generation urban environment that aims to reduce energy consumption and carbon dioxide emissions by using ICT to optimize the infrastructures of power, communications, and so on, on which it is based. As the global population continues to increase, people in both developed and developing countries are moving into cities in search of better living standards. As a result, cities all over the world are saddled with a wide range of problems as they become excessively populated, which include worsening public safety, deteriorating living environments, chronic traffic

---

N. Tokoro (✉)
Nihon University, College of Commerce, Tokyo, Japan
e-mail: tokoro.nobuyuki@nihon-u.ac.jp

congestion, and aging populations. Smart cities aim to optimize energy usage for the sake of the environment at the same time as solving these problems.

Among the various aspects of smart cities, this chapter looks at healthcare. As populations are rapidly aging in developed countries, in particular in Japan, the urgent problems of healthcare and nursing, caused by a lack of financial and human resources, require a societal approach. There are high expectations of smart cities being able to deliver comprehensive and efficient local care systems using ICT. This chapter analyzes the construction of healthcare systems in smart cities from the perspective of business co-creation through the "collaborative dynamic capabilities" (DC) of players in different industries.

5.2 Research Question and Methodological Discussion

Research on smart cities has been done from multi-faceted perspectives and backgrounds, with the bulk of analysis from the perspectives of urban planning and city engineering (Rassia and Pardalos 2014; Ercoskum 2012); and some from the perspectives of urban governance and urban civilization (Herrschel 2013; Gibbs et al. 2013; Townsend 2013). This chapter approaches it from the perspective of "value co-creation by businesses in different industries"—existing research from this perspective includes that by Tokoro (2015). Smart city construction entails the involvement of companies in various industries whose technologies and know-how collide, interact, and fuse to create new values, the sum of which forms the smart city. This chapter addresses three research questions based on this analytical approach.

(1) *Ba* enables new value to be created through the collision, exchange, and fusion of the technologies and know-how from the individual companies.
(2) The individual companies must correctly understand open and closed strategies to create new value in the interaction and fusing of their technologies and know-how.

(3) There must be leaders with the collaborative DC to sublimate the technologies and know-how of the individual companies into value creation.

To enlarge on open and closed strategies. In general, collaboration between companies is mutually complementary of the weaknesses and strengths of their technologies and know-how. The concept of "open innovation" does not stop at mutual complement, but aims to cause "chemical reactions" through the bringing together of the strengths of individual companies that lead to innovation (Chesbrough 2003a, b, 2006). However, making judgments about which pieces of a company's technology and know-how should be open and which should be closed requires caution. Opening everything risks excessive leakage of technology or know-how, whereas being too closed can hinder innovation. These judgments require high-quality strategic thinking. Hence, it is difficult to create value if the companies involved do not have this kind of strategic thinking.

This chapter uses case studies as its analytical methodology. Other analytical methodologies include quantitative analysis using statistical software to process large data samples. However, since this chapter is looking at the details of the processes of value creation between companies in different industries, we have determined that case studies, with a microanalysis of individual cases, have a greater affinity with this research issue than macroscopically ascertaining facts through quantitative analysis.

5.3 Smart Cities Around the World

Interest has grown in smart cities as a prescription for solving the various problems faced by cities, and smart city construction projects are ongoing all over the world. For example, the Tianjin Eco-city project in the suburbs of Tianjin, China, entails the construction of a new 400,000 person city on the former saltpans of the Bohai Sea, and the plan is to attract industry adjacent to the residential area. In India there is a plan to lay a dedicated freight railway line for about 1500 km between Delhi and Mumbai—150 km of which includes residential and commercial areas on both sides—and infrastructure, such as industrial areas, distribution bases, power generation, roads, and harbors. In Abu Dhabi in the United Arab Emirates, the Masdar City project is an artificial city for about 50,000 people in the desert suburbs of Abu Dhabi, which is to be completely powered by renewable energy sources, such as solar power. These smart city projects in developing countries are characterized by urban development in parallel with enticements for industry. These are new, large-scale urban developments on unused or reclaimed land, replete with infrastructure, attractive to industry, and with residential areas. In short, this can be called the developing country smart city model.

In contrast, in developed countries, smart cities are strongly characterized by the redevelopment of existing cities and technical demonstration and verification. There are projects in Leon in France, Amsterdam in the Netherlands, Melbourne in Australia, and Yokohama in Japan, which involve efforts to convert existing urban infrastructure to smart infrastructure; while projects in New Mexico and the island of Maui, Hawaii in the United States are to demonstrate technologies.

According to the Japan Economic Center (2016), the scale of smart community-related markets will reach JPY 1040 trillion globally by the year 2030. This figure is calculated to include JPY 242 trillion for power transmission and distribution, JPY 145 trillion for solar and wind power generation, JPY 471 trillion for storage battery systems, and JPY 105 trillion for ecological cars such as electric vehicles. It appears that smart communities are going to be built in 11,700 locations around the world by 2025.

5.4 Case Study: Fujisawa Sustainable Smart Town Project

Using a case study, this section will verify the processes of value creation by companies in different industries within the smart city project of Fujisawa Sustainable Smart Town (Fujisawa SST). This is an ongoing construction by major Japanese electronics manufacturer Panasonic on the former site of one of its factories in the town of Fujisawa, Kanagawa Prefecture. Panasonic's business was related to the production and sales of consumer electronics—such as TVs, refrigerators, washing machines, and video recorders—but it had not had any involvement in the area of smart city construction. However, around the year 2000, with the rapid modularization and digitization of products, Japanese major electronics manufacturers lost their market competitiveness and suffered revenue losses. Panasonic was no exception. Hence, given these conditions, Panasonic embarked on smart city construction as a new growth strategy.

5.4.1 Overview of Fujisawa SST

Fujisawa SST is on a former Panasonic factory site of roughly 19 ha in Fujisawa, Kanagawa Prefecture. It aims to be an advanced urban development, housing around 3000 people in 1000 households.[1] Begun in 2011, the total cost of the project is JPY 60 billion and it is due for completion in FY 2018. The details of this urban project are as follows.

All sections of Fujisawa SST, such as housing, facilities and public zones, are equipped with solar power generation systems and domestic storage batteries. In the public zones, "eco-cycle pack" infrastructure has been implemented, such as charging facilities for electric and plug-in hybrid vehicles, electric assisted bicycles, and solar parking stations. The town has thought about diversity by including electric vehicle mobility sharing services, security services with optimized control of lighting, sensors, surveillance cameras, and healthcare services—including facilities to enable the elderly to live comfortably. There is a community platform supporting these mechanisms, so that residents can apply to use the services through a one-stop portal and terminals, linked to a "smart energy gateway" (a device for the unified management of networked appliances in residences), which enables: energy consumption visualization; Fujisawa SST commercial facility sales notifications; and booking of facilities from residential living rooms. Through these approaches, Fujisawa SST has targets to reduce carbon dioxide emissions by 70% and domestic water consumption by 30%, compared to 1990 levels.

To drive the processes of the Fujisawa SST project, Panasonic has taken the lead in creating visions and drafting plans through to their execution. This project is being undertaken under the Panasonic strategy of "solutions for the whole house, the whole facility, and the whole town," and the company intends to pioneer global markets based on the knowledge obtained from Fujisawa SST. Since Panasonic was originally a consumer electronics manufacturer with no experience or knowledge in urban development it could not have executed this project by itself. Therefore the project has been promoted since its inception with Panasonic as the lead corporation, in collaboration with eight other diverse companies involved in housing construction, real estate, gas, finance, trading, consulting, and so on.

As residents began to move in the project entered a new stage. In conjunction, the participating companies have changed, and new companies have joined. The following section verifies the healthcare support system that is one aspect of value creation in Fujisawa SST.

5.4.2 Healthcare Support System

Healthcare and nursing have been traditionally recognized as separate fields with unique, respective systems. However, these fields are linked in Fujisawa SST, with the aim of creating a comprehensive local care system that can provide uninterrupted services appropriate to the needs of residents. For example, in the past, when patients left a hospital and requested home care, they had to search themselves for a home care service provider. If homecare service providers are linked with a hospital, the patient's hospital can introduce an appropriate provider and give them data on the patient's state of health. In other words, linking home care service providers with hospitals means patients can seamlessly continue to receive services. With this concept, healthcare, nursing, and pharmacy are mutually linked in a way that transcends boundaries in Fujisawa SST—the town includes a common server that stores data such as the health status of its residents and their medical information which can be accessed as necessary (Fig. 5.1).

This comprehensive local care system has been built in an area in Fujisawa SST called Wellness SQUARE. Using ICT and cutting-edge technologies, high-quality services have been developed for residents by linking information between various facilities. Wellness SQUARE consists of two buildings, the North Hall and the South Hall. The North

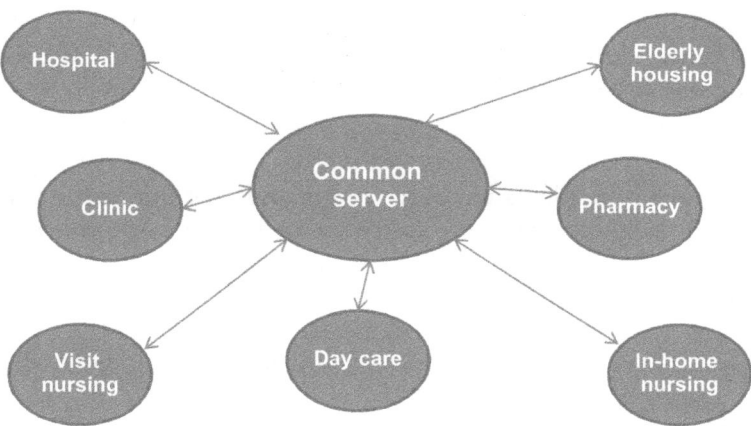

Fig. 5.1 Concept of the local comprehensive care system at Fujisawa SST

Hall features a special nursing home for the elderly and short-term residential care facilities. The South Hall features serviced elderly housing, in-home nursing support, visit nursing, day care, clinics, pharmacies, licensed daycare for children, after school childcare, study facilities, an exchange hall to encourage intergenerational interaction, and a café. There are plans for events with participation by the elderly and children, club activities, and study groups on healthcare and welfare. Plans for encouraging intergenerational exchange and promoting the health of residents are under consideration.

Gakken Coco Fan Holdings Co., Ltd. plays the lead role in configuring this comprehensive local care system in the Wellness SQUARE. In focusing on serviced housing for the elderly, the company has led the construction of this comprehensive local care system by linking information from the pharmacy, day nursing, care visits, and visiting nurses with ICT and promoting human exchange between various places of business. With Gakken Coco Fan Holdings as the axis, other companies are proactively participating in the construction of this comprehensive local care system. For example, Ain Pharmaciez Inc. provides linkages with electronic medical records and the information services provided by Fujisawa SST to its residents to provide them with services such as appropriate medicine dosage methods and seasonal health support information. Social welfare corporation Camellia has partnered with the special home for the elderly to provide nursing services tailored to the needs of its residents. Meanwhile, Panasonic has equipped all rooms in the residences for the elderly with its "Smart air conditioner watching service," in which smart air conditioners and sensors monitor the activity levels and presence of residents to collect and provide the information necessary for nursing care without burdening facility staff or residents. The following describes details of the facilities and services in the Fujisawa SST Wellness SQUARE.[2]

(1) Serviced housing for the elderly "Coco Fan Fujisawa SST" (run by Gakken Coco Fan Holdings)

   Provides secure living for patients requiring intensive nursing and dementia patients, with staff available 24 hours a day. Provision of comprehensive care seamlessly linking care, medical, and nursing services in associated facilities using ICT.

(2) In-house care support "Gakken Coco Fan Fujisawa SST" (run by Gakken Coco Fan Holdings)

   Care managers create care plans for elderly residents and the elderly living in the area. Has comprehensive contact functions for nurses to co-ordinate with elderly requiring nursing.

(3) Visiting nursing "Gakken Coco Fan Fujisawa SST-HC" (run by Gakken Coco Fan Holdings)

   Helpers provide nursing support for daily activities such as meals, bathing, and moving. Staff in the halls are on duty 24 hours a day to monitor the state of residents and provide appropriate care services linked to medicine and nursing.

(4) Day nursing services "Day Service Coco Fan Fujisawa SST" (run by Gakken Coco Fan Holdings)

   A day service deploying Gakken's proprietary dementia prevention program "*Nou Genki* Time" (healthy brain time).

(5) Visit nursing "Gakken Coco Fan Nursing Fujisawa SST" (run by Gakken Coco Fan Nursing)

   Supplying 24-hour, 365-day support services, providing nurse visits to residents, health management, and medical treatment consultation so that the ill and disabled can live at home and in familiar

surroundings. Partners with pharmacies and clinics for preventive care, intensive nursing, and palliative care.
(6) "Fujisawa Smart Town Clinic" (run by Yamanouchi Ryoma Foundation)

A clinic opened in Fujisawa SST by Yamauchi Hospital, the hospital is located in front of Fujisawa station and has been providing medical services to the area for a long time. It provides internal medicine, pediatrics, orthopedics, and in-home treatment.
(7) "Ain pharmacy Fujisawa SST branch" (run by Ain Pharmaciez)

Provides services by comprehensively understanding patient pharmaceutical records and lifestyles. Provides in-home treatment, and practices healthcare linking and information management.
(8) Special nursing home "Camellia Fujisawa SST" (run by social welfare corporation Camellia)

Provides nutritional care management through registered dietitians, and meals in partnership with the kitchen operated by the company. A café on the first floor of the event hall provides a communications space with music.
(9) Short-term residency care "Short stay Camellia Fujisawa SST" (run by social welfare corporation Camellia)

Enables short-term, in-facility residence, that is, living in the facility while receiving services such as daily life nursing, meals, recreation, functional training, and health checks.

5.5 The Process of Co-creating Value

This section aims to verify the value creation processes between companies in different industries involved in the comprehensive local care system in the Fujisawa SST Wellness SQUARE. Table 5.1 describes the members of the Fujisawa SST council.

The author traveled to Panasonic's Tokyo headquarters on two occasions to hear the Fujisawa SST project director talk (February 26, 2014; September 6, 2016). The project director clarified that the project is centered on the Fujisawa SST council, whose members are companies participating in the Fujisawa SST project. As the leader of the project,

Table 5.1 Fujisawa SST council

Secretariat	Panasonic
Committee members	Gakken Holdings, Culture Convenience Club, Social Welfare Corporation Camellia, Dentsu Gakken Coco Fan Holdings Tokyo Gas, Panahome, NTT East, Sumitomo Mitsui Trust Bank, Mitsui & Co., Mitsui Fudosan Mitsui Fudosan Residential, Yamato Transport
General members	Ain Pharmaciez, Accenture, SUN AUTAS, ALSOK, Nihon Sekkei
Advisers	Keio Research Institute at SFC, Tokyo Electric Power, Fujisawa City, Fujisawa SST Management

Panasonic acts as the council's representative secretary and leads the organization. Panasonic has the role of leader of the Fujisawa SST project, based on the company's strategies, but is not involved in every single aspect of the project. This is because Panasonic is a consumer electronics manufacturer and does not have the rich knowledge required to build a town such as Fujisawa SST. In relation to the comprehensive local care system discussed in this chapter, it is not Panasonic that has the central role in driving the project, but Gakken Coco Fan Holdings. As well as being involved in managing the serviced housing for the elderly, Gakken Coco Fan Holdings plays a central role in the creation of new healthcare value at Fujisawa SST in partnership with social welfare corporation Camellia, Ain Pharmaciez, Yamauchi Ryoma Foundation and participating members. Panasonic's role is to provide support in building the comprehensive local care system.

According to the Panasonic director, the Fujisawa SST project is led by Panasonic, but it is also a place for the participating members to create value. Panasonic fully recognizes that it is impossible for it to create value at Fujisawa SST alone and it expects value to be created among other participating members. For this reason, the role of the Fujisawa SST Council, in which all the project members participate, is crucial. In the hearing attended by the author, the operation of the Fujisawa SST Council was described as follows.

Basic project policies come from Panasonic as project lead company and representative secretary of the Fujisawa SST Council. These are illustrated by: the Fujisawa SST concepts of "A town where energy to live is born," "building a town as an origin of technology through to an origin of lifestyle," and "A town that will last a hundred years"; and by the specific town building guidelines based on these concepts. These basic policies were based on Panasonic's business strategy, and project members are required to understand and act in line with them. These are binding conditions on project members and as long as members do not deviate from these basic project policies they are guaranteed opportunities to fully demonstrate their knowledge. Fujisawa SST aims for value creation in the five areas of energy, security, mobility, wellness, and community, to which project members contribute by raising quality standards through free debate in the Fujisawa SST Council.

In other words, the Fujisawa SST Council is a *ba* where project members can pit their intellectual resources against each other, such as technologies and know-how, and exchange and converge them. In verifying the processes of knowledge creation and value co-creation, the *ba* is an extremely important concept. As shown in existing research, the concept does not simply describe a place, but also includes mental aspects, such as shared values, will, and interpersonal bonds (Nishida 1965; Shimizu 2000, 2003; Nonaka and Takeuchi 1995; Nonaka and Konno 1998; Nonaka et al. 2008). For example, if there is not a shared objective among members gathered in a meeting, meaningful value will not be generated, even if the meeting takes a long time. On the other hand, if peoples' sense of values and will are shared, even across physically remote locations, meaningful value can be generated and communicated through exchange. In other words, a *ba* is not just a physical location, such as a meeting room, but it is a concept of extensive relationships based on "meaning." Fujisawa SST Council is a body that brings together companies in different industries with the common objective of creating value in the five areas mentioned through the construction of Fujisawa SST and has the characteristics of a *ba*.

According to Itami (1999, 2000, 2004), the creation of a *ba* does not mean that value will be created. A ba must have requirements prepared so that it is dynamic and animated, and members can actively engage in exchanges with each other. These requirements entail respect for the autonomy of members and leaders who steer the *ba*. Most importantly, respect for member autonomy entails enabling them to freely state their opinions and guaranteeing them their right to act in the *ba*. At first glance, this seems only natural, but in reality there are many situations in which such rights are not guaranteed. The most common is when powerful members control the *ba* and force other members to conform. Project planning and operations get decided by particular members and others are unable to disagree, which makes free exchange difficult and as a result hinders the generation of worthwhile value. There are also patterns in which things cannot be stated freely among members due to relationships with capital, trading, or business power relationships, which also have a negative effect on value creation. In the hearings attended by the author, the operation of the Fujisawa SST Council was described as guaranteeing member autonomy by preventing such situations from occurring. An important factor here is that the project leader company, Panasonic, welcomes free and vigorous debate and exchange among the members. As mentioned, Panasonic indicates basic policies but relies on the exchange of intellectual resources among other members in individual areas, and fully understands that it is this exchange that leads to the creation of new value. Thus, the construction of the comprehensive local care system lies in the hands of Gakken Coco Fan Holdings, which is given the opportunity and freedom to play an active role.

One more requirement is for leaders who can steer the *ba*—but what kind of people are these? While a *ba* must not constrain the utterances and actions of participating members, and must preserve their autonomy, on the flip side, there is always a danger that disordered or directionless discussions might occur and serious conflicts of interest may occur instead of value creation. To avoid falling into those situations, there has to be a leadership that can steers the process of exchange to avoid such conflicts of interest and create value. To do this, leaders of a *ba* must be equipped with DC, particularly collaborative DC (Teece 2007, 2009, 2014).

Collaborative DC are those that can skillfully lead the intellectual resource exchange among dissimilar actors so that new value is created in the process. As discussed in Chaps. 1 and 2, this concept includes the three elements of: (1) building relationships of trust through strategic collaborations; (2) asset co-specialization; and (3) capabilities synthesis with ecosystem partners. For relationships of trust a framework for collaboration is embedded in Fujisawa SST Council and residents. The emergence of new business models as co-specialization was accelerated in Fujisawa SST by integrating (composite) systems and services, enabled by synergies between products and industries. To achieve this, stakeholders in Fujisawa SST Council had to demonstrate DC and collaborative DC for initiatives in knowledge integration as convergence between dissimilar services and technologies (Kodama 2009). Stakeholders also engaged in strategic learning processes for asset co-specialization and capability synthesis between differing organizations.

In addition, it is necessary to understand the difference between a "manager" and a "leader" by correctly understanding collaborative DC. A manager is an administrator who manages routine operational work, efficiently allocates tasks to organizational members, and analyzes and administrates the execution of tasks. This position can be characterized as an "analyst" looking "from the whole to the parts." In contrast, a leader has clear vision and acts as a catalyst of organizational members, inspiring emergence and leading the way to the creation of value. This is characterized by a "synthesis" role that looks "from the parts to towards the whole." Collaborative DC are capabilities of synthesis that lead emergence among organizational members to value creation—hence, leaders of a *ba* must be equipped with the comprehensive capabilities of "holistic leadership" (Kodama 2017a). While Gakken Coco Fan Holdings plays the lead role in structuring the comprehensive local care system at Fujisawa SST, it does not play the role of leader in a *ba*. The role of the company is limited to operations, and it can be said in the position of manager of the construction of the comprehensive local care system. It is thus Panasonic who supplies the project visions and plays the role of leader to value creation (Fig. 5.2).

5.6 Implications

This section looks at the implications gained from the discussions in this chapter, which has used a case study analysis methodology, and has examined the three research questions through hearings and an analysis of published materials. As a result, hypotheses (1) and (3) can be maintained. Regarding (1), to enable the creation of new value through the

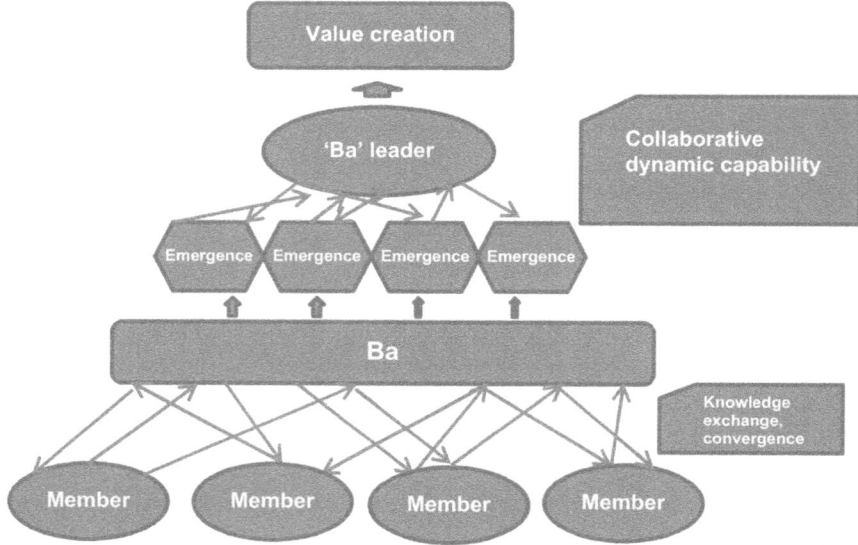

Fig. 5.2 The process of value co-creation

interaction and convergence of the knowledge and know-how of differing actors, existing research on knowledge creation theory and so forth verifies that it is necessary to create a *ba* to enable such new value creation. An analysis of Fujisawa SST confirms that this is conceptually correct. However, to reiterate, a *ba* does not simply mean a formal or physical gathering such as a meeting or a council. In society, such gatherings are innumerable, but how many of them create new value? There is no shortage of meaningless meetings. In other words, the hurdle is high for configuring a *ba* that fulfills the conditions to promote the exchange of knowledge resources between dissimilar actors and to sublimate these for value creation through resonance and co-creation.

The above perspective is deeply related to hypothesis (3). In other words, for a *ba* to create value it needs a *ba* leader with collaborative DC. Not a leader who is simply a manager in charge of operational business. These leaders must have "synthesis" capabilities to present clear visions, promote the exchange of knowledge resources among members, and sublimate these for value creation. At Fujisawa SST, the project lead corporation Panasonic presents its clear visions of "a town where energy to live is born" and "a town that will continue for 100 years," and presents a direction towards the creation of the five values of energy, security, mobility, wellness, and community. To generate these five values and achieve a town that can grow sustainably, the project requires strategic innovation, which entails the demonstration of DC and collaborative DC by project leaders to generate new value through the dynamic formation of *ba* (Kodama 2017b).

At the same time, the management of the Fujisawa SST Council, with the participation of all project members, ensures autonomous member activity. This is not characterized by Panasonic managing top-down so that other members conform or that the roles of members are so clearly defined that they only take on operational business. This point was clarified through the author's survey of Panasonic that showed that a *ba* for value creation has been structured at Fujisawa SST.

In contrast, it was not possible to draw any clear implications from these observations regarding (2). Historically, many Japanese corporations have been wary of leakage of their technologies and know-how to other companies and have adopted defensive strategies through patents. Accordingly, not many companies properly understand and practice open and closed strategies. In short, it seems there is a lack of strategy to correctly analyze which intellectual resources should be open and which should be closed to reap more benefits. In hearings with Panasonic, a clear response to this point was not obtained, clarification of which remains an issue for the future.

Notes

1. The descriptions of Fujisawa SST are based on materials provided by the directors to the author in hearings held in Panasonic's Tokyo headquarters, and materials published on the company's website.
2. The descriptions of facilities and services of the Fujisawa SST Wellness SQUARE are based on a Fujisawa SST press release dated August 25, 2016.

References

Chesbrough, H. (2003a). The Era of Open Innovation. *Sloan Management Review, 44*(3), 35–41.
Chesbrough, H. (2003b). Open Innovation: How Companies Actually Do It. *Harvard Business Review, 81*(7), 12–14.
Chesbrough, H. (2006). *Open Business Models: How to Thrive in the New Innovation Landscape*. Boston: Harvard Business School Press.
Ercoskum, O. Y. (Ed.). (2012). *Green and Ecological Technologies for Urban Planning: Creating Smart Cities*. Hershey: Information Science Reference.
Gibbs, D., Krueger, R., & MacLeod, G. (2013). Grappling with Smart City Politics in an Era of Market Triumphalism. *Urban Studies, 50*(11), 2151–2157.
Herrschel, T. (2013). Competitiveness and Sustainability: Can 'Smart City Regionalism' Square the Circle? *Urban Studies, 50*(11), 2332–2348.
Itami, H. (1999). *Management of 'Ba': A New Management Paradigm* (in Japanese). Tokyo: NTT Publishing.
Itami, H., & Karube, M. (Eds.). (2004). *Strategy and Logic of Invisible Assets* (in Japanese). Tokyo: Nihon Keizai Shinbun-sha.
Itami, H., Nishiguchi, T., & Nonaka, I. (Eds.). (2000). *The Dynamism of 'Ba' and the Company* (in Japanese). Tokyo: Toyo Keizai Shinpou-sha.
Japan Economic Center Co., LTD. (2016). *The Actual State and Future Prospects of the Smart Community Market: Smart Energy, Electricity Deregulation, Smart City Market Forecast/Technology* (in Japanese). Tokyo: Tsusan Shiryo Press.
Kodama, M. (2009). Boundaries Innovation and Knowledge Integration in the Japanese Firm. *Long Range Planning, 42*(4), 463–494.
Kodama, M. (2017a). *Developing Holistic Leadership: A Source of Business Innovation*. London: Emerald.
Kodama, M. (2017b). Developing Strategic Innovation in Large Corporations—The Dynamic Capability View of the Firm. *Knowledge and Process Management, 24*(4), 221–246.
Nishida, K. (1965). *A Full of Collection of Kitaro Nishida's Work* (in Japanese). Tokyo: Iwanami Shoten.
Nonaka, I., & Konno, N. (1998). The Concept of 'Ba': Building a Foundation for Knowledge Creation. *California Management Review, 40*, 40–54.
Nonaka, I., & Takeuchi, H. (1995). *The Knowledge Creating Company*. New York: Oxford University Press.
Nonaka, I., Toyama, R., & Hirata, T. (2008). *Managing Flow: A Process Theory of the Knowledge-Based Firm*. London: Palgrave Macmillan.

Rassia, S. T., & Pardalos, P. M. (Eds.). (2014). *Cities for Smart Environmental and Energy Future: Impacts on Architecture and Technology*. Heidelberg/New York/Dordrecht/London: Springer.

Shimizu, H. (2000). *"Ba" and Co-creation* (in Japanese). Tokyo: NTT Publishing.

Shimizu, H. (2003). *The Concept of "Ba"* (in Japanese). Tokyo: University of Tokyo Press.

Teece, D. J. (2007). Explicating Dynamic Capabilities: The Nature and Microfoundations of (Sustainable) Enterprise Performance. *Strategic Management Journal, 28*(13), 1319–1350.

Teece, D. J. (2009). *Dynamic Capabilities and Strategic Management: Organizing for Innovation and Growth*. New York: Oxford University Press.

Teece, D. J. (2014). A Dynamic Capabilities-Based Entrepreneurial Theory of the Multinational Enterprise. *Journal of International Business Studies, 45*(1), 8–37.

Tokoro, N. (2015). *The Smart City and the Co-creation of Value: A Source of New Competitiveness in a Low-Carbon Society*. Tokyo/Heidelberg/New York/Dordrecht/London: Springer.

Townsend, A. M. (2013). *Smart Cities: Big Data, Civic Hackers, and the Quest for a New Utopia*. New York/London: W.W. Norton and Co.

6

Business Model Changes Through Collaborative Dynamic Capabilities Through Insurance Company Use of IT (InsurTech) in the Medical and Health Sectors

Futoshi Okada

6.1 Trends in the Use of IT by Insurance Companies in the Medical and Healthcare Sectors

The use of information technology (IT) by insurance companies in the medical and healthcare sectors is a major area of Insurance Technology (InsurTech). InsurTech is a concept represented by the convergence of insurance with science and technology, in other words, the insurance version of financial technology (FinTech). InsurTech is advantageous because it enables insurance companies to provide new products and services through the use of IT that were not conventionally possible while enabling advanced and efficient business. According to the Yano Research Institute, the Japanese InsurTech market was worth 46 billion yen in

F. Okada (✉)
Nihon University, College of Commerce, Tokyo, Japan
e-mail: okada.futoshi@nihon-u.ac.jp

financial year (FY) 2016, and is predicted to grow to 110 billion yen by FY 2020 (Yano Research Institute 2017). Japan, which has lagged behind leading overseas companies, arrived at its first year of InsurTech in the medical and healthcare sectors in 2016. Following is an overview of health promotion-type (wellness) insurance, which is currently gaining attention as a new insurance product.

6.1.1 Health Promotion-Type Insurance

In June 2016, Kenko-Nenrei Shogaku Tanki Hoken, a group subsidiary of Noritsu Koki, began selling medical insurance interlocked with health age. Unlike conventional health insurance which is issued according to the actual age of the customer, this insurance is characterized by coverage according to the "health age" of the customer.[1] This is a health indicator that uses a statistical model that is based on health diagnosis data of 1.6 million people and statements for treatment costs (receipts), developed by the group's Japan Medical Data Center. Specifically, 12 items of data including body mass index (BMI), systolic blood pressure (high blood pressure measurement), diastolic blood pressure (low blood pressure measurement), and neutral fat are collected by examining the customer's health, and these are then used in conjunction with gender and actual age to calculate the health age of the customer. For example, if a customer (the insured) with an actual age of 50 is found to have a health age of 48, the insurance premium will be cheaper than that for the customer's actual age. In other words, these insurance premiums are subdivided into categories depending on risk. Furthermore, if the length of healthy life can be measured, customers can be insured after making a simple declaration, even if they have some chronic condition. After getting insurance coverage, the premiums change according to the state of the customer's health based on their health age, which is recalculated every year. This gives the customer (the insured) an incentive to take actions to increase and maintain their level of health.

Similarly, in December 2016 Neo First Life Insurance, a group company of Dai-ichi Life Insurance, released a health insurance product called Karada Kakumei (body revolution) that also uses health age.[2] However, actual age is used on signing a contract for this insurance, and health age is used when the contract is renewed every three years.³ The health age of each customer is also a unique indicator created by analysis of medical big data of the Japan Medical Data Center by Mizuho-DL Financial Technology, and is not the same as the health age interlocked-type health insurance described earlier.

In April 2017, Tokio Marine Group company Tokio Marine & Nichido Anshin Life Insurance released a health insurance product called Aruku Hoken (walk insurance) that offers premium cashbacks in line with the health promotion activities of the customer.⁴ This insurance plan has a set premium cashback mechanism that acts as an incentive to promote health, which is paid after two years according to six-monthly achievements—if the customer walks an average of more than 8000 paces per day. Specifically, the two-year period is divided into six-monthly sections, and the average number of paces the customer walks is calculated using a wearable terminal specified by the company. These policies are characterized by the type of health data—customers' health information (the life log) is acquired instead of health examination data.

Regarding life insurance, the foreign-owned NN Life Insurance released its Emergency Plus term insurance product aimed at customers insuring for a maximum of 100 million yen in November 2017. With only three items to report, this product quantifies the risk of death using anonymized and accumulated medical big data held by Medical Data Vision on details of hospital treatments.

The development and release of health promotion-type insurance has been limited to small amount and short term insurance companies, the so-called mini insurance companies, and insurance group subsidiaries. The major insurance companies are in the preparatory stages of achieving these sorts of insurance products. Among them, the Japan Vitality Project initiative launched jointly by Sumitomo Life Insurance, Discovery, a financial services company in South Africa, and SoftBank in July 2016 has been gaining attention. This initiative refers to the development of the Japanese-version of Discovery's Vitality wellness program, which began in South Africa in 1997 and has approximately 3.5 million subscribers in more than ten countries around the world. The basic concept of the Japan Vitality Project is to promote behavioral change to improve the health of insurance customers, which entails incentives for health improvement activities and so forth, through which points can be earned throughout the year and then used for insurance premium discounts or exchanged for various services offered by partner corporations.

6.1.2 Promoting Health Through Applications (Loss Control)

While these are not yet insurance products, there is a wide variety of initiatives that use smartphone applications and so on to promote health improvement activities in society in general, including insurance customers. In October 2014, AXA Life Insurance introduced the Health U app into its AXA Medical Assistance Service. As users can understand their health stages through the app, they can also gain support for improving their lifestyles. In May 2016, Manulife Life Insurance opened the Manulife Wellness Lab and began offering the Manulife Walk app under the theme of promoting physical and mental health. This enables users to participate in social contribution activities by donating shoes to Cambodian children when the user reaches a certain number of paces. In addition, in October 2016 Taiyo Life Insurance began offering its customers a dementia prevention application that alerts users to future symptoms of dementia and so forth by measuring and analyzing normal walking speed. As well as that, in November 2016, SBI Life Insurance began providing health tech venture FiNC's health management and lifestyle improvement app to its whole life health insurance customers, and in June 2017 expanded this service to all its insurance customers. In March 2017, major life insurance company Dai-ichi Life Insurance released its Kenko Daiichi health promotion app to the public, and then added improved functionality enabling health age measuring and calorie calculation of meals using photographs and so on in October of that year.[5]

6.1.3 Corporate Services

Health improvement support services aimed at corporations have commenced. In July 2016, Sompo Japan Nipponkoa Himawari Life Insurance teamed up with DeSC Healthcare, a health tech company, with the aim of expanding its partnerships and forming a healthcare ecosystem. Also in June 2017, Meiji Yasuda Life Insurance began providing its MY health promotion service, a health management support program aimed at small to medium-sized businesses.

6.2 Changes in Life Insurance Company Business Models and Collaborative Dynamic Capabilities

6.2.1 Changes in Business Models

Generally, a business model is defined as the way a company generates value, provides it to customers and uses the payments it receives to generate profit (Teece 2010, p. 173). In the medical and healthcare sectors, how does InsurTech affect the value offered by insurance companies?

One type of value common to all life insurance companies is peace of mind, provided as the intangible services of guarantees in case of emergencies. Although some customers who receive an insurance payout can feel the value of insurance (they are glad that they were insured), most customers do not receive insurance payouts and do not easily feel the value of this peace of mind.

Apart from peace of mind, insurance also has value that can be had by all its customers. These are supplementary and related services to insurance products, and include such things as insurance review upon application for new insurance, financial planning, consultation on health and nursing, and second opinion services. However, these services only play supportive roles to insurance products.

Health promotion-type insurance and services have the potential to transform conventional perspectives. Insurance companies' services that support health promotion are positioned as a type of loss control service designed to prevent accidents before they happen and avoid serious disadvantages. Generally, insurance customers have a lower awareness and make less effort with regard to preventing accidents than before they bought insurance. To hedge against such moral hazards, insurance companies have to build loss control and premium discounts into insurance contracts to give customers incentives to avoid accidents. Furthermore, because the size of insurance premiums depends on the health risk of the customer, they are made easy to understand and fairness is ensured. Hence, the value of health promotion, in other words health improvement and such initiatives, is returned (awarded) to customers by discounting the insurance premium (an experience value). Meanwhile, insurance payments that insurance companies have to make are reduced by reducing death and disease risks. From the social perspective, these approaches bring about longer average life spans and healthy life spans, and reduce medical expenses. Hence, the provision of health promotion value, which can be felt by the majority of insurance customers who do not normally receive insurance payments, is the core of these business models.

Another major change in business models is the change in business partners. Conventionally, life insurance companies have developed insurance products based on external statistical data and their own data. However, in developing health promotion-type insurance products, partnerships with companies that have medical big data storage and analytical capabilities, and health tech companies that can manage health using apps and cloud services are indispensable because there are no models for assessing the necessary information and risk. In addition, as with Discovery's Vitality, partnerships with companies that can grant benefits are required to implement point systems that reflect on health promotion.

6.2.2 Collaborative Dynamic Capabilities

Dynamic capabilities (DC) are the capabilities of organizations and managers to integrate, configure and reposition internal and external capabilities to respond to rapidly changing environments (Teece 2013, p. xvii). Although generally it is not easy to discuss InsurTech in the healthcare and medical sector from the perspective of DC, we can focus on Kenko-Nenrei Shogaku Tanki Hoken that released Japan's first health promotion-type insurance. This means exploring why Kenko-Nenrei, a company established in November 2014, was able to pioneer this area.

The Japan Medical Data Center, which holds the medical big data indispensable for the development of this insurance and creation of the business model, is a Noritsu Koki group company, as is Kenko-Nenrei. The many Noritsu Koki group companies in healthcare have various IT capabilities in the medical and health insurance sector. While it might have been possible to partner with existing insurance companies to develop health promotion-type insurance and release it to the market, in efforts to change the historical common thinking behind insurance, maybe the company determined that there would be time and cost involved in partnering with an existing insurance company. Perhaps this is why they established the Kenko-Nenrei, a mini insurance company. The case of Neo First Life Insurance, a subsidiary of Dai-ichi Life Insurance, suggests the partnership runs smoothly thanks to Mizuho DL-Financial Technology, a company in which Dai-ichi Life Insurance has a 30% stake.

In contrast, Sumitomo Life Insurance started the Japan Vitality Project initiative in partnership with Discovery and SoftBank, companies in which it has no equity stake. Thus it is probably not easy to demonstrate DC, and those partnerships require time. Meanwhile, the DC of Nippon Life Insurance, a giant in the industry in Japan, is gaining attention for its response to environmental changes because the company has formed a wide range of partnerships with the Australian insurer MLC, Nomura Research Institute, companies in Silicon Valley and NTT DOCOMO, partnerships which it must lead.

6.3 Conclusion

This chapter has described an overview of InsurTech trends in the medical and healthcare sector, and briefly described business model changes and collaborative DC. As future issues, first is the problem of increased insurance premiums if customer health deteriorates, even though they have made efforts to improve their health, because health promotion-type insurance is risk subdivision-type insurance. While it is advantageous for new insurance companies to acquire customers with good risk profiles, it is not easy for the major insurers, which have the majority of customers, to raise insurance premiums when health deteriorates. With automotive insurance, risk subdivision-type insurance has been introduced with direct insurance companies, although there has not been much progress in this regard with major loss insurers for similar reasons.

Second, the promise of IT in the medical and healthcare sectors is similar for public health insurance. Major life insurance companies have many corporate customers through group insurance. Hence, business developments should accelerate with the tailwind of "health management," although perhaps in terms of insurance premiums these developments could amount to nothing more than support services through health apps.

Third, life insurance companies require new partnerships with InsurTech. It seems that differences appear at the outset depending on whether these companies have relationships with companies that are good at digital health. The way the leadership of major insurance companies deploys DC to co-create value with partners is a fascinating topic.

Notes

1. The insurance guarantees JPY 800,000 in case of hospitalization for treatment for specific conditions such as cancer, stroke or myocardial infarction.
2. The insurance guarantees payment of JPY 1,000,000 in case of hospitalization for treatment for seven major lifestyle-related diseases, such as cancer. Hospitalization benefits are paid once per year and can be received a total of ten times. In addition, customers who turned 70 on contract renewal can transfer to lifetime protection.
3. The company released its Neo-de kenko-yell product in October 2017, in which insurance premiums are decided according to health age on contract signing.
4. 2017 Good Design Award Winner. This was awarded to Lifenet Insurance for its smartphone insurance application service released in FY 2013, the first of its kind in the life insurance industry. Furthermore, in 2014 French major insurer AXA distributed compact pedometers to its customers, and began a service offering substantial insurance discounts entailing distribu-

tion of coupons exchangeable for products in hospitals valued at 50 Euros for an average of 7,000 paces or 100 Euros for an average of 10,000 paces per day within a set period. The Nikkei (2015, p. 5).
5. Using a photo captured with a smartphone, this is the first time a Face AI function has been added to a Japanese app to check on one's future self through changes in BMI and aging to promote current lifestyle improvements.

References

AXA Life Insurance. (2014, September 30). *AXA Releases the Insurance Industry's First Health Application "Heath U"* (in Japanese). http://www2.axa.co.jp/info/news/2014/pdf/140930c.pdf

Dai-ichi Life Insurance. (2017a, March 21). *"Health First" App Offered and Start Campaign Launched Promoting "Living Healthily and Happily"* (in Japanese). http://www.dai-ichi-life.co.jp/company/news/pdf/2016_092.pdf

Dai-ichi Life Insurance. (2017b, October 5). *Smart Phone App "Health First" for Long Healthy Life Society Improved – Uses the Latest Technology to Enable Health Age Measurement and Calculation of Meal Calories with Photographs* (in Japanese). http://www.dai-ichi-life.co.jp/company/news/pdf/2017_037.pdf

IoT NEWS. *IoT-Related Terminology: Smart Healthcare*. https://iotnews.jp/keywords/スマートヘルスケア. Last viewed on 1 Jan 2018 (in Japanese).

Japan Association of Corporate Executives. (2015). *Digital Health – Healthcare and Nursing Improvements Through Innovations at System Level* (in Japanese). https://www.doyukai.or.jp/policyproposals/articles/2015/pdf/150424a.pdf

Manulife Life Insurance. (2016, May 19). *Manulife Announces "Manulife WALK" App Enabling Fun Walking and Social Contribution* (in Japanese). https://www.manulife.co.jp/servlet/servlet.FileDownload?file=-00P1000000bc9oQEAQ

Meiji Yasuda Life Insurance. (2017, June 21). *Regarding the Launch of "MY Health Promotion Service", a Health Management Support Program Aimed at Small to Medium Businesses* (in Japanese). http://www.meijiyasuda.co.jp/profile/news/release/2017/pdf/20170621_01.pdf

Neo First Life Insurance Co., Ltd. https://www.neofirst.co.jp/

Next-Generation Healthcare Industry Council. (2016). *Next-Generation Healthcare Industry Council Progress Report on Studies and "Action Plan 2016"* (in Japanese). http://www.meti.go.jp/committee/kenkyukai/shoujo/jisedai_healthcare/pdf/005_02_00.pdf

Nikkei Business Online Edition. (2010). *The e-Heath Revolution – The Changing Future of Health and Medical with IT in Japan*. Nikkei BP (in Japanese).

SBI Life Insurance. (2017, June 27). *SBI Life Insurance and FiNC Provide the Health Management and Lifestyle Improvement "FiNC App" to all SBI Life Insurance Customers, Accelerating Development of "Personal Insurance"* (in Japanese). http://www.sbigroup.co.jp/news/pr/2017/0627_10709.html

Sumitomo Life Insurance. (2016). *Japan Vitality Project "Health Promotion-Type Insurance" Making Japan Healthier*. July 21, 2016 news release (in Japanese). http://www.sumitomolife.co.jp/about/newsrelease/pdf/2016/160721a.pdf

Taiyo Life Insurance. (2016, October 20). *Taiyo Life Insurance – Japan's First "Dementia Prevention App" Available to Customers from October 20!* (in Japanese). https://www.taiyo-seimei.co.jp/company/notice/download/press_article/h28/281020.pdf

Teece, D. J. (2010). Business Models, Business Strategy and Innovation. *Long Range Planning, 43*, 172–194.

Teece, D. J. (2013). (Translation by Taniguchi, K. and others) "Dynamic Capabilities" Diamond (in Japanese).

The Nikkei. (2015, October 12). *AXA of France Uses Big Data for Insurance, Discounts for Safe Driving, Introduction Considered in Japan* (morning ed.), p. 5.

Tokio Marine & Nichido Fire Insurance Co., Ltd. www.tokiomarine-nichido.co.jp/

Yano Research Institute. (2017, May 29). *Investigation on the InsurTech Market in Japan in the Life Insurance Sector* (in Japanese). http://www.yano.co.jp/press/press.php/001694. Kenko-Nenrei Shogaku Tanki Hoken, https://kenko-nenrei.co.jp/

7
Telemedicine System Developments Through Strategic Collaboration Between Industry, Government and Academia

Rumiko Azuma and Mitsuru Kodama

7.1 Innovative Customers

Including the concept of user innovation (Hippel 1998) or customers as innovators (Hippel and Katz 2002; Thompke and Von Hippel 2002), this chapter looks at certain users who are customers of manufacturers (vendors) and bring about new innovations through trial and error and practical experience (e.g., Rosenberg 1982) using (or not using) diverse tools (hardware and software) as "innovative customers." In short, customers who have the high-level knowledge and competences needed to achieve user innovation through rich learning experiences in particular fields of specialization can be called innovative customers.

From the perspective of dynamic capabilities (DC), this kind of user innovation or customers as innovators can be considered as follows.

R. Azuma (✉) • M. Kodama
Nihon University, College of Commerce, Tokyo, Japan
e-mail: azuma.rumiko@nihon-u.ac.jp; kodama.mitsuru@nihon-u.ac.jp

Customers who have high-level knowledge and competencies are innovative customers who personally have outstanding DC. Existing research reports that some DC exist in individual managers and top executives, and are the most remarkable characteristics of companies where, at certain definitive crossroads, chief executive officers and top managers recognize important developments and trends, and work to move companies forward by proposing responses and instructing entire companies (Adner and Helfat 2003).

Thus, Collins (1994) called DC a higher order capability to acquire sustainable competitiveness, and it represents a process of infinite regression to even higher order capabilities. Accordingly, regardless of the level of capabilities reached, this implies that it is impossible to acquire a permanent advantage. Furthermore, while Zollo and Winter (2002) mainly focused on primary and secondary capabilities, they also presented the implication of something like infinite regression, arguing that in constantly changing and unpredictable contexts even the higher learning approach itself would have to be constantly updated.

In response to this, Teece (2014) argued that if the concept of non-routine manager activity (Teece 2012) is introduced, the prospects for regression become very low. In many cases, the creative and innovative actions of managers, businesspersons and innovative customers described in this chapter are characteristically non-routine. According to Teece (2014), in reality many of the strategic actions and reformations require non-routine activities that cannot be copied (Teece 2012, p. 1397). Accordingly, competitive advantage theories that do not deal with the possibility of non-routine actions by top management, particular practitioners in organizations and certain customers with high levels of experience and knowledge (e.g., innovative customers) are unnatural, and hence it can be proposed that the source of the demonstration of DC is strategic non-routine activities. As presented in Chap. 2, in contrast to routine activities through the demonstration of ordinary capabilities (OC) in formal organizations, the formation of strategic communities (SC) through the strategic non-routine activities of practitioners triggers DC.

7.2 Collaborative Innovation Through DC Centered on Telecommunications Carriers

As the second answer to the question we have raised about who the main players in e-healthcare are, this section discusses existing research into the proposition that project teams at telecommunications carriers are leading main players.

In recent years, business systems have changed rapidly, with changing industrial structures and business environments, and the development of ICT. Many businesses face the challenge of developing strategic business that takes into account resources such as knowledge and personnel that exist across diverse industries, both those in the company and outside—not only resources limited to existing business units, but resources accessible through strategic alliances, mergers and acquisitions (M&A), corporate ventures, and strategic outsourcing.

Particularly in leading business fields such as IT, e-business, contents, electronics, and bio-tech, leading core technologies and diverse business models are becoming more and more dispersed throughout the world and are innovating. It is becoming more and more difficult for old-style hierarchical organizations of the mass production era or companies with closed and autonomous systems to retain independent and full control over their innovations. The theoretical frameworks of open innovation (Chesbrough 2003), distributed innovation (Haour 2004) and hybrid innovation (Kodama 2011b) point to the importance of managing various assets both inside and outside a company (core competencies or core capabilities) and generating new collaborative innovation (Kodama 2015) across businesses and industries.

Despite playing a central role in configuring e-healthcare systems, before the emergence of the internet telecommunications carriers worked with business models centered on providing telephone services. In the old era of telephone services, the business models of telecommunications carriers were technologically well defined, and core technologies and know-how were developed, with results of the development being retained in closed systems within the company, or in *keiretsu*-type alliances with communications equipment manufacturers. In addition, product and service development cycles were comparatively longer than they are today. This was an era in which companies could independently offer vertically integrated telephone services. This is illustrated by "asset orchestration architecture" of the vertical value chain model in vertical integrated architecture, illustrated in Table 9.1 in Chap. 9.

With the rapid technical innovations such as digital technologies, internet, broadband, and the mobile internet of the 1990s, conventional business models were dramatically transformed. Figure 7.1 illustrates how the vertically integrated, telephone service technology-centered business models were destroyed in the internet protocol (IP) era, to be replaced by new opportunities to pioneer and expand markets, with entry by a wide range of players into individual layers, such as the terminal layer with its personal computer, mobile music players, mobile telephones, smartphones, tablets, mobile information devices, and so forth, the network layer offering optical fiber communications and high-speed mobile communications through long-term evolution, the platform layer

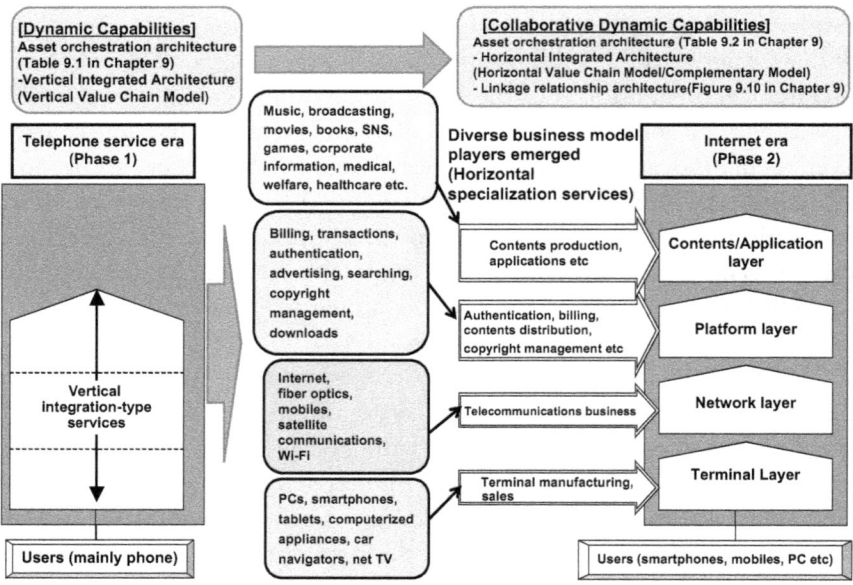

Fig. 7.1 The transforming business models of telecommunications carriers around the world (fixed and mobile networks)

having functions for contents authentication (music, video, games software, e-commerce, etc.), billing, content delivery, and copyright management, as well as the contents and application layers providing diversified contents and wide-ranging application services typified by social networking services to various end user terminals (including medical, welfare, healthcare, and educational services).

In short, the advent of the internet has caused a massive shift from vertically integrated business models to horizontal specialization business models. While competing on layers, players on the individual layers also engage in strategic alliances and M&A with players on adjacent layers to expand business opportunities (see Fig. 7.1). In these cases, companies and organizations have to pour their efforts into "asset orchestration architecture" of the horizontal value chain model and the complementary model in horizontal integrated architecture, as shown in Table 9.2 in Chap. 9, or linkage relationship architecture, as shown in Fig. 9.10.

This means that with these changing business models, telecommunications carriers have to create new assets by orchestrating not only their own core research and development (R&D) assets in telecommunications technologies accumulated over time, but also assets outside the company across a range of different businesses and industries (diverse information terminals, software, contents, applications, etc.) through DC.

The massive changes to business models such as those above are a common business model framework found in telecommunications carriers (both fixed line and mobile) all over the world. In particular, collaborative innovation through collaborative DC between main player telecommunications carriers and collaborating partners in related businesses and industries to plan and develop diverse social services by combining ICT with medical, welfare, and healthcare is creating new markets in Western developed countries and Japan.

7.3 Asset Orchestration Through Collaborative DC

These massive business model changes have a profound impact on the capabilities of these telecommunications carriers. As discussed in Chap. 2, collaborative DC among partners brings about capability synthesis as win–win synergies of strategies through platform building capabilities with strategic (co-specialized/complementary) partners. Teece (2007, pp. 1332–1333) identifies the importance of "managing complements and platforms" to build co-specialized assets.

In addition, against the backdrop of the advance of ICT business in recent years, from the perspective of business models and corporate strategies, platform strategies are becoming increasingly important (Kodama 2009a, b, 2013). Since platforms are the foundations of products and services, configuring complementary products and services on platforms is considered a way to provide even more value to customers. Microsoft in the software industry with its Windows operating system and Intel in the hardware industry with its microprocessor unit (MPU) semiconductors have created a situation in which both companies are platform leaders (Gawer and Cusmano 2004). Thus, both companies are maintaining strong competitiveness with Windows and MPUs, because positive feedback through network effects functions as partners, as complementary parties provide applications and software to run on the systems.

The win–win relationships built between these platform leaders and complementary parties bring about "business ecosystems." Other major platform strategies (products) in the ICT business include the iPhone iOS application platform and the Google Android operating system for smartphones, providing operating environments on which a range of authentication, finance and transaction functions, diverse applications, and software run.

For companies that aim to become platform leaders, it is important to decide upon a platform architecture that will encourage autonomous growth of various complementary commercial technologies, products, and services on the platform. Then, at the same time as selecting and building a platform in product development, an important issue is to set down suitable vertical boundaries with external partners that are complementing one's company to develop an attractive platform on which the platform leader can encourage autonomous growth of those external partners.

As described above, the core capabilities that drive the overall system made up of technologies, products, and services developed autonomously by individual partner companies centered on a company ICT platform, co-specialized assets of the company, while skillfully deriving and co-ordinating the co-specialized assets of partner companies (or customers or competitors) in relationships with the company is called DC. Companies that are main players in business ecosystems such as Microsoft, Google, Intel, Qualcomm, NVIDIA, Apple, Sony Computer Entertainment, Nintendo, and TSMC are called "platform companies."

Platform companies maintain power over their own businesses and enable them to grow long term by building open (or hybrid or half-open) platforms as modular systems. If it is possible to skillfully deploy these platform strategies through collaborative DC among partners, businesses can be opened up that would be difficult for a company alone to embark upon, which enables bringing about a business ecosystem involving "co-creation and co-evolution" among the companies and their partners, customers, and even its competitors (see Fig. 7.2).

Moreover, DC entail contexts in which there are synergies between diverse strategies. In particular, multi-national enterprises have to orchestrate co-specialized assets on a global scale. Teece (2007, p. 168) identifies

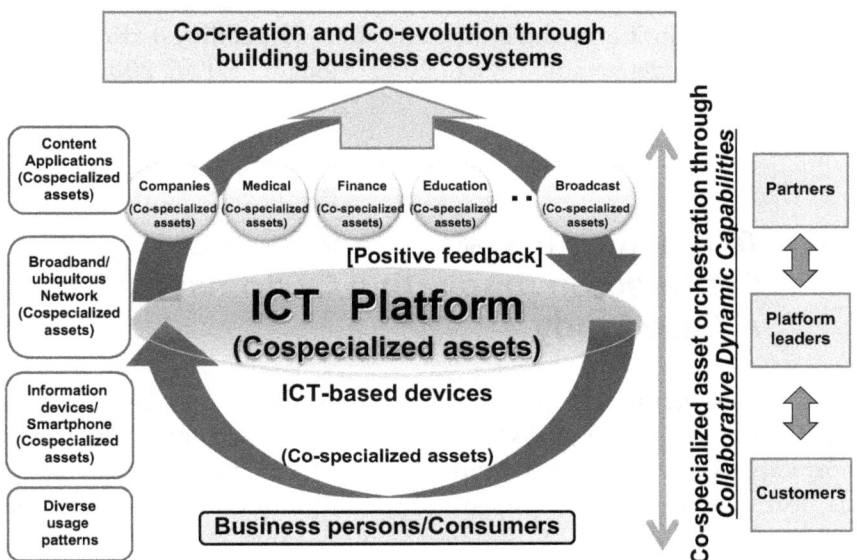

Fig. 7.2 Building business ecosystems through collaborative DC

"replication capabilities" that bring about two types of strategic values (the ability to support geographic expansion and the ability to support production-line expansion) as another element of DC. The replication, redeployment and reconfiguration (or recombination) of these intangible assets can also be thought of as bringing about co-specialization, as synergies of global strategies enabled by DC.

For example, like the business models of Japanese general trading companies discussed in Chap. 9, these could be strategic synergies accompanying strategic expansion upstream and/or downstream in a value chain expansion through vertical integration, global geographical expansion through a horizontal integration across domains, strategic synergies accompanying expansion of successful business models into adjacent industries, strategic synergies accompanying group company partnering through integration of group company strategies, or strategic synergies through the integration of a company itself through joint ventures or M&A. Moreover, strategic synergies can be brought about through collaborative DC by integrating different business models of different partners (e.g., fabless and foundry, ICT, and education/healthcare services). Integration of these different assets (capabilities) (Kogut and Zander 1992; Helfat and Peteraf 2003; Kodama 2000, 2002, 2003, 2004, 2005c, 2007d, 2011a, 2014, 2017a, b, 2018) also requires the orchestration of co-specialized assets.

7.4 Telemedicine System Development Centered on Innovative Customers: A Case Study

First, in answering the question about who the main players are in e-healthcare, this section discusses the case of physicians in university hospitals who are "innovative customers" with high levels of experiential learning. This section presents a case of product innovation in the healthcare field using ICT centered on Asahikawa Medical University in Japan.

7.4.1 Innovation at Asahikawa Medical University of Japan

The Japanese population is entering a period of serious aging, the likes of which the world has never seen. In particular, Hokkaido is five years ahead of the national level in Japan, with one in four people predicted to be 65 or over by the year 2020. In addition to this, the aging of the population appears to be accelerating faster in rural areas than urban areas. Healthcare facilities with advanced medical equipment tend to concentrate in urban areas, so to receive sufficient healthcare treatment there is currently an unavoidable reliance on urban medical institutions. This puts a heavy physical, economic and time load on patients and their families—people from the vast rural areas of Hokkaido with its harsh winter or those from remote islands have to find accommodation when they come to visit physicians. Thus, patients wanting access to optimal healthcare but living in the so-called remote areas are disadvantaged physically, economically, and time-wise even before they have received any treatments.

While many of the medical facilities in these localities have CT and MRI equipment, and can perform operations, many of them do not have radiologists or pathologists. This often leads to the delayed discovery of critical diseases or provision of appropriate treatment. Aiming to correct for the differences in treatment between rural and urban areas, in 1994, Asahikawa Medical University introduced ophthalmology telemedicine by moving image transmission of slit lamp microscope and sharing ophthalmoscopic findings between ophthalmology-affiliated hospitals and the university.

Further correcting healthcare disparities between regions and relieving an unfavorable situation, a telemedicine center was established in 1999 in Asahikawa Medical University Hospital, ahead of the rest of Japan. Asahikawa Medical University Hospital drives this telemedicine using the ICT in its center to respond to the expectations of localities. In recent years, 3D hi-vision (3D-HD) video methods using optical fiber networks have been introduced for video image-based diagnosis, ophthalmology care, and surgical support. These networks connect some 50 medical institutions both in and outside Hokkaido.

Internationally, in addition to projects in the USA, Singapore and Thailand, Asahikawa Medical University Hospital has begun telemedicine projects linking four healthcare institutions with the Chinese government. In light of these achievements, the university has embarked on the expansion of exports of telemedicine systems. In 2015–2016, it provided image diagnosis technologies and know-how fostered both in Japan and overseas to Russia, and provided healthcare information management systems to India. As well as these systems that mitigate the problem of doctor shortages and disparities between regional healthcare facilities, the university has also developed systems to operate telemedicine in disaster-hit areas during large-scale disasters, and is proceeding with the international networking of these.

There are new plans for exports to Russia in order to further internationalize these telemedicine systems. Asahikawa Medical University anticipates granting its technologies, devices, software, and operational know-how, and linking with telemedicine centers to provide medical guidance through the viewing of videos that take into account the number of images needed or differences compared with assessing for individual diseases with the naked eye. Russia, Sakhalin, and Hokkaido are connected through the medical field, and the demand for telemedicine is high. Asahikawa Medical University also has strategies to provide support for building and maintaining networks to medically isolated areas in order to spread these technologies throughout Russia.

As well as this, the university plans to grant its healthcare information management system to India. It will provide its "Wellnet link," which has been developed and operated by its telemedicine center, with Indian specifications. This system began as a server for storing and sharing patient medical records. As there are many cases of paper medical records being carried around in India, there is an urgent necessity to manage medical records using ICT. Hence, this system aims for a future in which Indian citizens can connect to a site as required, and input, save, and manage information such as healthcare diagnoses. The university is aiming to build a system that as well as enabling patients to get information from medical institutions, or advice from dietitians for example, will also be a system that doctors can use with their examinations. To achieve this, driving strategic collaboration among different stakeholders (collaborating partners) such as governments, medical institutions, private companies, and local administrations will be key.

In October 2016, Asahikawa Medical University began to offer telemedicine to patients in six hospitals in Hokkaido using smartphones. This service is aimed at emergency and critical care for cardiovascular surgery such as ruptured aneurysms. The system enables the diagnosis of conditions and preparation for surgery while the patient is being transported to the Asahikawa Medical University Hospital even if a physician is not present in the hospital. This shortens the time before surgery can commence, which improves survival rates and reduces medical costs. The system is also useful for reducing medical disparities between different localities.

The six hospitals involved are Kitami Red Cross Hospital (Kitami-city), Hokkaido Kitami Hospital (Kitami-city), Fukagawa Municipal Hospital, Rumoi Municipal Hospital, Furano Hospital (Furano Association, Furano-city), and Engaru-Kosei General Hospital (Engaru town), which all now transport emergency patients to Asahikawa Medical University Hospital if no surgeon is available or if they are short of staff. Telemedicine using a smartphone is undertaken using the following procedure. The six hospitals send diagnostic images of patients to an external cloud server. Physicians at Asahikawa Medical University access the server before the patient arrives, to view the symptoms of affected areas and diagnose the disease. Doctors use a ruler function to measure the size of the affected areas to determine the seriousness of the condition and determine what surgical tools will be required. This is a revolutionary system that enables doctors, anesthetists, and surgical staff to instruct each other using chat. As described above, Table 7.1 provides a summary of the main historical initiatives taken by the university with its telemedicine systems.

The successful case of this university centered on ophthalmology professor Dr. Akitoshi Yoshida (currently the University President), an "innovative customer" who was heavily involved in the chain of processes from planning and development of the telemedicine system through to experiments, verification, and commercialization. While performing the formal, routine activities of providing healthcare and educating as both a physician and a professor, Prof. Yoshida worked with all his might on the

Table 7.1 Asahikawa Medical University Hospital telemedicine initiatives

Year	Key topics
1994	Ophthalmology telemedicine by moving image transmission of slit lamp microscope and ophthalmoscopic findings between ophthalmology affiliated hospitals and universities. Trails and experiments with ISDN lines (128 kbps/384 kbps/1.5 Mbps/3.0 Mbps)
1999	Remote medical center established in Asahikawa Medical College Hospital, 1999
2001	In 3D image transmission experiments using broadband network between Asahikawa Medical University Hospital surgical suites and Sapporo Kōsei Hospital Opthalmology Dept., experienced surgeons confirm faithful 3D imaging performing operations live
2004	Asahikawa Medical University Telemedicine Center and Hakodate Goryokaku Hospital connect for high-definition (HD) operation image transmission to provide surgical support from the center during an operation being performed in Hakodate Goryokaku Hospital in real time
2005	IP begins with telemedicine centers (migration from ISDN communications to IP communications)
2006	Asahikawa Medical University connected to Singapore National Eye Center for successful transmission of high-resolution 3D images to Singapore with ABB 3D-HD telemedicine ophthalmology experiment using broadband
2007	"Home telemedicine" begins in ophthalmology after hospital discharge. Asahikawa Medical University ophthalmology ward and patients connected via internet for health management and monitoring after hospital discharge. Confirmation that providing full health management systems to patients far from the inpatient hospital can contribute to driving early hospital discharge. Virtual ophthalmology symposium held using 3D high-vision connecting the three Asian countries of Japan, Singapore, and Thailand
2011	Asahikawa Medical University and the Chinese Ministry of Health agree on Japan–China telemedicine project grant aid. Asahikawa Medical University's telemedicine operations know-how and technologies provided to four hospitals—Ministry of Health China—Japan Friendship Hospital (Beijing), Shanghai Jiaotong University School of Medicine Ruijin Hospital (Shanghai), Shenmu Hospital (Shaanxi), and Dujiangyan People's Hospital (Sichuan)
2015–16	Telemedicine system and healthcare and medical information management system technologies exported to India and Russia

Source: Created from Asahikawa Medical University Hospital publications

telemedicine system R&D through to commercialization, demonstrating an entrepreneurial spirit and aiming to create a society with no healthcare disparities, providing it equally to people throughout Japan and the world. In other words, he continually demonstrated routine and OC while at the same time demonstrating DC to take a long-term view, research and develop the telemedicine system, and then commercialize it to achieve his philosophy and vision.

In observing and analyzing the processes of R&D through to commercialization at the university, strategic collaboration through the formation of close-knit strategic communities across industry, government, and academia such as communications equipment manufacturers, medical equipment manufacturers, telecommunications carriers, and government research institutions centered on Prof. Yoshida's project team is observed. This was also a period in which proactive R&D investments were made in R&D through to commercialization toward entry into a new practical ICT field involving the stakeholders—communications equipment manufacturers, medical equipment manufacturers, telecommunications carriers, and government-related research institutions—who got the project to develop a new telemedicine system up and running through their own project teams' demonstration of DC to drive the planning and development of new business. The success of Prof. Yoshida's project team can be interpreted as a major achievement of the demonstration of collaborative DC between the team and the collaborating partner companies, the stakeholders. As discussed in Chaps. 2 and 7, the boundaries of synchronization and synchronization of the strategic innovation loops on the individual Capabilities Maps of Asahikawa Medical University, the main player and collaborating partners, brought about collaborative DC from R&D through to commercialization.

7.4.2 Promotion of Creative Dialog and Collaborative Innovation with Innovative Customers

As is typified by ICT, providing products and services to customers essentially entails companies marketing and developing commercial products, services and business models from the perspective of the customer, as well as absorbing a wide range of opinions, hopes, and criticisms from customers familiar with related products and services.

In particular, as the most important perspective found in this case study, the formation of strategic communities from innovative customers and companies (manufacturers and vendors) to bring about new products and business models through proactive dialog and collaboration within these communities, and horizontal expansion to other related customers of the results of these community activities has become a business process of previously unseen importance.

For a company, the first issue is the promotion of close dialog with innovative customers through proactive contact with them. Unlike the business models of the era of mass production and mass marketing in which companies one-sidedly created products and business models and provided products to customers, modern companies must work to conceptualize new business models and products by engaging in dialog with innovative customers. In other words, innovative customers are just like company staff who do nothing other than jointly develop business models and product concepts. The important point is for development project leaders in companies (called community leaders in this chapter) and innovative customers to share and resonate their visions and values with each other toward bringing about new product concepts and business models.

Innovative customers have ideas and visions about many customers (in this case, patients and the healthy) being able to enjoy high-quality, low-cost products and services (in this case, medical services) brought about through new products and business models. Thus it is the mission of the company, as the community leader, to provide competitive products and services to as many customers as possible (in this case, hospitals and healthcare professionals), and achieve high levels of customer satisfaction. Here, community leaders and innovative customers must repeatedly engage in dialog to share and resonate their values with each other so that they can establish new concepts. It is also important to form strategic communities that include innovative customers and company project teams. Members of these strategic communities must share their values with each other, and the innovative customers must be treated as members of the project team, while business processes must be driven so that

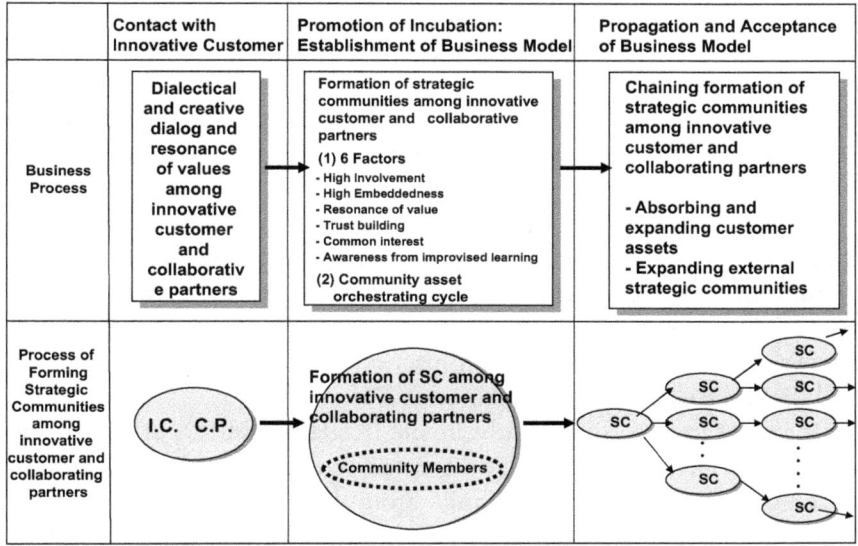

Fig. 7.3 Creating strategic communities among innovative customers and collaborating partners. (*IC* innovative customer, *CP* collaborating partners, *SC* strategic communities)

innovative customers are regarded as community members, and think and take action together with them (See Fig. 7.3).

In this case, the R&D project that was centered on Prof. Yoshida, the innovative customer of Asahikawa Medical University, entailed motivating and co-ordinating the collaborating players, the manufacturers and telecommunications carriers, and led to the building of a new telemedicine system. Moreover, the university's success has become a template for telemedicine systems representative of Japan, and is positioned as part of the export of Japanese ICT technologies. This was underpinned by Prof. Yoshida's strong vision about equal access to healthcare services and the informatization of medical data. The persuasiveness and ability of the innovative customer to paint a picture of the future of telemedicine that both end-user customers (patients, and the healthy) and hospitals involved in healthcare could understand, along with the promotion of collaborative innovation through collaborative DC and creative dialog among collaborating partners across industries were extremely important. In this sense, through working to share and resonate values among all community members in strategic communities formed of a main player and collaborating partners, the contributions of the innovative customers and the university research staff to this business venture were of major significance.

Moreover, having analyzed this case in detail, we have extracted the following perspectives as being important aspects of this resilient strategic community structure, which can be illustrated by the "six factors" in Fig. 2.7 in Chap. 2. These six factors drive boundary synchronization in strategic communities, the synchronization of strategic innovation loops, and the three elements of collaborative DC.

The first factor is "high involvement" (Kodama 2005a). This increases the commitment to strategic non-routine activities in strategic communities. Strategic communities built around "Ba" (Kodama 2005a, b) entail the sharing of contexts through mutual interaction with others, and bring about a space and time where new knowledge is inspired by and based on the new meanings and actions that come about through these dynamically changing contexts. As well as this, strategic communities create a space and time where tacit knowledge can be shared, which is the source of commitment.

Strategic communities are fundamentally different to "communities of practice" (e.g., Wenger 2000; Kodama 2007a, c). This is because, as seen in this case, communities that are motivated by issues in business or social activities are also groups that instigate action relating to pressing issues and problems. Pressing problems are problems that immediately generate interest and are also business opportunities that will disappear if not grasped quickly. Therefore, these communities are required to move in an instant. Communities that are motivated by business issues in this way are qualitatively completely different to "communities of practice," in that there are major differences in the sense of urgency and diversification between these two types of communities. In general, a community of practice has few members, and does not have the same sense of urgency as the community motivated by issues (e.g., Buckman 2003; Kodama 2007b).

The second factor is "high embeddedness" (e.g., Granovetter 1985). This deepens the level of sharing of knowledge and information within the strategic community. In other words, it illustrates the qualities of deeply connected human networks. The third factor is "resonance of values" (Kodama 2001). This brings about shared values related to the project objectives between project members and innovative customers, and promotes the sharing and resonating of these within strategic communities. Through the process of resonating values, community members build trust with each other, which is the fourth factor.

From the perspective of those involved with the university hospital, such as innovative customers, there are currently serious deficiencies in medical practices and hospital information systems that must be overcome, and there is an interest in achieving R&D for highly effective systems for healthcare professionals and administrators, as well as interest in academic and practical contributions through the publication of unique research papers in new areas of research and the acquisition of patents as intellectual property. In addition, values are used to raise the level of the university's contribution to society through its responsibility for social contribution and through the telemedicine system.

Conversely, the value for manufacturers and telecommunications carriers from a business perspective is how these companies can invigorate their ICT-related businesses. For this reason, these companies research, develop, and market hardware and software that will contribute as their sense of value accelerates the process of new product development, and ultimately contributes to the success of their ICT businesses. Thus, these shared values between the university as the main player and collaborating partners regarding the project objective of the telemedicine system led to the formation of resilient strategic communities (see Fig. 7.3).

Nevertheless, as a fifth factor, it is necessary for the university as the main player and collaborating partners to have common interests (Kodama 2007c) to bring about high involvement and high embeddedness. Here, repeated and mutual dialectical and creative dialog (Kodama 2007a) is important. High-quality productive dialog is a medium that leads to the discovery of shared solutions and the establishment of shared objectives. These processes result in the discovery and sharing of common interests, which can act as a trigger for the process of resonating values.

Moreover, resonating values promote learning among the university as the main player and the collaborating partners. Organizational learning is an important process that brings about new assets (knowledge) and drives best practice within organizations (e.g., Huber 1991; Walsh and Ungson 1991). "Awareness gained from improvised learning" is inspired by the processes of ad-lib formation of these assets (knowledge). The processes of handling assets embedded among individual members of communities becomes an important perspective that gives the members awareness gained through improvised learning, the fifth factor, and brings about the orchestration of new assets.

In this case, originally under the guidance of Asahikawa Medical University, the innovative customer schemes to verify real-time communication tools such as TV conferencing with the medical workplace were executed. From the perspective of the innovative customer, tools like this had already been commercialized (although at the time only designed for some business applications), but there had not been much testing regarding its applicability to the healthcare field. Manufacturers could have continued on their own path through normal sales planning in-house and existing sales channels, although project team members at these manufacturers were inspired by the new awareness that was drawn from the perspective of new application development. At the same time, to provide fair healthcare services around Japan, the innovative customer also gained a significant awareness of strong philosophy and ideas for pioneering the field of telemedicine, for which there had not been much progress in R&D in Japan at the time.

According to existing research, the "knowledge process" entails knowledge transfer (e.g., Szulanski 2000), knowledge access (Grant and Baden-Fuller 1995), knowledge acquisitions, knowledge storage, knowledge retrieval (Hargadon and Sutton 1997), knowledge creation (Nonaka and Takeuchi 1995), knowledge transformation (Carlile and Rebentisch 2003), and knowledge integration (Kodama 2009a, 2011a), which are the process systems of knowledge embedded in practitioners and organizations (e.g., Hargadon and Sutton 1997; Kodama 2001; Carlile and Rebentisch 2003). As this knowledge process, the process axes of such important core factors as the asset orchestration process in the perspective of this case are also the factors of knowledge accumulation, knowledge sharing, knowledge inspiration, and knowledge creation (which includes knowledge integration and knowledge transformation) (e.g., Kodama 2006, 2011a). In addition, in its individual meanings, knowledge can mean both tacit and explicit knowledge (or tangible and intangible assets) and is considered to be an asset in the perspective of asset orchestration through DC.

Through the formation of strategic communities with the university as the main player and other companies as collaborating partners, new co-specialized assets (specifically new products, services, or business models) are created by community members and practiced in worksite organizations. Thus assets such as competences, skills, and know-how (tacit knowledge and explicit knowledge) become embedded and accumulate in and between community members. We call this chain of asset handling processes the "community asset creating cycle."

We describe these six factors and the community asset orchestrating cycle as an important core concept in the next section.

7.4.3 Innovation Processes of Innovative Customers and Collaborating Players

The issue faced by strategic communities is producing specific incubation and surefooted commercialization of the service models they have constructed or the products they have invented through trial and error. To drive this incubation and commercialization, innovative customers as main players are the central characters who are driving projects to execute such things as incubation planning and scheduling. This enables the extraction of issues required for incubation through the valuable core assets of innovative customers.

For example, this entails including specific strategy and tactics for actual field monitoring of customers and methods of execution. Thus, through collaborative DC among collaborating partners in strategic communities centered on innovative customers, performing experiments in the actual field, and then through surveys and interviews with many customers, the appropriateness of a new system or business model is confirmed and the level of product and service quality is moved toward commercialization.

(1) Community Asset Orchestrating Cycle

In this incubation stage, community asset innovation and co-specialization are important as part of the learning and creative process in communities. This specifically entails the sharing of existing assets held by members in the community, including innovative customers, and then creating new community assets through mutual inspiration and propagation, which is then accumulated organizationally (see Fig. 7.4).

As an example, these processes can be described through a case study. The first step of sharing community assets is the stage at which innovative customers and collaborating partners thoroughly discuss mutual objectives in the community, and share and understand each other's assets. This was the stage of experimenting and verifying telemedicine systems through communications tools such as TV conferencing systems. A major achievement was the development of compression transmission and viewing technology for 3D images, as well as 3D imaging transmissions that could be used with a 1.5 Mbps communications line enabled by the new compression technology. In addition, it was confirmed that

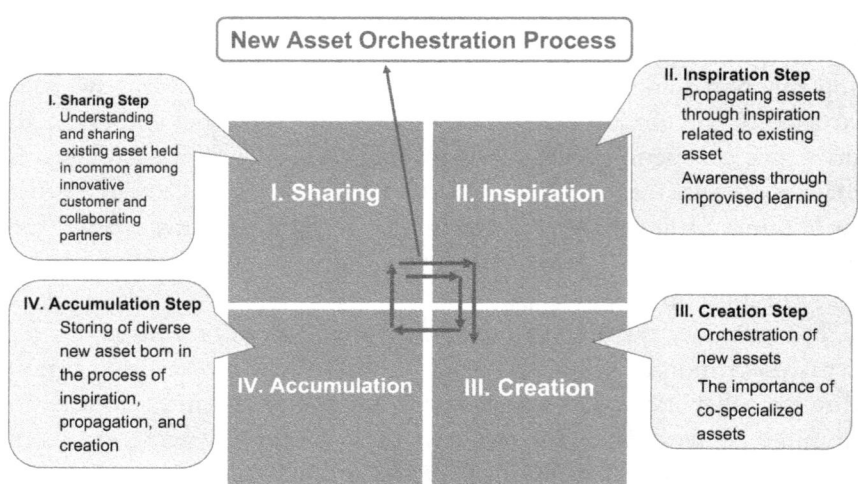

Fig. 7.4 Community asset orchestrating cycle among innovative customers and collaborating partners through the strategic communities creation

medical high-resolution imaging transmission was possible with a 3.0 Mbps communications line. As a result, innovative customers and community members became confident that they could expect to achieve remote medicine through high-quality imaging transmission in the internal medicine and surgical fields by proceeding with the construction of an affordable ultra-high-speed network, and the use of surgical imaging, endoscopy and laparoscopy. However, at the time, telecommunications carriers only provided ISDN lines (128 kbps, 384 kbps, 1.5 Mbps and 3.0 Mbps) as network infrastructure, and so qualitative details of telemedicine encountered certain restrictions. Because of these technical limitations, manufacturers recognized that they should concentrate on developing technologies to improve image quality, while telecommunications carriers recognized that they should concentrate on developing broadband through the use of IP.

Thorough communal sharing and understanding of the clinical and medical information assets of the physicians as the innovative customers with the ICT and imaging technology assets of manufacturers, telecommunications carriers, and government research institutions was therefore crucial at the beginning of the incubation stage. The innovative customers understood the technologies that the collaborative partners had, and wondered how they could be used to achieve a telemedicine system. In contrast, the collaborating partner community members thoroughly understood the opinions and requirements of the innovative customers, considered the level of image quality and transmission quality that could be brought about with the technologies the company had, and engaged in planning for a new product development for the fully fledged incubation of the telemedicine system.

The second step in the inspiration of community asset was the stage in which a wide range of community assets were mutually inspired and propagated to uncover problems and issues, their solutions allowing the establishment of new products and business models for a telemedicine service based on these shared community assets. Specifically, through incubation trials, many issues and demands were extracted by the healthcare workers, institutions, and patients involved, which acted as feedback for improving the product and service. However, in this case study, the community members faced a wide range of problems and issues in executing the trial experiment process. These issues included image quality, network quality, cost efficiency, lack of telemedicine staff in the university hospital, disparities between localities and home healthcare—there were various serious issues, and the community members had to deal with all these problems rationally.

In contrast, awareness came about through improvised learning among the community members and a process of trial and error during this inspiration step. In the sharing and inspiration steps, community members had to have the capabilities of dialectical and creative dialog (Kodama 2007a), creative confrontations or abrasion (Leonard-Barton 1995), productive friction (Hagel III and Brown 2005), and political negotiating practice (Brown and Duguid 2001), because high-quality dialog and practice is crucial for the third process, which was asset orchestration.

Asset orchestration is the stage in which new community assets (co-specialized assets are especially important) are created based on the assets inspired and propagated in the community. Specifically, this means product and service improvements and upgrades through incubation, new services and products that are created to provide healthcare professionals and patients with sufficient satisfaction, and the establishment of new business models.

The fourth step, accumulation, is the stage in which community assets acquired through the process of sharing, inspiration, and creation accumulate in organizations as valuable know-how. Specifically, these are a range of accumulated developmental processes, operations skills and technical know-how related to telemedicine services obtained through incubation. Through these community asset innovation processes, the quality of incubation was raised, and the creation of new products and services that would help many healthcare professionals and patients was enabled.

(2) Chaining Strategic Communities Formation with Many Partners

The next issue faced by the strategic communities was popularizing, expanding, and establishing the products and business models created through incubation. In this case study, the achievements of community assets accumulated through the activities of the strategic communities, including innovative customers, such as wide-ranging developmental processes, operating skills and technical know-how related to telemedicine services, were effectively used through the formation of strategic communities with other related partners and customers. As a result, new value could be offered to many partners and customers through the telemedicine system developed, which in turn enabled the smooth popularization and deployment of the business models through the continuous formation of strategic communities with customers. Specifically, through expansion of the R&D of Asahikawa Medical University to external strategic communities with hospitals around Japan and in other countries, innovative customers and project teams orchestrated community assets through the absorption of core assets, and accumulated new skills and know-how (see Fig. 7.3).

7.5 Capabilities Synthesis Through Collaborative DC Centered on Telecommunications Carriers: A Case Study

As a case study, in answering the question "who are the leading main players in e-healthcare?" this section discusses the processes of Nippon Telegraph and Telephone Corporation (NTT), Japan's largest telecommunications carrier, in its gaining of governmental support and that of local administrations in order to engage in DC synthesis, leading to the introduction of an e-healthcare system in a doctorless area in Japan.

7.5.1 Promotion of Diffusion of ICT in Regions of Japan: The World's First Multimedia Village Project Uses Multimedia to Vitalize Depopulated Areas

(1) Background and Aims of Measure

Multimedia-based enrichment of regional community is becoming an important topic in the twenty-first century. As population declines owing to the falling birth rate and society continues to age, progress is being made in the social structure with regard to internationalization and the decentralization of authority to the local level. For village residents in various regions to lead secure, healthy, and enjoyable lives, we must work to enrich local, intra-village communities, encourage active extra-village intercourse, and improve the environment for lifelong learning, beginning our efforts with enrichment in fields such as health insurance, social welfare, medical care, and education, and the improvement of regional government services. The Multimedia Village Project is an initiative in which the government and private sector (the Ministry of Posts and Telecommunications, regional governments, Japan's largest telecommunications carrier NTT, and others) are collaborating and co-ordinating their efforts. It is based upon a special project concerned with working to improve the depopulation problem, to improve the living environment in rural villages and to vitalize them, while investigating the question, "what kind of multimedia would village residents like to use?"

(2) Formation of Networked Strategic Communities

(a) Mission and Challenges

In September 1997, NTT launched a new-generation videophone throughout Japan. Business and virtual classroom communications was its initially targeted market, but its use in household circles began to gradually catch on, helped by the product's features that allowed, at the world's lowest price of JPY 198,000 a pair, the enjoyment of a high-quality two-way video communication.

The vision and concept under which the NTT project leader pursued the popularization of the videophone called for offering a helping hand in the areas of medical care, insurance, social welfare, and education for the aged populations, bed-ridden folk among them, in remote regions. To make an impact, one remote village in Japan was selected, and all the households in it were connected by videophone to the rest of the country. A larger frame of the project concept, called the Multimedia Village Project, envisioned the creation and provision to large numbers of the aged, of new values, through a number of applications in the areas of medical care, health insurance, social welfare, and education. The vision and concept of the project leader was to realize a multimedia village in Japan and create a new template—the first of its kind in the world.

The project, however, faced some initial obstacles:

- Financial difficulties with the installation of equipment to support the videophone and associated systems. The problem of how to secure government subsidies from the Ministry of Posts and Telecommunications and other sources.
- Selection of one village from among many. Consensus-building among the villagers concerning the introduction of the videophone to each household.
- Problem of how to provide an extensive application of the videophone to the areas of medical care, insurance, social welfare, and education.
- The videophone debuted with the catchphrase "So easy to use, anyone can use it," but it was not certain if gadget-allergic aged people would take to it.
- In addition, a host of other problems needed addressing.

(b) Decision-Making Based on Past Accomplishments

For the project leader, selecting a village posed a major challenge. It was additionally important to secure the consensus and co-operation of those concerned at the local prefectural government level, under whose jurisdiction the village was hosting such a large-scale project, if it were to begin. NTT had a track record of working with Fukushima Prefecture in a multimedia-supported, virtual-format, life-long learning program. The Koriyama Women's University, which celebrated the 50th anniversary of its foundation as an educational corporation in 1996, launched a Multimedia Telecommunications-Based Life-Long Continuing Education Service as one of its commemorative projects (Fukushima Minpo Shimbun 1997).

Under this program, a PC-based teleconferencing system was put in place, a multi-room teleconference system that enabled participation via a regular TV set or by simple monitor hook-up, thereby allowing an interactive life-long continuing education course to be made accessible to subscribers through multiple-point-of-access teleconference hook-up. Specifically, multimedia-based two-way classes were inaugurated with a network that linked the Life-Long Learning Center with citizen centers in various farming communities.

Under the slogan of "Attend College Courses Near Your Home," the program promoted life-long learning while contributing to ending the dwindling in opportunities for education. A course linking the center to three citizens' centers in the prefecture in real time offered a total of five lectures centering around the general theme of "Respecting Regional Needs" and focusing on such specific topics as "Real-life problems in day-to-day living," "Themes that make our lives worth living" and "Events of topical social interest." The participants took part with enthusiasm, and fever-pitch debates unfolded. Satisfying exchanges of information and knowledge took place between participants and lecturers, and among the participants themselves. Co-ordinated by NTT, a linkup between Fukushima Prefecture and faraway Brazil was realized using the teleconferencing system in August 1997, providing an opportunity for, among other things, an exchange of opinions between the Fukushima governor and Fukushima-born residents of Brazil.

In view of this background, the first thought on the project leader's mind was to target a village in Fukushima.

> I believed there was in Fukushima Prefecture a sufficiently deep-rooted culture receptive to the teleconferencing system and the videophone. The telecommunications-based life-long continuing education course had won acclaim from the aged and housewife sets, and I was aware that we had made the Fukushima Governor, the highest-ranking official of the prefecture, sufficiently aware of the value of video communication. We were thus to choose a village in Fukushima as the primary candidate. Of the several villages in the prefecture, we chose one in which was located Katsurao Middle School, known for its emphasis on Internet utilization in its curricular program, which caught our attention, leading us to eye Katsurao Village as the Multimedia Village Project site. We believed that a leadership of the Governor, the prefecture's highest-ranking official, would be key in the startup of the large-scale project that was the Multimedia Village Project. Our first, most important task, then, was to make a presentation of the vision and concept for the project before the Governor and secure his consent.

(3) Formation of a Networked Strategic Communities

In January 1998, the NTT project leader made a presentation of the vision and concept for the project before a panel of executive-level core leaders including the Fukushima Prefectural Governor and the Mayor of Katsurao Village. Following exhaustive discussions, the sympathy and positive response of the core leaders was obtained in support of the project, and a Strategic Community (SC, specifically SC-a) could be formed (See Fig. 7.5). Keeping pace with the formation of SC-a, NTT project leader made a presentation of the vision and concept for the project to the executive director and senior officials of the Ministry of Posts and Telecommunications (MPT), to try to gain financial support for the project. Then SC-b, between NTT and MPT, could be formed. At this stage, several problems regarding the allocation of funds and the effects of the project on social welfare were discussed within the SC-b (Fig. 7.6, Phase 1).

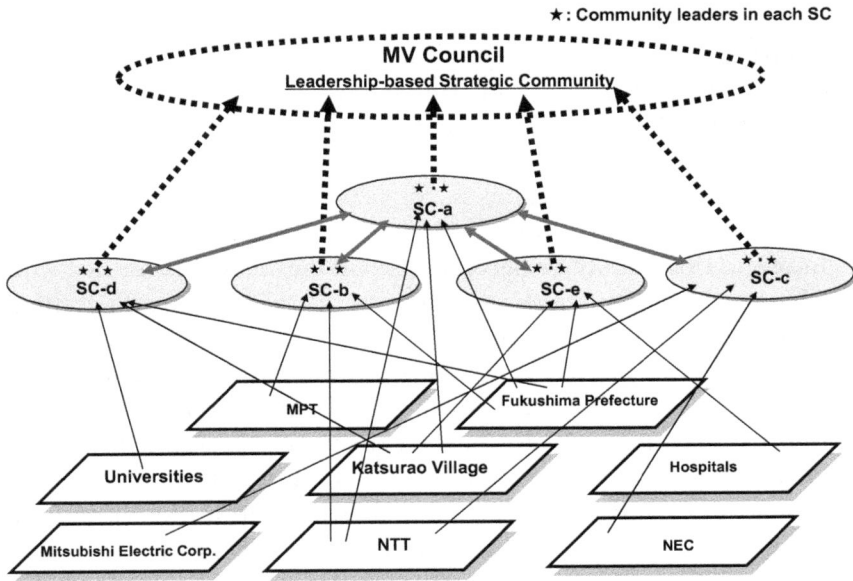

Fig. 7.5 Formation of strategic community and networked SCs

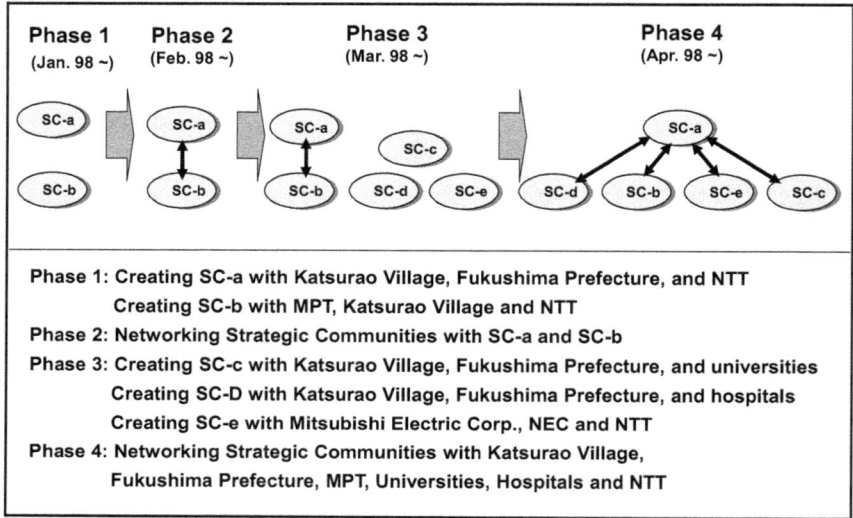

Fig. 7.6 Networked strategic communities at the big project

In the process of pursuing political and financial issues in greater detail and solving a number of real problems in Katsurao village households, NTT actively collected data on village needs for the videophone and other related multimedia systems, and discussed with MPT including the Fukushima Prefectural Governor and Katsurao village the realization of this project. Through this process, SC networks linking between SC-a and SC-b were formed in this phase (Fig. 7.6, Phase 2).

In connection with these negotiations and the consensus reached with MPT to achieve the large-scale project, the Fukushima Prefectural Governor and Katsurao village officials were trying to finalize the completion of proposals in which experiments for e-learning, remote healthcare, and telemedicine were planned through deep collaboration with universities and hospitals. To this end they made presentations of the vision and concept for the project to several universities and hospitals. In this process, they formed the new SCs with universities (Koriyama Women's University and Fukushima University) (SC-c) and hospitals outside the village (SC-d) for deep collaborations (see Fig. 7.5). The NTT project team, on the other hand, could form an SC with system vendors

(Mitsubishi Electric Corp. and NEC) (SC-e) to realize the concept of the multimedia village from the standpoint of the technology, using IT and multimedia. A variety of technical issues related to video communication and transmission of educational and medical contents were thoroughly discussed (Fig. 7.6, Phase 3).

Accordingly, an umbrella network project centered on Katsurao village in SC-a, which was linked through SC-e, was formed that would co-ordinate the interworkings of different entities toward the realization of the Multimedia Village Project, and a decision was taken to work out the details (Fig. 7.6, Phase 4). A proposal based on a vision and concept developed by an NTT project leader triggered the realization of a community as an executive-created project, which in turn provided a vehicle for the mutual sharing of values held by the core leaders.

In April 1998, an organization named Katsurao Village Multimedia Village Promotion Council (MV Council) was formed that worked across various organizations, hospitals and schools among them, such as the Ministry of Posts and Telecommunications, the Ministry of Education, Fukushima Prefecture, the village of Katsurao, the University of Fukushima, Koriyama Women's University, hospitals, medical associations, villagers' livelihood co-operatives, and NTT (see Fig. 7.3). The purpose was to take further steps toward the accomplishment of the project. The MV Council, consisting of the core leaders from each organization (in this chapter, the MV Council is referred to as a Leadership-based Strategic Community, LSC), was formed to enthusiastically promote and verify the experiment, and instigate the introduction of the videophone-based multimedia system to remote village communities across the nation. With this initiative, it was hoped that the Multimedia Village Project idea would be accepted throughout the country. The core leaders of the various organizations (government agencies, Fukushima Prefecture, the village of Katsurao, universities, hospitals, medical associations, NPOs, etc.) were referred to as community leaders.

As part of the experiment, a Health Maintenance and Well-Being Subcommittee and an Education Subcommittee were formed. The former was to provide care, medical consultation, health counseling, and other services for the aged while verifying the possibility of realizing videophone-based remote medical care and consultation services. It was decided that the Education Subcommittee should organize videophone-aided remote classrooms, seminars, and interschool student exchanges, and provide support for life-long learning in farming communities to create an educational environment that would eliminate regional disparities.

In this way, a community was created together with the MV Council bringing strategic organization to the initial core leadership approach. To bring the Multimedia Village Project closer to reality, the MV Council studied details relating to its conceptual foundations, the design of the system structure, matters pertaining to medical care, insurance, social welfare, and education, and prepared presentations for villagers to build consensus and test run schedules. Thanks to the swift action of the community, the village residents, the customers of the project, were able to deepen their understanding. By June 1998, equipment installation had been completed, and under a three-year plan, to end at the end of March 2001, a test run of the videophone-aided Multimedia Village Project got under way (Fig. 7.7 shows a conceptual drawing of the video network in Katsurao Village.) (*New York Times* 1999).

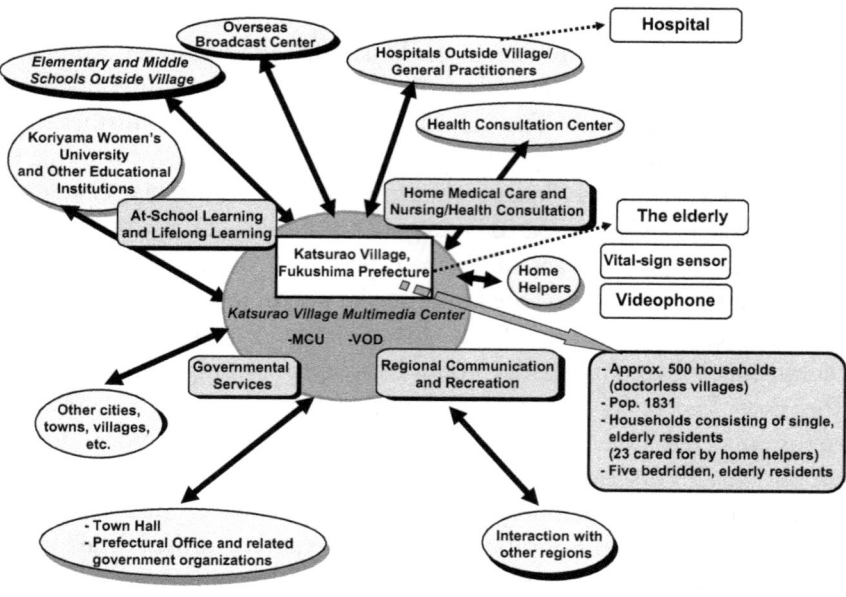

Fig. 7.7 Video-Net in Katsurao village, Fukushima Prefecture [conceptual diagram]

By laying digital access lines to all 473 households in Katsurao village, to the schools, the town hall, and other public facilities, organizers prepared an environment in which videophones could be used freely under the Multimedia Village System (MV System). Equipment installed consisted of a multi-point connection unit (MCU) (Kodama 1999, 2008), which enabled a maximum of 94 locations to be simultaneously connected to the multimedia center in the town hall to make arrangements and hold meetings, and a video on demand (VOD) (Kodama 1999, 2008) server, which enabled searching and retrieval of graphical information using a videophone. Residents expressed numerous opinions, such as, "I'd like them to put a lot of information closely related to daily life on the video server," "Aren't there any applications that let children play and have a good time?" and "I want to use my videophone to talk to family and friends outside the village."

In the experiment, as an initiative to revitalize rural village regions, multimedia that could be easily, cheaply and readily used by anyone was put to practical use, and methods were examined for applying multimedia in various fields such as medical care, social welfare, education, and government services with the objective of promoting the diffusion of information technology. Specifically, the experiment verified how efforts can be made to put to practical use bi-directional communication through easy-to-understand videophone-based graphical information to improve the depopulation situation, improve the living environment in rural villages and revitalize them.

This project raised the information and knowledge levels of individual residents using the video network between public facilities and their homes and provided various services that met the individual needs of village residents, forming a society in which everyone from children to the elderly could feel secure and lead a life worth living. Amid a rapidly shrinking and aging population, and in an effort to form a regional society in which village residents could live healthy, secure lives, a multimedia center was installed in the Katsurao village town hall and public facilities were networked to each home using digital access lines to make available health preservation, social welfare, education services, and government information services.

Thus, with the vision and concept proposed by an NTT project leader triggering sympathetic resonance among the value systems of core leaders, organized community creation on a grand scale grew from group-level community-creating efforts, resulting in services to the village population, the customers.

(d) Innovation in New Asset Orchestration

The biggest challenge for the MV Council, which was an LSC, was how to provide worthwhile content and applications for the village residents, the customers, using the completed MV system as the platform. Put differently, this challenge addressed the human aspects of providing inspiration (software) through the MV system (the hardware).

The initial challenges faced by the LSC were the consolidation of the Multimedia Village Project and conceptualization, design, and construction of the MV system. Following the initial stages, existing content and applications for services in medical care, insurance, social welfare, and education were made available to villagers through the MV system as virtual knowledge-based services (Kodama 1999). Then project leaders had to work out how to gain acceptance for the system across the community. Services were provided in the fields of medical care, insurance, and education.

7.5.2 Capabilities Synthesis Through Collaborative DC of Community Leaders

Struggles and conflicts are a common occurrence among networked SCs. These elements are harmful factors in the effort to synthesize their capabilities. This synthesis is thus promoted by the LSC, which we describe below.

The role of the LSC is to synthesize the capabilities of all SCs on the networks formed by community leaders (made up of personnel from various levels of participating organizations: top management, middle management, etc.) and to generate capabilities synthesis through collab-

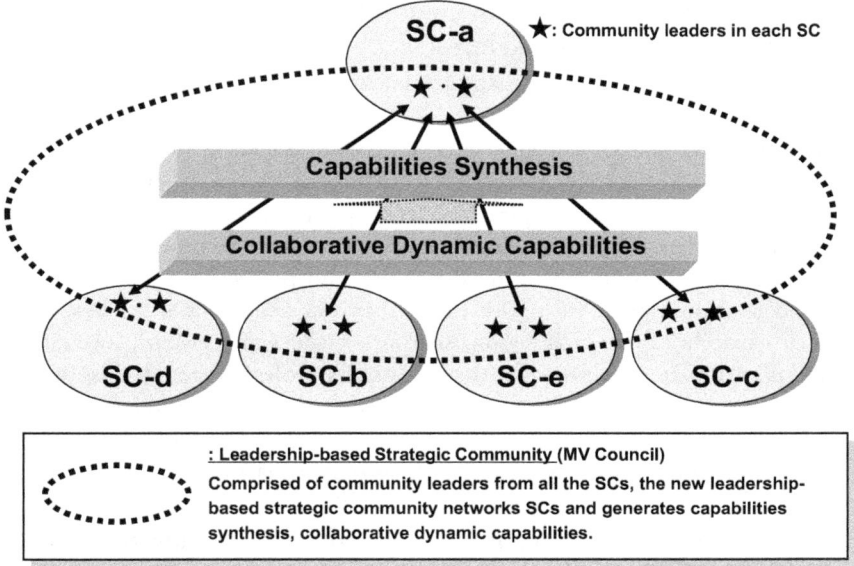

Fig. 7.8 Capabilities synthesis through collaborative DC of community leaders

orative DC, the combined network power of all SCs (see Fig. 7.8). Solid LSCs give rise to the group ties of community leaders in SCs. As shown in Fig. 2.7 in Chap. 2, solid LSCs entail the six factors of high involvement, high embeddedness, high resonance of values, trust-building, common interest, and awareness through improvised learning. To reach the ultimate target of networked SCs, that of knowledge creation, the capabilities of each SC must be thoroughly and mutually understood and shared among community leaders. This is equivalent to high involvement among community leaders. In addition, solid LSCs entail the factor of high embeddedness to bring about new asset orchestration in networked SCs by orchestrating the shared different assets of each SC. To bring about high involvement and high embeddedness in LSCs, the high resonance of values and trust-building among community leaders is crucial. Thus, for community leaders and community members, an important issue is that of new discovery and achievement through dynamic trial and error based on new common values and interests through common interests and awareness through improvised learning.

For example, a Katsurao village leader says:

> it's critical to build relationships of trust between leaders in various organizations to make these large-scale projects succeed. A variety of dissimilar specialized knowledge is required to execute the project. For example, professional leaders in various fields such as government, finance, education, healthcare, welfare, technical development, and political aspect, need to build relationships of trust with each other and demonstrate the best of their capabilities. For this reason, sharing of values and visions, interests and empathy are important for the success of a project. Through this, specialized knowledge in various fields is shared for new awareness and ideas. Furthermore, by engaging in trial and error, and by fusing and converging them, new concepts can be materialized as the ultimate aim of a project.

Having the above six factors, these solid LSCs provide the driving force that brings about capabilities synthesis through asset orchestration.

As well as this, the LSC needs to balance the various paradoxical elements and issues within SCs on the network to achieve capabilities synthesis. The LSC also needs to enable community leaders to consciously conduct dialectical management based on collaborative DC and engage in dialectical dialog to solve the various differences and issues that result from learning among the community leaders. As a result, the LSC actively analyzes problems and resolves issues, forms an arena for the resonance of new values and creates a higher level of capabilities. Dialectical management is based on the Hegelian approach, which is a practical method of resolving conflict within an organization (Benson 1977; Peng and Nisbett 1999; Seo and Creed 2002).

The balancing of paradoxical elements and issues involves the synthesis of mutually divergent views among organization members coming from different corporate cultures on the one hand and the synthesis of a variety of divergent business as well as social issues (such as the procedures of different management, technologies or customers' needs) on the other. In the case of the MV Council, for example, synthesis was required in three areas: (1) the values of many employees with a broad diversity of viewpoints and knowledge (assets) shaped by the different organizational cultures to which they belong, (2) balancing customer needs and high technology presented by firms, and (3) balancing political aspects and social needs. Thus, the LSC plays a central role in synthesizing the paradoxical elements and issues in the specific areas of human resources, elements of seeds and needs, and political issues. The collaborative DC with the new ideas and approaches of the community leaders who have adopted the methods of dialectical management based on deep strategic collaboration in their efforts to synthesize paradoxical elements and issues make new asset orchestration and innovation possible.

The LSC promotes dialectical dialog and discussion among community leaders to cultivate a thorough understanding of any problems. By communicating and collaborating with each other, community leaders become aware of the roles and values of each others' work. As a result, community leaders are able to transform the various conflicts that have arisen among them into constructive conflicts (Robbins 1974). This process requires community leaders to follow a pattern of dialectical thought and action in which they ask themselves what sorts of actions they themselves would take, what sorts of strategies or tactics they would adopt and what they could contribute toward achieving the large project and innovation through asset orchestration. Then, in achieving new asset orchestration and innovation, the LSC promotes empathy and resonance of community leader values. The combined synergy and collaborative DC among the community leaders resulted in the high levels of capabilities synthesis that enabled the MV Council to achieve its goal and form new virtual knowledge-based services in medical and educational fields. In another sense, it can be seen that the MV Council used the resonance of values among community leaders in their SCs and their leadership synergies to form the LSC and high levels of capabilities synthesis, based on collaborative DC, which in turn generated a solid network of SCs (see Fig. 7.8).

Through the analysis of these in-depth case studies, we would like to emphasize that innovative organizations in the twenty-first century need to be strategic community-based organizations. In other words, we believe that it is important for innovative organizations to create ongoing innovation through business as well as non-profit activities that involve the formation of SCs based on creative assets and the networking of these SCs. Assets, or management resources aimed at innovation, are created from SCs, and a wide range of assets both inside and outside the company, including customers and strategic partners, are synthesized via the network, creating new and never-before-seen assets as new sources of competitive advantage. It is therefore important for community leaders who form LSCs to find new value for innovation with customers and leaders of strategic partners inside and outside the organization as the organization endeavors to achieve its desired vision and mission. The newly created value is then shared, empathized and resonated among all community members through dialectical dialog and discussion within the LSC. The philosophy of an interactive learning-based strategic community, where members teach and learn from each other, is an important part of this process. This approach promotes further collaborative DC based on dialectical consideration, and becomes the driving force for producing high levels of capabilities synthesis.

7.6 Conclusion

This chapter has discussed management processes that entail the formation of strategic communities through strategic collaboration across wide-ranging business types and industries such as university hospitals, private companies, and government research institutions, as projects involving medical professionals with high levels of learning experiences and innovative private companies pioneer new businesses engaging in the asset orchestration process to bring about a new telemedicine system. The formation of strategic communities drives collaborative DC among stakeholders across industry, government, and academia, and achieves capability synthesis for new asset orchestration.

References

Adner, R., & Helfat, C. E. (2003). Corporate Effects and Dynamic Managerial Capabilities. *Strategic Management Journal, 24*(10), 1011–1025.
Benson, J. (1977). Organization: A Dialectical View. *Administrative Science Quarterly, 22*, 221–242.

Brown, J. S., & Duguid, P. (2001). Knowledge and Organization: A Social-Practice Perspective. *Organization Science, 12*(6), 198–213.

Buckman, R. (2003). *Building a Knowledge-Driven Organization.* New York: McGraw Hill.

Carlile, P. R., & Rebentisch, E. S. (2003). Into the Black Box: The Knowledge Transformation Cycle. *Management Science, 49*(9), 1180–1195.

Chesbrough, H. (2003). *Open Innovation.* Boston: Harvard Business School Press.

Collins, R. (1994). *Four Sociological Traditions.* Oxford: Oxford University Press.

Fukushima Minpo Shimbun. (1997). Kooriyama Women's University Offers Distance/Lifelong Learning Courses Featuring University Lectures Over Television Monitors. 11 June, 3.

Gawer, A., & Cusmano, M. A. (2004). *Platform Leadership.* Boston: Harvard Business School Publishing.

Granovetter, M. (1985). Economic Action and Social Structure: The Problem of Embeddedness. *American Journal of Sociology, 91,* 481–510.

Grant, M., & Baden-Fuller, C. (1995). A Knowledge-Based Theory of Inter-Firm Collaboration. *Academy of Management Best Paper Proceedings, 38,* 17–21.

Hagel, I. I. I., & Brown, J. S. (2005). Productive Friction. *Harvard Business Review, 83*(2), 139–145.

Haour, G. (2004). *Resolving the Innovation Paradox.* London: Palgrave Macmillan.

Hargadon, A., & Sutton, R. (1997). Technology Brokering and Innovation in a Product Development Firm. *Administration Science Quarterly, 42,* 716–749.

Helfat, C. E., & Peteraf, M. A. (2003). The Dynamic Resource-Based View: Capability Lifecycles. *Strategic Management Journal, 24*(10), 997–1010.

Huber, G. P. (1991). Organizational Learning: The Contributing Processes and the Literatures. *Organization Science, 2*(1), 88–115.

Kodama, M. (1999). Customer Value Creation Through Community-Based Information Networks. *International Journal of Information Management, 19*(6), 495–508.

Kodama, M. (2000). New Multimedia Services in the Education, Medical and Welfare Sectors. *Technovation, 20*(6), 321–331.

Kodama, M. (2001). New Regional Community Creation, Medical and Educational Applications Through Video-Based Information Networks. *Systems Research and Behavioral Science, 18*(3), 225–240.

Kodama, M. (2002). Strategic Partnership with Innovative Customers: A Japanese Case Study. *Information Systems Management, 19*(2), 31–52.

Kodama, M. (2003). Strategic Innovation in Traditional Big Business. *Organization Studies, 24*(2), 235–268.

Kodama, M. (2004). Strategic Community-Based Theory of Firms: Case Study of Dialectical Management at NTT DoCoMo. *Systems Research and Behavioral Science, 21*(6), 603–634.

Kodama, M. (2005a). Knowledge Creation Through Networked Strategic Communities: Case Studies on New Product Development in Japanese Companies. *Long Range Planning, 38*(1), 27–49.

Kodama, M. (2005b). How Two Japanese High-Tech Companies Achieved Rapid Innovation Via Strategic Community Networks. *Strategy & Leadership, 33*(6), 39–47.

Kodama, M. (2005c). New Knowledge Creation Through Leadership-Based Strategic Community—A Case of New Product Development in IT and Multimedia Business Fields. *Technovation, 25*(8), 895–908.

Kodama, M. (2006). Knowledge-Based View of Corporate Strategy. *Technovation, 26*(12), 1390–1406.

Kodama, M. (2007a). *The Strategic Community-Based Firm*. London: Palgrave Macmillan.

Kodama, M. (2007b). *Knowledge Innovation –Strategic Management as Practice*. Cheltenham: Edward Elgar Publishing.

Kodama, M. (2007c). *Project-Based Organization in the Knowledge-Based Society*. London: Imperial College Press.

Kodama, M. (2007d). Innovation and Knowledge Creation Through Leadership-Based Strategic Community: Case Study on High-Tech Company in Japan. *Technovation, 27*(3), 115–132.

Kodama, M. (2008). *New Knowledge Creation Through ICT Dynamic Capability Creating Knowledge Communities Using Broadband*. Charlotte: Information Age Publishing.

Kodama, M. (2009a). Boundaries Innovation and Knowledge Integration in the Japanese Firm. *Long Range Planning, 42*(4), 463–494.

Kodama, M. (2009b). *Innovation Networks in Knowledge-Based Firm –Developing ICT-Based Integrative Competences*. Cheltenham: Edward Elgar Publishing.

Kodama, M. (2011a). *Knowledge Integration Dynamics –Developing Strategic Innovation Capability*. Singapore: World Scientific Publishing.

Kodama, M. (2011b). *Interactive Business Communities -Accelerating Corporate Innovation Through Boundary Networks*. London: Gower Publishing.

Kodama, M. (2013). *Competing Through ICT Capability*. Basingstoke: Palgrave Macmillan.

Kodama, M. (2014). *Winning Through Boundaries Innovation –Communities of Boundaries Generate Convergence*. Oxford: Peter Lang.

Kodama, M. (Ed.). (2015). *Collaborative Innovation: Developing Health Support Ecosystems* (Vol. 39). London: Routledge.

Kodama, M. (2017a). *Developing Holistic Leadership: A Source of Business Innovation*. Bingley: Emerald.

Kodama, M. (2017b). Developing Strategic Innovation in Large Corporations—The Dynamic Capability View of the Firm. *Knowledge and Process Management, 24*(4), 221–246.

Kodama, M. (2018). *Sustainable Growth Through Strategic Innovation: Driving Congruence in Capabilities*. Cheltenham: Edward Elgar Publishing.

Kogut, B., & Zander, U. (1992). Knowledge of the Firm, Combinative Capabilities and the Replication of Technology. *Organization Science, 5*(2), 383–397.

Leonard-Barton, D. (1995). *Wellsprings of Knowledge: Building and Sustaining the Sources of Innovation*. Boston: Harvard Business School Press.

New York Times. (1999, August 30). Japan Bets on a Wired World to Win Back Its Global Niche.

Nonaka, I., & Takeuchi, H. (1995). *The Knowledge-Creating Company*. New York: Oxford University Press.

Peng, K., & Nisbett, R. E. (1999). Culture, Dialectics, and Reasoning About Contradiction. *American Psychologist, 54*(9), 741.

Robbins, S. P. (1974). *Managing Organizational Conflict: A Non-traditional Approach*. Englewood Cliffs: Prentice Hall.

Rosenberg, N. (1982). *Inside the Black Box: Technology and Economics*. Cambridge: Cambridge University Press.

Seo, G., & Creed, W. (2002). Institutional Contradictions, Praxis, and Institutional Change: A Dialectical Perspective. *Academy of Management Review, 27*, 222–247.

Szulanski, G. (2000). The Process of Knowledge Transfer: A Diachronic Analysis of Stickiness. *Organizational Behavior and Human Decision Processes, 82*(1), 9–27.

Teece, D. J. (2007). Explicating Dynamic Capabilities: The Nature and Microfoundations of (Sustainable) Enterprise Performance. *Strategic Management Journal, 28*(13), 1319–1350.

Teece, D. J. (2012). Dynamic Capabilities: Routines Versus Entrepreneurial Action. *Journal of Management Studies, 49*(8), 1395–1401.

Teece, D. J. (2014). The Foundations of Enterprise Performance: Dynamic and Ordinary Capabilities in an (Economic) Theory of Firms. *The Academy of Management Perspectives, 28*(4), 328–352.

Thompke, S., & Von Hippel, E. (2002). Customers as Innovators. *Harvard Business Review, 80*(4), 74–81.

Von Hippel, E. (1998). Economics of Product Development by Users: The Impact of "Sticky" Local Information. *Management Science, 44*(5), 629–644.

Von Hippel, E., & Katz, R. (2002). Shifting Innovation to Users Via Toolkits. *Management Science, 48*(7), 821–833.

Walsh, J. P., & Ungson, G. R. (1991). Organizational Memory. *Academy of Management Review, 16*(1), 57–91.

Wenger, W. (2000). Communities of Practice: The Organizational Frontier. *Harvard Business Review, 78*, 139–145.

Zollo, M., & Winter, S. G. (2002). Deliberate Learning and the Evolution of Dynamic Capabilities. *Organization Science, 13*(3), 339–351.

8

Pharmacy Service Innovation from the Standpoint of Collaborative Dynamic Capabilities

Takuya Akikawa

8.1 Introduction

Japan's rapidly aging society has necessitated a transformation of the country's pharmacies. Most Japanese pharmacies currently specialize in drug dispensing, focusing on fulfilling prescriptions for patients. However, they need to adjust to become partners that are familiar with drugs and their usage. As a result, there has been a progressive shift in the medical framework from treatment being completed in a single hospital to that within a region, referred to as integrated community care. In order to adapt to this change, Japanese pharmacies need to be innovative, not only in terms of changing their work content, but also by redefining the role of the pharmacist. The aim of this chapter is to discuss how pharmacies' dynamic capabilities (DC) contribute to such innovation.

T. Akikawa (✉)
Nihon University, College of Commerce, Tokyo, Japan
e-mail: akikawa.takuya@nihon-u.ac.jp

8.2 The Current State of Japanese Pharmacies and the Transformation Required

Japanese medical expenditure has reached 42 trillion yen, which corresponds to over 10% of the gross domestic product. Ever since universal health insurance coverage was introduced in Japan, the burden on citizens to secure the necessary financial resources has increased. Of the total medical costs, dispensing accounts for 7.5 trillion yen (approximately 18%). The Japanese median age was 46.9 years in 2016, the second highest worldwide (Central Intelligence Agency 2017), indicating a rapidly aging society. As a result, the number of elderly people with multiple chronic diseases is increasing.

The number of pharmacies in Japan has increased consistently over time, with approximately 58,000 in operation as of 2016. This increase is attributed not only to the aging society, but also to the change in the pharmacy regulations. Following the Western model, the Japanese government has separated dispensaries from medical practices. Physicians provide patients with a prescription, based on which pharmacists dispense drugs in order to manage patients' drug history appropriately and to guide drug administration. This system enables the use of the expertise of both professions. Pharmacies and clinics were previously integrated in Japan, where dispensing occurred within a hospital. However, polypharmacy, prescribed by physicians, has become a social problem, promoting the separation of dispensing and prescribing. The medical fees covered by insurance were revised and physicians' technical fees for external prescriptions were increased. As a result, the rate of the separation of dispensing and prescribing has increased since the 1970s, with external prescriptions for outpatients currently at approximately 70% (Ministry of Health, Labour, and Welfare [MHLW] 2015).

However, the rapid change to the separation of dispensing and prescribing caused a new problem, namely the so-called "monzen pharmacies," located near hospitals in order to meet the demand of dispensing hospital prescriptions. "Monzen" means "in front of a gate" in Japanese. Thus a monzen pharmacy refers to a pharmacy located near a hospital or a clinic. The problem with these is that, by specializing in dispensing drugs, they have made this their core business. Previously, Japanese pharmacies not only sold drugs, but also provided local residents with advice on health or hygiene issues. As such, they were regarded as regional hubs. However, the number of regional pharmacies has gradually declined, replaced by centers that simply dispense prescribed drugs, with the spread of monzen pharmacies and the rise of drugstores selling over-the-counter (OTC) drugs at lower prices. The oligopoly of monzen pharmacies has weakened the function of health consultations in regions that previously had pharmacies. Therefore, the increasing number of monzen pharmacies has had the negative effect of promoting self-medication. In Japan, the number of patients who visit a hospital to receive prescribed drugs covered by insurance, even in cases of mild symptoms, is considered a problem. Thus it is inferred that the problems caused by monzen pharmacies may also be attributed to the changes in the functions of a pharmacy. In addition to being a supplier or dispenser of drugs, the World Health Organization defines a pharmacist as a team member engaged in the provision of healthcare services (World Health Organization 1994). The deviation from these principles is a side effect of the separation of dispensing and prescribing.

In terms of the spread of integrated community care, as introduced by the government, the oligopoly of monzen pharmacies is an unsuitable situation. According to the MHLW, the aim of integrated community care is to support the elderly so that they can live an independent life and continue to live in familiar regions, as much as this is possible. It also means the system in each region needs to provide a comprehensive set of professional services, such as healthcare, caregiving, and prophylaxis. The "Dankai no Sedai," the baby-boom generation born immediately after World War II, accounts for the largest proportion of the demographic composition by age, and will turn 75 years of age or older in 2025. As a result, the issue of healthcare provided to the elderly is predicted to become more serious. The conventional healthcare provision system in Japan used to be provided by a single hospital. However, this system could not be maintained because of the rapidly aging society, stringent financial conditions of health insurance, and lack or uneven distribution of physicians across regions. With the exception of hospitalized treatment or advanced medical care, the provision of primary care needs changed to the specialization and co-operation of regional healthcare institutions. This is considered a transformation of the ecosystem comprising healthcare providers. Integrated community care assumes that regional issues are discussed by all stakeholders, such as healthcare or caregiving organizations, government, and local residents, in order to determine and implement countermeasures. Pharmacists or pharmacies are required to be actively involved in such regional co-operation. As a result, the function of a pharmacy has also changed (i.e., to that of a monzen pharmacy), now being operated in relation to a specific hospital, and cannot respond to these changes. Most of the elderly have multiple diseases and visit multiple medical institutions. Patients' drug information needs to be handled in an integrated manner in order to realize accurate personal care.

The MHLW also depicts the spread of "kakaritsuke pharmacies" as a vision of future pharmacies (MHLW 2015). The Japanese word "kakaritsuke" refers to a person's "regular place, where they can always receive healthcare services." Therefore, a kakaritsuke pharmacy represents a specific pharmacy where patients request dispensing, even if they visit multiple medical institutions. Kakaritsuke pharmacies provide the following functions: (1) patients' drug information, in an integrated and continuous manner, based on which pharmaceutical management and instruction are performed; (2) 24-hour response and home visit care; and (3) enhanced co-operation with medical institutions, including kakaritsuke doctors. The government is promoting a review of the dispensing fee system in order to encourage pharmacies to transform in a way that medical fees can reflect the functions or services they provide, consistent with those of a kakaritsuke pharmacy.

However, pharmacies need many additional resources or capabilities in order to provide the aforementioned three functions, which hinders the spread of kakaritsuke pharmacies. We discuss this problem in the following section.

8.3 Resources Necessary for the Transformation of Pharmacies

Introducing information and communication technology (ICT) is essential to unifying drug information. A paper-based medication notebook is currently used in Japan to record prescription information. Patients are required to carry the notebook with them, and to submit it when requesting dispensed drugs. However, patients do not always do so, which hampers the information-sharing function of the system. In addition, the notebook does not allow the sharing of information such as patients' diagnostic results, laboratory data, and drug history on admission, preventing pharmacies from co-operating with medical institutions in the region, as required by integrated community care. Thus, a network needs to be built centering on a cloud-based database that allows regional healthcare participants to manage and share patients' drug information in an integrated fashion. Specifically, the following ICTs are necessary: an electronic health record, serving as the platform for healthcare co-operation, and a personal health record to manage patients' medical histories in a unified manner.

However, pharmacies such as monzen pharmacies, which specialize in dispensing, have a poor record of investing in and operating ICT. Such pharmacies typically use a closed network, which is limited in terms of an online presence to health insurance claims. Prescriptions are mostly handled using a paper-based system. This has introduced problems with the standardization of information and the identification of patients. However, pharmacies lack the capability to invest in and operate such networks. Whether these costs can be covered in order to realize the necessary investment and capabilities is key to promoting kakaritsuke pharmacies.

Realizing 24-hour response and homecare visits depends on co-operation between pharmacies in a region. The chronic shortage of hospital beds and the aging society mean that integrated community care enables patients with severe diseases to receive medical care at their homes. Thus pharmacists in kakaritsuke pharmacies are consulted on drug therapy, and can dispense drugs or visit patients' homes to provide care, irrespective of whether this occurs within the operating hours of the pharmacy. However, because Japanese small-scale pharmacies tend to have a poor human resources function, responding to such requests independently is difficult. Therefore, it is conceivable that these pharmacies will build a co-operative system with nearby pharmacies, responding to requests by rotating among the co-operating regional or extensive pharmacist associations.

Enhancing co-operation among medical institutions, including kakaritsuke doctors, is a major challenge. Kakaritsuke pharmacies are required to conduct a prescription inquiry, as well as to send feedback on drug administration information, propose or prescribe prescriptions for patients, and instruct patients on residual drugs, as needed. In addition, kakaritsuke pharmacies need to be able to refer patients to relevant institutions after being consulted by local residents on health or caregiving issues. Building co-operative relationships with regional medical institutions is therefore required. However, because there are only a few medical institutions providing prescriptions per monzen pharmacy, the relationships with medical institutions that should be built through prescription inquiries or proposals of prescription change also tend to be limited. Therefore, monzen pharmacies are required to make a sustained effort to build relationships with regional medical institutions in order to participate in the integrated community care system.

In summary, a successful change to kakaritsuke pharmacies depends on whether pharmacies have the capabilities to operate ICT and to build relationships within the region. Substantial changes in recognition are required to transition from monzen pharmacies to kakaritsuke pharmacies. A conventional monzen pharmacy can maintain its business based on income from the public insurance system, because patients visit them from nearby hospitals to fulfill their prescriptions. However, under the integrated community care system, a pharmacy unable to become a kakaritsuke pharmacy would be differentiated based on medical fees, and would find it difficult to continue its business. The transformation from a monzen pharmacy to a kakaritsuke pharmacy is associated with a change in providing patients with services, rather than objects. This means pharmacies are forced to fundamentally change their operational processes in order to succeed in the new asset orchestration process. Furthermore, this corresponds to change management, which is difficult to realize. Thus it is necessary to identify those factors that promote change management.

8.4 Formulation of Hypotheses

As a factor to promote change management, we focus on the concept of DC. Integrated community care and kakaritsuke pharmacies are just concepts, and many factors will determine how well the concept is realized, including identifying target local patients, designing operational processes or services, earnings structures, methods to introduce the techniques, and how well leadership monitors employees' performance. Because pharmacies specializing in dispensing tend to have insufficient human resources, these decision-making processes pose a substantial burden in terms of economy and capabilities. If pharmacies continue to specialize in dispensing, they might downgrade their decision-making related to the associated risks. Neutralizing this decision-making bias is also included in the functions of DC.

Thus the following hypothesis is derived.

H1   The DC of a pharmacy exert a positive effect on the effectiveness of integrated community care.

A pharmacy must capture the opportunities to meet the two challenges of contributing to regional healthcare and maintaining the management of the pharmacy organization. To realize these opportunities, pharmacies need to dynamically reallocate their assets. However, pharmacies have poor resources, because they do not function in the context of healthcare, but rather provide complementary resources in the ecosystem. Therefore, under the vision of integrating regional healthcare, it is inevitable that healthcare organizations will share complementary resources. To do so, they will need to build and maintain fundamental relationships. Dyer and Kale (2007) refer to the capability of accommodating resources belonging to other organizations as "relational capabilities." According to Dyer & Kale, there are four factors enabling relational rent: (1) relationship-specific assets; (2) complementarity capabilities; (3) knowledge-sharing routines; and (4) effective governance. These factors are important in providing regional patients with an integrated service process. The DC required by pharmacies should include relational capabilities to dynamically deal with these factors.

A pharmacy that is recognized as a regional healthcare provider always seeks access to external resources to complement its own limited resources. Thus the pharmacy should build relationships with participants (e.g., hospitals, clinics, other pharmacies, care facilities, government, local residents, etc.) in regional healthcare in order to make external resources available. These relationships would serve as the basis for developing integrated community care. Therefore, the following hypotheses are derived.

H2   The DC of a pharmacy exert a positive effect on a regional relationship.
H3   The regional relationship of a pharmacy exerts a positive effect on the capabilities of integrated community care.

Pharmacies typically do not have the ICT resources necessary to share information with external institutions. As mentioned above, because pharmacies specializing in dispensing have management systems operating on closed networks, they have not been required to operate effective ICT systems. Here, the important issue seems to be the capability to mobilize and develop ICT resources rather than physical ICT resources (Bharadwaj 2000; Kodama 2008, 2013). That is, pharmacies lack the personal and organizational capabilities to build, operate, and maintain such systems and to achieve targeted effects by integrating ICT resources with the process. Because ICT resources rapidly become obsolete and have environment-dependent characteristics, ICT capabilities need to be dynamic and updated continuously. This includes updating ICT resources, and building and operating an information platform for information sharing so that the capabilities play a role in the integrated community care.

Therefore, the following hypothesis are derived.

H4   The DC of a pharmacy exert a positive effect on the capabilities of the information-sharing network.
H5   The capabilities of an information-sharing network of a pharmacy exert a positive effect on the capabilities of integrated community care.

Additionally, a high-level regional relationship should enable participants in regional healthcare to build the information platform.

Therefore, the following hypothesis is derived.

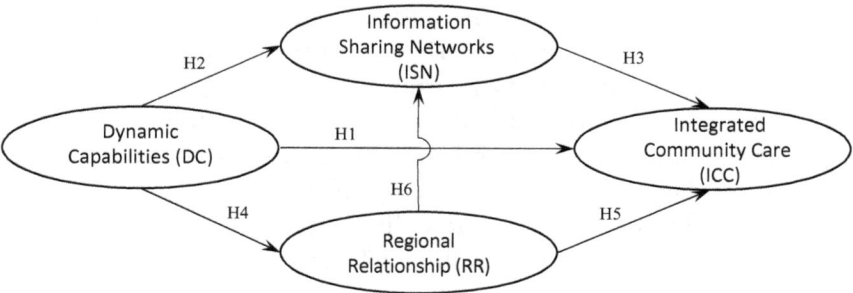

Fig. 8.1 Conceptual model

H6   The regional relationships of a pharmacy exert a positive effect on the capabilities of the information-sharing network.

Figure 8.1 shows the relationship between the hypotheses.

8.5 Verification of the Hypotheses

In order to verify the models, structural equation modeling is used, with relevant data collected via a questionnaire survey of pharmacists.

8.5.1 The Measures and the Questionnaire

The measures of DC were developed using the method of Pavlou and El Sawy (2011). Other measures for the construct are newly developed, owing to the lack of such measures in related studies, based on case studies and a report published by the MHLW (2015). The measure for the capabilities of the information-sharing network was developed using parameters related to the level of the sharing of patient information, which is considered necessary in integrated community care. The measure for regional relationship was developed using parameters in which the relationship can be visualized (e.g., participation in a healthcare event within a region). To evaluate the integrated community care, the measure for the functionality of a pharmacy was developed based on existing cases or policies. The measures all use seven scores, corresponding to the evaluated levels. These constructs might be influenced by the organizational scale of a pharmacy or its participation in a group of pharmacies. As control variables, I use a dummy variable representing participation in a group and the average number of prescriptions handled per day to indicate the scale of a pharmacy.

The data were obtained from an online questionnaire of pharmacists, conducted in February 2017, resulting in 554 samples. The profiles of the pharmacies of the respondents are shown in Table 8.1.

Table 8.1 Profile of respondents

Types of pharmacy to which the respondents belong	%
Insurance pharmacy, focusing on dispensing	80.5
Insurance pharmacy where both OTC and dispensing are handled	19.0
Other	0.5
Total	100.0
Location of pharmacy to which the respondents belong	%
Monzen pharmacy	76.3
Inside hospitals or clinics	6.7
Inside commercial facility	6.7
Other	10.3
Total	100.0
The maximum rate of dependence on prescription from one medical institution	%
100%	4.3
80–99%	50.9
60–79%	17.9
40–59%	12.3
20–39%	9.0
0–19%	0.4
Unknown	5.2
Total	100.0
The number of pharmacists who work for the pharmacy	%
1	13.0
2	27.1
3	22.7
4	15.0
5–9	18.4
10 or more	3.8
Total	100.0

Two kinds of verification were performed to check for possible bias. First, non-respondent bias was checked. The samples were categorized in the order of response into a "respondent group of the former period" (n = 277) and a "respondent group of the latter period" (n = 277). The two groups were then compared in terms of the types of pharmacy in which the respondents work and the distribution of the number of prescriptions. The results showed no significant difference. Thus no problems of bias were considered.

Then the common method bias was checked using Harman's one-factor test (Podsakoff and Organ 1986). An exploratory factor analysis was performed using the principal factor method, where the criterion for factor extraction is an eigenvalue > 1.00, with all questionnaire items included. As a result, three factors were extracted, with the contribution of the principal factor being lower than 50% (46.9%). Therefore, no problems with bias were demonstrated.

8.5.2 The Verification Results

Based on the approach of Anderson and Gerbing (1988), reliability and validity were verified. The analytical results are shown in Table 8.2. A confirmatory factor analysis was performed to analyze reliability, with the following results: χ^2 (degrees of freedom (df) = 49) = 75.398; $p < 0.001$; χ^2/df = 1.539, goodness of fit (GFI) = 0.977, adjusted goodness of fit index (AGFI) = 0.964, incremental fit index (IFI) = 0.994, Tucker-Lewis index (TLI) = 0.992, comparative fit index (CFI) = 0.994, and root mean square error of approximation (RMSEA) = 0.031, showing valid fitness. This confirms the one-dimensional nature of the measures.

All factor loadings for convergent validity are required to be over 0.5, based on the results of the confirmatory factor analysis conducted using the maximum likelihood method (Bagozzi and Yi 1988). This requirement is satisfied in this study. In addition, Cronbach's alpha needs to be 0.7 or more (Nunnally 1978), the composite reliability (CR) should be 0.6 or more, and the average variance extracted (AVE) should be 0.5 or more (Bagozzi and Yi 1988; Fornell and Larcker 1981). The results show that the criteria for all the constructs are satisfied, and thus there are no problems with the convergent validity.

Table 8.2 Measurement model and descriptive statistics

Constructs and items	Means	Std. dev.	Std. loadings	Cronbach's alpha	AVE	CR
Dynamic Capabilities (DC) To what degree was the following effective in reconsidering the operation of pharmacy to respond to the environment:				0.781	0.641	0.696
The resources in the pharmacy are reorganized and new services to patients are created	4.148	1.128	0.810			
The resources in the pharmacy are often replaced to respond to requests from patients	4.096	1.163	0.791			
Information-Sharing Networks (ISN) Whether the following are shared with local medical institutions and utilized through the network:				0.953	0.875	0.949
Sharing dispensing information	1.675	1.548	0.900			

(continued)

Table 8.2 (continued)

Constructs and items	Means	Std. dev.	Std. loadings	Cronbach's alpha	AVE	CR
Sharing disease name information	1.558	1.426	0.950			
Sharing laboratory test information	1.578	1.414	0.956			
Regional Relationship (RR)				0.883	0.672	0.846
To what degree are the following characteristics applicable:						
Face-to-face relationships have been built with nearby medical and caregiving institutions	3.848	1.794	0.750			
Proactive participation in business activities for local residents, conducted by administrative institutions or medical associations	3.455	1.709	0.920			
Proactive participation in local activities relating to healthcare, based on requests from administrative institutions or schools	3.442	1.764	0.887			

(continued)

Table 8.2 (continued)

Constructs and items	Means	Std. dev.	Std. loadings	Cronbach's alpha	AVE	CR
Proactive participation in pharmacy operation response during holidays or at night, with the co-operation of administrative institutions or the pharmacist association	3.625	1.956	0.701			
Integrated Community Care (ICC)				0.755	0.511	0.616
Whether you are superior to other pharmacies in terms of the following aspects:						
Promoting appointment of kakaritsuke pharmacist	3.448	1.566	0.752			
Co-operating with patients' kakaritsuke doctors	3.962	1.354	0.721			
Pharmaceutical management and instruction by visiting patients' homes	3.357	1.622	0.670			
Participation in pharmacy group (dummy variable)	0.769	0.422				
Number of prescriptions handled per day	1826.966	4835.708				

Table 8.3 AVE and correlation matrix

Constructs	AVE	1	2	3	4
1. DC	0.641	0.801			
2. ISN	0.875	0.398	0.936		
3. RR	0.672	0.541	0.508	0.820	
4. ICC	0.511	0.704	0.454	0.703	0.715

Note: The diagonal values represent the square root of the AVE

Table 8.4 Results of hypothesis tests

Hypothesis	Path			Path co-efficients	t-value	Outcome
H1	DC	→	ICC	0.564	7.611***	Supported
H2	DC	→	ISN	0.232	2.902***	Supported
H3	ISN	→	ICC	0.034	0.881	Rejected
H4	DC	→	RR	0.757	9.548***	Supported
H5	RR	→	ICC	0.379	7.824***	Supported
H6	RR	→	ISN	0.370	7.119***	Supported

Note: ***$p < 1\%$, **$p < 5\%$, *$p < 10\%$

Two kinds of tests were performed for the discriminant validity. First, the absolute values of the correlation co-efficients of the constructs do not exceed the square root of the AVE (see Table 8.3). Second, the χ^2 values of the model in which the correlation co-efficients of each construct are fixed as one are compared with those of the model in which the co-efficients are free estimations (Hair et al. 2010). The results show significant differences in all the models (χ^2 of models are between 8.001 and 344.632), indicating that there are no problems with discriminant validity.

Structural equation modeling using the maximum likelihood method is used to infer the hypothetical model. The fitness indices of the model are as follows: χ^2 (df = 64) = 84.878; $p < 0.004$; $\chi^2/df = 1.326$, GFI = 0.978, AGFI = 0.965, IFI = 0.995, TLI = 0.993, CFI = 0.995, RMSEA = 0.024. The general goodness of fit criteria are as follows: GFI and AGFI of 0.9 or more, TLI or CFI of 0.95 or more, CFI of less than 0.97, RMSEA of less than 0.7 (Hair et al. 2010), and IFI of 0.90 or more (Bagozzi and Yi 1988). Thus the results show there are no problems present in the goodness of fit.

The inference results related to the path co-efficients of the structural equation are shown in Table 8.4. The path co-efficients are standardized. The results show that the five hypotheses other than H3 are supported.

Table 8.5 Total effects on ICC

	DP	RR	ISN
Direct effects	0.441	0.433	0.039
Indirect effects	0.238	0.014	0.000
Total effects	0.679	0.447	0.039

Note: All values are standardized

Table 8.6 Paths of controlled variables

Path			Path co-efficients	t-value
Participation in pharmacy group	⇒	DP	0.062	1.305
Participation in pharmacy group	⇒	ISN	0.117	3.061***
Participation in pharmacy group	⇒	RR	−0.021	−0.527
Participation in pharmacy group	⇒	RCC	0.085	2.290**
Number of prescriptions handled per day	⇒	DP	0.166	3.453***
Number of prescriptions handled per day	⇒	ISN	0.081	2.078**
Number of prescriptions handled per day	⇒	RR	0.048	1.170
Number of prescriptions handled per day	⇒	RCC	0.044	1.172

***$p < 1\%$, **$p < 5\%$, *$p < 10\%$

Table 8.5 shows the effect each construct has on integrated care capability. As shown, the contribution of DC is the largest of the constructs. Most of the indirect effects are exerted through the regional relationship (RR), with almost no effect noted through the information-sharing network. Table 8.6 shows the path co-efficients between the control variables and each construct.

8.6 Discussion

This research focuses on DC. A causal modeling analysis is conducted using structural equation modeling to examine the effect of DC on integrated community care. The hypotheses were examined based on the results of a questionnaire survey of pharmacists working for pharmacies. The results show that the five hypotheses H1, H2, H4, H5, and H6 are supported, but that H3 is rejected. Despite one hypothesis being rejected, DC seem to contribute to building the capabilities of integrated community care.

8.6.1 Formation of Dynamic Capabilities

The examined models suggest that DC potentially contribute to improving the capabilities of integrated community care, both directly and indirectly. Thus the significance of the existence of DC is demonstrated in terms of a pharmacy management strategy. The next issue is how DC can be promoted within a pharmacy.

Significant positive correlations are shown between DC and the number of prescriptions handled and the participation in a pharmacy group (see Table 8.6). This result suggests that the scale of an organization and the participation in a pharmacy group have an effect on building DC.

Most pharmacies in Japan are small, with most personnel playing a role in the operation of the business, and often with no personnel specialized in management. Thus three steps appear to be required for the effective application of DC: sensing, seizing, and reconfiguring (Teece 2009). In particular, there appear to be some challenges of sensing threats and opportunities for which top management needs to be responsible, largely because this kind of recognition needs to happen from local and distant perspectives (Nelson and Winter 1982). The latter perspective is difficult to cultivate in personnel engaged in the daily operation of the pharmacy. Even if such personnel exist, they often lack the time to put this into action. Given that the social requirements of pharmacies and their management environment have changed significantly, pharmacies need personnel who focus on external contacts and update the methods used to scan or interpret information, and thus have the ability to sense such changes. However, it is difficult for small pharmacies to employ personnel of this type.

As an additional explanation of the above-stated statistical significance, increasing the scale of an organization would be an effective way for a pharmacy to secure personnel who can develop their DC. A large-scale organization would have higher productivity owing to the advantage of scale, and thus can employ personnel specialized in management. As another option, having pharmacies group together or building a chain of pharmacies would enable the headquarters to exercise the management function. In Japan, pharmacy chains have already begun to be created. If these chains successfully adapt to the regions, they might become leading providers of regional healthcare.

From the perspective of small-scale pharmacies, what options are there for them to adapt to the environment by exercising DC? First, there would be an option to participate in a group of pharmacies. In this way, time could be freed up to reallocate to management. Japanese regulations specify that pharmacies have one pharmacist per 40 prescriptions they handle. The Japanese retail pharmacy industry has adhered to these regulations, leading to discounting improvements in labor productivity. Therefore, automating dispensing or clerical functions would allow room for an improvement in labor productivity. This, in turn, could free resources, enabling management to develop and exercise DC.

8.6.2 Dynamic Capabilities and Building Relationships

DC can potentially contribute to improving the capabilities of integrated community care through the building of relationships (H2 and H3). Because integrated community care functions within a region, a good relationship between healthcare providers and care givers is an essential condition. The results indicate that DC are involved in such a relationship. Therefore, a detailed discussion is necessary on how this relationship is involved in the formation of DC.

It may be effective to apply the concept of collaborative DC (Chap. 1) to such a discussion. This concept has three factors: (1) establishment of trust relationships through strategic collaboration with ecosystem partners; (2) asset co-specialization; and (3) capabilities synthesis. The trust relationship described in (1) can be put in place where collaboration frameworks have already been embedded in local communities. However, because the issues to be resolved are specific to regions, the integration of resources between organizations, referred to in (2) and (3), will require a learning process characterized by trial and error. According to Kolb (1984), the experiential learning cycle model includes concrete experience, reflective observation, abstract conceptualization, and active experimentation. In other words, it is a process in which shared experience is reflected co-operatively to generate awareness, a group of it is aligned coherently to develop independent hypothesis, and it is demonstrated with the practice. As a result of this learning, the cospecializing of resources and appropriate integration can be attempted. The parties participating in the integrated community care will need to review the activity, plan or redesign the process, and build a community in which to practice the experienced learning process. Thus it is desirable that pharmacists are actively involved in these learning opportunities.

8.6.3 Dynamic Capabilities and ICT

Although the correlation between DC and the information-sharing network was demonstrated (H4), the potential of the correlation to contribute to integrated community care (H5), which is the purpose of the demonstration, could not be demonstrated. Therefore, one of the indirect effects of DC cannot be fully realized. The reason for this seems to be the low level of involvement in the information-sharing network, as shown in Table 8.2. The two control variables (the number of prescriptions handled and participation of the pharmacy group) were significantly positively correlated with the information-sharing network (Table 8.6). This suggests that smaller organizations have little involvement in the information-sharing network.

As pointed out earlier, there are problems of environment insufficiency, such as the standardization of information, identification of patients, and security. In terms of standardization of information, the delayed diffusion of an electronic health record is a serious problem. According to the survey of medical institutions conducted by the MHLW, the diffusion rate of electronic health record systems in hospitals is only about 34%. However, among the large hospitals (400 or more beds) the rate is 78%, showing a steady diffusion of the system. The issue of patient identification is likely to be resolved owing to the introduction of the "My Number" system in 2015, which numbered all individuals in Japan who have a residence certificate. The biggest challenge is security. Because the risks associated with the information system have been diversified and have increased significantly, it would be technically difficult to build an information platform that can meet the challenges of system availability and the protection of personal information. Smaller pharmacies would have to make a substantial effort to participate in building such a platform. With the fund utilizing consumption tax as a financial resource, the government is improving the environment in which the network exists and is supporting private healthcare providers responsible for building the network. However, as indicated in the results of the questionnaire (Table 8.2), little progress has been made.

Medical information is required to ensure the confidentiality, credibility, and availability of information. Building a network for this kind of information is evidently associated with a high-cost investment. Therefore, in Japan, as pointed out by Eguchi (2016), building and operating an information platform that serves as a regional healthcare infrastructure should be advanced at the initiative of the government, as has happened in the United States and Europe, rather than delegating the duties to private companies. In Canada, government-funded organizations play a central role in building the electronic health record, with the diffusion rate increasing rapidly as a result. Therefore, Japan could learn from the experience of Canada.

Even if an information platform is created by the government, pharmacies must not remain non-responsive. As stated above, pharmacies need human and organizational resource capabilities in order to operate ICT. Therefore, these abilities need to be developed.

References

Anderson, J. C., & Gerbing, D. W. (1988). Structural Equation Modeling in Practice: A Review and Recommended Two-Step Approach. *Psychological Bulletin, 103*(3), 411.

Bagozzi, R. P., & Yi, Y. (1988). On the Evaluation of Structural Equation Models. *Journal of the Academy of Marketing Science, 16*(1), 74–94.

Bharadwaj, A. S. (2000). A Resource-Based Perspective on Information Technology Capability and Firm Performance: An Empirical Investigation. *MIS Quarterly, 24*, 169–196.

Central Intelligence Agency. (2017). *The World Fact Book*. Retrieved November 6, 2017, from https://www.cia.gov/library/publications/the-world-factbook/fields/2177.html

Dyer, J., & Kale, P. (2007). Relational Capabilities: Drivers and Implications. In C. E. Helfat, S. Finkelstein, W. Mitchell, M. Peteraf, H. Singh, D. Teece, & S. G. Winter (Eds.), *Dynamic Capabilities: Understanding Strategic Change in Organizations* (pp. 65–79). Blackwell: Wiley-Blackwell.

Eguchi, M. (2016). *From Separation to Cooperation in Pharmacies and Clinics: Present Status and Issues of Cooperation of Pharmacies and Clinics from a View on Institutional Analysis of Separation of Dispensing and Prescribing* (Doctor Thesis of Graduate School of Economics, Shiga University) (Japanese).

Fornell, C., & Larcker, D. F. (1981). Structural Equation Models with Unobservable Variables and Measurement Error: Algebra and Statistics. *Journal of Marketing Research, 18*, 382–388.

Hair, J. F., Black, W. C., Babin, B. J., & Anderson, R. E. (2010). *Multivariate Data Analysis* (7th ed.). Upper Saddle River: Prentice Hall.

Kodama, M. (2008). *New Knowledge Creation Through ICT Dynamic Capability Creating Knowledge Communities Using Broadband*. Charlotte: Information Age Publishing.

Kodama, M. (2013). *Competing Through ICT Capability*. London: Palgrave Macmillan.

Kolb, D. A. (1984). *Experiential Learning*. Englewood Cliffs: Prentice Hall.

Ministry of Health, Labour, and Welfare [MHLW]. (2015). *Pharmacy Vision for Patients: From monzen to kakaritsuke and Region* (Japanese). Retrieved November 6, 2017, from http://www.mhlw.go.jp/file/04-Houdouhappyou-11121000-Iyakushokuhinkyoku-Soumuka/vision_1.pdf

Nelson, R. R., & Winter, S. G. (1982). *An Evolutionary Theory of Economic Change*. Cambridge: Harvard Business School Press.

Nunnally, J. C. (1978). *Psychometric Theory*. New York: McGraw-Hill.

Pavlou, P. A., & El Sawy, O. A. (2011). Understanding the Elusive Black Box of Dynamic Capabilities. *Decision Sciences, 42*(1), 239–273.

Podsakoff, P. M., & Organ, D. W. (1986). Self-Reports in Organizational Research: Problems and Prospects. *Journal of Management, 12*(4), 531–544.

Teece, D. J. (2009). *Dynamic Capabilities and Strategic Management: Organizing for Innovation and Growth*. Oxford: Oxford University Press on Demand.

World Health Organization. (1994). *The Role of the Pharmacist in the Health Care System*. Retrieved November 6, 2017, from http://apps.who.int/medicinedocs/en/d/Jwhozip32e/4.html

9

Building Healthcare Ecosystems Through Strategic Collaboration Across Different Industries

Mitsuru Kodama

9.1 The Dynamic Capabilities and Business Models of Japanese General Trading Companies

Japanese general trading companies have adapted to environmental changes by transforming their business models. The traditional business model of a trading company was to act as an intermediary between trading partners to acquire commissions and brokerage fees, and to act as a low-risk, low-return agency (trader) investing to further complement revenues. However with changing business environments, the trading business further evolved so that in the overall view of the upstream and downstream in the value chains of various types of businesses and industries, these companies participate in a supervising role in sections required to meet customer needs aiming for enhanced competitiveness and business value of traders and investors, which entailed them making efforts to

---

M. Kodama (✉)
Nihon University, College of Commerce, Tokyo, Japan
e-mail: kodama.mitsuru@nihon-u.ac.jp

shift to business models to acquire profits in various areas of the value chain. For example, the cases of the business model transformation of the healthcare services of Mitsubishi (see Box 9.1), or the expansion of healthcare and medical services of Mitsui & Co. Ltd. (Mitsui hereinafter) in Asia (see Box 9.2) are typical cases of this.

In this way, the traditional business models of trading companies entailed the further advancement of the trading business model as an agency for simple products, to participation in supervising roles in sections required to meet customer needs, from upstream to downstream, in the value chains of various types of businesses and industries in order to generate profits in various areas of the value chain, which has become an important pursuit of general trading companies.

In general trading companies, the basic concept behind the building of value chains is the existence of diverse networks around the world. The existence of human resources and networks of personnel that can sense, converge, integrate, and use a wide range of knowledge on a global scale is the wellspring of value chain building. In other words, this entails demonstrating dynamic capabilities (DC) as the processes of sensing high quality assets distributed all over the world, and seizing and transforming to dynamically formulate and properly implement suitable configuration and reconfiguration of them.

As expertise required in a general trading company, Mitsubishi expresses itself as a matrix of three axes, the axis of products and industries, the axis of regions and the axis of functions, whereas Mitsui expresses itself as place x people x goods x services x information to raise the quality and quantity of business. Hence, business creators (or value chain creators) as entrepreneurial human resources require the capabilities to bring together and integrate products, regions, and functions as place x people x goods x services x information on a global scale.

The trading company business models typified by Mitsubishi and Mitsui entail trading support, financial services, and strategic investment across entire value chains from resource development, raw materials trading and manufacturer of final products through to wholesale and retail. Hence the most important issue is to create profits by building win–win relationships with partners and by optimizing entire value chains. To achieve this, based on the company's own professional knowledge and know-how (products and industries x regions x functions or place x people x goods x services x information), these companies identify bottlenecks and dams in business processes through hypothesis testing of optimal target value chains, select the best partners both in Japan and around the world to solve these bottlenecks and dams, and provide business solutions through collaboration with the partners. Thus, as a total co-ordinator of a business model, the greatest strategic objective of a general trading company is to raise the level of both customer and partner satisfaction (Fig. 9.1).

For general trading companies to design entire value chains, the existence of networks of various partners, customers, and regions covering a wide range is important. These are "alliance networks" with partners both in Japan and around the world (manufacturers, service industries, funds, large corporations, ventures, governments and governing bodies, and non-profit organizations, etc.), and are global business networks with various bases (general trading company overseas bases, group companies, and related companies), and investment destinations around the world. These trading companies provide joint venture business with a wide range of partners in Japan and around the world; hence how business networks

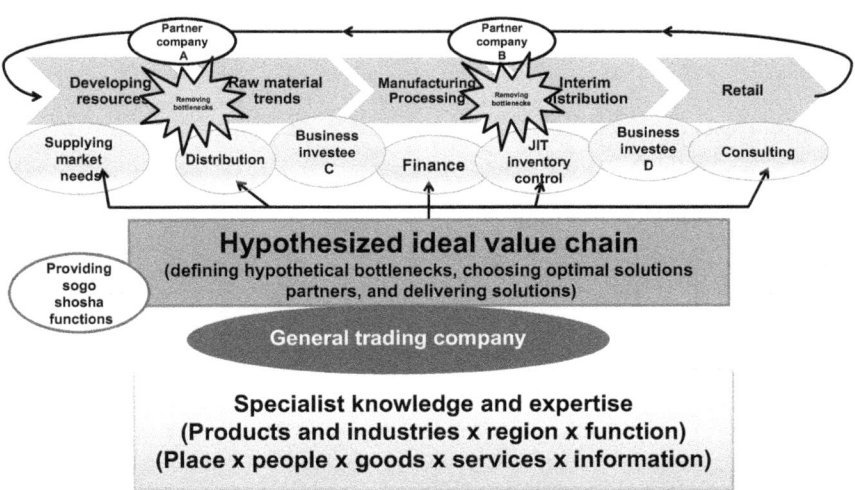

Fig. 9.1 General trading company business model. (Source: Mitsubishi and Mitsui publicly released materials)

are built with which partners affects business performance. In other words, the asset orchestration of these trading companies, a DC, is also the capability of building these networks.

In this way, the business models of general trading companies are clearly different to those of other types of business. Mitsubishi, a general trading company, is providing information on the characteristics of its business systems, and, for example, describes the differences between itself and consulting firms and investment funds as follows (see Fig. 9.2). Mitsubishi puts the focus on thinking and action to grasp markets and new needs of latent technologies. Hence, focusing on its business value chain, Mitsubishi engages in various activities to respond to customer needs, and depending on the situation the company dispatches experts in the relevant technical fields, financial experts and legal experts, has equity and commits itself to actual business over the long term while taking risks. In this regard, the business models of general trading companies typified by Mitsubishi are clearly different from the business models of consulting firms aiming for no risk, short-term profits by selling off

General trading companies acquire business value through completion bonuses for consulting and risk-taking

Fig. 9.2 Mitsubishi corporation's business model: comparison with other business structures. (Source: Mitsubishi Corp.'s publicly released materials)

knowledge and know-how to meet specific customer needs, or the business models of investment funds looking to garner returns in the short to medium term by uncovering investment projects without getting involved in specific details of business models.

Mitsubishi has been demonstrating investment fund capabilities since the late 1980s, and consulting capabilities in house or through consulting subsidiaries. In recent years, there has been a trend observed towards investment banks and consultancy companies becoming general trading companies. Examples include an investment banking firm moving from derivatives trading to involvement in the aviation fuel procurement business, or consulting companies and investment funds linking up and fusing. In this way, the business model of the trading company Mitsubishi can be said to entail business processes of uncovering customer needs, leveraging the company's suite of functions (finance, investment, marketing, distribution, information technology [IT], etc.) and acquiring profits through long-term commitment to business while taking on risk.

Box 9.1 Mitsubishi's Business Transformation and Its Healthcare Business

With the ongoing rapid aging and depopulation in Japan, the soaring costs of healthcare and nursing have become an urgent national issue. Mitsubishi offers total solutions from management support to healthcare institutions through to related services, in the fields of healthcare, nursing, and preventive health, and has a mission to contribute to improving the quality of healthcare and nursing, and controlling rising costs.

As discussed later, after Mitsubishi began fully fledged initiatives in healthcare-related fields in the 1970s, the company has been actively developing projects such as solutions businesses oriented towards Japanese medical institutions, import and export of medical equipment, nursing and care-related businesses, and initiatives in overseas markets including those of North America and China.

As a specific initiative, Mitsubishi began its healthcare-related businesses with the establishment of MC Medical in 1989 as a medical equipment import agency. Grasping the needs of the healthcare workplace in Japan early on, Mitsubishi quickly introduced cutting-edge technologies, products and services from around the world into Japan. After that in 1995, responding to the needs of hospital and medical providers, the company established Japan Hospital Service Co., a company comprehensively

(continued)

Box 9.1 (continued)

involved in pharmaceuticals and medical materials procurement for hospitals and management of goods. Thus the company has been proposing its Just In Time & Stockless (JITS) system, a system developed with cutting-edge IT, multi-dimensional database and distribution know-how fostered through its operations as a trading company, as a method of improving hospital management.

After that, in 2001, Aprecia was established as a hospital management consulting company providing medical equipment maintenance, procurement support and contract support. The aim of establishing this company was to import, export and sell healthcare tools, equipment and healthcare expendables in the dramatically changing healthcare environment of Japan, and also to expand business by providing optimized solutions for customer medical institutions to support managerial perspectives on expanding revenues and reducing costs, transparency and the business health of hospitals, and so on.

In 2000, Mitsubishi established Lifetime Partners Co as a comprehensive business consulting and financial support company engaged in preventive healthcare, acute and chronic disease care, nursing facilities and home nursing, and providing assistance with creation of systems to provide total healthcare to medical institutions and nursing care companies. In 2007, Mitsubishi established Healthcare Management Partners Co., a company involved in discretionary fund operation for investment in assets related to healthcare in the medical and nursing fields, and management of fund-invested assets. In this way, Mitsubishi built new value chains and business models by extending its business functions across everything from medical equipment sales agency business to healthcare services, business support services, and healthcare funding businesses.

Mitsubishi has been demonstrating investment fund capabilities since the late 1980s, and consulting capabilities using in-house and consulting subsidiaries. In this way, its business model entails business processes that uncover customer needs, make use of the company's various functions (finance, investment, marketing, distribution, IT, consulting, etc.) and acquire profits through long-term commitment to business while taking on risk.

As well as this, in April 2010 the aforementioned Japan Hospital Service (healthcare materials-related business, established 1995), Aprecia (healthcare equipment and systems procurement support, healthcare equipment maintenance, established 2001) and MC Medical (medical equipment imports and sales, established 1989) were merged to form MC Healthcare. With this merger, the functions scattered throughout the three companies were brought together, and in addition to creating systems to comprehensively respond to the advanced and diverse needs of medical institutions,

(continued)

Box 9.1 (continued)

the company is now one of the largest in Japan providing solutions to medical institutions, with business growing steadily. Currently, MC Healthcare is mainly involved in businesses related to (1) medical materials, (2) medical equipment, (3) joint purchasing, and (4) advanced medical equipment and private brand (PB) products (see Fig. 9.3).

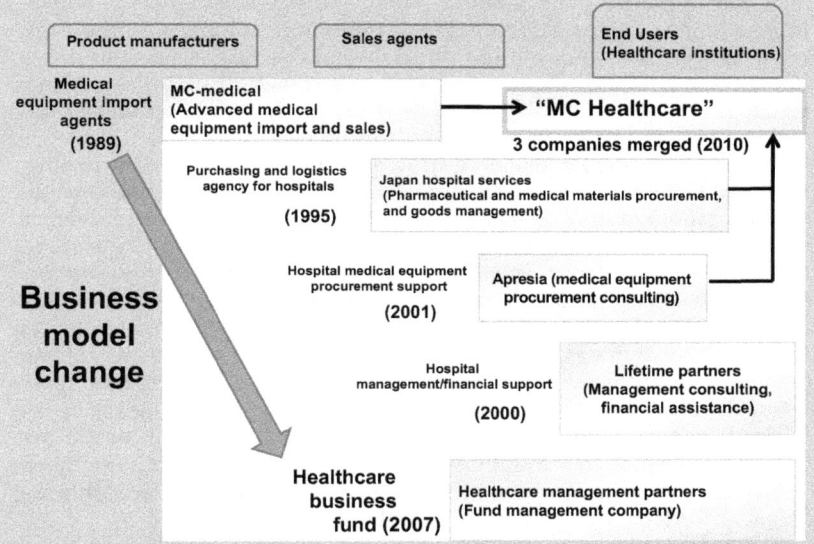

Fig. 9.3 The transforming business model of Mitsubishi—the healthcare business case

Box 9.2 Mitsui Healthcare and Medical Businesses

Currently, medical needs in various countries and regions around the world are increasing and diversifying rapidly. Mitsui is currently taking initiatives to provide solutions by building a healthcare ecosystem that organically ties together core hospital businesses with businesses on the periphery of healthcare. According to the population estimates announced by the

(continued)

Box 9.2 (continued)

United Nations in 2011, there were 200 million people over 60 years of age in 1950, which rose to 800 million by 2012 and is expected to rise sharply to 1 billion by 2020 and 2 billion by 2050. This aging, coupled with longer lifespans, is going to greatly increase the medical expense load.

Notably in Asia, where populations are increasing and living standards are rising with economic development, countries are facing serious problems with rapid and high levels of aging, and sharp increases in lifestyle-related illnesses that require long-term treatment. Moreover, as there are many areas of Asia that did not originally have sufficient hospitals, there are not enough hospitals to provide treatment that satisfies international standards, and healthcare supply faces no small number of problems both in terms of quantity and quality.

With the remarkable economic growth of Asia in recent years, populations are increasing and aging in developing countries. Lifestyle changes are also causing a shift away from patients with acute diseases to patients with chronic diseases that require ongoing medical treatment. There is also an emerging lack of medical institutions that can respond to this situation. In addition, owing to various reasons such as the advanced technology and more attractive healthcare costs in Asia, and the pinch of medical expenses in developed countries, there are increasing numbers of patients coming from other countries to healthcare institutions in Asia to receive treatment: the so-called "medical tourism market" is beginning to show signs of development. Against the backdrop of these situations, the current healthcare industries in major countries in Asia are said to be worth about 80 trillion yen, and are expected to grow by 15–20% year on year. Thus the healthcare business in Asia is a giant market about to awaken.

Anticipating these trends, Mitsui has embarked on a new field called "hospital network business" in Asia. In 2008, the company established a medical and healthcare division by bringing together businesses and divisions related to healthcare and pharmaceuticals. Mitsui demonstrated the "sensing" function of DC to uncover a business chance to eliminate the demand and supply gap in medical infrastructure in Asia by engaging in a range of trial and error while investigating and analyzing world healthcare environments. Mitsui aimed to contribute to solving various healthcare issues by building its own healthcare ecosystem by building hospitals in areas with insufficient healthcare facilities, taking initiatives with peripheral businesses such as specialist clinic facilities centered on the hospitals, healthcare and pharmaceutical information services, healthcare personnel introduction services, facility management, and hospital catering businesses, and orchestrating these core assets.

As a specific initiative, in the early 2000s the company forged relationships with Asia's largest private hospital group IHH through pharmaceutical

(continued)

> **Box 9.2 (continued)**
>
> manufacture and clinical trials support businesses. Then in May 2011 Mitsui acquired 30% (18.1% as of September 2016) of IHH stocks from Khazanah Nasional Berhad, the Malaysian government investment fund company, an IHH stockholder. IHH has under its umbrella the largest Singapore hospital group, Parkway Holdings, and Malaysia's second-largest hospital group Pantai Holdings. IHH has also invested in India's second largest hospital group, Apollo Hospital. Through its partnering with IHH, Mitsui is able to participate in healthcare-related businesses throughout Asia.
>
> These companies have had a previous relationship. Originally, Mitsui and IHH's subsidiary Parkway were involved in pharmaceutical research and development, and Mitsui engaged in a joint venture with pharmaceutical manufacturer for drug research and development business, which also involved partnering with Parkway; so their human relationships and relationships of trust had already been built through business. As discussed in Chap. 2, this factor drives boundaries synchronization between the partners. This partnership had strong mutual benefits, and IHH wanted to move into China, where the healthcare business is predicted to expand. However, essential networks and know-how about entering the Chinese market were lacking. Nevertheless, Mitsui, who wanted to reinforce the medical and healthcare services area, searched for a healthcare-related company to partner with. This means that these needs drove the co-specialization of assets, or strengths, of both companies.
>
> Moreover, Mitsui's entry into the healthcare field was highly significant for its focus on non-resource sectors and strengthening of downstream businesses. Currently, although a high proportion of Mitsui's revenues come from the resources sector, it will require a good balance of a variety of fields to increase revenues so that it can develop sustainably and stably in the future.
>
> At that time, Mitsui was the only Japanese general trading company that had interests in overseas hospital businesses, but as it had only been involved in the trading of pharmaceuticals and so forth, there were aspects in which it was lagging behind in the healthcare field, and the company was not able to take full advantage of its strengths. This was as a result of starting late and thus not being able to do the same as other companies, Mitsui arrived at its response with hospital infrastructure. Because the company started relatively late, it did not cower in the background but took up a major challenge. With this attitude, Mitsui tied up with the largest hospital group in Asia, IHH, and boldly extended itself into the business of developing hospital infrastructure in foreign countries. In this way, Mitsui exhibited the entrepreneurial spirit to demonstrate DC in its business activities.
>
> Thus, with its participation in IHH management, Mitsui raised its profile to that of a major player in the healthcare business, and in October 2015 it made participatory investments in MIMS Group, a major healthcare infor-

(continued)

Box 9.2 (continued)

mation service. In addition, after launching its healthcare service business division by restructuring its healthcare-related businesses, pharmaceutical businesses, outsourcing service businesses and personnel training services in April 2016, Mitsui bought 20% of the stock of DaVita Care, a subsidiary of American major dialysis clinic business DaVita Healthcare Partners Inc. in August of the same year, and entered into the Asian dialysis business.

Thus, with its entry in 2011, the scale of IHH was 3500 beds in 16 hospitals, but by initial public offering and acquisitions, this rose to about 10,000 beds in 52 hospitals by the end of September 2016. Having become the world's second largest private hospital company in terms of market capitalization (as of June 30, 2016), IHH has begun to accept high net worth patients seeking advanced treatments, and at the same time contributes to the development of national healthcare systems by sharing roles with public hospitals, and thus is contributing to the development of Asia's medical infrastructure.

Moreover, in July 2016, Mitsui invested in Columbia Asia Group, Asia's largest middle-income group hospital. Columbia Asia Group operates 27 hospitals and two clinics and boasts around 2300 beds in Malaysia, India, Indonesia, Vietnam and Kenya. With its healthcare ecosystem centered on the two hospital groups of IHH and Columbia Asia, Mitsui has achieved a system through which it can respond to wide-ranging healthcare demands in Asia from the wealthy through to middle income earners.

Currently, with healthcare said to be costing roughly 500 trillion yen annually, modern healthcare faces a range of issues. Mitsui is currently engaging in never-before-seen concepts to solve modern healthcare issues such as eliminating shortages of hospitals, doctors, and pharmaceuticals, strengthening the connections between healthcare institutions and making improvements to business efficiency. By demonstrating DC, Mitsui is involved in management in a range of fields such as hospitals specializing in high-level treatments, specialist clinics handling chronic disease treatment, supplying human resources such as doctors, development, manufacture and sales of pharmaceuticals, and providing services such as hospital catering and medical information. Through these participations, Mitsui is able to acquire and link together information and know-how acquired from various worksites, and bring about more efficient next-generation healthcare mechanisms.

By organically linking individual assets and building a healthcare ecosystem as a sustainable global healthcare network, Mitsui is creating the healthcare of the future in Japan, Asia and the world. A healthcare ecosystem (see Fig. 9.4) is a platform centered on a hospital, and is also a next-generation healthcare infrastructure that contributes to society by raising the quality and efficiency of healthcare by organically bringing together various peripheral businesses such as specialized treatment, pharmaceuticals, information, and services. At the center of a healthcare ecosystem is a hospital providing

(continued)

Box 9.2 (continued)

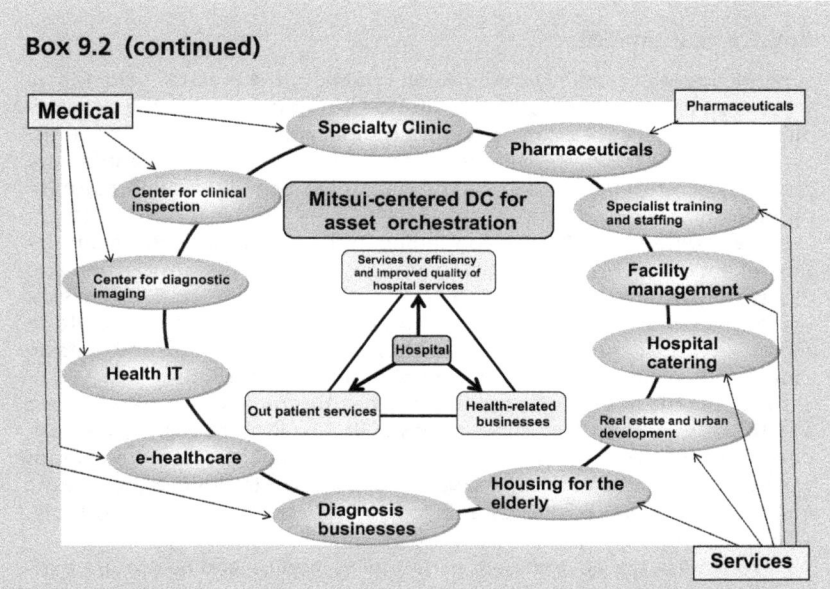

Fig. 9.4 Mitsui healthcare ecosystem—global healthcare network. (Source: Created by the authors from Mitsui publications)

treatment, and around it are various peripheral businesses such as primary care clinics, specialty clinics such as diagnosis centers and dialysis centers, and pharmacies. As well as this, there are also important roles played by a wide variety of companies, such as pharmaceutical companies involved in development and manufacture of drugs and infusions used in those businesses, management-supporting businesses providing various kinds of services such as medical staffing and training and healthcare-related various information provision, and outsourcing businesses involved in facility management and maintenance including hospital cleaning, catering for both patients and staff, and electricals. Through the asset orchestration process, Mitsui seizes initiatives to build new healthcare infrastructure in order to bring about diverse overall value to both patients and medical service providers, and sustainably provide optimized treatment by networking these peripheral businesses with hospitals.

To build this kind of healthcare ecosystem and sustainably maintain it, Mitsui focuses on hospitals and clinic businesses and their peripheral businesses, medical information service businesses and healthcare management

(continued)

Box 9.2 (continued)

support businesses, mainly in the Asian region. In the medical field, Mitsui focuses on entire value chains that include businesses supporting development of pharmaceuticals, manufacturing support businesses, and manufacturing and sales businesses with involvement in development, manufacture and sales of pharmaceuticals, thus providing solutions in the pharmaceutical industry.

In the service field, Mitsui is continuing initiatives in the personnel training field and is involved in global operations that include introduction and dispatch of highly specialized persons and training-related businesses, while also being involved in contract food services (catering) and uniform rental services in hospitals and healthcare facilities both in and outside Japan, and facility management of public and sports facilities.

To handle the business functions of the healthcare field, the medical field and the services field, the company has built a healthcare and service business division as an organizational system. The company therefore extends itself globally by focusing on growth areas that aim to achieve the healthy lifestyles demanded by society and provide services that are comfortable, safe, and secure.

Nevertheless, the environment surrounding medical and healthcare businesses is changing rapidly with the rising number of patent expirations, the emergence of generic pharmaceuticals, the ongoing aging of populations around the world and the changing of disease structures. Moreover, against the backdrop of population increase, improved living standards and changing lifestyles, the structure of consumer markets is changing more and more rapidly all over the world. With this healthcare environment, and while keeping a close eye on these changes, the company's healthcare and services business division is driving the global development of hospitals and periphery businesses, pharmaceutical development, manufacture and sales businesses, and outsourcing businesses, and is taking up the challenge of pioneering adjacent regions and new businesses using IT to meet various needs in Japan and around the world.

Currently, as its main projects, the company has involvement in a variety of businesses such as hospitals, clinics, periphery businesses (in Malaysia, Singapore, and Turkey, etc.), medical information services for health professionals (in Singapore, Malaysia, Hong Kong, Australia, India, and China, etc.), pharmaceutical support for development, manufacturing (CMO) and sales, and pharmaceutical manufacturing and sales (in Japan, the United States, Europe, China, and India), contract food service (catering)-related businesses (in Japan and China), personnel introduction and dispatch services for healthcare professionals and IT technicians, and other training-related businesses (in Japan, the United States, England, and Brazil).

9.2 The Business Domains and Value Chains of General Trading Companies

In describing the business domains and value chains of general trading companies, which have a particular and unique form in Japan, this section gives the example of the general trading company Mitsubishi (other general trading companies such as Mitsui are quite similar). Mitsubishi defines its business on a strategic classification map, segregating it on a matrix of business domains and value chains (see Fig. 9.5). First, "Existing business expansion model" depicts businesses already existing in business domains and value chains, which means these are the main existing businesses that the company makes efforts to expand through the growth of sales forces and channels. Examples of these are the company's traditional main businesses of the past, including natural gas (maintenance and expansion of existing liquid natural gas (LNG) projects, and driving the Tangguh LNG project in Sakhalin), metals (iron and steel, methacryloyloxydecyl dihydrogen phos-

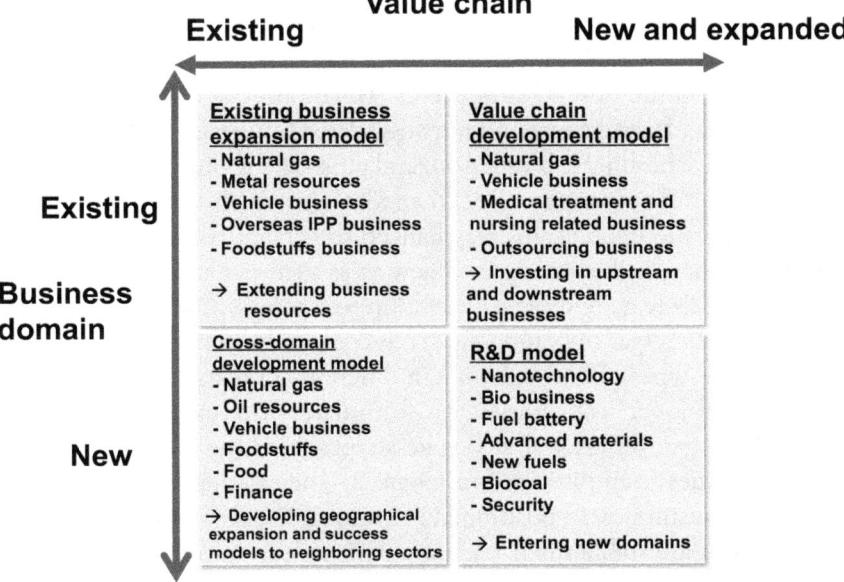

Fig. 9.5 Mitsubishi corporation's business model by category. (Source: Created from Mitsubishi Corp.'s publicly released materials)

phate (MDP), non-ferrous metals), automotives (Mitsubishi Motors Corp. (MMC) existing overseas businesses, Isuzu Thailand business), overseas Independent Power Producer (IPP) businesses (Mexico, America, Asia, Australia), chemical resources (Saudi petrochemicals), and foodstuffs (value chain reinforcement through investment capital existing businesses).

Second is "Cross-domain development model," in which value chains exist as they are and only the business domains are changed. This entails models of geographical expansion of existing businesses or deployment of successful existing business models to adjacent industries. For example, these include natural gas (LNG in Venezuela and others), petroleum (petroleum gas exploration and development industries in West Africa, the Gulf of Mexico in the USA and others), automotive (European sales and financial services, deployment in China, Russia, and Eastern Europe, etc.), foodstuffs (investments in China and Southeast Asia), and comestibles (strengthened full line national distribution system, supply chain management (SCM) system construction in China) and finance (business restructuring support, asset finance, etc.).

Third is "Value chain development model," in which business domains exist as they are and only the value chains are changed, while investments are made in upstream and downstream businesses. These include natural gas (LNG bases on the west coast of the USA), automotive businesses (export base in Thailand), healthcare and nursing-related businesses (expansion into comprehensive healthcare businesses), and outsourcing businesses. Fourth is "Research and development (R&D) model," in which both the business domains and the value chains are changed to generate business models in new areas. These include entry into new areas such as nano-tech, bio-businesses, fuel cells (e.g., hydrogen generation technologies), advanced materials and new fuels (gas to liquids, etc.), bio-core, and security.

These four types of business exist in different contexts, and require different practitioner capabilities to formulate and execute strategies. Figure 9.6 organizes these four business types from the relationship with the Capabilities Map discussed in Chap. 2. The existing business expansion model businesses are positioned in Domain IV, the strategic efficiency domain, and are stable main businesses with clear corporate boundaries and established value chains. They require efficient and sustainable expansion through slow incremental innovation in order to improve and upgrade existing business through ordinary capabilities (OC) in sluggish

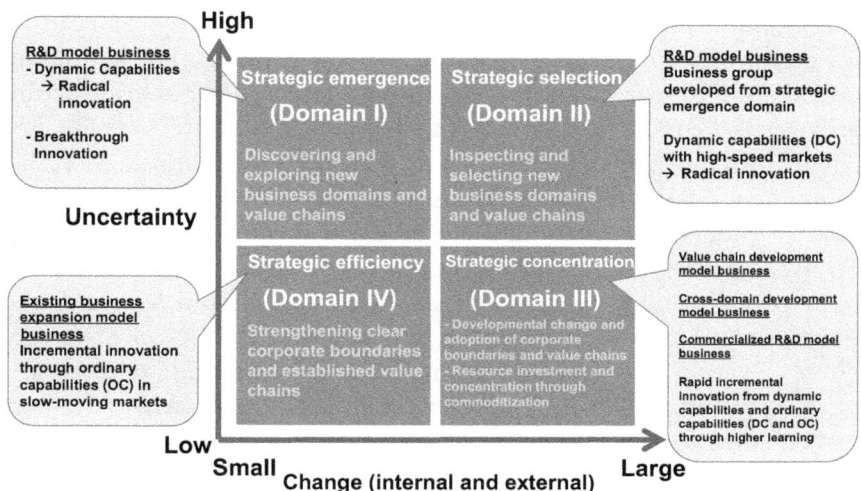

Fig. 9.6 General trading company capabilities map

markets. These existing business expansion model businesses originated through the Domain I → Domain II → Domain III shift. Hence these traditional main businesses give rise to value chain development model businesses and cross-domain development model businesses that are developed and established in the changing market environments of Domain III, as discussed later.

Value chain development model businesses and cross-domain development model businesses are growing businesses positioned in Domain III, the strategic concentration domain, and require developmental adjustment and application of corporate boundaries and value chains. Here, business expansion is required through strategic investment via dynamic (rapid) incremental innovation as development and application activities of existing businesses to respond to the dynamically changing customers and competitive environments through DC born through transforming experiences and OC fostered via high-level learning.

R&D model businesses are positioned in the strategic emergence and strategic selection domains of Domains I and II, in which the processes of searching, discovering, verifying and selecting new business domains and value chains occurs dynamically over time. In both these domains, DC are particularly required as organizational capabilities. On the other hand, R&D model businesses break into competitive markets as uncertainty is lower, and they shift to the strategic concentration domain of Domain III, in which resource input is made to bring about fully fledged commercialization. These R&D model businesses are different from the main existing business expansion model businesses, the value chain development model businesses and the cross-domain development model businesses, and are executed in new value chains and business domains, being born through radical innovation.

In general trading companies such as Mitsubishi and Mitsui, businesses of these four types are driven in house, while at the same time in-house performance assessment and risk management models are established and applied in response to each model type. General trading companies therefore have four different capabilities to respond to each domain, and engage in dialectical management to combine both radical and incremental innovation.

Mitsubishi expresses its business model as a multi-layering of basic and new functions, and has externally published this concept (see Fig. 9.7).

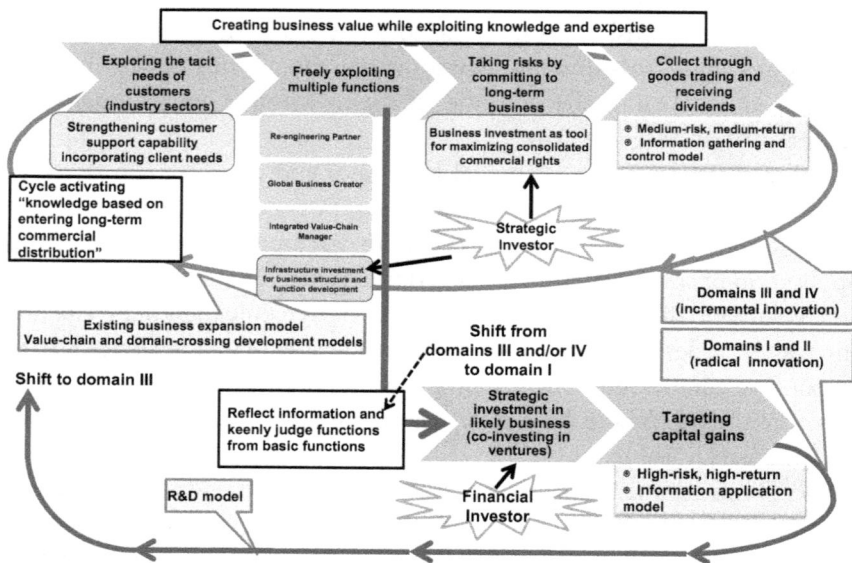

Fig. 9.7 Mitsubishi corporation's multi-layered functions (basic and new). (Source: Created from Mitsubishi Corp.'s publicly released materials)

Business with these basic functions is equivalent to the three business models of existing business expansion model businesses, value chain development model businesses, and cross-domain development model businesses that entail incremental innovation. Main businesses are reinforced, and development and application of them is propelled forward. Business done with basic functions entails strengthening and embedding of value chains to match customer needs through commitment to long-term business based on mid-risk and mid-returns. According to Mitsubishi's description of basic function businesses, these are equivalent to Domains III and IV on the Capabilities Map in Fig. 9.6.

In contrast, new functions are equivalent to R&D businesses involved in radical innovation, and entail hypothesizing and verification of business models to attain capital gain through strategic investment in promising businesses with a high-risk, high-return base. These new functions are triggered by insight and information collection through the basic functions of existing business or core competencies (inspiration of new knowledge and sensing, etc.). The trigger for new functions from basic functions is illustrated by the shift from Domain III and/or Domain IV to Domain I in the strategic innovation loop (see Fig. 9.6). According to Mitsubishi's description of new function businesses, these are equivalent to businesses that have shifted to Domains I, II, or III on the Capabilities Map in Fig. 9.6.

Much of this domain shifting (from Domain III or IV to Domain I) through sensing or inspiration of new knowledge is due to asset (knowledge) inspiration processes (the asset orchestration process) via Mitsubishi's global network. Differing from the businesses embedded in existing value chains (manufacturers, distributors, and so forth), Mitsubishi inspires and induces new assets (knowledge) based on new perspectives from outside Mitsubishi's existing value chains, and generates the seeds of innovation such as building new value chains and business models. In this sense, Mitsubishi's globally dispersed bases can be said be a "knowledge discovery and transmission centers" driving emergent and entrepreneurial strategies (Mintzberg 1978). Hence the concept of "multi-layered basic and new functions" can be interpreted as dialectical management through strategic innovation loops combining both the radical and incremental innovation, as described above.

Currently, general trading companies such as Mitsubishi and Mitsui propel incremental innovation businesses in Domains III and IV at the same time as incubating and starting up R&D model businesses in Domains I and II to then concentrate on fully fledged commercial businesses. Whether these general trading companies can succeed with strategic innovation as new business is thus key to their sustainable growth into the future. In this sense, general trading companies do not only grow main businesses with diverse types and function, but also bring about strategic innovation capabilities to pioneer new businesses at the same time. The next section considers the asset orchestration process, a central DC function of general trading companies in handling each domain.

9.3 Asset Orchestration Processes at General Trading Companies

The asset orchestration processes of general trading companies are deeply related to formation of their value chains. General trading companies use their multiple functions upstream and downstream in the value chain (finance, investment, consulting, distribution, etc.), and make efforts to optimize their vertical value chain models (see Box 9.4) through collaboration with both internal and external leading partners, and at the same time drive the co-evolution model to build win–win relationships with partners.

The architecture on which value chains are built is the diverse strategic communities spread widely around the world. The sources of these strategic communities are the people and human resource networks that can sense, converge, integrate and use diverse, global-scale assets through DC functions (sensing, seizing, transforming). In short, the dynamic configuring of strategic communities (SC) and networked SC is an important factor for Mitsubishi. In this way, specialties of personnel required for innovation in general trading companies are indicated by the three axis-matrix of products and industry, region, and function, the know-how of place x people x goods x services x information shown in Fig. 9.1 and entrepreneurial persons in step with ideal products, regions, and functions orchestrating assets around the world.

Both the strategic emergence and strategic selection domains in the Capabilities Map of the general trading company in Fig. 9.6 represent the commercialization processes of R&D model business, and differing from closed innovation by traditional manufacturers the asset orchestration process is executed in these domains as open innovation (Chesbrough 2003) to seek out leading internal and external partnerships; hence the asset orchestration through integration and convergence of multiple assets is dominant. Figure 9.8 depicts a map of the asset orchestration process to handle each domain.

How should companies construct vertical value chain models to commit to upstream, midstream, downstream and co-evolution models through vertical integrated architecture as "asset architectural thinking" (see Box 9.4: Asset architectural thinking)? As in the IT industry, in industry structures with horizontal specialization business models how should companies concentrate their business resources, in particular

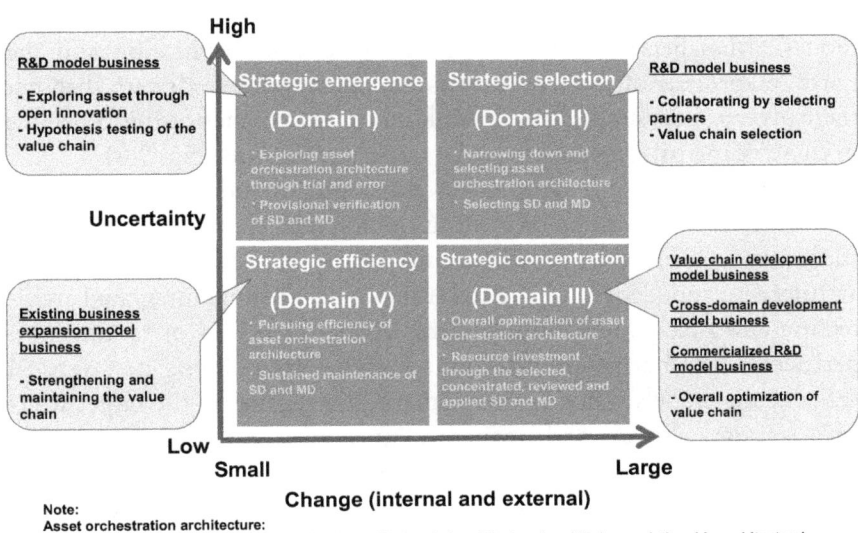

Fig. 9.8 General trading company asset orchestration map. (Note: Asset orchestration architecture: → "vertical integrated architecture," "horizontal integrated architecture" and "linkage relationship architecture"; *SD* strategy drivers, *MD* management drivers)

value chain functions, and collaborate with other companies to build entire target value chains (vertical value chain model and co-evolution model)? Does this entail maximizing profits by only focusing resources on particular specialized areas of the company through horizontal integrated architecture or linkage relationship architecture? While seeking out ties with other companies (strong or weak) and supplementing weaknesses, how should new value chains be configured through the convergence and integration of the strengths of one's own company with those of another through strategic collaboration across different industries? To pioneer new business, general trading companies have to think about how to find business models and value chains in Domains I and II.

Accordingly, managers of general trading companies allow various expansions of asset orchestration architecture (vertical integrated architecture, horizontal integrated architecture, linkage relationship architecture; see Box 9.4) as asset architectural thinking, and must concentrate on core businesses selection process through experiments and trials to build optimized value chains (vertical value chain model and co-evolution model). Managers also have to pursue hypothesis verification and the selection process of strategy drivers and management drivers through their diverse asset architectural thinking in asset orchestration processes in these domains, depending on the target strategy (see Fig. 9.8).

On the other hand, value chain development model businesses are positioned in the strategic concentration domain. Here, the asset orchestration process entails a developmental review of the vertical integrated architecture and, depending on the situation, horizontal integrated architecture and linkage relationship architecture to uncover or rethink new partners in the horizontal direction, and thereby building new vertical value chain models. Thus in this domain, depending on the target strategy, strategy drivers and management drivers are developmentally reviewed in the asset orchestration process.

Cross-domain development model businesses are also positioned in the strategic concentration domain. Here, existing vertical integrated architecture is adopted as an applied asset model, strategy drivers and management drivers are almost unchanged and partners are selected from geographical considerations. Or successful models are applied and adopted to adjacent areas, horizontal boundaries are extended in strategy drivers and existing vertical value chain models are adapted and applied to horizontal boundaries. On the other hand, regarding the shift of R&D model businesses from the strategic selection domain of Domain II to the strategic concentration domain of Domain III, strategy drivers and management drivers are defined and concentrated, and the asset orchestration architecture selected in Domain II, the strategic selection domain, is further optimized in its entirety.

Finally, the existing business expansion model businesses are positioned in the strategic efficiency domain of Domain IV, in which strategy drivers and management drivers are sustainably maintained. Hence, asset orchestration architecture pursues efficiency to strengthen and maintain the value chains of existing business. As discussed above, general trading companies configure vertical value chain models and co-evolution models by deftly and flexibly choosing and using their asset orchestration processes to respond with capabilities to achieve strategies in target business domains and value chains.

Box 9.3 The Asset Orchestration Process Map

In relation to the Capabilities Map presented in Chap. 2, this section describes the asset orchestration process (asset orchestration process map, see Fig. 9.9).

At the initial stage of radical innovation, in Domain I, slow (or extremely slow) environmental changes and high uncertainties are observed, and new ideas, business concepts and new technologies are created from new discoveries and inventions through the exploration process via DC. In this domain, here are diverse patterns for asset orchestration with strategic emergence. Most traditional large corporations drive closed innovation with in-house research laboratories and development departments under conventional hierarchical systems. To develop sustainable innovation with path-dependent assets accumulated throughout company history, closed innovation processes are important. In traditional hi-tech fields such as heavy electrical, nuclear power generation, aviation, vehicle equipment, machine tools, medical, and semiconductor machinery industries, closed innovation plays a critical role.

In contrast, in industries in which technologies are rapidly advancing, such as IT, the best technical achievements and know-how are becoming increasingly spread out across the globe. In environments like this, which

(continued)

Box 9.3 (continued)

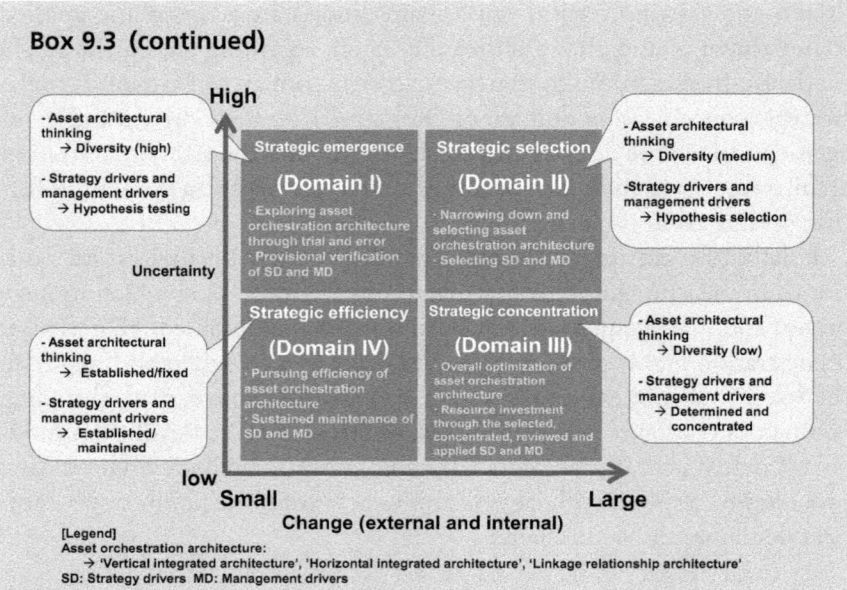

Fig. 9.9 Asset orchestration process map. ([Legend] Asset orchestration architecture: → "Vertical integrated architecture," "Horizontal integrated architecture" and "Linkage relationship architecture"; *SD* strategy drivers, *MD* management drivers)

are changing rapidly, asset orchestration through converging and integrating knowledge both inside and outside companies is effective by adopting open innovation or partially incorporating external core assets.

Should a company adopt a vertical integration model with vertically integrated architecture? Should a company concentrate on particular specialized areas through horizontal integrated architecture or linkage relationship architecture? Or, while seeking out ties with other companies (strong or weak) and supplementing weaknesses, how should new value chains be configured through the convergence and integration of the strengths of one's own company with those of another through strategic collaboration across different industries? Thinking about what business models a company should pursue is required in this domain. Accordingly, practitioners have to allow for high diversity of asset orchestration architecture as asset architectural thinking (vertical integrated architecture, horizontal integrated architecture and linkage relationship architecture; see Box 9.4), and concentrate on trial and error, experiments, and trial activities.

(continued)

Box 9.3 (continued)

In whatever case, in strategic emergence domain, companies have to hypothetically test their corporate boundaries, in other words strategy drivers in response to strategic objectives or business environments (see Fig. 2.7 in Chap. 2) and make attempts at various asset orchestration processes through these processes of trial and error. If it is advantageous to develop or manufacture in house, then it is better to configure a vertical value chain model through the functioning of management drivers with a focus on creativity (see Fig. 2.7 in Chap. 2). In contrast, if another company has achieved more with its developments than those in-house, there are many cases in which a company must abandon its development efforts, and access and acquire external intangible assets through partnership or mergers and acquisitions through the functioning of management drivers focusing on efficiency. Accordingly, as asset orchestration process in this domain, practitioners pursue the asset orchestration through hypothesis testing of strategy drivers and management drivers depending on strategic objectives and diverse asset architectural thinking (See Fig. 9.9).

Next, to incubate core technologies and business concepts that have shifted from sluggish environments in Domain, staff are acquired in house (sometimes externally) and organizations are reshuffled and quickly change. With ongoing uncertainty, these core technologies and business concepts are shifted to Domain II, environments of great change. In asset orchestration process processes in Domain II, the strategic selection domain, various asset orchestration processes that were tested and experimented with in the strategic emergence domain are selected and narrowed down. This is a stage in which the level of completion of asset orchestration is raised as products, services and business models. Accordingly, strategy driver and management driver elements are generally selected. In addition, the diversity of elements of asset orchestration architecture (vertical integrated architecture, horizontal integrated architecture and linkage relationship architecture) is lowered (to a medium level) compared with the strategic emergence domain. Moreover, depending on the situation, sometimes companies review their structural architecture (whether vertical integrated architecture or horizontal integrated architecture) or review their relationships with other partner companies by changing their linkage relationship architecture (see Fig. 9.9).

Hence, new businesses (including new products and businesses) with future prospects that to some degree eliminate uncertainty, and that have come through the strategic selection domain of Domain II, are shifted to Domain III, which has relatively lower uncertainty, although change that is external (environmental) and internal to a company is ongoing. This strategic concentration domain is the stage in which the level of completion of products and services is raised through asset orchestration to commercialize

(continued)

Box 9.3 (continued)

products and services through definition and concentration of asset orchestration and business elements that determine the asset orchestration (strategy drivers and management drivers) to complete business value chains. The degree of change of vertical integrated architecture, horizontal integrated architecture and linkage relationship architecture is minor (low) compared with the strategic selection domain, while co-ordination to optimize entire asset orchestration architecture is the most important issue (see Fig. 9.9).

However, as discussed in the strategic innovation loop concept in the next section, in the strategic concentration domain, companies must strategically and continually raise the level of their technologies and review their business models to raise the value of their products and services in order to respond to fast and competitive environments. Hence, as companies have shifted their new businesses from Domain I → Domain II → Domain III for commercialization in the Domain III stage, owing to the new businesses shifted from the strategic selection domain and existing products and businesses being given major upgrades (because of new technical developments or new business models), new asset orchestration processes arise.

Domain III also includes the original concept of DC to drive incremental innovation, which can be interpreted as capabilities to generate high performance through the evolution and diversification of operating routines through high-level learning to generate profits in response to internal and external changes.

In contrast, for many existing businesses positioned in Domain IV with its low levels of change and uncertainty and sluggish market environments, companies drive incremental innovation for thorough efficiency of business through processes of upgrading and improving existing business with existing organizations (main streams). The asset orchestration in this strategic efficiency domain, efficiency of existing routines and operations, is pursued in the framework of established and fixed vertical integrated architecture, horizontal integrated architecture and linkage relationship architecture under continually maintained strategy and management drivers (See Fig. 9.9).

Box 9.4 Asset Orchestration Thinking

How are different assets orchestrated through the formation of SC and networked SC? In this regard, this section would like to systemize these based on empirical cases of existing research. This is because the network structures of SC are small world structures, which determine the patterns of asset orchestration processes. What are the mechanisms for forming SC and network SC inside and outside organizations? Alternatively, what kinds of patterns do practitioners use to intentionally form networks? In this regard,

(continued)

Building Healthcare Ecosystems Through Strategic... 249

Box 9.4 (continued)

Table 9.1 Vertical integrated architecture

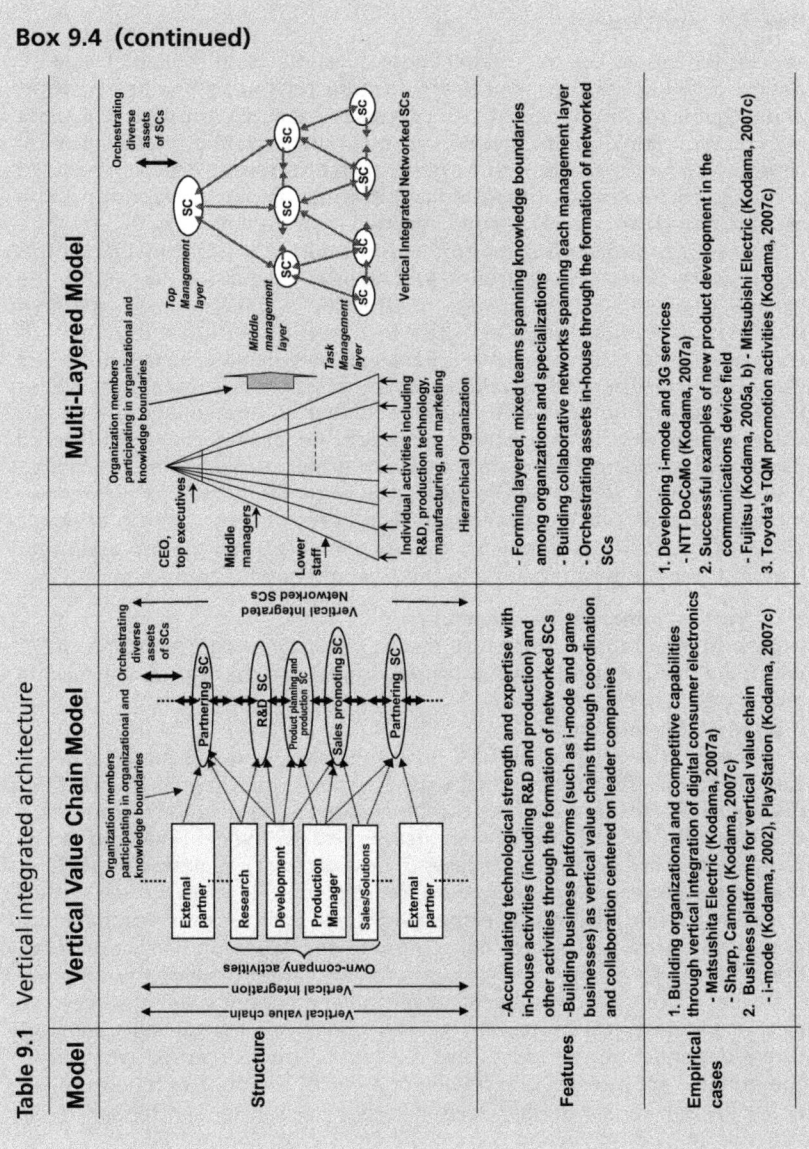

Model	Vertical Value Chain Model	Multi-Layered Model
Structure	(diagram)	(diagram)
Features	- Accumulating technological strength and expertise with in-house activities (including R&D and production) and other activities in the formation of networked SCs - Building business platforms (such as i-mode and game businesses) as vertical value chains through coordination and collaboration centered on leader companies	- Forming layered, mixed teams spanning knowledge boundaries among organizations and specializations - Building collaborative networks spanning each management layer - Orchestrating assets in-house through the formation of networked SCs
Empirical cases	1. Building organizational and competitive capabilities through vertical integration of digital consumer electronics - Matsushita Electric (Kodama, 2007a) - Sharp, Cannon (Kodama, 2007c) 2. Business platforms for vertical value chain - i-mode (Kodama, 2002), PlayStation (Kodama, 2007c)	1. Developing i-mode and 3G services - NTT DoCoMo (Kodama, 2007a) 2. Successful examples of new product development in the communications device field - Fujitsu (Kodama, 2005a, b) - Mitsubishi Electric (Kodama, 2007c) 3. Toyota's TQM promotion activities (Kodama, 2007c)

(continued)

Box 9.4 (continued)

this section would like to consider these questions from the perspective of design thinking, in other words architecture related to human networks and organizational networks. As processes executed through the asset architectural thinking of practitioners, asset orchestration in our empirical cases has so far consisted of three general architectures (vertical integrated architecture, horizontal integrated architecture, linkage relationship architecture), which are clearly divided into two individual models.

The research process leading to the derivation of the framework for this architecture of asset orchestration will be briefly described. Regarding the vertical chain model and linkage relationship architecture, we analyzed synergies between business activities (the level of vertical integration) in companies, the transactional relationships between businesses (contract details, contract periods of validity, power relationships, etc.), the level of knowledge sharing (levels of information sharing and collaboration) and value networks to create business models. Regarding the multi-layered model, we conducted structural analysis of project organizations in companies. In addition, regarding the horizontal value chain and complementary model, we analyzed the formation of business models through strategic alliances and joint development among companies, and the processes that lead to these business models and the level of knowledge sharing.

(1) Vertical integrated architecture

Vertical integrated architecture means vertically integrated forms of SC, which are divided into the multi-layered model and the vertical value chain model (see Table 9.1).

(a) Multi-layered model

In the multi-layered model, SC have hierarchy, and this model is structured through the formation of cross-functional multiple SC by practitioners in various sections within a company at the same time as the formation of hierarchical SC networks in management levels. The multi-layered model is often observed in large-scale cases of new product development (NPD) or large-scale projects. For example, in the NPD multi-layered model, professionals in various divisions and specialist areas such as overall architecture design, various subsystems design, software development, hardware development, and production technologies for the target developmental product collaborate and formulate SC at each management level, and these SC exist in a hierarchical structure. The reason for this is that product architecture is dependent on product functions and product structure (whether its components are integral or modular, or a mix of the two), and because the entire systems can be broken down into many subsystems with hierarchical structure (e.g., Baldwin and Clark 2000; Clark 1985; Simon 1996).

In a specific empirical case, the case of Fujitsu NPD by Kodama (2005a, b), asset orchestration of dissimilar technical elements was required (technology

(continued)

Box 9.4 (continued)

such as image and audio compression, semiconductor design, semiconductor software, communications interfaces, computers, software, and human interfaces). To achieve this, Fujitsu engaged in collaboration with external partners (other companies in the same industries) to absorb their technologies, and at the same time formed a multi-layered model within Fujitsu to mobilize the company's own dispersed and internal elemental technical assets.

As another example, the i-mode development and deployment system (Kodama 2002, 2003, 2004, 2007a, 2014, 2017) was a large-scale project of NTT DOCOMO, in which the company formed multi-layered and hierarchical networked SC with vertical integration in house to build value chains from its R&D through to implementation of its services. As Henderson and Clark (1990) identified, technical structures that make up the internal structure of a development organization may be reflected on it, although when basic technologies move, company response may be held back by these existing organizational structures (e.g., when business models or product and service architecture changes). In taking on such a massive challenge, there were huge constraints in the DOCOMO case in its existing organizational systems, but the company was able to handle the new development by creating flexible and organic networked SC in house.

This multi-layered model was an effective organizational architecture for achieving Fujitsu's NPD, which required convergence and integration of a wide range of technologies or large-scale business models such as the i-mode. In this multi-layered model, individual and autonomous SC consisting of groups of professionals secure creativity and flexibility when developing new products or business models for specific tasks. SC hierarchy has the advantage of securing efficiency in executing tasks and speed of decision-making.

(b) Vertical value chain model

The vertical value chain model means the formation of SC and networked SC as vertical integration for co-ordination and collaboration for various tasks to achieve vertical integration in tasks, such as R&D, product technologies, manufacturing, and sales. Empirical cases of network SC that achieve in-house vertical integration in Japanese manufacturers have been reported. As discussed in existing research, networks of SC between different organizations and specialist areas in appliance and communications equipment manufacturers orchestrate internal assets and bring about vertical integration-type business models unique to Japanese companies.

Furthermore, these vertical value chain models function to network companies with strong ties in the Japanese mobile telephone industry and automotive industry. In networked SC creating vertical value chain models with high level of information and knowledge sharing in these industries, leader companies (e.g., DOCOMO and Toyota) have leadership and bargain-

(continued)

Box 9.4 (continued)

ing power in technologies and markets. These inter-company networks are typified by Japanese automakers (Toyota, etc.) and components manufacturers (e.g., Amasaka 2004; Dyer and Hatch 2004).

The aforementioned i-mode business model entails a vertically integrated value chain consisting of DOCOMO, mobile telephone manufacturers, and content providers (CPs). In DOCOMO's mobile telephone development, the detailed functions of mobile telephones and the technical architectures and detailed specifications needed to achieve these functions were decided, and the mobile telephone manufacturers delivered completed products to DOCOMO. This entailed the sharing of information and knowledge between DOCOMO and the mobile telephone manufacturers through strong networked SC. Moreover, DOCOMO controlled many CPs by exercising its authority to determine what content from which CPs would be adopted and posted on official i-mode websites. Hence, co-ordinating huge numbers of CPs through vertical integration is an important task for DOCOMO.

Behind the success of the mobile telephone business in Japan such as i-mode lay the formation of SC as "small world networks" between the entrepreneurial organizations and traditional organizations within DOCOMO, as well as the formation of a number of SC consisting of mobile telephone manufacturers and CPs. Thus, for DOCOMO, the way it formed clusters of SC as small world networks by creating links with certain external partners was key. The birth of the i-mode business model entailed the formation of numerous small world networks in house and with mobile telephone manufacturers and CPs to co-create new business models, while DOCOMO collaborated with its external partners. Hence, this vertical value chain model accelerated the asset orchestration process through the formation of networked SC centered on DOCOMO both inside and outside of DOCOMO, and was an important factor in driving the co-evolution of the new business model in the mobile telephone industry (business ecosystem).[1]

(c) The vertical integrated architecture and the "creativity view"

The unique creativity view of Japanese companies (Kodama 2009a, b) promotes the building of a vertical integrated architecture. In particular, Japanese corporations drive asset orchestration by mobilizing the assets of individuals in various locations through the formation of networked SC under a multi-layered model for creative technology innovation. In addition, Japanese companies accumulate the tacit knowledge of experience and know-how between tasks through a vertical value chain model, and raise the level of creativity to respond to new technical changes and to develop new technologies. As well as this, the vertical value chain model enabled through network SC transcending companies is a factor in the formation of unique business platforms, such as creative mobile telephone services (e.g., i-mode) or the Toyota production system.

(continued)

Box 9.4 (continued)

(2) Horizontal integrated architecture

Horizontal integrated architecture means horizontally integrated forms of SC, which are divided into the horizontal value chain model and the complementary model (see Table 9.2).

(a) Horizontal value chain model

The horizontal value chain model entails the construction of networked SC to expand business to new areas from existing business domains, and create new value chains. In other words, the horizontal value chain model decides corporate horizontal boundaries to provide answers to questions such as what kind of products and services should a company keep or how should a company bring about value through diversification of business. In particular, small world networks between different industries and businesses drive access to dissimilar knowledge and drive dialog on knowledge boundaries. Creative abrasion and productive friction on knowledge boundaries inspire new assets, and raise the creativity needed to achieve new business models. Apple's strategy transformation from its personal computer business to music distribution and smartphone businesses is a good example of this (Kodama 2011). New business models such as electronic money businesses, credit card businesses, businesses converging communications with broadcasting (television broadcast to mobile phone and internet business convergence) and businesses converging mobile telephones with automobiles (telematics) using mobile telephones, all observed in mobile telephone businesses centered in Japan, are enabled through the building of horizontal value chains through the formation of network SC among dissimilar businesses.

For example, Japanese mobile telephone carriers DOCOMO and au (KDDI) proactively promote strategic alliances or alliances through capital participation with the finance, credit card, broadcasting, railroad, distribution, healthcare, education, advertising, and automobile industries, at the same time as driving collaboration with business leaders in the internet field, such as Google, to achieve mobile internet businesses with new added value. The asset orchestration process through the formation of business networks including different business types is an important factor in building horizontal value chains to generate new business models.

(b) Complementary model

Complementary models entail collaborative SC and networked SC on an equal footing with external partners in the same industry (or in adjacent business areas), and do not have many of the hierarchical elements seen in vertical integrated architecture. This model entails cases of disseminating common knowledge with external partners, and engaging in joint development of new products and services on an equal footing. For example, DOCOMO widely spread knowledge created and accumulated in the com-

(continued)

Box 9.4 (continued)

Table 9.2 Horizontal integrated architecture

Model	Horizontal Value Chain Model	Complementary Model
Structure	Orchestrating diverse assets of SCs → Horizontal Value Chain → Horizontal Integrated Networked SCs. Inter-corporate networks created from different industries	Orchestrating diverse assets of SCs → Horizontal Integration → Horizontal Integrated Networked SCs. Inter-corporate networks created from the same and related industries
Features	- New asset orchestration through the formation of networked SCs among companies in different industries - Formation of new business platforms (such as mobile-EC services and telematics) among companies in different industry types	- Asset orchestration through the formation of networked SCs with externally distributed and in-house asset - New asset orchestration through collaborating in same or related (neighboring business domains) industries
Empirical cases	1. Mobile e-commerce - NTT DoCoMo (Kodama, 2007a) 2. Networks among companies in different industries - Network formation centered on NTT DoCoMo and au (KDDI) (Kodama, 2009a)	1. NTT DoCoMo's international strategy - Global development of Conexus Mobile Alliance and I-mode (Kodama, 2007a) 2. Examples of successful new product development in communications device and machine tool fields - Fujitsu (Kodama, 2005a,b) - Fanuc, NEC (Shibata and Kodama, 2007) 3. Formation of supplier networks - Supplier's learning networks (Dyer and Hatch, 2004) - The Toyota Group and the Aisin Fire (Nishiguchi et al, 1998)

(continued)

Box 9.4 (continued)

pany about i-mode and 3G mobile telephone systems with communication carriers in other countries through this complementary model. In addition, in Asian regions, DOCOMO and Far EasTone Telecommunications (Taiwan), Hutchison Essar (India), Hutchison Telecommunications (Hong Kong, Macao), KT Freetel (Korea), PT Indosat Tbk (Indonesia), StarHub (Singapore), and True Move Company (Thailand) formed the Asia-Pacific Mobile Alliance (Conexus Mobile Alliance), and agreed to proceed with business collaboration on international roaming and corporate services. With a 100 million subscriber base, these companies are partnering in the largest carrier alliance in Asia to improve services for travelers between these partners' countries and regions, enrich services for multinational corporations and raise customer convenience while strengthening the competitiveness of these companies in the Asian region.

This complementary model is also typified by the new product developments of Japanese manufacturers through joint development with competitors or related companies (Fujitsu, NEC, Fanuc, etc.) (Kodama and Shibata 2014), and the recent cases of joint procurement of LCD panels by Sony and Samsung Electronics, and joint development of next-generation organic EL panels between Japanese manufacturers (Hitachi and Canon, Sony and Toshiba). In the empirical cases of Fujitsu NPD discussed earlier (Kodama 2005a), NPD was successful through collaboration enabled by the formation of networked SC with a number of external partners. These appliance, communications equipment and machine tool manufacturers execute horizontal integration of external assets by absorbing the assets of external partners (specialist partners in business players with horizontal divisions of labor) through the formation of networked SC with external partners, while orchestrating assets through vertical integration via the formation of networked SC internally. In the Fujitsu case, networked SC are fundamental to the asset orchestration model in order to orchestrate external assets with those in house. Taking a case from the automotive industry, the learning networks that suppliers of Toyota continually form (empirical case in Table 9.2) are also examples of this complementary model. The case of other suppliers collaborating to form SC as small world networks to autonomously back up Aisin, a supplier for Toyota that had experienced a disastrous fire, can also be interpreted as this complementary model (empirical case in Table 9.2).

(c) **Horizontal integrated architecture and the "dialectic view"**

The unique dialectic view of Japanese companies (Kodama 2009a, 2014) promotes the building of a horizontal integrated architecture. To build win–win relationships in business models, Japanese companies drive the orchestration of diverse assets through the formation of networked SC with partners including companies in different industries. Furthermore,

(continued)

Box 9.4 (continued)

the dialectic view drives co-ordination and collaboration among partners (including competitive companies) through complementary model constructions, and achieves NPD and joint business. In addition, co-creation between dissimilar businesses through the formation of the horizontal value chain model generates new business models, and drives co-evolution across entire industries.

(3) Linkage relationship architecture

Boundaries are "asset platforms" that entail practitioners sharing dynamic contexts (time, location, relationships with people) to generate new knowledge. As boundaries, SC are represented by space and time generated and changed through the synergies between individuals sharing and changing contexts with each other. SC create space and time for tacit knowledge sharing and dialog and practice.

"Organizations" and "individuals" are in dialectic relationships with each other, hence practitioners change organizations with their humanity in environments where the "here and now" as SC and "practical consciousness," which is tacit knowledge in dynamic contexts, cyclically relate to organizations. While human beings are constrained by the organizations that they have created, they also have the practical power to transform those organizations (Giddens 1979; Giddens and Pierson 1998). SC are platforms that link individuals with organizations (companies), and human beings form (or eliminate) SC or link them together. In doing so, they influence macrostructures such as organizations, companies, industries and entire societies.

Accordingly, SC are not only important as micro–macrolinkages in social networks, but also critical units of analysis from the perspective of how they influence company performance through the generation and accumulation of social capital (Coleman 1988; Burt 1997; Nahapiet and Ghoshal 1998; Cohen and Prusak 2000) as individuals form and link SC in relationships between individuals, organizations, SC, companies and industries, and how they conversely influence individuals.

On the other hand, in the flow of knowledge management social capital as knowledge capital is born centered on SC, and SC are also important from the perspective of the clarification of various knowledge processes that transcend SC boundaries and are integrated. There is also practical significance for practitioners regarding a perspective on how new knowledge is born through the formation and linking of SC.

The new perspective obtained from the case of the aforementioned i-mode development is the fact that there are always differences in their context, diverse and multi-layered SC and networked structures. These are formed and linked together as practitioners proactively approach others in their environments (customers, etc.) and organizations. Practitioners intentionally (or emergently) form

(continued)

Box 9.4 (continued)

and link SC. In particular, as observed in the cases of Fujitsu and DOCOMO mentioned earlier, cases of new product development in hi-tech fields in recent years led to the necessity to converge and integrate dissimilar technologies. Until now, technological innovation has been developed through the pursuit of specialized knowledge; however, there are many cases of new products and services that have been developed with new and unconventional ideas that converge technologies from one area with those of another.

An important issue is how to integrate different and dispersed assets (from a technical perspective, this means how to integrate assets in different technological fields to achieve technology integration). Dispersed assets are embedded in SC dispersed in space and time. To orchestrate assets, individual assets must transcend the boundaries of SC and be networked. Put differently, distributed SC must join together in networks, and the knowledge dispersed throughout those SC must be deeply embedded in the networks. In terms of social network theory, SC can be interpreted as cliques of practitioners (collections of actors with close mutual ties), and the connections between SC and SC are also types of ties.

Actors committed to multiple SC play a central role in tying together SC with SC for asset orchestration. For dissimilar knowledge to be integrated, practitioners must deeply understand and share knowledge (tacit knowledge and explicit knowledge) in their respective SC, and also must deeply embed shared knowledge in networks that transcend the borders of SC (the factor of deep embeddedness is important) (Kodama 2005a, b). In particular, for tacit knowledge sharing, it is necessary to deeply share contexts on networks, and strongly tie SC together with each other.

In the aforementioned service development cases such as i-mode, SC were strongly tied together, and dissimilar assets were shared through deep embeddedness to generate new knowledge as technology integration for new products and services. In this way, building SC networks with strong ties is an important proposition in integrating dissimilar knowledge, and practitioners must intentionally consider SC relationships as these strong ties.

On the other hand, according to the teachings of social network theory, it is also possible to bridge new dissimilar information with weak ties (Granovetter 1973). Furthermore, Burt (1992) identified the high possibility of acquiring new business opportunities by actors accessing new information through weak ties with "structural holes." Hence, we are particularly conscious of the problem of situations in which building SC networks with weak ties will be effective (see Fig. 9.10).

Moreover, while there is not much case research in the field of business, the i-mode development case could be one of these. The i-mode business model consists of the integration of various knowledge such as mobile telephone development, technical platform development and contents development.

(continued)

Box 9.4 (continued)

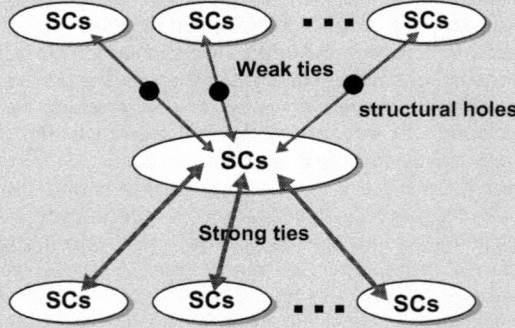

Relationships between SCs

Fig. 9.10 Linkage relationship architecture

Among these, mobile telephone development and technical platform development were produced in various strongly tied SC inside and outside DOCOMO organizations.

On the other hand, regarding the development of various contents (wide-ranging content such as text content, games, location information, music distribution, movie distribution or two-dimensional barcodes, and electronic money services such as i-mode FeliCa), DOCOMO does not have close network relationships with particular content providers (however, the DOCOMO i-mode official site content providers share knowledge deeply with DOCOMO). Instead, the company builds SC networks with weak ties to content providers aiming for access to new content information, and hence opportunities with new content business.

For example, behind the achievement of the i-mode FeliCa, the world's first electronic money service using mobile telephones, rather than by maintaining a close network relationship with the Sony Group, which was developing FeliCa, instead from the beginning DOCOMO maintained relationships with weak ties to various companies, including Sony, to uncover the mobile telephone electronic money service of the future. Practitioners from DOCOMO and Sony effectively filled in this structural whole to enable access to new information and knowledge from each other and achieve knowledge creation as a new service.

(continued)

> **Box 9.4 (continued)**
> As described above, in asset architecture to achieve asset orchestration, not only are strongly tied SC networks built, but also weakly tied SC networks are an important proposition to drive the development of new business, and hence practitioners must intentionally consider both these SC relationships and their ongoing combination (or usage). We call it language relationship architecture in asset orchestration. Maintaining SC networks with strong ties at the same time as building SC networks with weak ties and bridging structural holes in a timely manner enables the absorption and integration of dissimilar assets. The i-mode business model can be said to be an example of skillfully using the linkage relationship architecture of SC.

9.4 Strategic Innovation Capability of General Trading Companies

As discussed earlier, the four types of elements of general trading companies are divided into R&D model-type businesses as radical innovation pursuing exploratory activities, and value chain development model businesses, cross-domain development model businesses and existing business expansion model businesses as incremental innovation pursuing exploitative activities (see Fig. 9.11). As main businesses, the existing business expansion model requires the maintenance of long-term, high-profit structures, while the value chain development model and cross-domain development model businesses require middle risk, middle return results; both domains (Domain III and Domain IV in Fig. 9.11) not only requiring reinforced customer response, but also ongoing investments in business and infrastructure.

On the other hand, R&D model businesses in Domains I and II aim for high risk and high return from promising projects through strategic investment in business and infrastructure (including venture investments), and require development processes that entail seeking out new business models through emergent activities to uncover latent customer needs. The DC required of general trading companies aim for recovery and capital gain through trading of goods and receiving dividends while committing to business over the long term and taking on risk, by making use of the knowledge and know-how of its various complex functions (distribution, finance, marketing, IT, etc.).

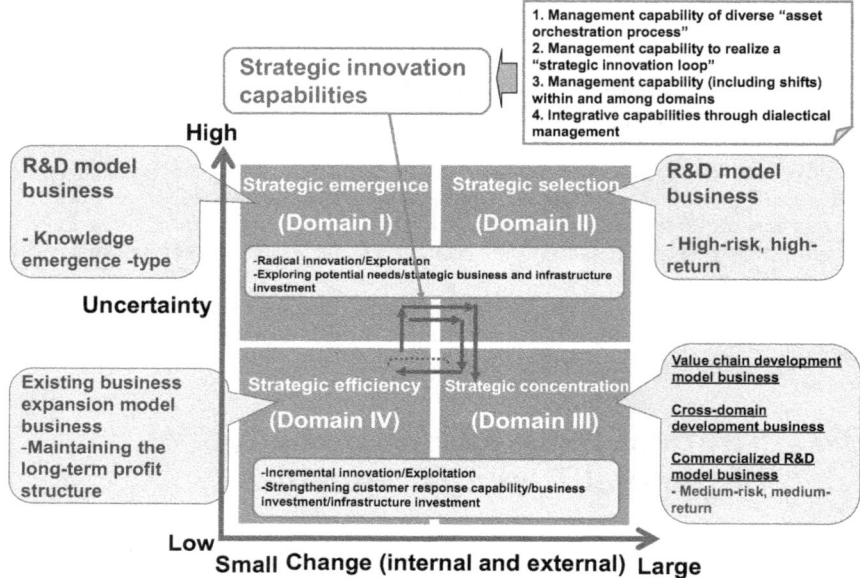

Fig. 9.11 General trading company strategic innovation system

As illustrated in Figs. 9.8 and 9.9 earlier, general trading companies require different asset orchestration processes in these four domains. This is equivalent to management capabilities for diverse asset orchestration processes, an element of strategic innovation capabilities. Major in-house organizational reform can stimulate the acquisition of management capabilities to build strategic innovation capabilities.

9.5 Boundaries Synchronization Among Collaborating Players

Finally, we would like to provide a new perspective on healthcare ecosystems through the Mitsui case. As described in Box 9.2, Mitsui is a company that built the healthcare ecosystem as a global healthcare network with its newly developed hospital businesses in Asia (see Fig. 9.4). At the center of this global healthcare network are hospitals, which are surrounded by a range of diverse services. The healthcare ecosystem illustrates how these various services support the various hospitals. In the Mitsui-centered healthcare ecosystem, various practitioners execute their business through deep interactions across organizational groups of wide-ranging collaborating players such as those involved in planning, development, manufacture, sales, and services. The healthcare business faces highly volatile circumstances in which markets rapidly change and technologies speedily advance. Nevertheless, high-quality and timely healthcare services must be continually provided to customers.

Thus, in forming a global healthcare network, the formation of SC as platforms for deeply sharing contexts and knowledge among collaborating players is an important action for practitioners in different organizations and with different areas of expertise. Mitsui's value chain concept consists of healthcare, pharmaceutical and service SC in its global healthcare network, as described by Fig. 9.12.

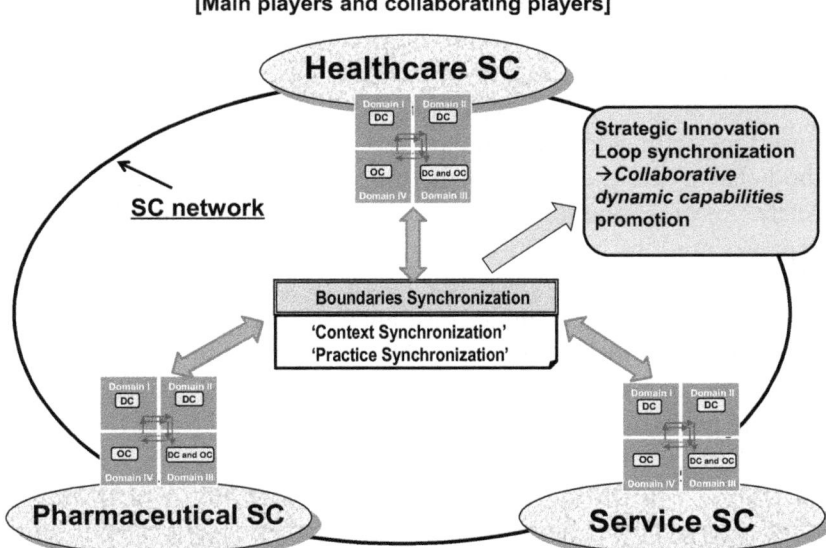

Fig. 9.12 Collaborative DC through boundaries synchronization

The strategic collaboration among the collaborating partners involved in hospitals, clinic businesses and their peripheries, medical information services, medical management support services and so forth in Asia provides valuable information and medical services to both healthcare professionals and patients. In the pharmaceutical SC, the strategic collaboration of collaborating players involved in the entire value chain from pharmaceutical development support, manufacturing support (CMO) and manufacture and sales business through to pharmaceuticals development, manufacture, and sales supports physicians in their provision of high-quality healthcare services to patients.

In the service SC, Mitsui is continuing initiatives in the personnel training field and is involved in global operations that include the introduction and dispatch of highly specialized persons and training-related businesses, while also being involved in contract food services (catering) and uniform rental services in hospitals and healthcare facilities both inside and outside Japan, and facility management of public and sports facilities. A typical example of a service surrounding a hospital is hospital catering, and a Mitsui-related company is currently involved in this service to deliver meals to patients. Facility management includes hospital cleaning, sheet and nurse uniform laundry, and rental services. There is also a wide range of other services, such as housing for the elderly that accepts long-term elderly hospital patients. Mitsui provides these services in both Japan and the USA. So that hospital medical professionals can specialize in providing high-quality healthcare, Mitsui and other related companies are also involved in other businesses. These are typified by healthcare management services that entail the use of computers to manage healthcare costs and complex insurance fee billing practices, as well as managing patient medical history using electronic medical records. The strategic collaboration of these groups of collaborating players provides healthcare professionals, healthcare administrators and patients with efficient and effective services.

As well as this, Mitsui also aims to "export" the advanced healthcare technologies of Japan, which is typified by Japanese surgeons performing operations in hospitals overseas. For example, Parkway Hospitals Singapore provides space for a doctor who is a leading Japanese authority on liver transplants to provide treatment and perform liver transplant operations. In terms of personnel exchange, the company also engages in partnerships in the education and training field for young doctors to study in famous Western hospitals—educating excellent physicians is also an important part of the strategy of hospital management. In other words, a hospital is not just created by getting some funds and building a box—if it does not have excellent physicians, it is meaningless. IHH also has university hospitals under its umbrella, and engages in ongoing doctor education as well as dispatching doctors to Mitsui-related hospitals.

The strong links between these three SC integrates the chain of business processes of healthcare, pharmaceuticals and services, and at the same time as optimizing the entire value chain provides high-quality, total healthcare solutions to customers that are differentiated from other medical services. The hospital management capabilities of Mitsui and IHH, the main players in this healthcare ecosystem, are underpinned by the formation of SC and their network integration capabilities.[2]

Thus, practitioners in organizations in the various collaborating partner companies carry out their work mainly through these individual SC to build this solid healthcare ecosystem. In the individual SC, these practitioners make decisions about specific strategy and tactics broken down into their roles, and play their part with the goal of building a value chain.

However, if the business decided in each individual SC was inconsistently and incompletely executed on the time axis, there would be no optimization of the overall value chain. In particular, upper management, including project leaders and middle managers in individual collaborating player companies in SC, must always participate in multiple SC, disseminate information and knowledge, and deeply share and practice contexts among practitioners in different organizations and dissimilar areas of expertise. In other words, there is a dynamic sharing of knowledge and context between SC, which not only serves individuals as they work towards targets, but also triggers "creative collaboration" among members (Kodama 2007c) that engenders mutual support. In this way, creative collaboration not only serves to optimize SC partially, but also enables overall optimization of the SC and hence overall optimization of the value chain through rigid SC networking via SC linkages.

Put differently, the mutually rhythmical synchronization of context and practice in the individual SC achieves partial optimization of SC, overall optimization of networked SC and hence optimization of entire value chains. This is the "boundary synchronization" discussed in Chap. 2. Boundary synchronization drives collaborative DC through the synchronization of strategic innovation loops among collaborating partners for building and sustainable growth of the healthcare ecosystem (see Fig. 9.12).

To achieve boundary synchronization, practitioners in the diverse organizations discuss specifics about what needs to be done. The enormous number of actions that form overarching strategy and tactics are broken down into specific tasks to be executed in numerous sections such as marketing, public relations, advertising, sales, service design, development, production technology, manufacturing, distribution, and services in the healthcare, pharmaceutical, and service areas. Of particular importance among this massive number of actions are those that cannot be self-contained in the business framework of a single organization. These include actions that must be executed through co-ordination and linkage with other organizations and other collaborating players, or actions that must be executed based on the outputs of collaborating players or other organizations; and so on.

All actions that cannot be completed within the framework of a single organization must be achieved through the formation of SC that transcend organizational and knowledge boundaries. In SC, practitioners reach consensus by discussing specific targets, meaning, time frames, and methods about who will do what (what actions need to be executed), why, when, with whom and how actions should be done. These are the practical strategic actions that practitioners execute at the microlevel to carry out specific strategic and tactical measures. Moreover, these practical strategic actions of practitioners are often characterized by a dynamism that entails trial and error as times change. Practitioners must always have a dynamic view of strategy, and not only execute planned deliberate strategies but also execute emergent strategies flexibly. Moreover, practitioners have to be able to improvise to deal with rapidly changing circumstances.

In SC, practitioners deeply share context and knowledge through creative dialog, and execute actions that have strong mutual dependencies with collaborating partners and other organizations. As practitioners execute practical strategic actions that have been decided in each SC, the progress towards achieving objectives is continually monitored among themselves. Furthermore, the practical strategic actions in individual SC are interdependent with those of other SC. This means that collaboration and co-ordination with practitioners in different organizations is required to answer questions such as when, with whom, and how.

Accordingly, practitioners who participate in a number of SC (particularly upper management) and commit to objectives must match the pitch and rhythm of progress towards the targets for each practical strategic action of the SC on the time axis, as they aim for the goals of the entire project. In executing business in each of the SC, practitioners get in step with each other to match rhythm and pitch. This boundary synchronization is the mechanism that achieves concurrent practical strategic action in each of the SC. Boundary synchronization is an important mechanism to achieve overall value chain optimization. The thinking and actions of practitioners in this way are the element of collaborative DC at the microlevel.

For practitioners, SC and networked SC are knowledge platforms that bring about new knowledge through the sharing of dynamic contexts. An SC provides the space and time for the creation and sharing of assets (tacit and explicit knowledge), and dialog and practice. The new perspective obtained from the case of Mitsui is the fact that there are always differ in context, diverse and multi-layered SC and networked SC. These are formed and linked together as practitioners proactively approach others in their environments (customers, etc.) and organizations. Practitioners consciously form and link SC (SC networking). Here, an important perspective is that SC and networked SC are collectives of practitioners in different specialist areas, and these collectives have knowledge boundaries that can always act as a source of innovation.

As factors of uncertainty and novelty such as new business models or value chain building increase, these knowledge boundaries will have a pragmatic boundary nature (Kodama 2007a, b, 2015). To transform the energy generated from these pragmatic boundaries into innovation, a strong common intention among practitioners is required. Practitioners need not only use boundary objects (Star 1989) as tools to trigger innovation or common knowledge among them, such as common language, common meaning, and common interest (Carlile 2002; Cramton 2001;

Star 1989), but even more importantly they also need a strong common intention that is rooted in their common values (Kodama 2002, 2007c). Practitioners in the main players Mitsui and IHH, and in many of the collaborating partners, have this strong common intention, and demonstrate collaborative DC through boundary synchronization by building resilient SC networks to succeed with new business models and value chains.

9.6 Conclusion

Through case studies of healthcare businesses enabled by strategic collaboration across dissimilar industries centered around Japanese general trading companies, this chapter has analyzed mechanisms for building new value chains and business models from the perspectives of DC and collaborative DC. Against the background of the demonstration of the asset orchestration process across different industries, through DC executed in general trading companies, this chapter has demonstrated the boundary synchronization between stakeholders (collaborating partners) that makes up the value chain and drives collaborative DC among stakeholders, and at the same time drives the asset orchestration process of the general trading companies as value chain co-ordinator.

Notes

1. The DOCOMO-centered small-world networks have hubs and a network structure resembling a scale-free network (Barabasi 2002) consisting of a huge number of links. Barabasi (2002) also observes a similar trend, in which 80% of all World Wide Web connections are "occupied" by only 20% of "hub" websites. Realistically, however, the number of business-related partners is limited. At the same time, a company comprising micropractitioners who think subjectively must discuss the pros and cons as well as transaction costs of building relationships with partners. This is why the networked SC formation differs somewhat (Watts 2003) from the highly centralized, scale-free network (Cole and Cole 2007; Barabási and Albert 1999).

2. Carlile (2004: 566) had the following to say: "Instead of viewing the firm as a bundle of resources (Wernerfelt 1984; Barney 1991), it will be viewed as a bundle of different boundaries where knowledge must be shared and assessed."

References

Amasaka, K. (2004). Development of "Science TQM", a New Principle of Quality Management: Effectiveness of Strategic Stratified Task Team at Toyota. *International Journal of Production Research, 42*(17), 3691–3706.

Baldwin, Y., & Clark, B. (2000). *Design Rules, Vol. 1: The Power of Modularity*. Cambridge, MA: MIT Press.

Barabasi, A. (2002). *Linked: The New Science of Networks*. Cambridge, MA: Perseus Books Group.

Barabási, A. L., & Albert, R. (1999). Emergence of Scaling in Random Networks. *Science, 286*(5439), 509–512.

Barney, J. (1991). Firm Resources and Sustained Competitive Advantage. *Journal of Management, 17*(3), 99–120.

Burt, S. (1992). *Structural Holes: The Social Structure of Competition*. Cambridge, MA/London: Harvard University Press.

Burt, R. S. (1997). A Note on Social Capital and Network Content. *Social Networks, 19*(4), 355–373.

Carlile, P. (2002). A Pragmatic View of Knowledge and Boundaries: Boundary Objects in New Product Development. *Organization Science, 13*(4), 442–455.

Carlile, P. (2004). Transferring, Translating, and Transforming: An Integrative Framework for Managing Knowledge Across Boundaries. *Organization Science, 15*(5), 555–568.

Chesbrough, H. (2003). *Open Innovation*. Boston: Harvard Business School Press.

Clark, B. (1985). The Interaction of Design Hierarchies and Market Concepts in Technological Evolution. *Research Policy, 14*(2), 235–251.

Cohen, D., & Prusak, L. (2000). *Good Company: How Social Capital Makes Organizations Work*. Boston: Harvard Business School Press.

Cole, R., & Cole, S. (2007). *Social Stratification in Science*. Chicago: University of Chicago Press.

Coleman, J. (1988). Social Capital in the Creation of Human Capital. *American Journal of Sociology, 94*, 95–120.

Cramton, C. (2001). The Mutual Knowledge Problem and Its Consequences for Dispersed Collaboration. *Organization Science, 12*(3), 346–371.

Dyer, J., & Hatch, N. (2004). Using Supplier Networks to Learn Faster. *Sloan Management Review, 45*(3), 57–63.

Giddens, A. (1979). *Central Problems in Social Theory: Action, Structure, and Contradiction in Social Analysis*. Berkeley: University of California Press.

Giddens, A., & Pierson, C. (1998). *Conversation with Anthony Giddens: Making Sense of Modernity*. Oxford: Blackwell Publishers Ltd.

Granovetter, M. (1973). The Strength of Weak Ties. *American Journal of Sociology, 78*(6), 1360–1380.

Henderson, R., & Clark, K. (1990). Architectural Innovation: The Reconfiguration of Existing Product Technologies and the Failure of Established Firms. *Administrative Science Quarterly, 35*, 9–30.

Kodama, M. (2002). Transforming an Old Economy Company Through Strategic Communities. *Long Range Planning, 35*(4), 349–365.

Kodama, M. (2003). Strategic Innovation in Traditional Big Business. *Organization Studies, 24*(2), 235–268.

Kodama, M. (2004). Strategic Community-Based Theory of Firms: Case Study of Dialectical Management at NTT DoCoMo. *Systems Research and Behavioral Science, 21*(6), 603–634.

Kodama, M. (2005a). Knowledge Creation Through Networked Strategic Communities: Case Studies on New Product Development in Japanese Companies. *Long Range Planning, 38*(1), 27–49.

Kodama, M. (2005b). How Two Japanese High-Tech Companies Achieved Rapid Innovation Via Strategic Community Networks. *Strategy & Leadership, 33*(6), 39–47.

Kodama, M. (2007a). *The Strategic Community-Based Firm*. London: Palgrave Macmillan.

Kodama, M. (2007b). *Knowledge Innovation –Strategic Management as Practice*. Cheltenham: Edward Elgar Publishing.

Kodama, M. (2007c). *Project-Based Organization in the Knowledge-Based Society*. London: Imperial College Press.

Kodama, M. (2009a). Boundaries Innovation and Knowledge Integration in the Japanese Firm. *Long Range Planning, 42*(4), 463–494.

Kodama, M. (2009b). *Innovation Networks in Knowledge-Based Firm –Developing ICT-Based Integrative Competences*. Cheltenham: Edward Elgar Publishing.

Kodama, M. (2011). *Interactive Business Communities*. London: Gower Publishing.

Kodama, M. (2014). *Winning Through Boundaries Innovation –Communities of Boundaries Generate Convergence*. Oxford: Peter Lang.

Kodama, M. (Ed.). (2015). *Collaborative Innovation: Developing Health Support Ecosystems* (Vol. 39). London: Routledge.

Kodama, M. (2017). Developing Strategic Innovation in Large Corporations—The Dynamic Capability View of the Firm. *Knowledge and Process Management, 24*(4), 221–246.

Kodama, M., & Shibata, T. (2014). Strategy Transformation Through Strategic Innovation Capability–A Case Study of Fanuc. *R&D Management, 44*(1), 75–103.

Mintzberg, H. (1978). Patterns in Strategy Formation. *Management Science, 24*(4), 934–948.

Nahapiet, J., & Ghoshal, S. (1998). Social Capital, Intellectual Capital, and the Creation of Value in Firms. *Academy of Management Review, 23*(2), 242–266.

Simon, A. (1996). The Architecture of Complexity: Hierarchic Systems. In H. A. Simon (Ed.), *The Science of the Artificial* (3rd ed.). MIT Press: Cambridge, MA.

Star, S. L. (1989). The Structure of Ill-structured Solutions: Boundary Objects and Heterogeneous Distributed Problem Solving. In L. Gasser & M. N. Huhns (Eds.), *Distributed Artificial Intelligence* (pp. 37–54). London: Pitman.

Watts, J. (2003). *Six Degrees: The Science of a Connected Age*. New York: W.W. Norton and Company.

Wernerfelt, B. (1984). A Resource-Based View of the Firm. *Strategic Management Journal, 5*, 171–180.

10
Boundaries Synchronization and Capabilities Congruence: Discussion and Implications

Mitsuru Kodama

10.1 Knowledge Boundaries and (Collaborative) Dynamic Capabilities

This section aims to identify the knowledge (assets) born on the boundaries between people and between organizations as a wellspring of innovation. The dynamic view of strategy, in which the diverse boundaries that exist within and between companies and include their partners and clients are networked, brings about new dynamic capabilities (DC) (and collaborative dynamic capabilities, C-DC) to generate innovation. Through detailed case studies of collaborative innovation between companies and organizations (Kodama 2015), this section discusses the mechanisms of generating new innovation by executing organizational architecture as networked diverse pragmatic boundaries that dynamically orchestrate the various assets (knowledge) inside and outside companies (organizations).

M. Kodama (✉)
Nihon University, College of Commerce, Tokyo, Japan
e-mail: kodama.mitsuru@nihon-u.ac.jp

10.1.1 Capabilities on Knowledge Boundaries: Knowledge Boundaries Between Stakeholders

Business practitioners recognize a wide range of organizational boundaries in their daily business activities. Here, organizational boundaries mean the boundaries between the professions of formal organizations such as research, development, production, and sales, the boundaries between management layers within a company, and, as discussed in the research setting of this book, the boundaries between different businesses and industries, customers, external partners, and various business types. These boundaries are made up of actors with differing backgrounds and knowledge (see Fig. 10.1).

Carlile (2004) characterized knowledge of boundaries in three ways, as difference, dependency, and novelty (Carlile and Rebentisch 2003), and asserted that the correlating characteristics of these three kinds of knowledge can be expressed as an image of boundaries as vectors between two or more actors.

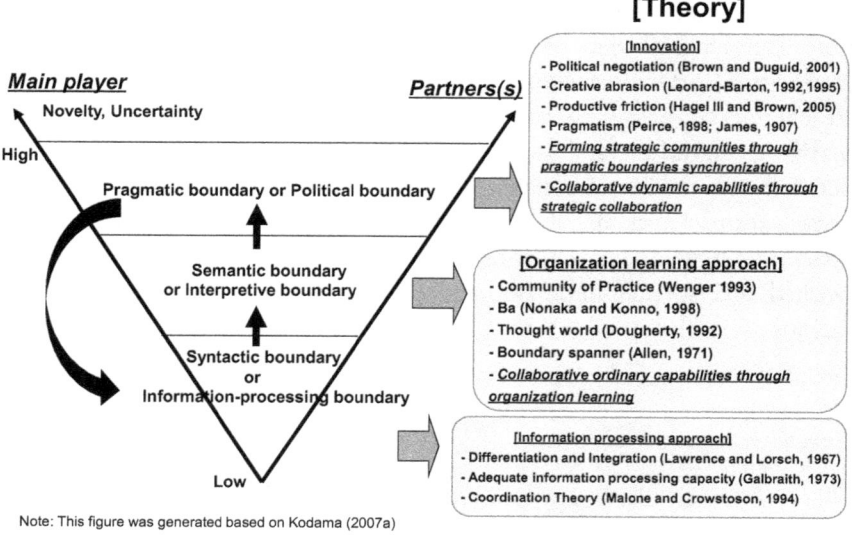

Fig. 10.1 Theory and characteristics of boundaries between main player(s) and partner(s). (Note: This figure was generated based on Kodama (2007a))

Generally, the characteristics of these boundaries consist of three layers (Shannon and Weaver 1949; Jantsch 1980; Carlile 2002, 2004) (see Fig. 10.1). In the first layer, syntactic or information-processing boundaries exist on which information and knowledge is transferred exactly between actors. Specifically, this entails routines as predetermined business processes or commercializing products through established development and production methods. On syntactic boundaries within corporations, the objectives are efficient production and business processes in which importance is placed on procedures and internally determined rules that follow business and management manuals and so on.

On the boundaries in the second layer (semantic and interpretive boundaries), actors engage in activities to generate new meanings and interpret (translate) new knowledge. Specifically, this entails activities along these semantic boundaries to incrementally continue to upgrade and improve existing business processes or development and production methods. On semantic boundaries within companies, importance is also placed on rules and company procedures of the syntactic boundaries, but these boundaries are also used to promote best company practice, business improvements, and upgrades such as total quality management and chains of organizational learning.

In the third layer of pragmatic and political boundaries, actors deal with new issues and objectives that have never existed, and work through conflict and friction between themselves, and even political power, in their activities to transform existing knowledge. These boundaries correspond to the specific achievement of completely new and unheard-of business concepts (new product and service developments to achieve new business models, new technical architecture or component developments, and new development and production methods). There is a high probability that new knowledge, the source of innovation, will be born on these pragmatic boundaries.

However, the boundaries in these three layers are interdependent, and their characteristics change dramatically with changes in the environment (customer needs, the competition, etc.) and the thoughts and interests of actors (syntactic boundary → semantic boundary → pragmatic boundary → syntactic boundary → semantic boundary →). In achieving innovation or corporate reform in particular, the boundaries among actors shift towards the pragmatic (syntactic boundary → semantic boundary → pragmatic boundary) when there are strong changes in circumstances or movements in the intentions of actors.

The vector of the syntactic boundary → semantic boundary → pragmatic boundary shift begins with the existing knowledge of deference and dependency among actors, and as novelty increases, the level of deference and dependency expands, and hence the amount of effort required with management of this increasing complexity and boundaries also grows. Existing knowledge of related deference and dependency have positive effects on the practical use of common knowledge (or mutual knowledge) (Cramton 2001) and has advantages for knowledge path dependency (Carlile 2004). However, on pragmatic boundaries in particular, there are many cases where the common knowledge of the past cannot express the novelty being currently faced (Carlile and Rebentisch 2003), and as novelty increases, knowledge path dependency conversely has negative effects (Hargadon and Sutton 1997).

In Fig. 10.1, there are clearly defined lines between the types of boundaries, but it is not easy for involved actors (main player and partners) to consciously (or unconsciously) distinguish where one line finishes and another starts in their actual practice. As well as that, the purpose of the hierarchical Fig. 10.1 is to express that actors' abilities on even more complex boundaries (e.g., pragmatic boundaries) with expanding complexity (expanding novelty) require abilities on their subordinate boundaries (e.g., semantic and syntactic boundaries). For example, on pragmatic boundaries this means the existence of common language, and common meaning is necessary to transform knowledge effectively.

Carlile (2004) states that multiple iterations are required between the three types of boundaries. It is impossible to achieve results in one go on pragmatic boundaries. In other words, actors must engage in repeated processes of mutual sharing of knowledge, evaluation, forming of new agreements and making changes where required. Thus as actors engaged in these repetition stages, it becomes easier to (skillfully) recognize important deference and dependency on boundaries, and reach integrated understanding and methods with more suitable common language, common meanings, and advantages and disadvantages of the problems and issues being faced. This ability to engage in repetition gives actors the ability to transform the characteristics of path-dependent knowledge.

Problematic scenarios found in corporations often occur owing to the use of path-dependent knowledge (or common knowledge) by administrators in positions of power that constrains the new knowledge of other managers who are expressing the novelty that they are facing. Such mismatches on boundaries result from managers with power putting themselves in even more powerful positions to demonstrate the unique knowledge of the fields in which they are involved. For example, these cases often entail actors creating conditions only for practical processes, boundaries transfer and syntactic processes, despite the fact that conditions for pragmatic and semantic boundaries are essentially necessary. These scenarios include, for example, disruptive innovation (Christensen 1997), in which exists the most dangerous strategic condition and one which actors fail to notice. As actors fail to recognize and resolve disruptive innovation, the novelty of it becomes critical with the passing of time.

Expanding the communications theories of Shannon and Weaver (1949) to organizational theories, Carlile's (2004) 3T (Transfer → Translate → Transform) model was reported as an analytical framework in case studies of product innovation or corporate reform done in the past. For example, existing research reports the Matsushita Electronics (Panasonic) corporate reform model (Kodama 2007d), new product development (NPD) between corporations (Kodama 2007e), knowledge-sharing processes between customers and suppliers in product development (Le Dain and Merminod 2014) and project management among stakeholders (Marjolein et al. 2016). As an organizational framework for promoting service development between companies and the building of ecosystems, this chapter uses Carlile's (2004) 3T model, analyzes capabilities on diverse knowledge boundaries between stakeholders and presents the new concept of boundary synchronization.

10.1.2 Synchronization of Pragmatic Boundaries by Forming Strategic Communities with the Main Player and Partners

New knowledge born on the various organizational boundaries that exist within and outside companies is a wellspring of organizational capability (Leonard-Barton 1995). In particular, integrating (orchestrating) new knowledge (assets) that arises on various pragmatic boundaries both inside and outside companies, and including their customers and partners (in other words synchronizing and orchestrating pragmatic boundaries that exist inside and outside companies), is a source of innovation, which in turn results in DC and C-DC to bring about sustainable competitiveness. Hence, this requires the synchronization of activities among stakeholders on knowledge boundaries (pragmatic boundaries) through strategic collaboration, an action that brings about synchronization of DC and C-DC. As stated in Chap. 2, C-DC brought about by DC synchronization lead to the synchronization of the strategic innovation loop (and boundaries synchronization) (see Fig. 10.1).

The concept I wish to propose in this book concerns a dynamic, practical method that corporate managers can use to orchestrate diverse asset distributed on networks, whether real or virtual, in order to develop new products or business models. At the core of the framework in this book is a concept known as strategic communities (SC) (Kodama 1999, 2005a; Kodama and Shibata 2014a, b), a theory for a practical method of accelerating innovation in a corporation. To obtain diverse and valuable assets, it is important to have a process in which managers from various strata of management both inside and outside the corporation can dynamically form SC as pragmatic boundaries with internal and external actors, without being restricted to existing formal organizations.

The SC is made up of four basic concepts. The first is that it possesses the element of *ba* as a constantly changing shared context in motion that allows corporations to respond to dynamic changes in market and technology environments (or to spontaneously create new market and technology environments) (Nonaka and Konno 1998). *Ba* is a place offering a shared context. Knowledge (assets) needs a context to be created, as it is context-specific. The context defines the participants and the nature of the participation. The context is social, cultural, and even historical, providing a basis for one to interpret information, thus creating meaning and becoming knowledge (assets). *Ba* is not necessarily just a physical space or even a geographical location or virtual space through information and communication technology (ICT) but a time–space nexus as much as a shared mental space. Any form of new knowledge (assets) can be created regardless of the business structure, as *ba* transcends formal business structures.

The second concept is that the SC is a community of practice (Wenger 2000) rooted in the resonance of values (2002, 2001, 2003, 2004) among the actors that form the SC. This aspect promotes mutual learning within the community by gaining an understanding of mutual contexts among members and resonating values, and continually generates new knowledge (assets). In the SC, the community membership and the community leader at the center of activities are gradually established, and these people dynamically produce the context in which they work toward fulfilling the community's mission. As shown by the case studies in this book, it involves the development of new products, services, and business models, and community members create new knowledge (assets) by learning from one another and sharing.

Third are the pragmatic boundary characteristics of SC to transform existing knowledge (assets) of actors in differing contexts (as discussed, pragmatic boundaries are positioned above the layers of syntactic and semantic boundaries. SC does not only have the characteristics of pragmatic boundaries) (Carlile 2002, 2004). As mentioned earlier, the concepts of *ba* and communities of practice (CoP) promote organizational learning and best practice through generation and sharing of new meaning among members on boundaries (e.g., Dougherty 1992) (This is equivalent to the semantic boundaries of the second layer mentioned above).

To promote best practice through regular routine upgrading and improvement, it's necessary to synchronize activities through organizational learning among stakeholders on semantic boundaries (between the main player and partners), which is an action that brings about ordinary capabilities (OC) synchronization and collaborative OC (C-OC) (see Fig. 10.1). C-OC brought about by OC synchronization in Domains III and IV on the Capabilities Map lead to the synchronization of the strategic innovation loop (and boundaries synchronization) (see Fig. 10.1). On the other hand, Teece (2014) suggests that organizational learning or best practice is not a contributor to the generation of DC, but rather is deeply involved in OC.

However, on knowledge boundaries between people and organizations on which high levels of novelty and uncertainty of innovation occur, new knowledge (assets) creation and existing knowledge (assets) transformation is required that transcends organizational learning and the meanings generated in the shared contexts of *ba* or CoP (this corresponds to the pragmatic boundaries of the third layer mentioned earlier).

On pragmatic boundaries, where various problems and issues are raised, actors must take up the challenge of solving such issues and problems, and generating new knowledge (assets). Actors need more practical creative abrasion (Leonard-Barton 1992), productive friction (Hagel III and Brown 2005) and negotiating practice (Brown and Duguid 2001) on boundaries. SC with pragmatic boundary characteristics formed by actors are sources of innovation, which also leads to DC (and C-DC), as self-organizing (companies) to bring about sustainable competitiveness as a result.

The fourth concept is that in which the actors, as hubs or connectors in an organization, dynamically bridge multiple different SC (or pragmatic boundaries) and form networks (or links) among the SC (Barabasi 2002; Watts 2003; Kodama 2005a, b, 2009a). In this way, multiple SC (or pragmatic boundaries) become orchestrated and enable corporations to create new knowledge (assets). In order to build NPD or business models, the actors then consciously network the SC that are pragmatic boundaries among various organizations in the corporation and integrate (orchestrate) multiple organizational boundaries. If needed, the actors also form SC through strategic alliances with external entities including customers and bond them deeply with SC within the corporation (Kodama 2003).

To achieve the innovation discussed in the case studies in this book, it is necessary to form SC by synchronizing the pragmatic boundaries between the main player and its partner(s). The formation of SC (and networked SC) that span within and between companies in this way leads to bringing about DC in one's own company, and C-DC (as well as C-OC) between companies (main player—partners—customers).

10.1.3 Dynamic Human Networks and the Architecture of the Asset Orchestration Process

As the fourth concept discussing SC characteristics as mentioned, network theories (e.g., Motter 2004; Watts 2003; Barabasi 2002) present the new perspective, which is a mechanism to dynamically integrate (orchestrate) knowledge (assets) dispersed both inside and outside companies. According to research done to date, networks linking people, groups, and organizations are important platforms for facilitating information and knowledge-based activities, in that the formation of organizations and networks has a major impact on the dissemination of knowledge and information (e.g., Owen-Smith and Powell 2004; Lin and Kulatilaka 2006). It is essential that companies form networks to acquire sustainable DC (e.g., Kodama 2007d), and dynamically reconfigure these networks to respond to changes in circumstances and strategic activities (e.g., Kodama 2006).

Network theories of nodes (e.g., individuals, groups of people, organizations of groups), network ties, or several networks topologies (e.g., small world structures, scale free structures) provide important knowledge and insight into practitioner behavior that transcends companies and the relationships between practitioners. As well as that, the thoughts and actions surrounding the formation of human networks by practitioners are the management drivers discussed in Fig. 2.7 in Chap. 2 (efficiency, creativity, resources, values, dialectics), and are important triggers for executing the asset orchestration process.

Network formations are generally classed as centralized or decentralized (Albert and Barabasi 2000; Ahuja and Carley 1999). Centralized networks are best adopted for vertical interaction and efficient execution, and routine information and knowledge flows (e.g., information and knowledge sent from central nodes to peripheral nodes) (e.g., Albert and Barabasi 2000; Tushman 1977). In contrast, decentralized networks are generally applied in uncertain conditions or when there are new challenges to be directly faced (e.g., smaller hubs) (e.g., Watts 2003).

Tight clustering and autonomy of workgroups is crucial to decentralized network formations. This structural design enhances information and knowledge exchange and interaction at the work group level, and can effectively facilitate mutual co-ordination and adjustments among peripheral local nodes (Tushman 1977). Furthermore, such local cluster co-ordination and collaboration reduces the information processing load assigned to the central node, as peripheral nodes do not need to communicate directly with the central authority whenever a decision-making situation arises.

"Small-world networks," in which a high degree of local clustering and only a small number of links between any two nodes exist, were found to enhance mutual dependence among cluster nodes and facilitate communications, co-ordination and collaboration among practitioners, especially when tight collaboration is necessary for connecting value chains in between organizations (e.g., Newman 2004). The availability of such short paths for "bridging" nodes enhances co-ordination and collaboration of the network, particularly when interacting in between organizations (e.g., Watts 2003; Baum et al. 2004). Moreover, such network properties are effective when creating new ideas and innovation in complex and dissimilar organizations (e.g., Braha and Bar-Yam 2004).

Moreover, small world networks provide organizations with robust network formations that can deal with sudden environmental changes such as concentrated information traffic, excessive overloads, bottlenecks or unexpected accidents, or environmental destruction (Newman 2004; Shah 2000). For example, the 1997 case of major Toyota supplier Aisin, which faced a destructive crisis that was averted by the mutual formation of emergent interorganizational networks among Toyota and its partner suppliers was precisely due to the formation of these "small-world networks" among the suppliers centered on Toyota (Watts 2003; Nishiguchi and Beaudet 1998).

Furthermore, SC, different from the concept of a community of practice (CoP) (e.g., Wenger 1998), is a form of cross-functionality by practitioners between different organizations and companies. SC itself is a "small-world structure" (see Fig. 10.2). Viewed from the perspective of social network theory, SC can be considered as clusters or cliques where people, the smallest nodes, come together (e.g., Roethlisberger and Dickson 1939; Roethlisberger 1977). While cliques are collectives of closely linked practitioners who interchange and share information, knowledge, and context, in SC, information is not simply exchanged among actor groups, but rather in collectives (teams and projects); new contexts and knowledge are generated dynamically in response to environmental changes.

The many specialized practitioners in an SC are a group of people who achieve new innovation to discover and solve problems on the pragmatic boundaries they face, execute creative strategies, and are formed as the

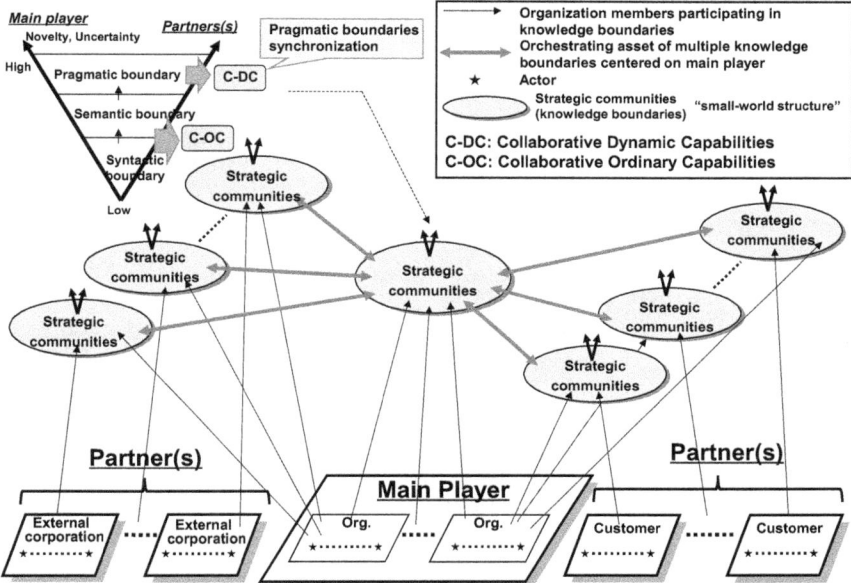

Fig. 10.2 Asset orchestration by forming SC between the main player and partner(s)

aforementioned "small-world networks." As discussed previously, the demonstration of collaborative DC requires synchronization of the pragmatic boundaries between stakeholders. In other words, this brings about synchronization of the players' DC, and hence brings about C-DC (see Fig. 10.2).

Small world networks are characterized by short connections between nodes (the smallest node is a person) and local clustering. For example, as nodes, the short path between practitioners belonging to dissimilar organizations enables access to practitioners within the company, belonging to other companies, and customers. Furthermore, each node in a small world network is embedded in the local cluster. Local clustering hence has the potential to foster reliable accessibility (White and Houseman 2003). A small-world network can be formed either by randomly rewiring a portion of an existing regular network or attaching each new node to a "neighborhood" that already exists (Watts and Strogatz 1998).

Furthermore, these are examples of two-mode networks (bipartite networks) and affiliation networks (e.g., Wasserman and Faust 1994; Faust 1997; Watts 2003) in social network theories, as shown in Fig. 10.2 (Kodama 2005a, 2009a). The author places particular focus on dynamically changing SC and network SC, whose network forms are called "group interlocked networks" by Watts (2003). Watts (2003) said actors have a relationship with a particular context, whereas in the real world of business, actors (practitioners) form groups subjectively in particular contexts, in which they incorporate other actors (practitioners) at the same time (in other words linking actors together). Accordingly, as a group, the SC changes dynamically in response to context, and at the same time as the networked form networked SC are dynamically formed and change.

Practitioners dynamically reconfigure SC as part of their daily activities, and multiple practitioners participate in multiple SC to share contexts, knowledge (assets), and information, and practitioners who also participate in other SC transfer contexts, knowledge (assets), and information, and share and transform it with those practitioners. Through this process, networked SC are formed as the above-mentioned group interlock networks. SC can be seen as nodes and hubs in the framework of this group-interlocked network. Practitioners who belong to hub or node SC inside or outside companies create networks among the SC (or link them together) by dynamically bridging multiple and different SC. In this way, multiple SC are integrated as networks, and new contexts and knowledge (assets) are orchestrated. To develop new products or configure new business processes, practitioners consciously network multiple SC between various organizations through pragmatic boundaries synchronization both inside and outside companies to make deep connections between the SC inside and outside their companies. This mechanism is the essence of the asset orchestration process (see Fig. 10.2).

In particular, as shown by the case studies in this book, to build an ecosystem through service innovation asset orchestration must be optimized within companies, between companies, and between industries. For this, pragmatic boundary synchronization among stakeholders promotes the formation of SC within companies and between companies and industries, and at the same time synchronization of the DC of the individual players brings about C-DC in companies, between companies, and between industries. As seen in the case studies in this book, these stakeholder actions lead to the realization of health support ecosystems.

10.2 Boundaries Synchronization Between Main Player(s) and Partner(s) on the Capabilities Map

Configuring SC (and networked SC) with the characteristics of pragmatic boundaries within and between companies is dependent on capabilities shifting between each domain in response to changes in the environment surrounding the company (uncertainty, risk, and speed). This section describes changes in boundaries characteristics accompanying the shifts between domains, and dynamic forms of informal organizations (SC and communities of practice) responding to the changes, from a framework of dynamic and OC.

In each domain in Fig. 10.3, an organizational form is indicated that demonstrates C-DC between the main player and partners or C-OC. In positioning in the domains, SC are close in character to the informal organizations in Domain I, which is where radical innovation is triggered. Particularly in building new business models spanning different industries or new product and service development, such as those described in this case study, practitioners in the main player company and partner companies belong to particular formal organizations, and there are many cases in which research and development (R&D) or new business planning and development is carried out informally, with very few specialists who have high level professional knowledge and techniques in a particular field. As discussed, in these workplaces pragmatic boundaries characteristic of organizations in which conflicts and discord occur are induced where the knowledge (assets) of different industries or areas of specializations intersect, and on these knowledge boundaries the probability of new innovation being brought about is raised (Kodama 2007a, e). Thus SC can also be called informal organizations characterized by pragmatic

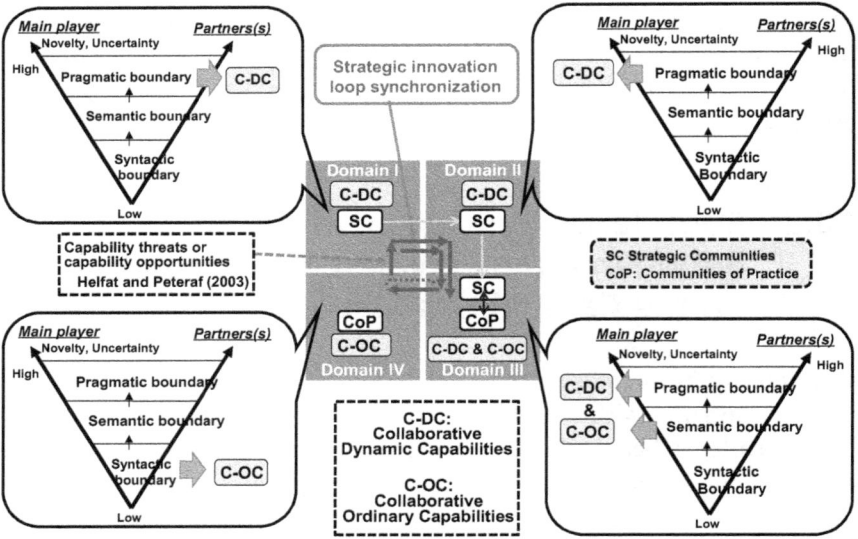

Fig. 10.3 Boundaries synchronization between main player(s) and partner(s) on the capabilities map—strategic innovation loop synchronization

boundaries, in which DC (and C-DC) can be easily demonstrated. For this reason, in Domain I demonstrating DC is critical, rather than OC (C-OC) with its focus on routine business.

Nevertheless, the members of SC are specialists, and at the same time these organizations are not devoid of a history of capabilities and do not start out with a blank slate. Naturally, there are cases in which each of the individuals in the founding team has human capital (context-specific knowledge, special skills, and experience), social capital (social ties within and outside the team), and cognition (Helfat and Peteraf 2003); and furthermore, sometimes as a group these individuals may possess team-specific human capital if they have worked together previously in another setting. However, as SC members between different companies lack common knowledge (Cramton 2001) they must create and share new community knowledge by sharing and understanding knowledge and experiences of their individual and dissimilar fields of specialization.

Members of SC spanning between companies (main players and partners) must therefore demonstrate C-DC by synchronizing DC for

"Sensing → Seizing → Transforming" to select new technologies and processes, and achieve R&D and new business development by searching out and detecting new potential markets, hence bringing about consistent results with R&D and new business model planning and development. However, there is a good chance of R&D or business development failure in Domain I where uncertainties and risks are high.

Nevertheless, the achievement of R&D and new business development in Domain I shift to Domain II for commercial development with demonstration of new DC (C-DC). Then in Domain II, new innovation measures are taken in to develop new products, services, and business through new technologies and processes to match market and technological innovations. Thus, similar to Domain I, there are many cases where informal organizations such as SC are formed as organizational systems in which DC and C-DC are demonstrated. In our investigations of a large corporation in Japan, I have seen many cases in which the members of SC involved in business in Domain I shift to Domain II and take with them their R&D achievements for commercial developments. Then, to succeed with commercial developments in Domain II, more resources are invested, and organizations become more formalized. Then, multi-layered SC are formed between formal organizations inside and outside companies. Here, as illustrated by Fig. 10.2, asset orchestration speeds up through the formation of networked SC via the demonstration of collaborative DC (C-DC).

However, it is in this domain that the "valley of death" exists, raising the likelihood of failure of commercial developments. There are even cases that lead to withdrawal in the prototype assessments or trial service stages or failure where chances are taken to attempt commercialization, despite high risk and uncertainty. There are also many cases in which the demonstration of DC and collaborative DC (C-DC) in Domain II has had negative effects (Kodama 2018).

In addition, the achievements of commercial development in Domain II shift to the establishment of new product value chains in Domain III by the enactment of new DC (and collaborative DC) (see Fig. 10.3). In Domain III, further improvements and upgrades of new products accelerate renewal processes (Helfat and Peteraf 2003), and bring about potentials of "replication/redeployment" (Helfat and Peteraf 2003) for commercial development duplication, transfer, or application in other business territories. As well as this, the possibilities for new products and services brought about by "recombination" (Helfat and Peteraf 2003) of one's company's products or services through those of another through strategic alliances or mergers and acquisitions (M&A) also increase.

Moreover, measures are required to achieve sustainable technological evolution and establish value chains in Domain III that can detect rapid market changes. Informal organizations enacting DC (and collaborative DC) in Domain III are often SC. The reason for this is the rapid incremental innovation of upgrading products and services that is unique to this domain (Kodama 2018). In other words, to succeed with rapid incremental innovation in Domain III, integration of CoP, organizations become characteristically more formal, and demonstrate OC to bring about improvements and upgrades to regular routines for best practice, with SC for new product and service version objectives being efficient and effective (see Fig. 10.3). This is thus the issue of combining efficiency with creativity. Mainly demonstrating DC (and collaborative DC), SC pursue novelty with new product versions, while CoP are organizations that mainly demonstrate OC (and collaborative OC) in pursuit of efficiency with improvements and upgrades to product manufacture and sales routines, which brings about a kind of co-specialization between organizations or between companies.

Furthermore, to successfully establish and sustainably expand sales of products in Domain III, further resources are invested and organizations further formalized in main player and partner companies. Multi-layered SC are then formed between these formal organizations inside and outside companies. Here, to upgrade products and services, asset orchestration speeds up through the formation of networked SC in which collaborative DC are enacted, as illustrated by Fig. 10.2.

In contrast, in Domain III, as discussed earlier, rapid incremental innovation where strong DC (and strong collaborative DC) must be demonstrated for unceasingly upgrading and improving products and services, is required to put newly developed products and services into orbit and win out over the competition. At the same time, supervisors and staff in departments downstream in the routine value chain (sales, technical management, procurement, production, and aftercare) must use strong OC (and strong collaborative OC) to upgrade and improve their operations management across companies. Therefore, since best practices through strong OC must be pursued, the key is the formation of CoP that spans the formal organizations within the companies (main player and partners). In Domain III, then, to strengthen the value chain upstream and downstream, strong interactive linkages are indispensable between the SC, demonstrating strong DC, and CoP, demonstrating strong OC (see Fig. 10.3).

Characteristically in many cases, formal organizations in Domain III adopt the form of an "integrated organization" (e.g., Kodama 2002, 2003, 2004, 2014) as organizational strategies to bring about strong C-DC and C-OC. This could mean, for example, merging project organizations with line organizations (functional organizations) since they easily bring about SC and CoP characteristics respectively.

In contrast, Domain IV contains the product lineups and services that have shifted from Domain III and may include flagship products. In general, in Domain IV there is a low level of uncertainty, the pace of environmental change is soft, and product lineups feature various models. There are plenty of necessities in the business to business and business to consumer fields. These include a variety of completed products, various parts of completed products, living ware, food, and so forth. As products that won out in Domain III to survive through to Domain IV, these also include traditional and classic products. In Domain IV, incremental innovation is repeated with existing technologies and routines to slowly improve them through the recognition of slow-moving markets (Kodama 2018). Thus, in Domain IV, strong OC in CoP and formal organizations in product value chains actuate best practices. Capability opportunities (Helfat and Peteraf 2003) are also a trigger for the Domain III → Domain IV shift (however, some products in Domain III are withdrawn owing to stiff competition, which leads to them being retrenched or retired). In the shift, processes of renewal through continuous and gentle incremental product innovation are mostly performed, but in some cases products might be replicated, transferred, or applied in other markets or business territories if market changes are sluggish (and the company has sufficient resources) (replication/redeployment (Helfat and Peteraf 2003)). Moreover, in slow-moving markets where there is not much uncertainty, there is also the potential to bring about synergies by creating new products (or services) through a recombination of company products or services with those of other companies through strategic alliances and M&A, by demonstrating strong OC as normal routines (see Fig. 10.3).

However, in Domain IV, product and service lineups gradually become more susceptible to influence from changes in customer tastes or technical innovations. For instance, there are good examples of analog products being pushed out by digital products over long periods, or telephone services shifting to become internet services. None of these have happened abruptly. In spite of this, there are plenty of cases that are lagging behind such developments. In other words, strong C-OC begins to become a hindrance, and as environmental changes loom, product lineups that lag behind go down the path to retrenchment or retirement.

For example, Kodama (2018) describes how Kodak was a company that took the path of retrenchment and retirement from Domain IV owing to the effects of digitalization, whereas Fujifilm successfully and strategically shifted from Domain IV to Domain I with redeployment/recombination. Kodak felt the threats from the market changes accompanying digitalization early on, but persisted in sticking to its existing strong OC, seeking to maximize its profits and shareholder value. Kodak consistently engaged in rigid strategies such as stock measures, using its own substantial capital to buy its own shares. Furthermore, at the time, Kodak's top management had no idea how to orchestrate the company's high-level intangible assets to respond to the changing environment of digitalization.

In contrast, Fujifilm used the high-grade photographic film technologies it already had to develop protective film for LCD screens, which the company successfully commercialized (applying its film technologies for LCD TVs—redeployment). And in another example of redeployment/recombination of existing technology, Fujifilm used its collagen technologies that it had used to prevent photographic film from drying out to develop a cosmetic product that is now a hit (Kodama and Shibata 2016). Hence, this company has successfully moved into the cosmetics business, a different field. As well as this, Fujifilm is also involved in medical product developments that are gaining attention in the fight against the Ebola virus. Differing from Kodak, Fujifilm did not set out to maximize profits and shareholder value, but avoided zero profits to survive, and by orchestrating (with strong DC) the existing high-level intangible assets that the company had accumulated it succeeded with radical innovation by shifting from Domain IV onto Domain I → Domain II → Domain III (where Domains I → II are the radical innovation and Domain III is the incremental innovation).

In the case of the shift from Domain III (or Domain IV) → Domain I, as the threats encroached the company engaged in higher-order learning as it was well aware of the dangers, and executed strategic collaboration through the formation of informal networks with differing areas of business (in other words, engaged in high-quality strategic non-routine activities), which led to the demonstration of strong DC (and strong C-DC) and raised the potential for a shift to Domain I. This is a good example of strategy transformation through capability threats (Helfat and Peteraf 2003).

In addition, as Winter (2000) describes, organizations faced with threats are likely to be motivated to raise the level of their capabilities. When capabilities are renewed, new methods are sought out and developed, and a stage of new progression comes about. In some cases, companies also redeploy their capabilities in markets for different products. Redeployment is not the same as replication, the application of the same products and services in a different regional market, but rather involves targeting markets for products and services with a strong association. Furthermore, when companies transfer capabilities to different businesses, but ones that have strong linkages to their current business, there are often cases that involve the recombining of capabilities with other capabilities instead of replication and redeployment (Helfat and Peteraf 2003). The success of Fujifilm can also be thought of as the result of the processes of renewal, redeployment, or recombination functioning through strong DC from beginning to end.

This can also be seen as a Domain III → Domain I shift. This is the concept of new radical innovation by discovering capability opportunities in rapidly changing environments and serious competition with rival companies. There are many cases of this, most remarkable in the world being the case of strategy transformation though strong DC with Apple's radical innovation in its business shift from the personal computer (PC) to the music distribution business. Apple succeeded in new business by moving from its Mac development methods (developed in house) to orchestration of the best intangible assets both inside and outside the company (co-specialized assets) (Kodama 2017b, 2018). This was the result of strong DC (strong C-DC) enabling processes of renewal, redeployment, or recombination to function through to the end. The new Nintendo Wii and DS concepts were also a radical innovation of gaming machines though redeployment to target customers in a completely different customer segment to the Sony PlayStation, a hugely popular product at the time (customers such as the elderly or housewives who had no previous interest in computerized games) (Kodama 2007c). The Domain III → Domain I shift is also the strategy of aiming for yet-to-be-pioneered markets or technologies, common to the so-called "blue ocean strategies" (Kim and Mauborgne 2005).

The above has considered the positioning of the four domains and their relationships in the Capabilities Map in the perspective of DC and OC (collaborative DC and collaborative OC). The capabilities that companies and organizations require to shift between each of these domains to respond to environmental changes (uncertainty and speed) change dynamically. Hence, collaborative DC bring about the synchronization of the DC of individual companies, while shifting between domains in response to changes in the environment brings synchronization to the strategic innovation loop (boundary synchronization).

10.3 The Five Capability Elements of Players

As a factor of C-DC, the concept of "capabilities congruence" among ecosystem partners to achieve capability synthesis for maximizing capabilities is important. As requirements for the five capabilities elements of ecosystem partners, (1) strategy capabilities, (2) organizational capabilities, (3) technology capabilities, (4) operational capabilities, and (5) leadership capabilities, this section presents the concept of congruence among capabilities elements, capabilities congruence among ecosystem partners, and new theoretical implications.

As discussed in Chap. 2, a business ecosystem can be thought of as a composite system consisting of subsystems with ultra-stable characteristics (e.g., Kramer and de Smit 1977), which include the various corporate systems (main players and groups of collaborating partners). In addition, these subsystems have to achieve capabilities congruence between their respective partial environments ([Insight-1], [Insight-2], and [Insight-3]). However, when dynamic changes occur in these partial environments, if it is possible to absorb and adapt to these changes through synergies between the corporate system, which is a subsystem, and the environment, and within the corporate system, then the assertions of [Insight-1], [Insight-2], and [Insight-3] will be satisfied (e.g., Kramer and de Smit 1977). Nevertheless, when significant changes occur that bring about new business ecosystems such as new service innovations, it is necessary to seek out stable conditions of new capabilities congruence for the entire system (a business ecosystem formed from the integrated systems of all the group companies).

On the other hand, at this time, while the business ecosystem, a competent system, is subjected, if a corporate system which is a subsystem (e.g., a main player) causes significant changes between environments it created, it will have significant influence on other corporate systems as subsystems (collaborating players). Hence, when this happens, the necessity inevitably arises to bring congruence to capabilities in subsystems ([Insight-1], [Insight-2], and [Insight-3]) through the interactions of capabilities between the subsystems (the corporate systems). At the same time, the synergies of capabilities between the various subsystems (between corporate systems) is equivalent to capabilities congruence among the various stakeholders ([Insight-4]), while dynamic congruence with the Capabilities Map in corporate systems is important.

Kodama (2018) defines the individual subsystem capabilities elements in a corporate system (subsystem elements required for capabilities congruence). Kodama (2018) extracts and analyzes elements of certain capabilities required for sustainable growth from interview data from large corporations that have achieved (or failed at) sustainable growth (in Asia and the West) through the practice of DC and published secondary materials.

Then, as empirical observations, business factors related to various core capabilities required for capabilities congruence in corporate systems are identified and categorized from first-order concepts related to the capabilities elements, and second-order themes are extracted from theoretical observations. As a result of analyzing and considering these second-order themes, I uncovered strong interactions between the various capabilities that were identified and categorized, as well as relationships of fitness and reinforcement.

Finally, these second-order themes led to the five core framework capabilities elements in a corporate system, the main aggregate theoretical concepts: (1) Strategy Capabilities, (2) Organizational Capabilities, (3) Technology Capabilities, (4) Operational Capabilities, (5) Leadership Capabilities (see Figs. 2.3 and 2.4 in Chap. 2).

These five capabilities elements in corporate systems can also be thought of as subsystem elements observed in the DC of corporate systems (i.e., the entire company) as entire systems. Processes are one factor of DC; however, since the performance of DC is also the processes used to apply DC (Eisenhardt and Martine 2000), these five capabilities can also be viewed as processes. In other words, they can be called "strategy processes," "organizational processes," "technological (creating) processes," "operational processes," and "leadership (the demonstration of) processes." These processes are thus similar to the signature processes unique to a company identified by Teece (2014).

Here, I would like to briefly describe why leadership capabilities (leadership processes) are related to processes. Leadership is not a matter of unique "style," but is also something that should be perceived as a constantly changing process. Put differently, in changing environments leaders engage in different leadership behaviors, moment by moment. Leadership as a process means particular leadership in situations that are always changing, which means unceasingly changing with each and every event or episode that occurs in innovation activities. As a process, then, leadership constantly changes as the intangible assets of human empirical knowledge are constantly renewed through the actual experience of humans moving from the fast, through the present, and into the future.

Thus the resources that bring about new intangible assets are the dynamic generation and nature of actual events and episodes made up of the interactions between individuals in a range of changing contexts as backgrounds (actual entities) (Whitehead 1978), and are by no means at all static. A fundamental analytical framework for perceiving dynamic corporate activity (e.g., the knowledge integration (convergence) process (Kodama 2011, 2014) lies in the dynamic processes of the innovations activities of individuals, associations, and organizations both inside and outside companies, thus, for sustainable corporate growth, it is important to perceive the corporate activities for sustainable growth as "processes" changing unceasingly in the past, the present and the future (Kodama 2018). Therefore, the leadership of leaders with good intangible assets dynamically change and strengthen as environments change while strategic collaboration with other leaders brings about leadership synergies (in other words, co-specialization of intangible assets related to the quality of leadership). As discussed later, leader teams (LT) formed from excellent leaders are co-specialized. Accordingly, the leadership of individual leaders are valuable co-specialized assets of organizations.

Furthermore, the operational capabilities (operation processes) discussed in this book do not mean exactly the same thing as a factor of the OC in corporate activities (daily routines) discussed in Chap. 2. Teece (2007, p. 1346) asserts "Yet it is perhaps an overstatement to say that 'operations management' tools and procedures cannot be the basis of competitive advantage, or work against it. If there is a significant, tacit, non-inimitable component of an enterprise's superior operational competence, it has the potential for a time to support superior performance (it will, in fact, generate Ricardian rents). Nevertheless, superior operational efficiency, while valuable, is not a dynamic capability." Teece (2014, p. 333) also gives the example of "fast food industry dynamic capabilities figuring out new products to put on the menu, new operating hours (e.g., late night), and new locations (central versus suburban)," and "operations strategy as developing resources and configuring processes so that there is good strategic fit with the business environment" (Van Mieghem 2008), thereby identifying DC in "operations."

Certainly, like Porter (1996), "operational management" tools and procedures cannot be identified as a source of competitiveness, although taking up the challenge of constantly innovating manufacturing (e.g., R&D for developing new technologies for production system automation, Internet of Things (IoT), artificial intelligence (AI), and robotics), as the Japanese Fanuc and Canon have done, can bring about operational and supply chain management mechanisms that are difficult for other companies to copy. The operational capabilities to bring about operational strategies that fit strategy and technology in this way are a factor of DC.

Teece (2007, p. 1338) also says that "Capturing co-specialization benefits may require integrated operations" (Teece 1980). In other words, new operational capabilities can be interpreted as unique corporate operational capabilities that are difficult for another company to copy, brought about with co-specialization occurring with technological capabilities resulting from technological innovation of production systems by operational management. Accordingly, I would like to emphasis that operational capabilities are not the OC discussed by Teece (2014), but are intangible assets which bring about co-specialization with other capabilities elements (e.g., technology and organizational capabilities). Therefore, I will call capabilities that give rise to operational processes that are difficult for other companies to copy "operational capabilities."

As signature processes also, these five individual process capabilities are unique to companies, and bring about specific DC that are difficult to copy by other companies through "Fit" (or alignment, consistency, congruence), by co-specialization between these many processes. Thus, this (dynamic) internal congruence appears when congruence (consistency) is generated between the five capabilities elements. The even stronger form of internal congruence in capabilities thus refers to a state in which not only has consistency between the five capabilities elements being achieved, but the co-specialization is reinforced (complemented) (discussed later) to optimize the corporate system.

In existing research, Miles and Snow (1994) refer to the necessity for a "tight fit" between strategy, structure, and process. Moreover, the five capabilities elements in a corporate system have commonalities with the theoretical models of existing research—"Organization Architecture" (Tushman and O'Reilly 1997) and the "Corporate Strategy Triangle" (Collis and Montgomery 1998). Thus, as a company drives the asset orchestration process through DC (Sensing → Seizing → Transforming), it also brings internal congruence among the five capabilities elements in the corporate system (see Fig. 2.4 in Chap. 2).

10.4 Congruence of the Five Capabilities Among Players

As three factors of the C-DC discussed in Chap. 1, capabilities congruence among stakeholders ([Insight-4]) leads to:

1) The building of enduring relationships of trust through strategic collaboration with ecosystem partners,
2) The realization of co-specialization with ecosystem partners, and
3) The realization of capabilities synthesis with ecosystem partners.

However, with [Insight-4], capabilities congruence among ecosystem partners, that is, among stakeholders it is crucial that the congruence of the individual five capabilities elements is optimized among ecosystem partners (stakeholders).

This section clarifies the importance of the concept of "capabilities congruence" among ecosystem partners in achieving capability synthesis for maximizing capabilities in ecosystems, a factor of C-DC. However, as discussed in Chap. 2, to achieve Insight-4, stakeholders must be synchronized when shifting between domains in the individual stages of Domains I to IV. Hence, Chap. 2 leads to the proposition that it is necessary to synchronize the strategic innovation loops on the Capabilities Map with capabilities congruence among stakeholders (Insight-4), and asserts that synchronization of strategic innovation loops promotes C-DC.

However, to synchronize the strategic innovation loops, it is crucial that the congruence of the individual five capabilities is optimized among ecosystem partners (stakeholders) (see Fig. 10.4).

To repeat, the asset orchestration process through DC (Sensing → Seizing → Transforming) is required to achieve internal congruence among the five capabilities elements in corporate systems and external congruence between the corporate system and the environment. Teece (2007, p. 1337) identifies the importance of "strategic fit" to strengthen corporate strategic management, and emphasizes co-specialization as an important aspect related to this "fit." In other words, orchestration of intangible assets such as co-specialized assets and complementary assets

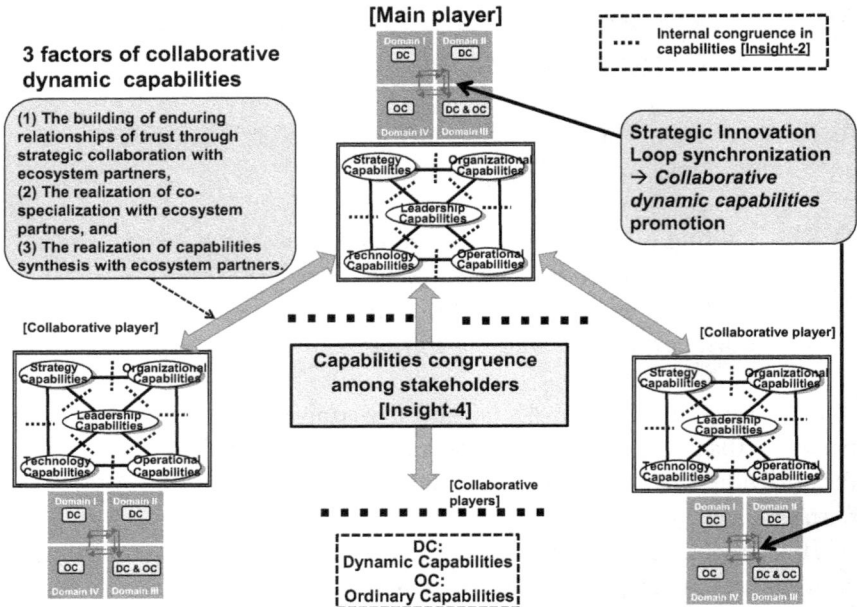

Fig. 10.4 Congruence of the five capabilities among players

are important for achieving this kind of strategic fit (Teece 2007; Helfat et al. 2007). This is because in systemic innovation, such as described by these service innovations of the case studies in this book, co-specialization between the subsystem elements that make up a system is crucial (Teece 1986). For example, focusing on technical aspects one can see that high-tech products are often systems that are made up of mutually interacting structural elements supported by platforms, and the importance of this co-specialization has been increasing in recent years.

Co-specialization involves some kind of complementary systems; for example, to meet customer demands for performance, co-specialization could describe part of a system in which technologies or other assets are closely integrated. Accordingly, with systems and networks, it is especially important to integrate not only company know-how (intangible assets), but also know-how from external sources for a business to succeed. This proposition is also closely related to congruence through orchestration of co-specialized assets inside and outside companies, as described by Insight 3.

Co-specialization can also be thought of as co-specialization between assets (e.g., technologies and capabilities) co-specialization between strategies and organizations, co-specialization between strategies and processes (e.g., operations), co-specialization between technologies, and co-specialization between technologies and other parts of the value chain. Co-specialized assets are a particular class of complementary assets where the value of an asset is a function of its use in conjunction with other particular assets. With co-specialization, joint use is value enhancing (Teece 2007, p. 1338).

Later, the five capability elements of corporate systems are described in detail.

10.4.1 Strategy Capabilities: Generating Strategic Collaboration, Co-specialization, and Capabilities Synthesis

Strategy capabilities bring about win–win synergies of strategies through platform building capabilities with strategic partners (co-specialized/complementary). Teece (2007, pp. 1332–1333) identifies the importance of "managing complements and platforms" to build co-specialized assets.

Against a background of the advance of ICT business in recent years, from the perspective of business models and corporate strategies, platform strategies are becoming increasingly important (Kodama 2009b, 2014). Since platforms are the foundations of products and services, configuring complementary services and products on platforms is considered as a way to provide even more value to customers. Microsoft, with its Windows operating system in the software industry and Intel with its microprocessor unit (MPU) semiconductors in the hardware industry have created a situation in which both companies are platform leaders (Gawer and Cusmano 2002). Thus, with both companies maintaining strong competitiveness with Windows and MPUs, positive feedback through network affects function as partners, as complementary parties provide applications and software to run on the platforms.

The win–win relationships enabled by strategic collaboration through the formation of SC built between these platform leaders and complementary parties go on to bring about "business ecosystems." Other classic platform (product) strategies in the ICT business include the iPhone iOS application platform and the Google Android operating system for smartphones on which a range of authentication, finance and transaction functions, diverse applications, and software are provided.

For companies that aim to become platform leaders, it is important to decide upon a platform architecture that will encourage autonomous growth on the platform of various complementary commercial technologies, products, and services. Then, at the same time as selecting and building a platform in product development, an important issue is to set down suitable vertical boundaries with external partners that are complementing one's company to develop an attractive platform on which the platform leader can encourage autonomous growth with those external partners (Kodama 2009b).

While skillfully co-ordinating the dynamic formation of SC from the co-specialized assets of partner companies (or customers or competitors) in relationships with one's own company, the core capabilities that drive the overall system centered on the company ICT platforms that are co-specialized assets, and made up of technologies, products, and services developed independently by individual partners, are strategy capabilities. Companies such as Microsoft, Google, Intel, Qualcomm, NVIDIA, Apple, Sony Computer Entertainment, Nintendo, and TSMC are typical examples of these platform companies.

Here I pick up the example of TSMC. Business models in the ICT and digital industries have shifted from the vertically integrated models of the past to horizontal divisions of labor. The semiconductor industry has changed to adopt a system of horizontally distributed tasks done by a range of players in the Large Scale Integration (LSI) design and development process such as customers (set manufacturers), semiconductor designers (fabless companies), and semiconductor manufacturers (foundries). Behind the success of the TSMC business model, a Taiwanese leading global foundry, lay the company's achievement of congruence between the corporate system and the environment [Insight-1], and congruence among individual capabilities within the corporate system [Insight-2] through congruence enabled by orchestration of co-specialized assets both inside and outside the company [Insight-3] (see Fig. 10.5).

TSMC focused on segmenting business processes in the semiconductor industry (in particular separating design and manufacture), and developed and built a standardized platform for semiconductor production. This standardized platform created a new value chain in semiconductor production and gave TSMC a lead over its competitors. TSMC dynamically achieved congruence with changing environments by configuring a vertically integrated value chain to orchestrate co-specialized assets (a platform strategy execution through strategy capabilities) between itself, its customers (fabless, design houses, Integrated Device Manufacturer (IDM), set manufacturers), and its partners (design houses, electronic design automation (EDA) vendors, Intellectual Property (IP)/library vendors, back-end vendors, etc.), and by optimizing the vertical boundaries as the corporate system.

Moreover, to bring about technology capabilities to respond to these strategy capabilities, TSMC developed and built a standardized platform

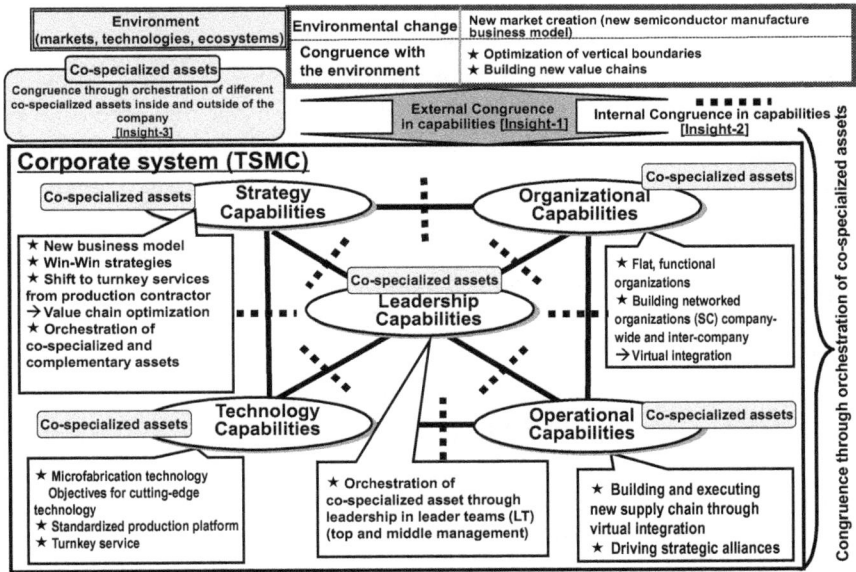

Fig. 10.5 Internal and external congruence through orchestration of co-specialized assets (The TSMC business model)

for the design and manufacture process as an environment creation strategy, and drove reuse and distribution of IP in design as well as providing it to meet common electronic characteristics and design rules—in other words, the company promoted open innovation. Thus, rather than produce semiconductors developed by themselves, set manufacturers can use the high-tech TSMC foundry with its large production capacity, giving themselves better competitiveness in terms of speed and costs by outsourcing more of their production to TSMC, and hence participate in a win–win strategy.

To properly demonstrate these strategy and technology capabilities, TSMC simultaneously achieved semiconductor design and manufacture using the best available specialist knowledge by strategically partnering with companies all over the world (design houses, EDA vendors, IP/library vendors, back-end vendors, etc.), while at the same time it used ICT to popularize these services and build a radically new supply chain through a solid chain of operational capabilities that entail simply taking consignments for production through to providing turnkey services.

TSMC's organizational forms that enabled its strategy, technology, and operational capabilities are characterized by the formation of cross functional teams as dynamic SC consisting of groups of specialists based on flat functional organizations within the company, at the same time as forming networked SC with partners to bring together diverse intangible and tangible assets dispersed outside the company. As dynamic organizational forms, these networked SC orchestrated co-specialized assets dispersed inside and outside the company, and acted as an organizational capabilities platform crucial to the achievement of the entire new business model and supply chain (turnkey services, etc.) through real and virtual integration (see Fig. 10.6).

Therefore, the execution of congruence between each of the capabilities elements—strategy, technology, operational, and organizational capabilities—was characterized by the mutual demonstration of synergies produced by specialist capabilities between functional organizations, through the demonstration of the leadership capabilities of in-house LT centered on TSMC. Co-specialized asset orchestration by leaders in the company (top and middle management) created virtual, vertically integrated value chains on a standardized production technology platform as well as successful win–win relationships between stakeholders including customers, through the sharing of values and building of trust between TSMC and its partners.

Platform companies such as TSMC build open (or hybrid or half-open) platforms as modular systems, which enables them to maintain power over their own businesses and grow long term. If it is possible to skillfully deploy these platform strategies, businesses can be opened up that would be difficult to embark upon with a single company's resources, and the possibility of bringing about a business ecosystem involving co-creation and co-evolution among the company, its partners, its customers and even its competitors (see Fig. 10.6). Considered from the perspective of capabilities congruence, the achievement of [Insight-2] with internal integration capability, [Insight-1] with external integration capability, and [Insight-3] with C-DC, strategic collaboration through the formation of networked SC among external partners, and fields of specializa-

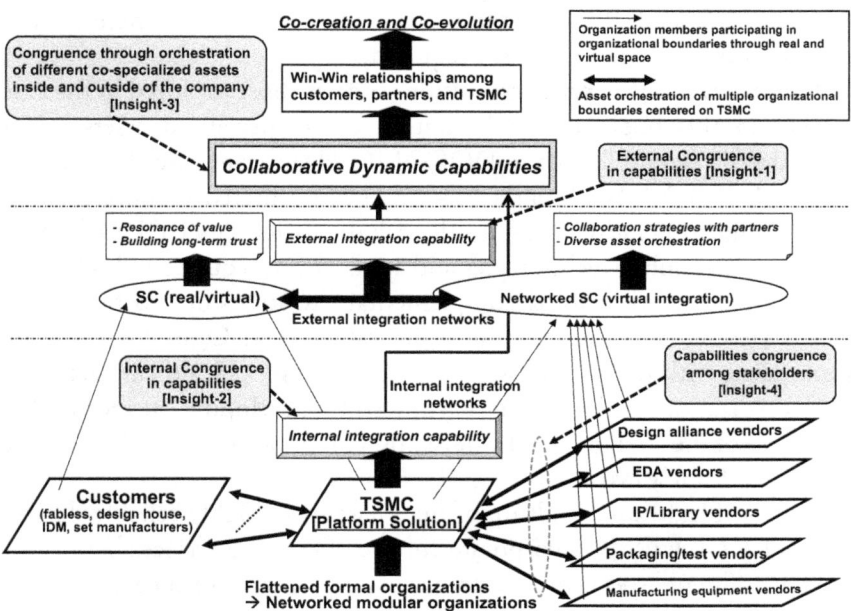

Fig. 10.6 TSMC's DC through asset orchestration

tion integrated in real and virtual space achieves [Insight-4] the demonstration of C-DC.

In this way, strategic capabilities have contexts of diverse strategic synergies. Orchestration of intangible assets brings about co-specialization, as synergies of strategies enabled by strategic capabilities. For example, these could be strategic synergies accompanying strategic expansion upstream and/or downstream in a value chain through vertical integration, global geographical expansion through a horizontal integration across domains, strategic synergies accompanying expansion of successful business models into adjacent industries, strategic synergies accompanying group company partnering through integration of group company strategies, or strategic synergies through integration of a company itself through joint ventures or M&A. Moreover, strategic synergies can be brought about through strategic capabilities by integrating different business models (e.g., fabless and foundry, IT, and education/healthcare services). These cases of integrating different capabilities, such as capability recombination (or knowledge integration) (Kogut and Zander 1992; Helfat and Peteraf 2003; Kodama 2011, 2014), are cases where orchestration of co-specialized assets is required.

Particularly, with service innovations such as those explored in the case studies in this book, the orchestration of co-specialized assets across industries is required. In the DOCOMO Healthcare case discussed in Chap. 3, DOCOMO Healthcare's smart life-centered corporate vision was "Connecting individual's health with the society." NTT DOCOMO had both the mobile technologies and applications required to build such a mechanism, and enabled complementary relationships to build new world views with Omron Healthcare, rather than Omron Healthcare proceeding with new businesses alone. DOCOMO Healthcare achieved co-specialization and capabilities synthesis by developing businesses that made use of the strengths of the developments at both Omron Healthcare and NTT DOCOMO.

Omron Healthcare's culture of manufacturing highly reliable devices and NTT DOCOMO's corporate culture of creating services have completely different aspects of investment concepts, sense of speed, and relationships with customers. Omron Healthcare could not easily build mechanisms as services, and as such strategic collaboration between

Omron Healthcare and NTT DOCOMO was required. These three factors of strategic collaboration, co-specialization, and capability synthesis led to the bringing about of C-DC with NTT DOCOMO.

10.4.2 Organizational Capabilities: Generating C-DC and C-OC

According to existing research, the ability to configure ambidextrous organizations (i.e., organizational capabilities) through DC enables the combination of both old and new business (O'Reilly and Tushman 2008). The aforementioned ability to configure informal, dynamic, organic organizations through SC brings about the organizational capabilities to demonstrate DC. Analyzing the cases of new business development with NTT DOCOMO and Omron in Chap. 3 and the Mitsubishi and Mitsui new businesses in the medical and healthcare fields in Chap. 9 from the perspective of organizational capabilities, the existence of unique networked SC (Triad SC model) in networks in and between companies was discovered. The following describes organizational capabilities in the representative example of the NTT DOCOMO case.

An organizational characteristic that brings about NTT DOCOMO's strategic innovation capabilities is the integration (synthesis) of the existing line organizations (traditional organizations) charged with exploitation as development of existing business and agile project organizations (e.g., Kodama 2007c) charged with exploration to develop new technologies and businesses (see Fig. 10.7). Project organizations both inside and outside companies mainly demonstrate DC (and collaborative DC) and specialize in R&D and service planning, new business development, whereas other related business is done by in-house line organizations demonstrating their existing OC (and collaborative OC).

In the new healthcare and medical business development described in Chap. 3, through NTT DOCOMO's demonstration of collaborative DC with differing companies in differing industries such as Omron, project organizations, which were good at creating knowledge (asset orchestration), were responsible for driving R&D activities and conceiving, planning, and developing new business, while through the compa-

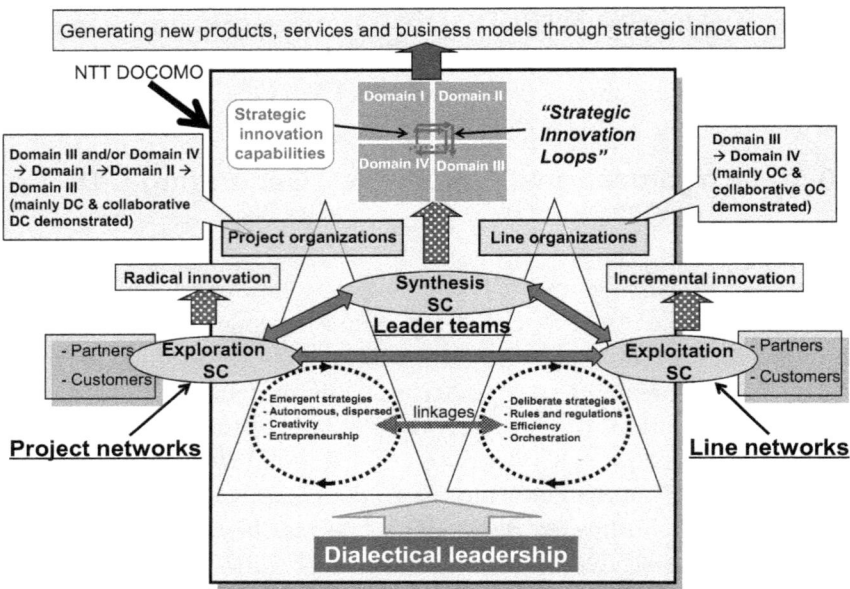

Fig. 10.7 Leader teams, project and line networks in NTT DOCOMO

ny's demonstration of collaborative OC with partner companies, existing line organizations, which were able to use existing knowledge efficiently, were put in charge of specific service operations, together bringing about optimization of the overall business value chain. In particular, strong integration of collaborative DC and collaborative OC is required in the high-speed markets in Domain III where competition is fierce.

For radical innovation in uncertain environments, project organizations inspire, create, and orchestrate new knowledge (assets) based on creativity, and bring about concepts for new technical developments and business models (new products, services, business frameworks, etc.) through trial and error. These activities induce the Domain III and/or Domain IV → Domain I shift of corporate capabilities. Here, companies drive radical innovation by practicing emergent and entrepreneurial strategies that entail the formation of multiple multi-layered SC with strategic business partners outside the company, and the uptake and orchestration of knowledge (assets) from both inside and outside the company in high risk environments. Individual projects in project organizations act autonomously and are dispersed as network organizations (Kodama 2003), but business activities are always monitored by the chief of the organization and the direction and objectives of business are controlled as entire project organizations. These project organizations demonstrate C-DC with partner companies to bring about new product and service concepts and prototypes one after the other, and then incubate a range of these to achieve commercialization (in other words, the Domain I → II → III shift).

Currently, NTT DOCOMO is working toward the creation of new smartphone-centered markets in the medical and healthcare fields to carve out the next i-mode "S-curve" following on from the era of conventional mobile telephones. For this, the company must simultaneously optimize its vertical boundaries, while redefining the horizontal boundaries of new business areas it moves into (e.g., Kodama 2009a, b). The Osaifu-Keitai (mobile wallet) and mobile phone credit business were stepping stones for the company's move into the finance business. NTT DOCOMO is also executing strategies to orchestrate new assets (knowledge) for never-before-seen markets (Kodama and Shibata 2016), by inducing, creating, and orchestrating new assets (knowledge) through the formation of project networks for radical innovation (exploration SC) with different businesses across different industries such as converged broadcast and communications businesses, automotive telematics businesses, ubiquitous business (IoT services), new personalized and social service business, medical and healthcare business, environment and ecology businesses, and safety and security business.

These kinds of organizational activities will continue to spread out NTT DOCOMO's horizontal boundaries into the future, and will trigger the forging of new business models. Not only does the company optimize its vertically integrated value chains as a conventional mobile phone carrier through smartphones for its external stakeholders, but it also places the utmost importance on creating business ecosystems that enable win–win relationships with stakeholders (e.g., Kodama 2015) while presenting new mobile business visions on its horizontal boundaries.

Nevertheless, the business processes of facilities construction, maintenance, sales, distribution, and after sales support are crucial for efficiently introducing to the market, popularizing and spreading new products and services in a timely manner. Line organizations (technology, facility, maintenance and sales departments, etc.) are in charge of these business processes (see Fig. 10.7). Line organizations drive the spiraling of popularization and embedding in new markets by releasing new services on to the market in Domain III that have been confirmed for marketability through the processes of concept-making, marketing, elemental, practical, and trial technology development, incubation, and commercialization done by project organizations (Domain I → Domain II → Domain III).

Line organizations drive efficient business process management cycles such as efficient and precise facilities investment planning to meet the projected demand of new services, new network operation systems set up to maintain high service quality, and nationwide sales, maintenance and after support systems establishment by creating "line networks" (exploitation SC) for collaboration with group and partner group companies and strategic outsourcing.

Based on knowledge assets built up over many years, line organizations, as bureaucratic organizations, engage in incremental innovation to make improvements and upgrades by forming line networks (exploitation SC) as multi-layered SC networks with group companies and groups of strategic partners. Well-thought-out and orchestrated strategy planning based on strategic rules are adopted by line organizations, and they proceed with routine business activities to pursue incremental improvements and upgrades, and efficiency in exiting business processes by demonstrating C-OC in Domains III and IV. Practice in line networks in this way requires thorough productivity and efficiency. These organizations then take the innovative new products and service concepts brought about through the project organizations, and efficiently and quickly get them onto the market, popularize, and expand them. This is the interlocking of Exploration SC and Exploitation SC (or shifting from Exploration to Exploitation).

Roughly classified, these two types of organizations (project organizations versus line organizations) and multi-layered SC networks (project network, exploration SC, versus line network, exploitation SC) have the contradictory elements of one practicing creativity and autonomy, while the other practices efficiency and control, which means there are always paradoxical conflicts and tugs of war occurring between these two types of organizations (e.g., Schad et al. 2016). These situations can inhibit synthesis of the knowledge of business practitioners in organizations. This is because line organizations and project organizations differ in many respects such as their ways of thinking, priorities, their values, and the degree of uncertainty that they allow. However, using creative abrasion and productive fiction (Hagel III and Brown 2005) through dialectical dialog (Kodama 2004), it is possible to sublate these contradictions. Driving this synthesis are LT, which are synthesis SC (see Fig. 10.7). At NTT DOCOMO, these LT are formed at all management levels (this means management teams, informal cross-functional teams, and task forces consisting of top, middle, and staff layers in project and line organizations), from the executive (the chief executive officer (CEO), executives and division directors) and senior management (department chiefs and directors), through to managers (managers and assistant managers), and staff.

At NTT DOCOMO, various leadership teams formed from leaders in the company's business organizations such as R&D, marketing, service planning and development, sales, technology, facilities, after sales support, and maintenance services between the project and line organizations, debate and make decisions about the timing, strategies, tactics, mechanisms, and resources for emergent and entrepreneurial strategies, and services to respond to these strategies. Through thorough dialectical and creative dialog, the leaders in LT select strategies and tactics to enable genuine radical innovation to blossom, and execute them through the execution of "dialectical leadership" (Kodama 2004, 2005a, b, 2006, 2017a).

The LT play the role of improving R&D and new business development performance by strengthening the characteristics of the cross-functional or inter-corporate integration of the exploration and exploitation SC. This means that leaders in LT are required to have dialectical leadership. As well as the elements of the participative leadership style and flexible approach discussed in literature on NPD (e.g., Dougherty 1996; McDonough and Barczak 1991), the combinations of creativity and efficiency, and factors of participative control and directive control (e.g., Eisenhardt and Tabrizi 1995) are also required.

There remains the issue that the behavior and dialectical management of leaders and between leaders has not been discussed much in the research on cross functional teams (CFT) and project management in NPD in the past. However, Lewis et al. (2002) argue that combining various paradoxes is necessary for successful product development. They clarify the frequent but ambiguous calls for subtle control as "Effective managers provide strong leadership to keep teams focused and on schedule, while empowering team members to foster motivation and creativity." In my field studies, I also acquired data on the dialectical thinking and actions of leaders from dialog and discussions with leaders. More than ever, it is clear that dialectical thinking and actions are required of leaders.

The synergies of dialectical leadership enabled by collaboration among leaders at all management levels, including the CEO and executives, drive dialectical dialog, and promote careful execution of deliberate strategy in response to carefully selected emergent or entrepreneurial strategies, and achieve synthesis of knowledge and strategy through the formation of multi-layered SC networks. These multi-layered SC networks form the triad model of SC from exploration SC, exploitation SC, and synthesis SC (see Fig. 10.7).

In analyzing organizational systems and strategies from the perspective of the strategic innovation process of NTT DOCOMO in Chap. 3 and Mitsubishi and Mitsui in Chap. 9, the multi-layered SC networks as the SC triad model are due to the existence of *ba* triad models, as discussed as follows. The *ba* triad model in leading companies and organizations was presented from case studies of Toyota, Fujifilm and Apple, in the "Dynamic fractal organizations for promoting knowledge-based transformation—A new paradigm for organizational theory" of Nonaka et al. (2014). For example, the case of the Prius NPD at Toyota was a radical innovation (exploration) that required the convergence of a wide range of technologies and dynamic synthesis of exploration and exploitation as incremental innovation (exploitation) to continually upgrade and improve this new product. For these reasons, Toyota's various project teams and existing line organizations had to form multi-layered *ba* networks both horizontally and vertically within and between organizations to simultaneously pursue the creation and utilization of knowledge.

What draws attention in this case is that *ba* to drive exploration activities for the knowledge creativity of radical innovation (called exploration *ba*) are responsible for processes to share tacit knowledge and convert it to explicit knowledge, while in contrast *ba* that drive exploitation activities to commercialize products and continually upgrade and improve commercialized products with knowledge efficiency (called exploitation *ba*) are responsible for processes of synthesis of explicit knowledge and internalization through personal experience. In other words, exploration *ba* have a strong tendency towards tacit knowledge, while exploitation *ba* strongly lean towards explicit knowledge. Nevertheless, both tacit knowledge and explicit knowledge are intrinsically linked in the spirals synthesis of the third type of knowledge, practical knowledge (phronesis) (Nonaka's so-called SECI process). Driving this spiral process to simultaneously achieve the creation and accumulation of knowledge is the "synthesis Ba." Teece (2014) sites, in actual fact, DC as complementary to "phronetic" leadership (Nonaka and Toyama 2007), whereas in contrast phronesis is in the background of source factors of dialectical leadership that manages different strategic and organizational characteristics at the same time in simultaneous pursuit of exploration and exploitation (see Fig. 10.8).

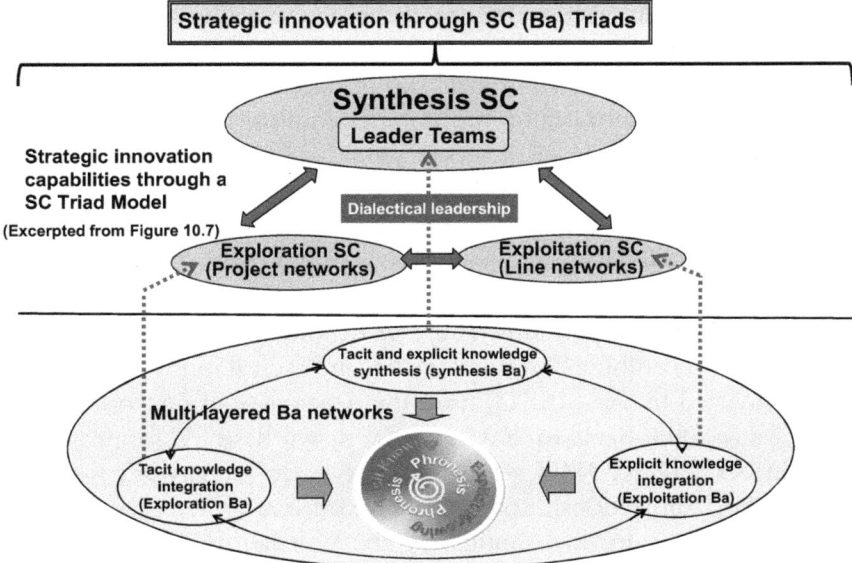

Fig. 10.8 Strategic innovation based on *ba* and SC triad model. (Source: Excerpted from Figure 4, Nonaka et al. (2014))

Hence, synthesis *ba* are mutually connected to exploration *ba* and exploitation *ba* to dynamically synthesize them, which forms the *ba* triad model. Then, the *ba* triad model also brings about the SC triad model of multi-layered SC networks with characteristics of *ba*. Accordingly, the SC triad model based on *ba* triad model is also a framework to achieve strategic innovation (see Fig. 10.8).

Though the SC triad model is similar to the "ambidextrous organization" (Tushman and O'Reilly 1997; O'Reilly and Tushman 2004), it offers the following new perspectives. In ambidextrous organizations, it is asserted that clear strategic objectives are set down in new business development organizations and organizations developing existing business, and the interaction between these organizations is heavily restricted at the operational level while upper management is responsible for both. In contrast, in the SC triad model close collaboration and interaction of exploration SC consisting of project networks aiming to pursue new R&D and build and develop new business, and exploitation SC consisting of line networks that continually improve and upgrade commercialized products and services are driven by synthesis SC centered on LT. Practitioners at levels of management (top, middle, and staff) drive smooth shifting between the domains to combine exploration and exploitation through the SC triad model. This perspective also contributes to a new theoretical framework for the ambidextrous organization.

LT synthesize knowledge of these organizations (project networks and line networks) at NTT DOCOMO, and play the role of bringing about strategic innovation capabilities throughout the entire company. To achieve strategic innovation capabilities, it is important that LT simultaneously combine and synthesize the apparently contradictory creative and planned strategic methods. Thus, for LT, the configuration of the SC triad model to combine both incremental and radical innovation is key.

As discussed in Sect. 10.1.3, from the perspective of network theory, (e.g., Watts 2003; Barabasi 2002), the LT as synthesis SC formed internally in NTT DOCOMO act as hubs and nodes in network space (in other words connections), and act to network multiple SC both inside and outside the company, configuring the SC triad model with project networks (exploration SC) and line networks (exploitation SC). The SC triad model brings about new contexts and knowledge, and promotes strategic innovation (see Fig. 10.8).

As described above, as is shown in Figs. 10.7 and 10.8, NTT DOCOMO has built an ambidextrous organization through the formation of the SC triad model, and has implemented dialectical management, an important factor of strategic innovation capabilities, which allows the two different archetypes to co-exist within the company, and as the company skillfully manages and combines both new technologies and services with existing services, the synergies that come about between both types of organization are a major factor in the success of strategic innovation in this large corporation. The existence of unique networked SC (Triad SC model) on networks in and between companies corresponds to the unique organizational capabilities of a company.

10.4.3 Technology Capabilities: Generating Co-specialized Assets Through Convergence

Fast-paced digital technology and ICT developments are bringing about new knowledge such as digital appliances, e-money, integrated circuit (IC) tag solutions, converged communications and broadcasting, wide-ranging content distribution to iPod and smartphone, and various business models that traverse differing industries and companies. As well as this, new business networks are forming between different industries as new value chains through the new technological and product developments that come about with technical convergence including ICT, and new competition rules and business models that cut across the boundaries between different businesses.

For example, as a technical background of the achievement of convergence in the ICT domain, value chains have come about through convergence between different platforms such as terminals (e.g., smartphones, mobile phones, tablets, and PCs), carrier networks (optical fiber, mobile wireless), platforms (e.g., finance, transactions, and e-commerce), applications (e.g., distribution and IC tag apps), contents (e.g., broadcasting, video, music, and advertising), and business applications (e.g., cloud services, e-learning, remote medicine, software as a service, the smart grid, etc.) through the co-ordination and collaboration between stakeholders.

These unique value chains have brought about business ecosystems such as content business and mobile commerce markets using smartphones and mobile telephones. These markets have continued to grow, creating co-evolution models in smartphone and mobile phone businesses (Moore 1993; Gawer and Cusmano 2002; Iansiti and Levien 2004; Kodama 2009a, b). Differing from older types of business structures, these new business networks are examples of how radical innovation moves beyond incremental innovation and simultaneously brings about both new competition and co-operation.

The phenomenon of convergence has added new layers of complexity to the traditional model of corporate and industry competitiveness. Convergence has accelerated strategic partnering and M&A between corporations, including customers, and has triggered dramatic changes to existing corporate boundaries (vertical and horizontal boundaries). This means that corporate strategies that transcend competition between differing industries and focus on alliances between industries are becoming increasingly important.

For example, as described by the case studies in this book, telemedicine, remote nursing, tele-health, and medical and pharmaceutical data management and support are new business processes and models that have been born through convergence between the ICT, health, welfare, nursing, and pharmaceutical industries. In other words, this means that switching away from strategies that focus on competition between companies or between different industries to collaboration strategies between diverse industries that include customers is becoming an important issue for modern companies. Modern examples resulting from convergence that have already been achieved include the new ICT-based markets enabled by technology capabilities spanning differing industries and technologies, such as the new e-book, e-learning, traceability, smart grid, electric vehicle, and remote healthcare business models.

Moreover, particularly in recent years, IoT, AI, big data, and robots are further advancing conventional internet technologies. The technical revolution of this advanced ICT is bringing never-before-seen impacts and speeds. The IoT enables two-way exchanges of all kinds of information in society via the internet, while big data technologies collect massive amounts of data for analysis (e.g., IoT/machine to machine data, cloud computing information, social network service data, real and virtual commercial information, location information, and so forth), which is bringing about new value. As well as that, the deep learning driving the rapid growth of AI is enabling AI self-learning and high-level judgment and execution that are beyond the capabilities of ordinary humans. Furthermore, various robotics technologies are enabling the automation of a wide range of complex tasks, which is not only bringing efficiency to business but also enabling achievement in societies that was previously thought to be impossible.

From the uniform services of conventional mass production, these technical innovations have the potential to dramatically change the structures of industry and employment, and have the potential to radically improve efficiency and productivity across entire supply chains by providing products customized to suit individual user needs and sharing data in real time. In future, advanced ICT will bring about new markets by combining the core technologies and business models of various different fields as common platforms (platform technologies) for technical revolution in all industries. For example, convergence of genome editing technologies and various biological data with advanced ICT will bring about new pharmaceutical, agriculture and bioenergy developments, and so forth.

In particular, the advances in IoT are driving the networking of products among dissimilar products and industries and dramatically expanding individual product functionality. This networking is organically connecting a diversity of big data sent and received in real time from people and things to core technologies and various individual business processes in wide-ranging industries across various professional areas. Hence the clearly delineated boundaries between products and industries of the past are becoming ambiguous, and the potential for new boundaries to be born is rising. In IoT, the focus needs to be on the acceleration of co-specialization as the creation of new business models such as services or integrated systems through synergies between differing products and industries, enabled by networking and convergence of things, people, data, technologies, and processes (see Fig. 10.9).[1]

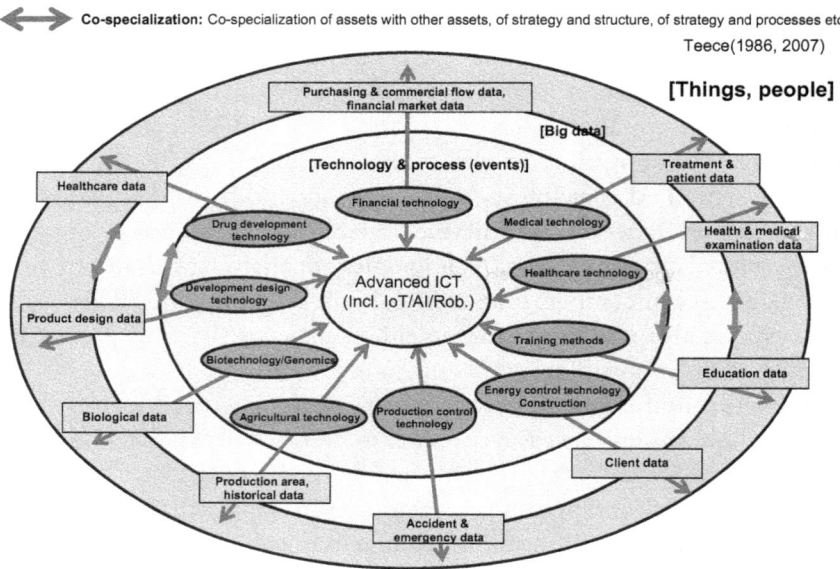

Fig. 10.9 Co-specialization through convergence

There exists a possibility of intangible assets being co-specialized in well-co-ordinated forms with other assets, because many intangible assets have specificity. Hence there is a potential for a company to create high value by creating special positions born of assets co-specialized by combining and reconfiguring intangible assets. Co-specialization has great importance in corporate strategy, and many of the technical convergences brought about by advanced ICT shown in Fig. 10.9 are the systems of high-tech products and services, and achieve co-specialization among multiple assets. These systems can also be said to be co-specialized assets that consist of interdependent elements supported by the platforms of advanced ICT.

Companies thus have to put convergence-based innovation processes at the core of their corporate strategies, and use the strong core competencies of their core business effectively, continually advancing them with incremental innovation, while at the same time engaging in radical innovation to pioneer peripheral businesses and businesses across different fields which trigger synergies with their core businesses to achieve sustainable competitiveness. Therefore, to raise core competences to a higher level, companies not only need to engage in new strategic activities to converge knowledge across wide-ranging boundaries within themselves, but also need technology capabilities to dynamically converge knowledge inside and outside the company, including that held by customers, to forge ahead with business in differing fields or on the periphery of their core competencies.

Technology capabilities are an important factor to achieve "systemic innovation" (Teece 2000). New products, services, and business models through integration and convergence of different technologies, or the Apple iPhone as an architectural innovation that fuses hardware and software, are good examples of orchestrating co-specialized assets through technological capabilities. With their developmental policy of unifying hardware and software (in other words, strengthening mutually dependent relationships and bundling, rather than modularizing individual technical elements), Apple has maintained a uniform identity since its foundation; while orchestrating its co-specialized assets with its technological capabilities that are difficult for other companies to imitate has enabled the company to bring to market numerous new products.

Teece (2000, 2007) points out the importance of building, aligning, and adapting co-specialized assets in platform products such as Apple iTMS or DRM, and wide-ranging digital products such as iPod, precision components, diesel-electric locomotives, and aircraft. With the iPod and so forth, Apple used its sensing functions to detect latent market needs, and used its technology capabilities to orchestrate unique component designs that comprised the best co-specialized assets from around the world. Integrating co-specialized assets through technology capabilities is an extremely important factor in the high tech field, which requires "capabilities congruence," in other words "fit" with the other elements of capabilities of (1) strategy capabilities, (2) organizational capabilities, (3) operational capabilities, and (4) leadership capabilities to achieve co-specialization of intangible assets related to these kinds of technologies.

10.4.4 Operational Capabilities

Operational capabilities do not have the same meaning as capabilities for regular routine activity (OC), as they bring about (or create) new operational processes. For example, the automation of manufacturing processes including ICT developments promoted by Fanuc and Canon of Japan brought about intangible assets that are difficult to copy with automated production systems and business processes. This led in turn to operational capabilities through the orchestration of co-specialized assets at Fanuc and Canon.

As a brief example of the relationship of ICT with such operational capabilities, Dell sells PCs online, but relies on many external companies for the PC components. Dell has to procure parts optimized to individual consumer needs and manufacture PCs at low cost. However, Dell simultaneously pursues the advantages of efficiency through vertical disintegration, with outsourcing in its business activities and the advantages of close-knit co-ordination activities through vertical integration.

For efficient assembly of PCs to meet its individual customer orders at Dell, external companies produce the required parts at the required time and deliver them to the Dell assembly plant (there are five around the world) in a timely manner, which enables the company to reduce the number of parts it has to hold in stock. Dell uses ICT to create interorganizational networks to promote the close sharing of information about the company's consumer-oriented mass customization and corporate customer solution businesses, and also share information and knowledge in real time with component manufacturers to reduce co-ordination costs and maintain supply chain efficiency.

In particular, the company configures close-knit teams of boundaries (SC) with component manufacturers and tight networks with certain corporate customers to collect information on customer needs in a timely manner and improve the quality of services, and hence promotes the sharing of information, contexts, and knowledge. In general, close co-ordination is possible with vertical integration in manufacturing organizations to develop and manufacture parts or completed products; however, Dell, in conjunction with its characteristic ICT use and strategic outsourcing partners, is able to reduce its governance costs as well as maintain quality in co-ordinating tasks by promoting the sharing of contexts and information between different companies. As in the Dell case, orchestration of ICT development as co-specialized assets and co-specialized operational processes in the company to respond to changes brings about operational capabilities and creates vertical boundaries as optimized value chains (see Fig. 10.10).

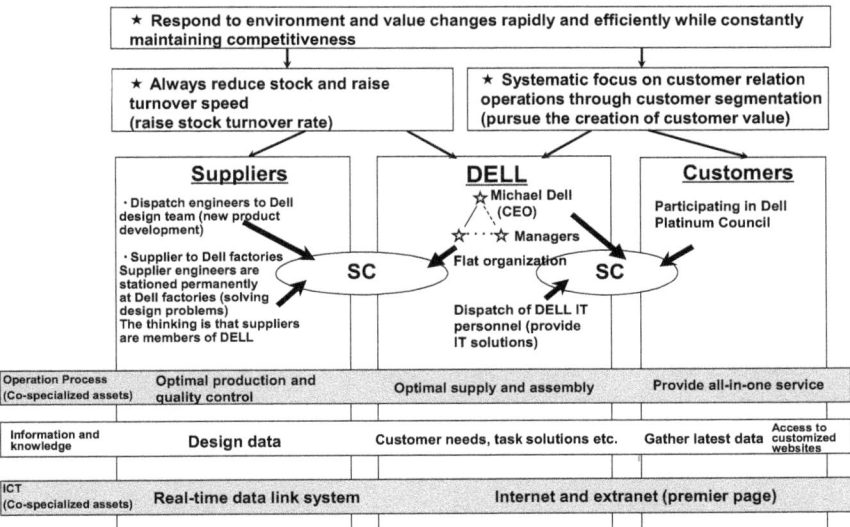

Fig. 10.10 Operational capabilities of Dell's virtual integration through the orchestration of co-specialized assets

10.4.5 Leadership Capabilities: Leadership Capabilities Across Different Companies

Convergences such as integration of dissimilar technologies and services, product and service developments, and business model planning across differing industries are becoming increasingly important. To formulate business strategies to deal with convergence, the need for leadership capabilities in main player and partner companies across differing companies is further increasing. A new theory of co-evolution and co-creation leadership that spans between companies, and includes customers, is required. The framework for such a theory of leadership capabilities stems from the "SC Triad model" that consists of the project networks (exploration SC), LT (synthesis SC), and line networks (exploitation SC) discussed as organizational capabilities. The existence of unique networked SC (Triad SC model) on networks in and between companies generates the unique leadership capabilities of a company.

Moreover, these leadership capabilities drive capabilities congruence among ecosystem partners, in other words the capabilities congruence among stakeholders [Insight-4]. This results in congruence of the aforementioned individual five capabilities becoming optimized among ecosystem partners (stakeholders). The following describes factors that make up leadership capabilities.

At local worksites where asset orchestration is performed, members belonging to project organizations with participation from multiple companies mainly demonstrate distributed leadership (Kodama 2004; Nonaka and Toyama 2004), and form and maintain project networks as SC based on Ba. Thus members drive communication and collaboration in SC, learn from each other, and deeply share knowledge (assets) for microstrategic contexts with each other. Furthermore, distributed leadership finds, captures, and mobilizes knowledge assets necessary for knowledge transformation (knowledge integration), and implements microstrategies through the asset orchestration process.

Leadership systems in project networks between dissimilar companies mainly differ from those within the same company in their necessity for boundary negotiations for the various individual issues that exist between the dissimilar companies. Individual companies have unique corporate cultures and values, and at the same time individual companies have leadership values that depend on the different organizational contexts embedded in the company. Sharing organizational culture and values creates company-specific systems, rules, and practices, and for staff this embeds thinking and perceptions unique to the company thinking and action, including leadership.

For example, Toyota is a company that has the values of wisdom and improvement and respect for people within itself. Based on this, Toyota's corporate culture is built on ideas and patterns of thinking and acting such as "With wisdom, even a dry towel will give up water. Observe actual production as if you were a blank piece of paper without prejudice. About everything you face, ask why five times. Don't settle on past success, but create higher goals, and strive unceasingly to be better." In Honda, the company infuses its staff with patterns of thinking and patterns of acting such as "Going to job sites, understanding actual things and conditions and being realistic. Respecting time for theories and ideas.

Asking the reasons why something is being done, what are the concepts, and what are the specifications?"

Building a unique corporate culture and promoting the sharing of values among staff is the responsibility of organizational top management (the CEO and executives), which mainly exercises centralized leadership (Kodama 2004). On the other hand, in the knowledge creation process (Nonaka and Takeuchi 1995) not only top management, but also staff such as middle management (including the lower layers), are involved in localized asset orchestration that requires distributed leadership.

Von Krogh et al. (2012) presented a framework for a new theory of leadership that ties together both centralized and distributed leadership with Ba, the SECI process (based on socialization, externalization, combination, and internalization), and knowledge assets. In their concept, they perceive leadership as a series of knowledge creation activities under certain conditions, and notably perceive leadership with a focus on activities (practice) rather than roles or characteristics. In other words, the importance of this framework lies in understanding the complex interactions between participants, processes, artifacts, and contexts shaping leadership. Their specific situated leadership can be understood as matching the thinking in contingency theory (e.g., Fiedler 1964; Fiedler and Chemers 1967; Fiedler and Garcia 1987), in which the existence of different types of leadership are recognized depending on the situation. In addition, expanding on this theory, it means it is possible that multiple layers of leadership exist simultaneously within an organization. Contingency theory tends to put a focus on the influence of central leaders on subordinates, although their framework enables the application of both centralized and distributed leadership as leadership activities in certain situations as situated leadership.

However, these systems of centralized and distributed leadership are all different owing to the differences in unique corporate cultures and values in individual companies. Integrated systems of leadership in individual companies are thus required as leadership systems that span between different companies. Figure 10.11 shows a leadership structure required for the asset orchestration process through SC formed through a corporate partnership between two companies. To simplify the leadership structure in Fig. 10.11, I describe a particular management layer (e.g., the middle management layer).[2]

In individual companies, the "SC Triad model" consists of project networks (exploration SC) that project organizations subjectively form, line networks (exploitation SC) that line organizations subjectively form, and LT (synthesis SC) that drive synthesis of exploration SC and exploitation SC. Project networks (exploration SC) mainly require distributed leadership, whereas line networks (exploitation SC) mainly require centralized leadership. Driving the synthesis of these two types of leadership requires the "dialectical leadership" (Kodama 2004, 2005a, b, 2006) of the LT, which are the synthesis SC. The LT play the role of improving R&D and new business development performance by strengthening the characteristics of the cross-functional or intercorporate integration of the exploration and exploitation SC.

In the joint development of two companies, at the same time as forming SC as project networks (exploration SC) for exploration activities for

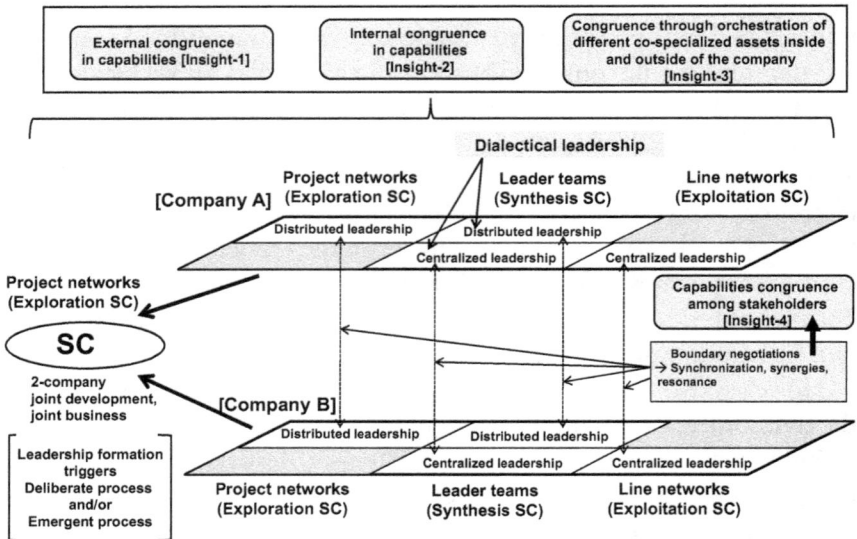

Fig. 10.11 Leadership capabilities—leadership interaction across different companies—leadership structures formed from multiple companies (middle-management layer)

radical innovation, individual project networks (exploration SC), LT (synthesis SC), and line networks (exploitation SC) exist in each company, while the centralized, distributed, and dialectical leadership of the two companies must be synchronized and integrated.

This synchronization and integration entails the distributed leadership of community leaders and members of both companies involved with the asset orchestration process in the worksite in project networks (exploration SC) and LT (synthesis SC), and also entails centralized leadership, with leaders and staff of both companies taking on the roles of support, management, and promotion of asset orchestration process in LT (synthesis SC) and line networks (exploration SC), which requires individual synchronization (or resonance) of these leaderships through boundary negotiations. Here, the factors of boundary negotiations are "synchronization," "resonance," and "synergies."

These factors of boundary negotiations were of particular importance in the relationships between NTT DOCOMO and Omron in Chap. 3, the relationship between Mitsubishi and Mitsui and various stakeholders described in Chap. 9, and the relationship between the Asahikawa Medical College and vendors described in Chap. 7.

Hence, in the SC and formal organizations of partnering companies, staff in different companies discuss specifics about how this "synchronization" should be conceptualized. Then the enormous number of actions are broken down into specific actions to be executed. Of particular importance among this massive number of actions are the details that cannot be self-contained in the business framework of a single company. These include actions that must be executed through co-ordination and linkage with other companies, or actions that are completed by a company but are dependent on the output of another company, and so on.

In the specific asset orchestration process, all actions that cannot be completed within the framework of a single company must be achieved through the formation of project networks as SC that transcend knowledge and organizational boundaries. In SC, members share the "six strategic contexts": who will do what (actions that need to be taken), why, when, who with, and how (Kodama 2007b), discussing specific targets, meaning, methods, and time frames, and then reaching consensus through co-ordination and collaboration between staff in different companies. As a result, shared strategies are executed. These are the practical actions that members take to form and carry out specific strategic and tactical measures for asset orchestration.

In particular, in project networks where asset orchestration is carried out, members of the companies demonstrate individual distributed leadership, and mutually synchronize these distributed leadership elements through dynamic trial and error over time. These community members must always have a "dynamic view of strategy," and execute not only "deliberate strategies" (planned asset orchestration processes) but also "emergent strategies" (situational asset orchestration processes) flexibly. Members also have to improvise to deal with rapidly changing circumstances as they mutually synchronize their distributed leadership.

In SC, members deeply share context and knowledge through creative dialog (Kodama 2007c), and execute actions that have strong mutual dependencies with other companies. Items for the asset orchestration process decided on by line networks and LT are executed by project networks, although support and level of achievement for these asset orchestration processes are constantly monitored and aided among staff with centralized leadership in the line networks and LT of different companies, information and knowledge are deeply shared, and the centralized leaderships of both companies are synchronized.

Accordingly, community members in companies (particularly upper management) who participate in SC through company partnerships and commit to strategic objectives must match the pitch and rhythm of progress towards the tasks of the asset orchestration process in the community, as it aims for the goals of the entire project. Synchronization means members of the companies being in step with each other, and a mechanism of concurrently achieving the tasks of asset orchestration and related tasks (e.g., advertising, sales, support and production, and so forth throughout the whole supply chain) in the project networks, LT, and line networks at a certain pitch and rhythm.

(a) Leadership Triggers: "Deliberate Processes" and "Emergent Processes"

A focus on forming SC between companies reveals the aspect of "leadership triggers." In other words, the building of Ba, the basics of SC, is triggered by particular processes. These processes are generally classified as "deliberate processes" and "emergent processes." With deliberate processes, initial leadership that acts as the trigger is the centralized leadership of mainly top and upper middle management. For example, a business-related context is developed by deliberate boundary negotiations enacted by the upper management of both companies, and strategies are configured and executed in both companies.

In this case, strategic targets, rules in both companies, and business processes are defined, and support is given by providing resources such as personnel and capital to build SC between the companies, and by providing the necessary knowledge assets through centralized leadership in line networks. On executing in-house centralized leadership in this way, designated and instructed members then demonstrate distributed leadership in LT, and through the building of *ba* among the members, macrostrategies for the inter-company partnership are formulated and broken down into microstrategies. Moreover, distributed leadership entails co-ordination and negotiation with the organizations of centralized leadership. In project networks, the building of *ba* enables the sharing of microstrategic contexts among members of different companies, and the gradual formation of SC. Then these community members go on to find and capture knowledge assets particularly required for co-specialization inside and outside their companies, and mobilize them for orchestrations through distributed leadership.

In contrast, "emergent processes" are completely opposite to the deliberate processes. This means members demonstrating distributed leadership in workplaces as project networks and driving everyday business become involved in sharing information through contact with potential partners. In this case, leader members demonstrating distributed leadership consider whether their localized microstrategies are congruent with the strategic visions, strategic objectives, and macrostrategies of the company with the aim of justifying the latent potential of new business in house. Hence, negotiations are held with centralized leadership members in LT on the formation of consensus of the new emergent and localized microstrategies.

Moreover, in line networks, centered on the centralized leadership of top management, in-house authorization is given for these sorts of emergent business, and resources, working environments, and incentives required for the asset orchestration process in SC. Emergent business on which consensus is reached through the boundary negotiations in line networks and LT drives the asset orchestration processed through the acquisition and mobilization of knowledge assets in project networks via the formation of SC based on the building of *ba* by distributed leadership. In contrast, centralized leadership continuously supports for providing project networks with the necessary knowledge assets and human support.

As described above, the asset orchestration process, with deliberate processes and emergent processes, clearly involves different leadership triggers. In the past, I have experienced both processes through my own participant observations and action research methods (e.g., Kodama 2007a, b). While both processes were in joint developments with American companies, the most important elements of emergent processes were the synergies of distributed and centralized leadership in LT and boundary negotiations. Justification in house for microstrategies through emergent processes often entails discord in the interactions between distributed and centralized leadership. Whether SC are formed based on the building of good *ba*, whether knowledge assets can be provided, and whether human involvement is achieved in LT are dependent on whether this discord can be converted into "creative abrasion" and "productive friction." This also affects the asset orchestration process in these project networks.

In contrast, with deliberate processes, the most important factor is the processes of forming SC based on the building of good *ba*, providing knowledge assets, and involving resources such as personnel. However, friction can occur in the interactions between distributed and centralized leadership in LT with deliberate processes. This is because discord arises among the organizations involved in the provision of the knowledge assets (in particular personnel) required to form SC. In such cases, the centralized leadership of top management in line networks plays a key role in enabling smooth boundary negotiations in LT.

While each of these processes has its own characteristics, in reality the process of forming SC between companies is complex, and both processes can be said to be mixed; however, management of distributed and centralized leadership in conflict with each other in LT is of particular importance, and the function of centralized leadership in line networks has a major involvement.

As discussed above, boundary negotiations as leadership interactions through deliberate processes or emergent processes (or processes where these processes are mixed) among stakeholders are crucial factors of leadership capabilities that drive capabilities congruence in subsystems (stakeholders); see Insight-1, Insight-2, and Insight-3. This also contributes to driving capabilities congruence among stakeholders at the same time: Insight-4 (see Fig. 10.11).

10.5 C-DC Through Capabilities Congruence Among the Various Stakeholders

As described above, for new service innovations (and ecosystem building), companies (main player and partners) must mobilize, align, and reconfigure intangible assets (including co-specialized and complementary assets) both inside and outside the company to dynamically adapt to environments. Thus, by orchestrating this diversity of co-specialized assets, groups of companies in ecosystems can bring about intangible assets as the unique corporate signature processes of (1) Strategy Capabilities, (2) Organizational Capabilities, (3) Technology Capabilities, (4) Operational Capabilities, and (5) Leadership Capabilities, to realize congruence among these capabilities elements and congruence with external environments (ecosystems covering a wide range of customers, partners, and so forth). Moreover, by driving co-specialization of these five capabilities with other capabilities, strong DC will function in the company, and at the same time bring congruence of these five capabilities among ecosystem partners, which also brings about C-DC.

On this point, Teece (2014, pp. 335–336) analyzed "strategic fit" in terms of existing strategy and organizational theories as follows: "The potential transformation envisioned when an enterprise has strong dynamic capabilities goes beyond narrow notions of 'strategic fit' seen as optimal in the 'adaptation' school of organizational change research. That school sees the environment as exogenous." Teece (2007) and Sirmon et al. (2007) emphasized a "fit" that is far broader and embraces (1) the firm's internal processes, (2) partners, (3) customers, and (4) the business environment. Achieving tight "fit" with all four is likely to require strong DC."

Interpreting further this perspective, to achieve strong DC (and strong C-DC), not only is "strategic fit" over a narrow range required, but also the five capabilities are mutually co-specialized, and at the same time mutually co-specialized among partners to bring "fit" over a wider range and to bring about strong congruence (see Fig. 10.4).

Through the orchestration of co-specialized assets through strong DC (and strong C-DC), companies can bring capabilities congruence to subsystems through the interactions of capabilities between the subsystems (between company systems), [Insight-1], [Insight-2], and [Insight-3], while the interactions between these capabilities between the subsystems (between corporate systems) brings capabilities congruence among stakeholders [Insight-4].

Notes

1. Changes to the frameworks that arise from the new boundaries between businesses and industries are bringing about products, product systems, services, and complex systems that integrate these products and systems. For example, such integrated (complex) systems can be found in the smart houses being promoted by the real estate industry and smart cities being driven by private enterprise (e.g., Fujisawa Sustainable Smart Town, Kashiwa-no-ha Smart city, and Funabashi Smart Share Town) in Japan.
2. The holistic leadership discussed by Kodama (2017a) entails dynamic usage and combination of centralized, distributed, and dialectical leader-

ship by practitioners (the three management layers of top management, middle management, staff) on the three practice layers of the formal organization layer, the psychological boundary layer, and the informal organization layer. As well as that, holistic leadership has a fractal quality. In other words, the three-layered structure of the leadership systems of the centralized, distributed, and dialectical leadership of practitioners in management layers (three practical layers) has a fractal nature. Moreover, leadership in entire corporate organizations that integrate top, middle, and lower management is also a three-layered leadership system in the same way.

References

Ahuja, M., & Carley, K. (1999). Network Structure in Virtual Organizations. *Organization Science, 10*(6), 741–757.

Albert, R., & Barabasi, A. (2000). Topology of Evolving Networks: Local Events and Universality. *Physical Review Letter, 85*(24), 5234–5237.

Barabasi, A.-L. (2002). *Linked: The New Science of Networks*. Boston: Perseus.

Baum, J. A. C., Rowley, T. J., & Shipilov, A. V. (2004). The Small World of Canadian Capital Markets: Statistical Mechanics of Investment Bank Syndicate Networks. *Canadian Journal of Administrative Sciences, 21*(4), 307–325.

Braha, D., & Bar-Yam, Y. (2004). Information Flow Structure in Large-Scale Product Development Organizational Networks. *Journal of Information Technology, 19*(4), 234–244.

Brown, J. S., & Duguid, P. (2001). Knowledge and Organization: A Social-Practice Perspective. *Organization Science, 12*(2), 198–213.

Carlile, P. (2002). A Pragmatic View of Knowledge and Boundaries: Boundary Objects in New Product Development. *Organization Science, 13*(4), 442–455.

Carlile, P. (2004). Transferring, Translating, and Transforming: An Integrative Framework for Managing Knowledge Across Boundaries. *Organization Science, 15*(5), 555–568.

Carlile, P. R., & Rebentisch, E. S. (2003). Into the Black Box: The Knowledge Transformation Cycle. *Management Science, 49*(9), 1180–1195.

Christensen, C. M. (1997). *The Innovator's Dilemma: When New Technologies Cause Great Firms to Fail*. Boston: Harvard Business School Press.

Collis, D. J., & Montgomery, C. A. (1998). *Corporate Strategy: A Resource-Based View*. Chicago: McGraw-Hill.

Cramton, C. D. (2001). The Mutual Knowledge Problem and Its Consequences for Dispersed Collaboration. *Organization Science, 12*(3), 346–371.

Dougherty, D. (1992). Interpretive Barriers to Successful Product Innovation in Large Firms. *Organization Science, 3*(2), 179–202.

Dougherty, D. (1996). Organizing for Innovation. In S. R. Clegg, C. Hardy, & W. R. Nord (Eds.), *Handbook of Organization Studies* (pp. 424–439). Thousand Oaks: Sage.

Eisenhardt, K., & Martine, J. (2000). Dynamic Capabilities: What Are They? *Strategic Management Journal, 21*(10–11), 1105–1121.

Eisenhardt, K. M., & Tabrizi, B. N. (1995). Accelerating Adaptive Processes: Product Innovation in the Global Computer Industry. *Administrative Science Quarterly, 40*, 84–110.

Faust, K. (1997). Centrality in Affiliation Networks. *Social Networks, 19*, 157–191.

Fiedler, F. E. (1964). A Contingency Model of Leadership Effectiveness. *Advances in Experimental Social Psychology, 1*, 149–190.

Fiedler, F. E., & Chemers, M. M. (1967). *A Theory of Leadership Effectiveness.* New York: McGraw-Hill.

Fiedler, F. E., & Garcia, J. E. (1987). *New Approaches to Effective Leadership: Cognitive Resources and Organizational Performance.* New York: Wiley.

Gawer, A., & Cusumano, M. A. (2002). *Platform Leadership: How Intel, Microsoft, and Cisco Drive Industry Innovation* (pp. 29–30). Boston: Harvard Business School Press.

Hagel, J., III, & Brown, J. S. (2005). Productive Friction. *Harvard Business Review, 83*(2), 139–145.

Hargadon, A., & Sutton, R. I. (1997). Technology Brokering and Innovation in a Product Development Firm. *Administrative Science Quarterly, 42*, 716–749.

Helfat, C. E., & Peteraf, M. A. (2003). The Dynamic Resource-Based View: Capability Lifecycles. *Strategic Management Journal, 24*(10), 997–1010.

Helfat, C. E., Finkelstein, S., Mitchell, W., Peteraf, M. A., Singh, H., Teece, D. J., & Winter, S. G. (2007). *Dynamic Capabilities: Understanding Strategic Change in Organizations.* Oxford: Blackwell.

Iansiti, M., & Levien, R. (2004). *The Keystone Advantage: What the New Dynamics of Business Ecosystems Mean for Strategy, Innovation, and Sustainability.* Boston: Harvard Business School Press.

Jantsch, E. (1980). *The Self-Organizing Universe.* Oxford: Pergamon Press.

Kim, W. C., & Mauborgne, R. (2005). *Blue Ocean Strategy.* Boston: Harvard Business School Publishing.

Kodama, M. (1999). Strategic Innovation at Large Companies Through Strategic Community Management–An NTT Multimedia Revolution Case Study. *European Journal of Innovation Management, 2*(3), 95–108.

Kodama, M. (2002). Transforming an Old Economy Company Through Strategic Communities. *Long Range Planning, 35*(4), 349–365.

Kodama, M. (2003). Strategic Innovation in Traditional Big Business. *Organization Studies, 24*(2), 235–268.

Kodama, M. (2004). Strategic Community-Based Theory of Firms: Case Study of Dialectical Management at NTT DoCoMo. *Systems Research and Behavioral Science, 21*(6), 603–634.

Kodama, M. (2005a). Knowledge Creation Through Networked Strategic Communities: Case Studies on New Product Development in Japanese Companies. *Long Range Planning, 38*(1), 27–49.

Kodama, M. (2005b). How Two Japanese High-Tech Companies Achieved Rapid Innovation Via Strategic Community Networks. *Strategy & Leadership, 33*(6), 39–47.

Kodama, M. (2006). Knowledge-Based View of Corporate Strategy. *Technovation, 26*(12), 1390–1406.

Kodama, M. (2007a). *The Strategic Community-Based Firm*. London: Palgrave Macmillan.

Kodama, M. (2007b). *Knowledge Innovation –Strategic Management as Practice*. Cheltenham: Edward Elgar Publishing.

Kodama, M. (2007c). *Project-Based Organization in the Knowledge-Based Society*. London: Imperial College Press.

Kodama, M. (2007d). Innovation Through Boundary Management—A Case Study in Reforms at Matsushita Electric. *Technovation, 27*(1), 15–29.

Kodama, M. (2007e). Innovation and Knowledge Creation Through Leadership-Based Strategic Community: Case Study on High-Tech Company in Japan. *Technovation, 27*(3), 115–132.

Kodama, M. (2009a). Boundaries Innovation and Knowledge Integration in the Japanese Firm. *Long Range Planning, 42*(4), 463–494.

Kodama, M. (2009b). *Innovation Networks in Knowledge-Based Firm –Developing ICT-Based Integrative Competences*. Cheltenham: Edward Elgar Publishing.

Kodama, M. (2011). *Interactive Business Communities*. London: Gower Publishing.

Kodama, M. (2014). *Winning Through Boundaries Innovation – Communities of Boundaries Generate Convergence*. Oxford: Peter Lang.

Kodama, M. (Ed.). (2015). *Collaborative Innovation: Developing Health Support Ecosystems* (Vol. 39). London: Routledge.

Kodama, M. (2017a). *Developing Holistic Leadership: A Source of Business Innovation*. Bingley: Emerald.

Kodama, M. (2017b). Developing Strategic Innovation in Large Corporations—The Dynamic Capability View of the Firm. *Knowledge and Process Management, 24*(4), 221–246.

Kodama, M. (2018). *Sustainable Growth Through Strategic Innovation: Driving Congruence in Capabilities*. Cheltenham: Edward Elgar Publishing.

Kodama, M., & Shibata, T. (2014a). Strategy Transformation Through Strategic Innovation Capability—A Case Study of Fanuc. *R&D Management, 44*(1), 75–103.

Kodama, M., & Shibata, T. (2014b). Research into Ambidextrous R&D in Product Development—New Product Development at a Precision Device Maker: A Case Study. *Technology Analysis & Strategic Management, 26*(3), 279–306.

Kodama, M., & Shibata, T. (2016). Developing Knowledge Convergence Through a Boundaries Vision—A Case Study of Fujifilm in Japan. *Knowledge and Process Management, 23*(4), 274–292.

Kogut, B., & Zander, U. (1992). Knowledge of the Firm, Combinative Capabilities, and the Replication of Technology. *Organization Science, 3*, 383–397.

Kramer, N., & de Smit, J. (1977). *Systems Thinking—Concepts and Notions*. Leiden: M Nijhoff Social Sciences Division.

Le Dain, M. A., & Merminod, V. (2014). A Knowledge Sharing Framework for Black, Grey and White Box Supplier Configurations in New Product Development. *Technovation, 34*(11), 688–701.

Leonard-Barton, D. (1992). Core Capabilities and Core Rigidities: A Paradox in Managing New Product Development. *Strategic Management Journal, 13*(S1), 111–125.

Leonard-Barton, D. (1995). *Wellsprings of Knowledge: Building and Sustaining the Source of Innovation*. Cambridge, MA: Harvard Business School Press.

Lewis, M. W., Welsh, M. A., Dehler, G. E., & Green, S. G. (2002). Product Development Tensions: Exploring Contrasting Styles of Project Management. *Academy of Management Journal, 45*(3), 546–564.

Lin, L., & Kulatilaka, N. (2006). Network Effects and Technology Licensing with Fixed Fee, Royalty, and Hybrid Contracts. *Journal of Management Information Systems, 23*(2), 91–118.

Marjolein, A. G., van Offenbeek, M. A., & Vos, J. F. (2016). An Integrative Framework for Managing Project Issues Across Stakeholder Groups. *International Journal of Project Management, 34*(1), 44–57.

McDonough, F. E., & Barczak, G. (1991). Speeding Up New Product Development: The Effects of Leadership Style and Source of Technology. *Journal of Product Innovation Development, 8*(2), 203–211.

Miles, R. E., & Snow, C. C. (1994). *Fit, Failure, and the Hall of Fame: How Companies Succeed or Fail.* New York: Free Press.

Moore, J. (1993). Predators and Prey: A New Ecology of Competition. *Harvard Business Review, 71*(3), 75–86.

Motter, A. E. (2004). Cascade Control and Defense in Complex Networks. *Physical Review Letter, 93*(098701), 1–4.

Newman, M. E. J. (2004). Fast Algorithm for Detecting Community Structure in Networks. *Physical Review E, 69*(6), 1–5.

Nishiguchi, T., & Beaudet, A. (1998). The Toyota Group and the Aisin Fire. *Sloan Management Review, 40*(1), 49.

Nonaka, I., & Konno, N. (1998). The Concept of "Ba": Building a Foundation for Knowledge Creation. *California Management Review, 40*(1), 40–54.

Nonaka, I., & Takeuchi, H. (1995). *The Knowledge-Creating Company.* New York: Oxford University Press.

Nonaka, I., & Toyama, R. (2004). Knowledge Creation as a Synthesizing Process. In H. Takeuchi & I. Nonaka (Eds.), *Hitotsubashi on Knowledge Management* (pp. 91–124). Singapore: Wiley.

Nonaka, I., & Toyama, R. (2007). Strategic Management as Distributed Practical Wisdom (Phronesis). *Industrial and Corporate Change, 16*(3), 371–394.

Nonaka, I., Kodama, M., Hirose, A., & Kohlbacher, F. (2014). Dynamic Fractal Organizations for Promoting Knowledge-Based Transformation—A New Paradigm for Organizational Theory. *European Management Journal, 32*(1), 137–146.

O'Reilly, C., & Tushman, M. (2004). The Ambidextrous Organization. *Harvard Business Review, 82*(4), 74–82.

O'Reilly, C., & Tushman, M. L. (2008). Ambidexterity as a Dynamic Capability: Resolving the Innovator's Dilemma. *Research in Organizational Behavior, 28*, 185–206.

Owen-Smith, J., & Powell, W. W. (2004). Knowledge Networks as Channels and Conduits: The Effects of Spillovers in the Boston Biotechnology Community. *Organization Science, 15*(1), 5–21.

Porter, M. (1996, November–December). What Is Strategy?. *Harvard Business Review, 74*, 61–78.

Roethlisberger, F. (1977). *The Elusive Phenomena: An Autobiographical Account of My Work in the Field of Organizational Behavior at the Harvard Business School*. Boston: Harvard Business School Press.

Roethlisberger, F., & Dickson, R. (1939). *Management and the Worker*. Cambridge, MA: Harvard University Press.

Schad, J., Lewis, M. W., Raisch, S., & Smith, W. K. (2016). Paradox Research in Management Science: Looking Back to Move Forward. *Academy of Management Annals, 10*(1), 5–64.

Shah, P. (2000). Network Destruction: The Structural Implications of Downsizing. *Academy of Management Journal, 43*(1), 101–112.

Shannon, C. E., & Weaver, W. (1949). *The Mathematical Theory of Information*. Urbana: University of Illinois Press.

Sirmon, D. G., Hitt, M. A., & Ireland, R. D. (2007). Managing Firm Resources in Dynamic Environments to Create Value: Looking Inside the Black Box. *Academy of Management Review, 32*(1), 273–292.

Teece, D. J. (1980). Economies of Scope and the Scope of the Enterprise. *Journal of Economic Behavior & Organization, 1*(3), 223–247.

Teece, D. J. (1986). Profiting from Technological Innovation: Implications for Integration, Collaboration, Licensing and Public Policy. *Research Policy, 15*(6), 285–305.

Teece, D. J. (2000). Strategies for Managing Knowledge Assets: The Role of Firm Structure and Industrial Context. *Long Range Planning, 33*(1), 35–54.

Teece, D. J. (2007). Explicating Dynamic Capabilities: The Nature and Microfoundations of (Sustainable) Enterprise Performance. *Strategic Management Journal, 28*(13), 1319–1350.

Teece, D. J. (2014). The Foundations of Enterprise Performance: Dynamic and Ordinary Capabilities in an (Economic) Theory of Firms. *The Academy of Management Perspectives, 28*(4), 328–352.

Tushman, M. L. (1977). Special Boundary Roles in the Innovation Process. *Administrative Science Quarterly, 22*, 587–605.

Tushman, M. L., & O'Reilly, C. A. (1997). *Winning Through Innovation*. Cambridge, MA: Harvard Business School Press.

Van Mieghem, J. A. (2008). *Operations Strategy: Principles and Practices*. Belmont: Dynamic Ideas.

van Offenbeek, M. A., & Vos, J. F. (2016). An Integrative Framework for Managing Project Issues Across Stakeholder Groups. *International Journal of Project Management, 34*(1), 44–57.

Von Krogh, G., Nonaka, I., & Rechsteiner, L. (2012). Leadership in Organizational Knowledge Creation: A Review and Framework. *Journal of Management Studies, 49*(1), 240–277.

Wasserman, S., & Faust, K. (1994). *Social Network Analysis: Methods and Applications*. New York: Cambridge University Press.

Watts, J. (2003). *Six Degrees: The Science of a Connected Age*. New York: W.W. Norton and Company.

Watts, J., & Strogatz, S. (1998). Collective Dynamics of "Small-World" Networks. *Nature, 393*(4), 440–442.

Wenger, E. (1998). *Community of Practice: Learning, Meaning and Identity*. Cambridge: Cambridge University Press.

Wenger, E. C. (2000). Communities of Practice: The Organizational Frontier. *Harvard Business Review, 78*(1), 139–145.

White, D., & Houseman, M. (2003). The Navigability of Strong Ties: Small Worlds, Tie Strength, and Network Topology. *Complexity, 8*(1), 82–86.

Whitehead, A. N. (1929/1978). *Process and Reality: An Essay in Cosmology* (D. R. Griffin & D. W. Sherburne, Eds.). New York: The Free Press.

Winter, S. (2000). The Satisficing Principle in Capability Learning. *Strategic Management Journal, 21*(10–11), 981–996.

11

Conclusions and Issues for Future Research

Mitsuru Kodama

11.1 Collaborative Dynamic Capabilities and Capabilities Congruence

What can be understood from the fact that many innovations arise on the boundaries between areas of specializations (Leonard-Barton 1995), a key discussion in this book, is that the effective orchestration of knowledge (assets) across the various boundaries within and between organizations and between companies gives rise to dynamic capabilities (DC) and collaborative dynamic capabilities (C-DC), thus bringing about a competitive edge. As discussed in Chap. 10, C-DC entail synchronization across the pragmatic boundaries between stakeholders to share, evaluate and orchestrate wide-ranging knowledge (assets). The promotion of synchronization of stakeholder activities on knowledge boundaries entails synchronization of the DC of the various individual players involved, which brings about C-DC. For this reason, pragmatic boundaries must

---

M. Kodama (✉)
Nihon University, College of Commerce, Tokyo, Japan
e-mail: kodama.mitsuru@nihon-u.ac.jp

be synchronized by forming strategic communities (SC) between the main player and partners. Moreover, pragmatic boundary synchronization between main player(s) and partner(s) on the Capabilities Map brings about synchronization of the strategic innovation loop (boundaries synchronization).

As Carlile (2004) discussed, perceiving the details of capabilities from the perspective of knowledge boundaries, rather than viewing corporate organizations as a bundle of resources (Barney 1991), we believe it is possible to describe corporate capabilities perfectly as bundles of various types of boundaries where knowledge sharing and evaluation (and orchestration) is required.

As observed in the case studies in this book, optimized asset orchestration in companies, between companies, and between industries, the formation of SC within companies, between companies, and between industries, and the acquisition of collaborative dynamic capabilities in companies, between companies, and between industries are important for success in building ecosystems with service innovations, and are factors in realizing construction of health support ecosystems.

As a factor of collaborative dynamic capabilities, the book has also clarified the importance of the concept of "capabilities congruence" among ecosystem partners in achieving capability synthesis to maximize capabilities in ecosystems. Moreover, as a prerequisite for five capabilities elements that ecosystem partners have, (1) strategy capabilities, (2) organizational capabilities, (3) technology capabilities, (4) operational capabilities, and (5) leadership capabilities, the book identifies the importance of the concept of "congruence among the capabilities elements."

11.2 Autopoiesis and Strategic Innovation Capabilities

One remaining research issue is that mentioned in Chap. 2—the management element of "autopoiesis" required for a sustainable ecosystem. Open systems that are self-regulating and self-organizing function to renew themselves and survive by constantly transforming their elements through "autopoiesis" (Maturana and Varela 1980). As Felix (2003) indicates, some types of systems learn through single loop feedback. However, if there are changes, there may be cases where this is not possible, or the system is strengthened for long-term survival. Questions arise on the aim of systems with double loop learning (e.g., Argyris and Schon 1978). If a system strays from a proper state, change begins and it attempts, as fast as is possible, to adapt to a new desirable state (passively or actively, through environment adaptive strategies and environment creation strategies) (Kodama 2015, 2018). This also includes jumps in system states (or discontinuity) depending on the level of environmental change.

In addition to this, Von Bertolanffy (1968) describes the concept of aiming for disequilibrium as flow equilibrium instead of aiming for equilibrium in most complex systems. For example, the shift from Domains III and/or IV to Domain I on the Capabilities Map describes the case of a corporate system transformation towards disequilibrium to generate new innovation. These orientations can actually be perceived in observations of large corporate systems. Flow equilibrium management systems can be characterized by equilibrium with constant movement. With both unrelenting positive and negative feedback, strategic direction can be given to corporate systems in rapidly changing and unpredictable environments (equivalent to the shifts between domains in the Capabilities Map).

In these recursive processes, for renewal and self-renewal of the business ecosystem feedback loops are formed, and stakeholders reconsider the management drivers in one's company, renew the four capabilities, and redesign and execute strategy-making processes to reconfigure SC (as Internal Strategic Communities (ISC) and External Strategic Communities (ESC)) and execute the shift of Domain III and/or Domain IV → Domain I → Domain II as new radical innovation, described in Fig. 2.7 in Chap. 2.

"Autopoiesis" (Maturana and Varela 1980) is composed of the self-sustenance of cellular, self-reference of neural systems and cognitive function as organisms. In other words, in one way organisms are characterized by accumulating metabolic functions, which then control biological systems. At the same time, nervous and immune systems are able to self-regulate the status of all their constituent parts. Then, through knowledge, organisms interact with others as independent systems.

Put differently, in neural systems as biological systems the basic concept of "autopoiesis" is not described as the range of forms from the fundamental elements of life, through to its complexes or the whole, but as the act of an entity that self-perpetuates its own behaviors, and through this perpetuation of its behaviors forms itself.

Autopoiesis as a theoretical model of the organism has also been used to build the theories of social systems by Niklas Luhmann, who endeavored to describe social systems (Luhmann 1984, 1990, 1995). Social systems are autopoietic systems in which continual communication gives rise to communication, and communication is the final indivisible element of the social system, where various events become issues. These are elements that only continue for a very short time. Communication disappears the moment it appears, and must be replaced by successive communications. Hence, unceasing reproduction of new communications brings about sustainable social systems.

Thinking from the perspective of autopoiesis or Luhmann's social systems, one of the characteristics of individual stakeholders as corporate systems bringing about sustainable ecosystems is the aforementioned recursive process. This is the reform of a corporate system towards disequilibrium to generate new innovations. In autopoiesis, momentary "events" (e.g., organizational activities such as communications and collaboration in corporate activities) are viewed as the elements of a system. For a corporate system to exist, these elements must therefore be continually and unceasingly produced. Through the generation and chaining of elements, corporate system boundaries are determined (i.e., the domains on the Capabilities Map), and the elements of each domains are configured based on the corporate system. Thus the recursive shifting between the domains on the Capabilities Map is nothing other than "autopoiesis."

As described by Figs. 2.6 and 2.7 in Chap. 2, for renewal and self-renewal of the business ecosystem, feedback loops are formed, and stakeholders carry out asset orchestration to reconfigure strategic communities (ISC and ESC) and execute the shift of Domain III and/or Domain IV → Domain I → Domain II as new radical innovations. Knowledge transformation through the asset orchestration and the strategic innovation loop enabled by strategic innovation capabilities can also be said to be autopoiesis.

The basic structural elements of Luhmann's social systems, communications systems, fit with the communications theory of Shannon and

Weaver (1949) discussed in Chap. 10, and are also the 3T model of Carlile (2004) expanded to organizational theory. In dealing with changes in situations, the dynamic changes of knowledge boundaries in and between companies (between stakeholders) (syntactic boundary → semantic boundary → pragmatic boundary → syntactic boundary →) enables the discovery of common knowledge (mutual knowledge) through new communications and collaboration, and recursively brings about boundaries synchronization among actors. Actions that demonstrate strategic innovation capabilities through this dynamic process can also be called autopoiesis.

11.3 Assets Orchestration Processes and Microstrategy Processes

11.3.1 Sensing Through Boundaries Vision

In the knowledge economy, diverse human knowledge is the source of valuable products, services, and business models that can give a company new competitiveness. Through convergence across different and diverse industries, co-specialized asset orchestration raises the potential to produce new products, services, and business models that span wide-ranging boundaries and value chains as new strategic models. Accordingly, for companies to configure new businesses, it is necessary to once again recognize the perspective of process-oriented management to create new intangible assets by transcending the organizational boundaries both in and between companies to dynamically share and integrate the intangible assets of people, groups, and organizations. Entire strategic processes must thus be optimized by dynamic assets orchestration on multiple organizational boundaries (which also means knowledge integration), through internal congruence in capabilities of the (1) strategy capabilities, (2) organizational capabilities, (3) technology capabilities, (4) operational capabilities, and (5) leadership capabilities that make up the corporate system: capabilities congruence among the various managerial elements of a corporate system [Insight-2] and external congruence in capabilities with the environment (dynamic external congruence, [Insight-1]).

As discussed in the case studies in this book, through the orchestration of co-specialized assets through DC (and collaborative dynamic capabilities), companies can bring capabilities congruence to subsystems (individual corporate systems) through the interactions of capabilities between the subsystems (between company systems), [Insight-1], [Insight-2], and [Insight-3], while the interactions between these capabilities between the subsystems (between corporate systems) bring capabilities congruence among stakeholders, [Insight-4].

For this, practitioners must use "sensing." Sensing functions to seek out, filter, and analyze business opportunities is dependent on the cognitive capabilities of individual practitioners, such as members of leader organizations in management layers. In the process of research and development (R&D) and selecting new technologies with innovation, the appropriate cognitive capabilities of management layers such as business opportunities are of extreme importance in responding to dynamic external environments.

In the seizing process, boundaries vision is an extremely important cognitive capability or intuition of practitioners which enables them to uncover the best intangible assets (and co-specialized assets). Moreover, practitioners need to drive the "four specific factors" (see Box 11.1) to promote capabilities congruence with the environment and practice the asset orchestration process (see Fig. 11.1).

To repeat, to create corporate value for new markets or dynamically changing markets, companies must drive capabilities congruence among capabilities elements (co-specialized assets) such as strategies, organizations, technologies, operations, and leadership in the companies (corporate systems) through the orchestration of co-specialized assets. Therefore, optimization of capabilities (capabilities congruence) achieved through the dynamic knowledge integration processes of assets (both intangible and tangible) inside and outside of the corporation (Kodama 2005a, b, 2009a, b) and knowledge convergence processes (Kodama 2014) is the most important factor, and practitioners must thus engage in sensing, seizing, and transforming through their "microstrategy view" (Kodama

Conclusions and Issues for Future Research

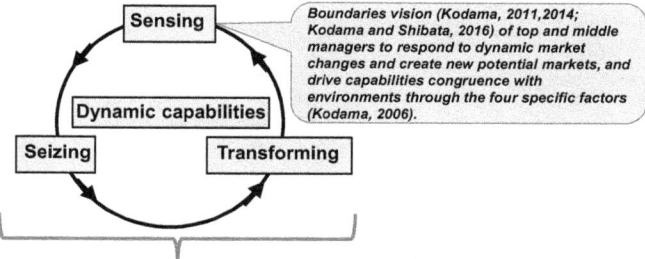

Level	Element	Who	Why	What	When	With whom	How
Practitioners' strategy context (micro strategy view)		Specific people - Who will do it? - Who will you have do it? - Which team members will you choose?	Specific contexts - Why do we do that? - Why does it work like that?	Specific contents - Set specific strategic goals - Focus on target customers, target products and services	Specific time - When to do it - Dynamics	Specific networks - Human networks - Tipping points - Connectors - Specific changing networks	Specific practices - How can we achieve it?

Fig. 11.1 Assets orchestration processes and microstrategy processes

> **Box 11.1 The Asset Orchestration Process for the Four Specific Factors**
>
> First is the context-specific factor. Practitioners have to constantly find new meaning in dynamic contexts to build and connect SC (Kodama 2005a, b). To achieve a business vision or mission, SC provide an organizational platform for creating and practicing new concepts through constructive and creative dialogue on questions such as why, how things should be, and how to achieve certain things. Moreover, one factor that determines the quality of strategic concepts is the quality of specific contexts. Overcoming contradictions originating in diverse contexts gives rise to other contexts, which at the same time forms and links SC. As a result, the quality of these specific contexts in turn determines the quality of the knowledge produced. According to Kodama (2018), the Apple case is an example of a vision for the future that entailed creating new markets, in which professionals with a range of backgrounds and skills have to question themselves and each other, and dynamically bring about and share specific contexts.

(continued)

> **Box 11.1 (continuted)**
>
> Second is the person-specific element. The origins of the context-specific elements described above are the SC formed and combined with specific persons. Not simply anybody: it is important that there be a number of certain people who have the capability of constantly pursuing innovation by themselves. These are specific people with "common knowledge" as expressed in engineering contexts. These people use their own ideas and beliefs to proactively bring about specific contexts and form and combine SC. Specific people means leaders and members of all organizational management layers, leaders and members of partner companies, and even leading customers (e.g., the lead users and core leaders centered on Steve Jobs in the Apple new product development cases) (see Kodama 2018).
>
> Third is the timing-specific element, an element related to the dynamism of SC generation and combination through time and space as a chronological aspect of SC. This means forming and linking SC by certain people with particular contexts at certain times. The element of timing is crucial for making decisions on strategy. How and when companies formulate and execute strategy greatly affect the results. The timing of SC formation and combination has a significant influence on decisions about new product and service developments and their release onto the market. In the Apple case (Kodama 2018), it was Napster that broke into the digital music distribution market, but Apple that came to dominate it through the formation of SC in and out of the company to orchestrate intangible assets and the well-timed development of iPod and iTunes Music Store.
>
> Fourth is the network-specific factor as a spacial characteristic of SC. This means specific networks for generating valuable knowledge; these are human networks as structural elements that form and combine SC. It is important for actors to reconfigure specific networks in time to suit strategic objectives. Thus, these can more precisely be called "specific networks that change." New business succeeded in the Apple case owing to the formation of specific networks necessary for the asset orchestration process (Kodama 2018).

2006, 2007b). The relationships between NTT DOCOMO and Omron described in Chap. 3, the relationship between Mitsubishi and Mitsui and various stakeholders described in Chap. 8 and the relationship between the Asahikawa Medical College and vendors described in Chap. 7 were the results of the demonstration of boundaries vision (Kodama and Shibata 2016) and these four specific factors.

11.3.2 Asset Orchestration Process Through Paradoxical Management

The important role for managers is to reposition and orchestrate certain assets both inside and outside the company by implementing system innovation (e.g., business ecosystems consisting of multiple stakeholders, as in the case studies in this book). As discussed, the importance of co-specialization corporate strategy is high, as many hi-tech products are systems. For success with systems and networks, it is especially important to integrate not only company know-how, but also integrate know-how from external sources. These systems and networks are structured from platform-centered and interdependent components, which means that congruence between the systems inside and outside a company including the environment is crucial for co-specialization of certain assets with others.

For a company to achieve co-specialization with subsystem elements that comprise a system, particularly to bring about radical innovation, managers' orchestration functions for reconfiguring intangible assets is important. For example, depending on the case, management layers may require open innovation (Chesbrough 2003) through the introduction of external technologies enabled by co-operation with suppliers to ascertain customer needs. Hence, companies need to dynamically reconfigure the aforementioned SC or networked SC to optimally execute asset orchestration both inside and outside the company.

According to existing research, systems integrators that proactively work on R&D, design, architecture, and assembly in product development (in the auto and hard disk industries for example) achieve efficient product development by configuring loosely coupled networks between many component suppliers. In contrast, it has been said that telecom manufacturing companies developing mobile phone systems find it better to configure tightly coupled and vertically integrated networks with component development manufacturers to respond to dramatic changes (Busoni et al. 2001; Busoni and Prencipe 2001). Theoretically, this seems to be a reasonable conclusion considering network structure from the perspective of co-ordination via vertical integration and co-ordination via systems integration. However, this can be interpreted differently in terms of other aspects such as the environments companies face (in particular diversifying customer needs or rapid technical developments), technical contexts (in technological or product fields) or the level of knowledge sharing among partners.

For example, in the context of the long experience I have had as a developer in the ICT field, or from the details gained through dialog with developers in electronics manufacturers, in reality when talking about system integrators it really means that for subtle adjustments to hardware and software under development, or integrity between architecture and components between parts manufacturers, numerous cases of close discussions and exchanges are necessary at the level of know-how (tacit knowledge) of many engineers (e.g., Kodama 2002, 2003, 2004, 2007a, b, c, d, 2011, 2014, 2017a, b, 2018). For example, once a tie-up with a vendor is decided, it can be confirmed that the once loose knowledge and information sharing relationships will transform into relationships demanding deep-level knowledge sharing when dense collaboration between engineers in their practice bases is entered (Kodama 2006).

Products areas such as terminals, multimedia devices, or software products where customer need and technologies change rapidly differ greatly from infrastructure communications equipment (switching and transmission equipment, etc.), not only because tight relationships must be encouraged and maintained, but also because there are cases where candidate partners must be sensed and partner companies often switched (particularly in mobile communications and software development).

Considering the characteristics of networks needed for the sharing of assets on loosely coupled and tightly coupled networks, in the strategy-making process for new product development where customer needs or technologies are changing rapidly, it is important to engage in sensing (Weick 1982) of diverse information and knowledge of other companies by forming multiple SC inside and outside the company as loosely coupled networks with wide-ranging vendors (Weick 1976; Morgan 1981; Orton and Weick 1990). Then it is a matter of choosing the best vendors for one's own company, and when strategic alliances are formed these SC loosely coupled networks transform into tightly coupled networks with deeper context and knowledge sharing and asset orchestration to achieve new product development. Then, to construct robust business processes, it is important for companies to tightly connect their SC with vendors to other SC inside and outside the company, such as sales and support departments, to promote understanding and sharing of different contexts and drive dissimilar knowledge sharing and the asset orchestration process.

However, tightly coupled SC networks with vendors are not necessarily continuous and must be reconfigured dynamically either intentionally by the company or in response to changes in the environment. Partner relationships are reviewed to handle changing customer needs and technologies, and SC formation is switched to different partners as SC with tightly coupled network properties change to loosely coupled networks or decoupled network relationships. In reality, there are many cases of long-term relationships coming to an end and transforming into decoupled networks, but then with new partnerships between companies sensing is mutually carried out in loosely coupled networks to share knowledge and information on new business opportunities.

In talking about these phenomena, first it should be noted that the character of partnerships in the perspective of the asset orchestration process is always changing in time between these tightly coupled and loosely coupled networks. Second, companies build tightly coupled networks with the best partners when deciding on strategic ties while maintaining loosely coupled networks with other vendors to seek out new business and hence make these two coupled network modes co-exist. The advantage of the paradoxical management of these networks between organizations in order to synthesize the different modes of SC formations in time and space is that is an effective method of avoiding the core rigidities that stem from path dependency (Leonard-Barton 1992) or competency traps (Levitt and March 1988).[1] In short, project leaders in charge of R&D maintain current product and service development through tightly coupled networks, while at the same time searching for future business opportunities through loosely coupled networks (see Fig. 11.2).

In other words, as group companies dynamically rebuild tightly coupled networks and loosely coupled networks, they orchestrate co-specialized assets through DC (and collaborative dynamic capabilities). At the same time, group companies can bring capabilities congruence to subsystems (individual corporate systems) through the interactions of capabilities between the subsystems (between company systems),

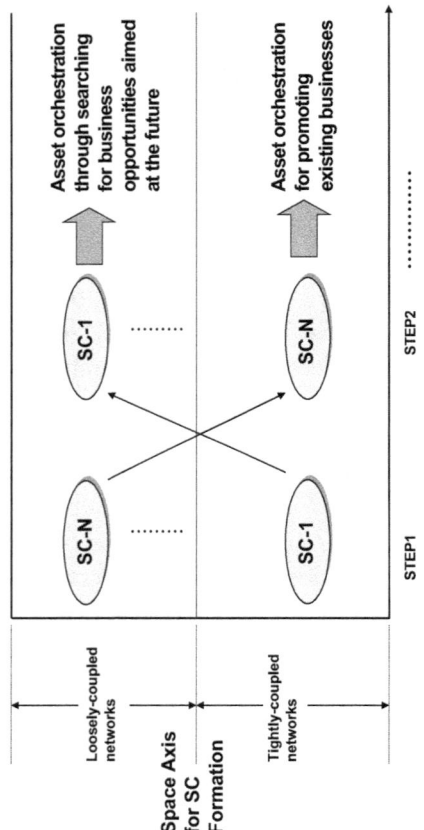

Fig. 11.2 Asset orchestration through dynamics of paradoxical SC formation. (Explanatory note: Loosely coupled network and tightly coupled network SC (SC-1 to SC-N) co-exist at each step of strategy execution. These network relationships change dynamically along the time axis according to environmental changes or deliberate corporate strategies)

[Insight-1], [Insight-2], and [Insight-3], while the interactions between these capabilities between the subsystems (between corporate systems) brings capabilities congruence among stakeholders, [Insight-4].

The bipolar mode utilization of this combination of tightly and loosely coupled corporate networks can also be interpreted as similar to concepts from the research findings of Pettigrew (Pettigrew and Fenton 2000). There is a long tradition in management and organization theory of using bipolar modes of thinking and action. The bipolar (or hybrid) concepts are variously explained and used as paradoxes and dualities. Pettigrew and Fenton (2000) report nine key dualities that innovative firms use to simultaneously build hierarchies and networks, seek greater performance accountability upward and greater horizontal integration, maintain the discipline to identify knowledge and the good citizenship to share knowledge, and attempt to centralize strategy and decentralize operations. Their survey also shows that some firms were innovating simultaneously in many of the elements of the three areas of structures, processes, and boundaries, and that many of the innovative firms were exposing themselves to a range of dualities.

Here, the important perspective is that the bipolar mode of tightly coupled networks as hierarchical vertical integration within a company and flexible network relationships between corporations is a factor that can bring about innovation (Pettigrew and Fenton 2000). SC that are tightly coupled networks are joined together with SC within companies through vertical integration, whereas SC that are loosely coupled networks with external partners can be interpreted as the flexible networks identified by Pettigrew and Fenton (2000). Nevertheless, paradoxical management of networks between these sorts of companies is likely dependent on the environments in which the companies are placed, business functions, products that should be developed, or new business developments, the details of which present further research issues.

As described above, the aforementioned four specific factors and paradoxical management of organizational networks does not entail independent relationships but interdependent relationships in the perspective of building SC and networked SC. Practitioners optimize these four individual factors partially and then entirely to build ideal SC and networked SC for the dynamic asset orchestration process, and achieve sustained practice to create superior products, services, and business processes. An optimal asset orchestration process is executed from a dynamic view of strategy that takes into account these four specific factors. In other words, the most important processes in practice is that of "specific people" dynamically creating and linking SC with "specific timing" as "specific networks" to dynamically generate "specific contexts" to orchestrate and share new assets.

11.4 Conclusion

This chapter has presented new research insights into and implications for "collaborative dynamic capabilities and capabilities congruence," "autopoiesis and strategic innovation capabilities," "assets orchestration processes and microstrategy processes," "sensing through boundaries vision," and "asset orchestration process through paradoxical management." In particular, this chapter has identified the importance of dynamic processes of capabilities to enable sustainable growth (strategic innovation capabilities and the strategic innovation loop) for corporate systems reflecting the concept of "autopoiesis" and groups of partner companies that make up business ecosystems. Moreover, for the sustainable growth of a business ecosystem, this chapter has identified the importance of boundaries vision as capabilities to bring about new knowledge from the combination (integration) of diverse boundaries and the execution of dynamic microstrategies and paradoxical management for successful asset orchestration processes.

Note

1. There is not much accumulated research on paradoxical management that considers networks between organizations in terms of time variation. Ford and Bockoff presented a paradoxical perspective on synchronic and diachronic organizational dualities. If such paradoxes provide corporations the chance for innovation, the content and quality of innovation must greatly be influenced by the nature of the paradox. Therefore, it may become more and more important to perceive paradoxical phenomena constructively and positively, and understand them as being the motive power for the radical transformation of corporations (Kodama 2003, 2004).

References

Argyris, C., & Schon, D. (1978). *Organizational Learning: A Theory of Action Approach.* Reading: Addison Wesley.

Barney, J. (1991). Firm Resources and Sustained Competitive Advantage. *Journal of Management, 17*(3), 99–120.

Busoni, S., & Prencipe, A. (2001). Exploring the Links Between Products and Knowledge Dynamics. *Journal of Management Studies, 38,* 1019–1035.

Busoni, S., Prencipe, A., & Pvatt, K. (2001). Knowledge Specialization, Organizational Coupling, and the Boundaries of the Firm: Why Do Firms Know More than They Make? *Administrative Science Quarterly, 46,* 1185–1200.

Carlile, P. (2004). Transferring, Translating, and Transforming: An Integrative Framework for Managing Knowledge Across Boundaries. *Organization Science, 15*(5), 555–568.

Chesbrough, H. (2003). *Open Innovation.* Boston: Harvard Business School Press.

Felix, R. (2003). A Proposed Taxonomy of Management Systems. *System Research and Behavioral Science, 20*(1), 21–29.

Kodama, M. (2002). Transforming an Old Economy Company Through Strategic Communities. *Long Range Planning, 35*(4), 349–365.

Kodama, M. (2003). Strategic Innovation in Traditional Big Business. *Organization Studies, 24*(2), 235–268.

Kodama, M. (2004). Strategic Community-Based Theory of Firms: Case Study of Dialectical Management at NTT DoCoMo. *Systems Research and Behavioral Science, 21*(6), 603–634.

Kodama, M. (2005a). Knowledge Creation Through Networked Strategic Communities: Case Studies on New Product Development in Japanese Companies. *Long Range Planning, 38*(1), 27–49.

Kodama, M. (2005b). How Two Japanese High-Tech Companies Achieved Rapid Innovation Via Strategic Community Networks. *Strategy & Leadership, 33*(6), 39–47.

Kodama, M. (2006). Knowledge-Based View of Corporate Strategy. *Technovation, 26*(12), 1390–1406.

Kodama, M. (2007a). *The Strategic Community-Based Firm.* London: Palgrave Macmillan.

Kodama, M. (2007b). *Knowledge Innovation – Strategic Management as Practice.* London: Edward Elgar Publishing.

Kodama, M. (2007c). *Project-Based Organization in the Knowledge-Based Society*. London: Imperial College Press.

Kodama, M. (2007d). Innovation and Knowledge Creation Through Leadership-Based Strategic Community: Case Study on High-Tech Company in Japan. *Technovation, 27*(3), 115–132.

Kodama, M. (2009a). Boundaries Innovation and Knowledge Integration in the Japanese Firm. *Long Range Planning, 42*(4), 463–494.

Kodama, M. (2009b). *Innovation Networks in Knowledge-Based Firm – Developing ICT-Based Integrative Competences*. Cheltenham: Edward Elgar Publishing.

Kodama, M. (2011). *Interactive Business Communities*. London: Gower Publishing.

Kodama, M. (2014). *Winning Through Boundaries Innovation – Communities of Boundaries Generate Convergence*. Oxford: Peter Lang.

Kodama, M. (Ed.). (2015). *Collaborative Innovation: Developing Health Support Ecosystems* (Vol. 39). London: Routledge.

Kodama, M. (2017a). *Developing Holistic Leadership: A Source of Business Innovation*. Bingley: Emerald.

Kodama, M. (2017b). Developing Strategic Innovation in Large Corporations – The Dynamic Capability View of the Firm. *Knowledge and Process Management, 24*(4), 221–246.

Kodama, M. (2018). *Sustainable Growth Through Strategic Innovation: Driving Congruence in Capabilities*. Cheltenham: Edward Elgar Publishing.

Kodama, M., & Shibata, T. (2016). Developing Knowledge Convergence Through a Boundaries Vision – A Case Study of Fujifilm in Japan. *Knowledge and Process Management, 23*(4), 274–292.

Leonard-Barton, D. (1992). Core Capabilities and Core Rigidities: A Paradox in Managing New Product Development. *Strategic Management Journal, 13*, 111–125.

Leonard-Barton, D. (1995). *Wellsprings of Knowledge: Building and Sustaining the Source of Innovation*. Cambridge, MA: Harvard Business School Press.

Levitt, B., & March, J. B. (1988). Organization Learning. In W. R. Scott & J. Blake (Eds.), *Annual Review of Sociology* (pp. 319–340). Palo Alto: Annual Reviews.

Luhmann, N. (1984). The Self-Description of Society: Crisis Fashion and Sociological Theory. *International Journal of Comparative Sociology, 25*, 59.

Luhmann, N. (1990). *Essays on Self-Reference*. New York: Columbia University Press.

Luhmann, N. (1995). *Social Systems*. Stanford: Stanford University Press.

Maturana, H. R., & Varela, F. J. (1980). Problems in the Neurophysiology of Cognition. In *Autopoiesis and Cognition* (pp. 41–47). Dordrecht: Springer.

Morgan, G. (1981). The Systematic Metaphor and Its Implications for Organizational Analysis. *Organization Studies, 2*, 23–44.

Orton, J. D., & Weick, K. E. (1990). Loosely Coupled Systems: A Reconceptualization. *Academy of Management Review, 15*(2), 203–223.

Pettigrew, A. M., & Fenton, E. M. (Eds.). (2000). *The Innovating Organization*. London: Sage.

Shannon, C. E., & Weaver, W. (1949). *The Mathematical Theory of Communication* (117p.). Urbana: University of Illinois Press.

Von Bertalanffy, L. (1968). General System Theory. *New York, 41973*(1968), 40.

Weick, K. E. (1976). Educational Organizations as Loosely Coupled Systems. *Administrative Science Quarterly, 21*, 1–19.

Weick, K. E. (1982). Management of Organizational Change Among Loosely Coupled Elements. *Change in Organizations, 375*, 408.

Index[1]

A
Abduction, 53, 81, 82
ABIM Foundation, 113
Acceleration, v, vii, 2, 4, 7, 20, 21, 27, 29–33, 37, 73, 99, 109, 147, 160, 171, 179, 252, 276, 285, 312, 313
Accountable Care Organizations (ACO), 113–129
Adaption dynamic capabilities, 35
Ambidextrous organization, 37, 303, 310, 311
Ambulatory Surgery Center (ASC), 118
Apple, v, 2, 8, 36, 50, 52, 68, 78, 84, 169, 253, 289, 298, 308, 315, 341, 342
Asahikawa Medical University, 170–175, 177, 180, 185
Asset architectural thinking, 243, 244, 246, 247, 250
Asset orchestration, vii, xvi, 4, 6, 7, 10, 13, 15, 17, 23–28, 31, 34–37, 47–54, 56–58, 60, 167–170, 181, 194, 196–198, 208, 228, 235, 241–255, 257, 259, 260, 266, 278–283, 285, 286, 294, 295, 300, 301, 303, 318, 319, 321, 322, 324, 336, 338–348
Asset orchestration architecture, 166, 167, 243–248
Asset orchestration process map, 245–246
Autopoiesis, 75, 84, 336–339, 348

---

[1] Note: Page numbers followed by 'n' refer to notes.

B

Ba, 136, 276
Balanced Score Card, 128
Barabasi, A., 266n1, 278, 279, 310
Barney, J., 13, 15, 61, 267n2, 336
Boundaries architects, 49
Boundaries conception, 63
Boundaries consolidation capabilities, 50, 51, 83
Boundaries synchronization, 76, 78, 80, 82, 84, 85, 106, 109, 110, 178, 233, 260–266, 271–326, 336, 339
Boundaries vision capabilities, 49, 50, 59, 83
Boundary vision, 34
Breakthrough innovation capability, 21, 23, 27, 38
Brown, A. D., 130n5
Bundled payments, 114
Burt, S., 257
Business communities, vii, 4, 7, 10
Business ecosystem, vi, viii, xvi, 2, 6, 9, 10, 20, 39, 54–56, 63, 65–77, 80, 83–85, 101, 106, 109, 110, 168, 169, 252, 290, 291, 298, 301, 305, 312, 337, 338, 343, 348
Business model matching, 7–10
Business synergy, 8, 10
Business transformation, 59, 229–231

C

Cannon, W. B., 55
Capabilities congruence, 47–78, 80, 83, 85, 106, 107, 109, 271–326, 335–336, 340, 345, 347, 348
Capabilities lifecycles, 30
Capabilities Map, 15–22, 30, 38, 39, 51, 55, 62, 71–73, 75, 77, 85, 101, 102, 104, 106, 107, 175, 238, 239, 241, 243, 245, 277, 283–291, 295, 336–338
Capabilities synthesis, 5–11, 71, 74, 96, 146, 185–198, 220, 295, 297–303
Capra, F., 54, 67, 72, 74, 75
Carlile, P., 12, 37, 50, 81, 265, 272–275, 277, 336, 339
Chain-linked model, 33
Checkland, P. B., 54
Chesbrough, H., 24, 49, 137, 165, 243, 343
Christensen, C.M., 2, 24, 34, 37, 275
Clark, K., 251
Closed innovation, 24, 49, 243, 245
Closed systems, 74, 75, 165
Co-creating value, 143–147
Co-creation, vi, vii, xvi, 2, 5, 10, 70, 76–85, 91–101, 103, 110, 136, 145, 148, 160, 169, 252, 301, 317
Co-evolution, vi, xvi, 2, 5, 10, 35, 63, 70, 76–85, 91–101, 110, 169, 242–245, 301, 312, 317
Cognitive capabilities, 48–50, 340
Collaborative dynamic capabilities (C-DC), vii, viii, xvi, 1–39, 47–85, 135–149, 153–160, 198, 203–222, 261, 264–266, 271–283, 335–336, 340, 345, 348
Collaborative ordinary capabilities (C-OC), 277, 278, 283, 284, 287, 288, 303–311

Common knowledge, 51, 81, 253, 265, 274, 275, 284, 339, 342
Community asset orchestrating cycle, 181–184
Community of practice (CoP), 178, 277, 278, 280, 286, 287
Competency traps, 345
Complementary model, 167, 250, 253–255
Complex adaptive systems, 75
Complex systems, 74, 75, 106, 326n1, 337
Context architect capabilities, 50, 51, 83
Context-specific, 276, 284, 341
Context synchronizing, 78, 105, 106, 109
Convergence, v, vi, viiin1, xv, xvi, xix, 2–4, 6, 7, 10, 13, 15, 47, 49, 53, 108, 128, 147, 148, 153, 213, 243, 244, 246, 251, 253, 293, 308, 311–315, 317, 339, 340
Core rigidities, 345
Corporate activity, vii, 4, 9, 17, 19, 55, 63, 293, 338
Corporate boundaries, 18, 24, 26, 49, 57, 62–65, 238, 239, 247, 312
Corporate capabilities, xvi, 4, 39, 304, 336
Corporate system, 31, 48, 53–61, 64, 66, 70–75, 85, 106, 291, 292, 294, 295, 297–299, 337–340, 345, 347, 348
Co-specialization, 5–10, 25, 36, 71, 74, 96, 97, 109, 146, 147, 170, 182, 220, 233, 286, 293–303, 313–315, 323, 325, 343

Co-specialized assets, 25, 47, 49, 50, 53, 64, 65, 85, 168–170, 181, 184, 290, 293, 295, 297–300, 302, 311–317, 325, 326, 339, 340, 345
Creative dialogue, 50, 82, 341
Creativity view, 63, 252–253
Cross innovation, 34

D

Darwinian sea, 27, 28
DC framework, 19, 21
Deliberate processes, 323–325
Dell, 316, 317
Destructive innovation, 34
Dialectical leadership, 307–309, 320, 321, 327n2
Dialectic management, 38
Dialectic view, 63, 68, 255
Digital health, 160
Discovery, 6, 20, 21, 23, 33, 35, 81, 155, 158, 159, 171, 179, 195, 241, 245, 339
Dissimilar knowledge, 49, 80, 81, 253, 257, 345
Doing the right things, 23, 26–28
Double loop learning, 75, 337
Dougherty, D., 59, 277, 307
Dynamic capabilities (DC), vii, xv, 1–39, 49, 52, 53, 55–64, 69–72, 74, 76, 77, 94–97, 101–105, 109, 110, 147, 149, 158–160, 163–167, 181, 185, 203, 208–211, 218–222, 225–235, 239, 242, 245, 248, 259, 266, 271, 276–279, 281, 282, 284–287, 289–295, 303, 309, 325, 326, 335, 340, 345

356   Index

Dynamic external congruence, 58, 64, 85, 340
Dynamic human networks, 278–283
Dynamic internal congruence, 58, 64, 294

E

Ecosystem partners, vii, 4–6, 8–10, 71, 74, 146, 220, 290, 295, 318, 326, 336
Ecosystems strategies, 15, 17
E-healthcare, viii, xvi, 91–110, 165, 170, 185
E-healthcare systems, 165, 185
Eisenhardt, K., 18–20, 63, 81, 292, 307
Embeddedness, 73, 80, 82, 108, 109, 179, 195, 257
Emergent processes, 323–325
Emergent strategies, 28, 51, 81, 104, 264, 322
Entrepreneurial strategies, 25, 28, 52, 77, 78, 81, 106, 241, 304, 307, 308
Equilibrium state, 106
Evidence-based healthcare, 118
Evidence-based management, 118
Evolutionary fitness, 57
Evolutionary theory, 34
Exploitation, 20, 27, 29, 31, 34, 37, 48, 68, 69, 82, 303, 306–310, 317, 320, 321
Exploitation Ba, 309, 310
Exploration, 20, 23, 25, 31, 34, 35, 37, 48, 68, 69, 82, 238, 245, 303, 305–310, 317, 320, 321

Exploration Ba, 308–310
External congruence, 25, 48, 58, 64, 65, 85, 295, 299, 340

F

Felix, R., 67, 74, 75, 337
Fujifilm, 50, 288, 289, 308
Fujisawa Sustainable Smart Town (SST), 138–149, 149n1, 149n2, 326n1

G

Giddens, A., 256
Google, v, 2, 7–10, 68, 78, 79, 84, 168, 169, 253, 298
Granovetter, M., 179, 257

H

Healthcare, viii, 4, 13, 91–101, 136, 139–144, 153–160, 165, 167, 170–172, 175–177, 179, 180, 183–185, 190, 196, 205–207, 209–211, 220, 222, 225–266, 302, 303, 305
Healthcare business, viii, 93, 98, 101, 103–106, 110, 229–233, 236, 238, 261, 266, 305, 312
Healthcare support system, 140
Health insurance company, 160
Health maintenance organizations (HMO), 7
Helfat, C, E., 17, 19, 30, 33, 48, 57, 164, 170, 284–287, 289, 296, 302
Henderson, R., 251

Higher-order learning, 29, 289
Higher-order routines, 36
High-speed markets, 304
Holistic leadership, 147, 326–327n2
Homeostasis, 55, 66, 73, 106
Horizontal integrated architecture, 167, 243, 244, 246–248, 250, 253–256
Horizontal value chain model, 167, 253, 256
Hybrid innovation, 49, 50, 165
Hypercompetition, 15, 17

I

I-mode, vi, 2, 8, 9, 92, 251, 252, 255, 257–259, 305
Improvisation, 20, 81
Improvised learning, 73, 81, 82, 108, 180, 184, 195, 196
Incremental innovation, 24, 27–29, 31, 34, 62, 76–80, 83, 238–242, 248, 259, 286, 287, 289, 306, 308, 312, 314
Incubation, 20, 21, 25, 26, 71, 72, 106, 181–184, 306
Information sharing system, 207
Innovation dynamic capabilities, 20, 35
Innovative customers, 163–164, 170–185
Intangible assets, 24, 25, 47, 49, 50, 61, 62, 104, 170, 181, 247, 288–290, 292–296, 302, 314–316, 325, 339, 340, 342, 343
Integrated community care, 203, 205–211, 218–221
Involvement, 36, 69, 73, 80, 82, 108–110, 120, 136, 139, 178, 179, 195, 221, 229, 236, 324, 325

J

Japanese general trading companies, 170, 225–235, 266

K

Knowledge boundaries, 51, 59, 81, 253, 264, 265, 271–283, 336, 339
Knowledge convergence processes, 53, 340
Knowledge creation, vii, 4, 11, 68, 145, 148, 180, 181, 195, 253, 258, 308, 319
Knowledge evolution process, 34
Knowledge integration, 13, 34, 49, 53, 68, 147, 180, 181, 293, 302, 318, 339, 340
Knowledge integration capability, 48, 49, 53, 302, 339, 340
Kodama, M., vi, xvi, 1, 2, 4, 11, 12, 19, 23–25, 27, 29, 33, 34, 37, 38, 48–59, 61–64, 68, 72, 73, 80–82, 92, 104, 105, 109, 124, 125, 128, 147, 165, 168, 170, 178–181, 184, 193, 194, 250–253, 255, 257, 263, 265, 266, 271, 272, 275, 276, 278, 279, 282, 283, 285–288, 290, 291, 293, 297, 298, 302, 303, 305, 307, 312, 318–322, 324, 326n2, 335–348

L

Leadership capabilities, 48, 58, 64, 66, 290, 292, 300, 315, 317–325, 336, 339
Leadership teams, 52, 53, 82, 105, 307
Leadership triggers, 323–325
Learning before doing, 18
Leonard-Barton, D., 14, 16, 38, 50, 81, 82, 184, 275, 278, 335, 345
Linkage relationship architecture, 167, 243, 244, 246, 247, 250, 256, 258, 259
Loosely coupled networks, 343–345, 347
Luhmann, N., 338

M

Mainstream reserve, 32
March, J., 20, 34, 35, 48, 68, 121, 274, 345
Markides, C., 29, 30, 32, 59
Maturana, H. R., 75, 84, 337
Mental model, 34, 48, 59
Mesarovic, M. D., 55
Microprocessor unit (MPU), 19, 20, 168, 297
Micro strategy processes, 339–348
MI dynamic capability, 20, 21, 38
Ministry of Health, Labour, and Welfare (MHLW), 204–206, 211, 221
Mintzberg, H., 51, 52, 104, 241
Mitsubishi, 191, 226–231, 237, 240–242, 303, 308, 321, 342
Mitsui, 226, 227, 231–235, 237, 240, 242, 260–263, 265, 266, 303, 308, 321, 342
Moore, J., 67, 68, 84, 312
Most stable state, 54
Multi-layered model, 250–252
Multimedia village project, 185–194
Multi-sided platform, 7–9
Multi-stable system, 54, 74, 106

N

Nelson, R., 20, 29, 36, 219
Networked strategic communities, 186–194
Network effects, 8, 9, 168
Network theory, 12, 84, 257, 278–280, 282, 310
Network-specific, 342
Next-generation competition, 15, 17
Nintendo, vi, 2, 8, 169, 290, 298
Nonaka, I., vii, xvi, 4, 11, 33, 73, 124, 125, 145, 180, 276, 308, 309, 318, 319
Non-routine, 33–37, 59, 164, 178, 289
NTT DOCOMO, vi, 2, 3, 8, 9, 68, 91–102, 159, 251, 302–305, 307, 308, 310, 311, 321, 342

O

Obamacare, 114, 115
O'Connor, G., 19–21, 23, 25–27, 31
OMRON, 94–97, 100, 101, 104–109, 302, 303, 321, 342
Open innovation, 24, 49, 137, 165, 243, 246, 300, 343
Open systems, 49, 73–75, 84, 106, 336
Operational processes, 208, 209, 292, 294, 315, 316

Operation capabilities, 48, 58, 64, 66
Optimized profit structure generation, 7–10
Ordinary capabilities (OCs), 17, 22, 52, 62, 101, 164, 175, 239, 277
O'Reilly, C., 34, 37, 38
Organisation for Economic Co-operation and Development (OECD), 92
Organizational networks, 250, 280, 316, 347
Organizational processes, 15, 17, 56, 292
Organization architecture, 294
Organization capabilities, 48, 58, 64, 66
Outstanding partners, vii, 4

P

P4P model, 117, 130n3
Panasonic, 103, 138–140, 142–147, 149, 149n1, 275
Paradoxical management, 343–348, 348n1
Partnership synergy, 10, 80
Path creation, 35
Path dependency, 14, 16, 77, 274, 345
Path-dependent knowledge, 274, 275
Patient centered medical homes (PCMH), 114, 115
Patient Protection and Affordable Care Act (PPCAC), 114, 129n2
Penrose, E.T., 13, 15
Peripheral vision, 34

Person-specific, 342
Peteraf, M.A., 30, 48, 170, 284–287, 289, 302
Pettigrew, A. M., 347
Pharmacy, 140, 141, 203–222, 235
Phronesis, 309
Phronetic leadership, 309
Platform innovators, 8, 9
Porter, M., 14, 15, 293
Practice synchronization, 82, 106, 109, 110
Pragmatic boundaries, 12, 37, 265, 271, 273–278, 280–284, 335, 336, 339

R

Radical innovation, 19–21, 23, 25, 27, 30–34, 37, 55, 56, 67, 72, 76–80, 82, 84, 102, 107, 240, 241, 245, 259, 283, 289, 290, 304, 305, 307, 308, 310, 312, 314, 321, 337, 338, 343
Regional relationship, 210, 211, 218
Resonance of values, 10, 73, 80, 82, 108, 109, 179, 195, 197, 277
Resource-based theories, 13–15
Rumelt, R., 13, 15, 28, 61

S

SC triad model, 308–311, 317, 320
SECI process, 309, 319
Seizing, 14, 16, 18, 21, 23, 25, 27, 36, 53, 58, 60, 76, 77, 94, 95, 103, 104, 219, 226, 242, 285, 294, 295, 340
Self-organization, 109
Self-organizing system, 55

Self-transcendence, 73, 109
Sensing, 14, 16, 18, 21, 23, 25, 36, 48, 50, 53, 58–60, 76, 94, 95, 103, 104, 219, 226, 232, 241, 242, 285, 294, 295, 315, 339–342, 345, 348
Service innovations, vi, viii, 2, 6, 7, 9, 13, 15, 23, 47–85, 91–110, 203–222, 282, 291, 296, 302, 325, 336
Shannon, C. E., 273, 275, 338
Signature processes, 23, 26, 28, 61, 292, 294, 325
Simon, A., 250
Simple rules, 18, 19
Small-world networks, 280, 281
Small-world structures, 12, 84, 280
Smart cities, 91, 136–138, 326n1
Social networking services (SNS), vi, 2
Sony, xvii, 2, 8, 10, 68, 169, 255, 258, 290, 298
Specific contexts, 50, 51, 341, 342, 348
Spiral feedback loops, 33
Stacey, R., 67, 75
Strategic alliances, 24, 25, 165, 250, 253, 278, 286, 288, 344
Strategic collaboration, vii, xvi, 4–6, 9, 13, 23, 24, 69, 71, 74, 78, 92, 94, 97, 99, 101, 103, 109, 110, 146, 163–198, 220, 225–266, 276, 289, 293, 295, 297–303
Strategic communities (SC), 7, 11–13, 34, 37, 51, 73, 74, 80–82, 84, 109, 164, 175–179, 181, 184–194, 197, 198, 242, 275–278, 336–338, 342
Strategic community-based firms, 52, 53, 104, 105
Strategic concentration, 27, 29, 31, 32, 72, 239, 240, 244, 245, 247, 248
Strategic efficiency, 29–32, 238, 245, 248
Strategic emergence, 23, 26, 31, 35, 239, 243, 245, 247
Strategic innovation capabilities, 31–38, 259–260, 303, 310, 311, 336–339, 348
Strategic innovation loop, 31–38, 72–79, 83, 85, 105–108, 175, 178, 241, 248, 264, 276, 277, 284, 290, 295, 336, 338, 348
Strategic innovation system, 22–31, 38, 39, 101–105, 260
Strategic objectives, 19, 24, 51, 59, 62, 64, 78, 80, 103, 247, 310, 322, 323, 342
Strategic selection, 26, 27, 72, 107, 239, 243, 245, 247, 248
Strategy architect capabilities, 50, 51, 53, 83
Strategy capabilities, 48, 58, 61, 63, 64, 66, 292, 297–303, 325, 336, 339
Strategy kernels, 61
Strategy processes, 61, 292, 339–348
Synthesis Ba, 309, 310
Systems approach, 38, 47–85
Systems theory, 54, 66, 67, 72, 74, 84, 85
Systems thinking, 55, 72

T

Takahashi, T., 125, 126, 128
Technological (creating) processes, 292
Technology capabilities, 48, 58, 64, 66, 290, 292, 299, 300, 311–315, 325, 336, 339
Technology synergy, 10
Teece, D. J., vii, 4, 14–19, 21, 23–25, 28, 29, 35, 36, 56, 57, 61, 62, 69, 124, 146, 157, 158, 164, 168, 170, 219, 277, 292–297, 309, 315, 326
Telecommunications carriers, 8, 78, 84, 94, 97, 99, 101, 103, 110, 165–167, 175, 177, 179, 183, 185–198
Telemedicine, 163–198, 312
Three-phase management, 21
Tightly coupled networks, 344, 345, 347
Timing-specific, 342
Tokoro,N., 136
Toyota, 251, 252, 255, 280, 308, 318
Transformational experience, 33
Transforming, 14, 16, 21, 23, 25, 27, 36, 53, 58, 60, 75–77, 84, 95, 103, 104, 166, 225, 226, 231, 239, 242, 285, 294, 295, 336, 340, 345
TSMC, 169, 298–301
Tushman, M., 29, 33, 34, 37, 38, 48, 279, 294, 303, 310
Two-sided platform, 7

U

Ultra-stable system, 54

V

Valley of death, 26, 285
Value based care (VBC), 121–122, 125
Value co-creation, 92, 136
Varela, F. J., 75, 84, 337
Vertical integrated architecture, 166, 243, 244, 246–253
Vertical value chain model, 25, 166, 242–245, 250–252
Von Bertalanffy, L., 55, 66, 67, 74, 75
Von Hippel, E., 163
Von Krogh, G., 319
VRIN, 61

W

Watts, J., 278–282, 310
Weaver, W., 273, 275, 338
Weick, K.E., 344
Wenger, E., 178, 277, 280
Wernerfelt, B., 13, 15, 267n2
Willpower, 28
Winter, S.G., 17, 19, 20, 29, 34, 36, 62, 164, 219, 289

Z

Zollo, M., 34, 164

CPSIA information can be obtained
at www.ICGtesting.com
Printed in the USA
LVHW02*2058060718
582930LV00013B/274/P